The Complete Book of
Papercrafts

The Complete Book of
Papercrafts

A TRULY COMPREHENSIVE

COLLECTION

OF PAPERCRAFT IDEAS,

DESIGNS AND TECHNIQUES,

WITH OVER 300 PROJECTS

HERMES
HOUSE

First published in 1998 by Hermes House

Hermes House is an imprint of
Anness Publishing Limited
Hermes House
88–89 Blackfriars Road
London SE1 8HA

© Anness Publishing Limited 1998

This edition published in the USA by Hermes House
Anness Publishing Inc.
27 West 20th Street
New York, NY 10011
(800) 354–9657

A CIP catalogue record for this book is available from the British Library

ISBN 1 84038 110 8

Publisher: Joanna Lorenz
Project Editor: Margaret Malone
Designer: Bill Mason
Consultant Editor: Jenny Matthews
Jacket designed by: Mark Stevens

Previously published as two separate volumes, *New Papercrafts* and *The Ultimate Papercraft and Origami Book*

Printed and bound in Germany

1 3 5 7 9 10 8 6 4 2

CONTENTS

INTRODUCTION

Paper is an unexpectedly versatile material. Not only is it available in dozens of variations, but the ways it can be used to make beautiful objects are seemingly limitless.

Over the centuries, diverse traditions of paperworking have been developed all around the world, each reflecting the essence of the culture in which it originated. In addition, craftworkers and artists have borrowed and adapted techniques to influence their own work. The result is a vast array of distinctive paper goods and decoration that is breathtaking in its scope and beauty.

This book has gathered together over 125 papercraft projects for you to make at home from paper construction projects to exquisite examples of decoupage, papier-mâché, paper cutting and collage. All the projects are easy to follow, relying on fairly basic materials and equipment. Each project is clearly illustrated with detailed step-by-step colour photography to guide you through every stage. A comprehensive section at the beginning of the book describes all the materials and equipment you will need, as well as essential paperworking techniques.

So start collecting those old newspapers, magazine cuttings, scraps of assorted papers and cardboard in readiness to try out some of the stunning projects shown on the following pages.

PAPERCRAFTS THROUGH THE CENTURIES

Invented in the second century BC by a Chinese court official, paper gradually spread westward, reaching Central Asia in 751AD. In 793, paper was first made in Baghdad, coinciding with the golden age of Islamic culture. From there the knowledge of papermaking spread further west, and by the fourteenth century a number of paper mills had sprung up across Europe. When printing was invented in the 1450s, the demand for paper rose dramatically. At this time linen and cotton rags were the basic raw materials and it was not until demand outstripped supply in the eighteenth century that a search for a new material which was in abundant supply began. In the early nineteenth century wood pulp began to be used.

Modern papermaking machines and processes also date back to the early nineteenth century, and have transformed the ancient craft into a highly technical industry. The basic processes remain the same, however: for those grades of paper requiring maximum strength, durability and permanence, cotton and linen fibres and clean, sorted rags are still used.

All over the world people have recognized the value of paper as a creative medium which can be used either to make objects or as a decorative feature. They have learned to craft paper into useful items which have their own elegance and beauty. They have also devised numerous ways of decorating with paper, either by folding and cutting intricate shapes, by colouring paper or by using coloured plain paper shapes or cut-out printed images to build up pictures. The Far East and Europe especially have strong traditions of using paper as a raw material and for recognizing its decorative potential.

PAPIER-MACHE

Papier-mâché (French for "chewed paper") is essentially pulped paper or paper strips mixed with glue or paste. It can be moulded into any number of shapes to create sturdy or delicate items, which can then be decorated in a variety of imaginative ways. Centuries before being introduced to Europe, the craft was raised to an art in the Far East, where carefully made items were exquisitely decorated and lacquered. Early in the eighteenth century, papier-mâché goods were being moulded in France, and later in Germany and England, where several different processes were used. One of these involved pressure-moulding several glued sheets of paper into trays and furniture panels. Although the production of papier-mâché goods in Europe declined in the nineteenth century, papier-mâché continued to be a popular material for toys, masks and models of various types. As one of the simplest and cheapest of craft techniques it is undergoing something of a revival today.

DECOUPAGE

Deriving from the French verb *découper*, meaning "to cut out", the craft of decoupage involves cutting and pasting black-and-white or coloured cut-outs on to a surface to create a picture or a pattern. Influenced by Siberian felt appliqué work and ancient Chinese and Polish folk-art paper cutting, it

surfaced in seventeenth century France as a form of furniture decoration. A century later, decoupage was well established throughout Europe as a popular pastime. Indeed, it was so fashionable that specially printed pictures were produced for cutting and applying to household and personal items such as hairbrushes, fans and screens. Recently, the craft has seen a resurgence of interest as a way of enlivening household objects such as wastepaper baskets, lampshades, screens, trays and boxes.

Many of today's decoupage designs derive from the heavy floral style of the Victorian era, but there is no reason why this fashion need dictate how modern decoupage should look. In this book there are projects that show the many different ways in which decoupage is used today. You can use any type of paper and image to suit your taste. Even black-and-white or tinted photocopies can be used to make up your own designs. The completed work should always be finished with several coats of varnish to protect the surface.

PAPER CUTTING

Paper cutting originated in the Far East. In China, where papercuts were first used for transferring embroidery patterns, they became extremely intricate and complicated. In Japan they were originally used as stencils for printing textiles. The craft eventually travelled along the trade routes of the Middle East to Europe where it was incorporated by monks into the art of manuscript illumination. Consequently, early secular European paper cutting focused on religious subjects, but as paper became more widely available, people began to depict scenes from everyday life instead. Polish folk artists have become famous for their charming and colourful depictions of rural life.

German and Swiss papercuts were complicated folded affairs called *scherenschnitte*. These symmetrical black on white images were taken by early European settlers to the New

World where they continued the practice. In Britain and France, a development of the Germanic style was to cut out paper silhouettes as portraits. The first silhouette likenesses were drawn life-size by lighting the model's head using candles and drawing the shadow on to paper. This was coloured black, cut out and mounted on white paper. As the fashion for paper cutting spread, well-bred ladies with plenty of leisure time realized that their small needlework scissors were perfect for cutting intricate lacy love tokens or Valentines and commemorative designs for family events. Paper cutting is still practised at traditional festivals in many parts of the world, such as Denmark, Mexico and the US. Depending on the type of paper used, the number of folds and the style of the design, paper cutting can produce a vast range of results.

DECORATING PAPER

Paper can be decorated in a number of ways to enhance the appearance of paper goods or to transform plain paper or cardboard. Stencilling enables decorative effects to be achieved which could not be created any other way. Popular for centuries as a simple but effective way of decorating interiors with repeating patterns, it can be applied to large or small articles alike, ranging from home-printed wallpaper to wrapping paper and stationery. Stamping, essentially a form of printing, is another excellent way to decorate paper. It can be applied to all sorts of paper and paper products. Today, stencilling and

stamping are being rediscovered as simple, cheap but impressive ways of beautifying or giving character to any surface. Ready-made stamps and stencils are widely available in many designs, but you can cut both yourself to your own patterns. You can cut stencils from waxed stencil cardboard or acetate, and you can cut your own stamps from potatoes or household sponges.

PAPER CONSTRUCTION

Paper can be cut and folded to make a surprising number of household items such as boxes, mobiles and lanterns. The art of folding paper to make decorative and useful objects probably had its origin in the even older art of cloth folding. Japanese origami must be the highest development of the art with hundreds of traditional paper folds being used to make spectacular three-dimensional objects and animals. Everything from an elephant to a vase of flowers can be constructed without using glue or adhesive tape to hold the paper together. Spain and South America also have paper-folding traditions. Folding coloured paper was introduced into the German kindergarten movement in the nineteenth century, and later the Bauhaus, the famous German school of design, taught paper folding in its commercial design courses.

Cardboard, normally dismissed as merely a packing material, can be made into a wide range of functional and decorative items. Early this century it was already being made into models and mock-ups for sculptures, furniture and architectural design. Some imaginative designers have even constructed entire pieces of furniture from it, which is a testament to its inherent strength. Cardboard became popular as a craft material during the Second World War, when it was widely used as packaging. Craftspeople were quick to make use of this newly available waste product but enthusiasm soon dwindled with the post-war advent of more exciting materials. Recently, however, interest in cardboard as a creative material has revived, and many artists are using it in novel ways to produce some remarkably diverse objects ranging from toys and handbags to chairs and tables. Corrugated cardboard, with its layered construction, is especially useful for making structures and several projects in this book make excellent use of it.

TYPES OF PAPER AND CARDBOARD

PAPER

Newspaper Cheap and widely available, newspapers are excellent for papier-mâché and some decorative work. For layering newspaper strips into moulds and on to armatures, broadsheets are preferable. Tabloids are better for making pulp. As newsprint creases and folds well, it is also good for papercuts.

Bond paper This quality stationery paper is made for repeated handling and resists ink well.

Laid paper This stationery paper has parallel lines running through it. It is useful for photocopying and for paper cutting projects.

Woven paper Woven paper is made with a mesh of slightly raised fine fibres running through it.

Coated papers The coloured coating may be on one or both sides. The colour can crack along folds, so experiment before starting a project.

Handmade Indian papers These exotic, lightweight papers are strong and easy to cut, but the visible flecks of wood and plant fibre may get in the way of folds. Sold in specialist paper outlets.

Coloured craft paper When only a couple of folds are required for a project, this strongly coloured paper is easy to use, and it cuts well.

Crêpe paper This crinkly, stretchy paper is manufactured in a range of bright colours. Adhesive tape does not stick well to it.

Tissue paper Good-quality tissue paper is very thin but quite strong. It is available in a range of vibrant colours and has a sheen. It is excellent for cutting even when folded many times. Tissue paper is also ideal for making papier-mâché pulp. Translucent objects can be made by pressing glue-covered paper into greased moulds.

Handmade Japanese papers Softer than Indian handmade papers, these are very strong and contain long threads of fibre. They cut well but their springiness makes them difficult to fold. They are expensive, but worth the money. Available from specialist shops.

Glassine paper When held up to the light, this glazed, coloured, heavy, tissue-type paper becomes mottled and transparent. It folds and cuts beautifully. Available from specialist paper dealers or some art shops.

Coated wrapping paper This is brown parcel paper coated on one or both sides with silver or another colour. It cuts and folds very well.

Metallic paper Sold as gift wrap, metallic paper has a real reflective shimmer. When it is made from foil-coated cellophane, it tends to slip and may tear. Some metallic papers fold well, but some won't unfold well once creased.

Brown wrapping paper Traditional parcel paper is strong, cheap and particularly good for hand-printing and stencilling.

CARDBOARD

Cardboard Because it folds easily this is ideal for greetings cards. It is available in various weights, thicknesses and colours.

Stencil cardboard Stencil cardboard and oiled stencil paper are easier to cut than acetate, but are less durable. Being opaque, they are less easy to position.

Flat cardboard Commonly used as a packaging material, this is useful for many paper construction projects. It is available in various thicknesses.

Corrugated cardboard This comes in different weights. Double-wall, or heavyweight, corrugated cardboard has two rows of corrugations or fluting which makes it excellent for

covering with papier-mâché. Single-wall, or lightweight, corrugated cardboard is good for moulding and paper construction. Available in large quantities from packaging suppliers or in small rolls from stationers and craft shops. Also available is a very fine version which is flexible, easy to cut and comes in bright colours. A medium-flute version, available in several colours and metallic finishes, is slightly less flexible.

Bleached cardboard This is very flexible with a slightly glazed surface. It is good for projects that need to be strong but curved.

Artist's mounting board Strong inflexible board used to mount photographs and paintings. Usually white (smooth side) with coloured paper (slightly textured side) laminated to one side. Available in a wide range of colours from art shops and graphic suppliers.

Unlined chipboard This is available in different weights – the thicker ones are less flexible. Thin chipboard is slightly flexible but bends and creases easily. Double-thickness chipboard is tough, smooth-sided and suitable for straight-sided projects. It can be easily painted. Cut with a very sharp blade.

Recycled newspaper board Slightly more flexible than the equivalent unlined chipboard, this has a more interesting and decorative finish.

Polyboard Two layers of smooth bleached card laminated over a layer of polystyrene, this strong board cannot be folded but has to be glued or pinned together.

Experiment with the full range of papers available today, including: marbled, textured, deckle-edged, mottled and embossed (*top left*), handmade papers, foil-coated, crêpe paper (*top right*), decorated, stamped and stencilled designs (*bottom right*) and corrugated, bleached and recycled cardboard (*bottom left*).

MATERIALS

In addition to paper and cardboard, papercrafts rely on many other materials. Many of these are used repeatedly in different projects, so it is a good idea to stock up on them and keep them ready to work with.

GLUES

Glues are used to stick paper and cardboard, either for decoration or for construction. Many types of glue produce similar results; personal preference is often the deciding factor when choosing. In addition to the glues listed below, a glue gun which applies melted glue is a useful tool.

Paper glue Although it may take longer to dry than some other glues, this golden-coloured liquid, is ideal for paper projects.

PVA (white) glue Because it dries quickly to a strong, clear finish, white glue is ideal for working with paper, especially papier-mâché. It can be used diluted with water to apply paper strips to a mould. It can also be used as a non-waterproof varnish or sealer on finished projects. Some glue can irritate the skin, so choose a non-toxic, child-safe type and apply it with a brush or wear rubber gloves.

Wood glue This is a stronger form of PVA (white) glue which is useful for heavyweight cardboard projects.

All-purpose glue This general adhesive is useful for gluing all types of materials together.

Powdered glue Non-toxic powdered glue granules are available from craft and hobby shops. They are mixed with water to a stiff consistency. This glue dries more slowly than PVA (white) glue, and it also makes papier-mâché more soggy.

Glue sticks Applied with a glue gun that melts the glue at point of contact.

Spray adhesive Spraying gives a light, even application of glue to a surface and is ideal for delicate projects, such as paper cutting. Always apply it in a well-ventilated area.

Wallpaper paste This is useful for larger projects, but it is not as strong as PVA (white) glue and takes longer to dry. Its slippery quality makes it useful for decoupage, allowing the motifs to be slid into exactly the right position. Wallpaper paste is also excellent for making papier-mâché, and as it contains fungicide it discourages mould. Fungicides may irritate the skin, however, so wear rubber gloves when using.

PAINTS

In papercrafts, paints are used to decorate a paper construction or to transform plain paper into something else, such as gift wrap. It is a good idea to apply two coats of undercoat

or primer to seal surfaces of cardboard or papier-mâché projects before applying the decorative finish.

Undercoat or primer Useful for sealing papier-mâché before painting. If you intend to decorate with poster or gouache paints, use white emulsion (latex), poster or powder paint. For acrylic paint, prime with white acrylic paint or acrylic gesso.

Acrylic paints These water-based paints dry to a plastic waterproof finish. They can be applied full strength or diluted with water or an acrylic medium. Acrylic stencil paints are quick-drying to reduce the possibility of paint seeping behind the stencil; they are available in a wide range of colours and can be mixed to extend the palette.

Emulsion (latex) paints Available in a vast range of colours, these water-based paints dry quickly. They can be

used for stencilling, but the cheaper varieties contain a lot of water and will seep through the stencil.

Poster paints These water-based paints do not dry to a waterproof finish so need sealing with varnish. Available in a wide range of colours.

Gouache paints Less exacting than pure watercolours, gouache paints have an opaque quality due to the addition of white body colour.

VARNISHES

Decorated and painted surfaces need to be protected from dirt and wear. Apply two coats, lightly sanding between applications.

Oil-based polyurethane varnish Available in gloss, satin or matt finishes, this low-solvent polyurethane varnish is suitable over poster, powder or gouache paints. Apply in a well-ventilated area.

Water-based acrylic varnish This is available in gloss, satin or matt finishes, and used to protect acrylic paints. Has the advantage over other varnishes of not yellowing with age. Apply in a well ventilated area.

Spray varnish This is useful for sealing small areas of paperwork. Wear a protective face mask when using.

OTHER MATERIALS

Dutch metal leaf A cheap alternative to real, and expensive, gold leaf, this extraordinarily thin material can be used to create spectacular decorative effects. It is is used in conjunction with gold size, which is applied first.

Fixative spray A design that is likely to smudge should be "fixed".

Blotting cardboard An absorbent material, use for removing excess paint off the brush before stencilling.

Clockwise opposite far left: fixative, felt-tipped pens, coloured pencils, marker pens, pastels, watercolour paints, gouache paints, poster paints, crayons (*centre*).

Clockwise opposite left: wood glue, strong glue, PVA (white) glue, spray paint, spray adhesive, masking tape, rubber solution.

Clockwise left: acrylic stencil paints, oil-based cream and metallic creams, fabric paints, oil-based stencil sticks, emulsion (latex) paints, gold leaf, acrylic varnish, gold size.

EQUIPMENT

Most of the equipment needed for working with paper is basic and easy to use. If you do not already possess them at home, most items can be bought cheaply from a stationer's or a craft shop. With the following tools, you should be able to tackle most of the projects shown in this book. Take good care of your tools, cleaning them immediately after use.

MEASURING TOOLS

In many projects, careful, accurate measuring will be crucial for obtaining good results.

Metal ruler This is essential for cutting straight lines with a sharp blade and can also be used in place of scissors when a softer edge is required.

Clear ruler This is useful if you need to see through a template while you are measuring and cutting.

Set (T) square One with 60 degree and 30 degree corners enables you to divide circles into sixths.

Protractor This enables you to divide circles into angles.

Pair of compasses (compass) Occasionally a pair of compasses (compass) is required for designing projects and marking out accurate circles with the centre spot marked.

CUTTING TOOLS

To cut paper and cardboard cleanly and easily, good-quality sharp tools are essential.

Scissors A pair of small, sharp scissors is indispensable for cutting around intricate motifs. Larger scissors can be used for cutting out templates and larger pieces of paper and cardboard. Pinking shears will give a zigzag edge to papercuts.

Craft knife For cutting out intricate patterns, the extremely sharp blade of a craft knife will give a good, clean outline. Also essential for cutting stamps out of sponge. Replace blades regularly as blunt knives can snag.

Cutting mat When using a craft knife, a self-healing cutting mat will protect the work surface, prevent slipping, and thus accidental cuts, and extend the life of the blade.

Lino (linoleum)-cutting tools These are necessary for cutting stamps from lino (linoleum) blocks.

DECORATING EQUIPMENT

When applying paint, it is important to use the correct paintbrush for the job. The three main types used in papercraft are decorator's, artist's and stencil brushes. Each type comes in a variety of shapes and sizes. Buy the best-quality brush you can afford: cheap brushes tend to shed hairs which will spoil your work. Clean, dry and store brushes and rollers carefully after use. Rinse brushes used for water-based paint or varnish in water, clean brushes used for oil-based paint or varnish in white spirit (paint thinner).

Decorator's brushes A 2.5 cm (1 in) paintbrush is ideal for priming and applying varnish. Never apply varnish with a brush that has been used for painting as the varnish will have paint flecks in it.

Artist's brushes Use these for fine paintwork, hand-tinting prints and adding intricate decoration. Available in a number of sizes, flat or pointed.

Stencil brushes Available in a wide range of sizes, these stiff-bristled brushes are purpose-made for applying paint through stencils.

Paint roller Small paint rollers can be used to apply paint and to load stamps. When stamping, use a different roller for each colour.

Sponge and foam Both can be cut to print designs. High-density sponge is best for detailed shapes and will give a smooth sharp print. Medium- or

Clockwise from top left: rubber (latex) gloves, protective mask, mould, petroleum jelly, scissors, masking tape, fine sandpaper, metal ruler, pencil, craft knife, modelling tool, bradawl, wire cutters, palette, decorator's paintbrushes, wire cake rack, leather gloves and cutting mat (*centre*).

low-density sponge will absorb more paint and give a more textured result.

Rubber stamps A huge selection of rubber stamps is widely available. Finely detailed motifs are best for small projects, while bolder ones are ideal for walls and furniture.

Inkpads Inkpads come in a wide range of shapes, sizes and colours.

Lino (linoleum) blocks Blocks for cutting stamps are available from art and craft shops.

OTHER EQUIPMENT

Masking tape This is used for masking off areas that are to be left unpainted, for temporarily securing motifs and for holding glued objects in place while they dry or have papier-mâché applied to them.

Low-tack reusable adhesive This can be used to hold and arrange cut-out images before gluing them permanently in position.

Glue gun Indispensable once tried, the glue gun delivers a small amount of hot, melted glue at the squeeze of a trigger. The glue dries almost instantly and is very strong.

Sandpaper Use fine-grade sandpaper for smoothing papier-mâché surfaces before priming and for rubbing down between coats of paint or varnish. A coarser grain can be used for preparing surfaces prior to decoupage.

Protective face mask A mask should be worn whenever dust is being created or powdered materials are being handled. A special mask to protect against fumes should be worn when working with strong-smelling glues and solvent-based products.

Tweezers Tweezers are useful for picking up delicate cut-outs.

Pencils A supply of both hard and soft pencils is essential. Soft pencils are best for transferring tracings.

Clockwise from top left: cutting mat, tweezers, scalpel, craft knife, pair of compasses (compass), metal ruler, tape measure, plastic ruler, felt-tipped pen, pencil, stencil brush, artist's paintbrushes, household paintbrushes, soft cloth, dish cloth, kitchen paper, medium-grade and fine-grade sandpaper, large scissors and small, sharp scissors (*centre*).

Felt-tipped pen Gives a good, clear outline when tracing. Use also for colouring photocopied gift-wrap.

Crayon A white crayon is useful for marking black paper.

Tracing paper This is essential for transferring designs.

Cloths and rags Soft cloths or rags are useful for rubbing down and cleaning work.

Spoon Useful for smoothing over the back of cut-outs to eliminate folds. A wooden spoon with a pointed end is useful for scoring cardboard without ripping the surface.

Bradawl This is a small pointed instrument used for starting holes.

Revolving hole punch A multi-sized hole punch will make neat holes. An eyelet punch gives a good finish.

Wire cake rack Resting objects on a cake rack will speed up drying time, as air can circulate freely.

Rubber gloves Wearing lightweight, close-fitting gloves when handling any form of adhesive or pulp will protect skin from becoming irritated.

Petroleum jelly A thin layer of petroleum jelly applied to the surface

of a mould for papier-mâché will ensure that it can be easily removed when dry. Cling film (plastic wrap) can also be used for this.

Adhesive tape Use clear adhesive tape for sticking ribbons. Double-sided tape enables you to join paper invisibly. Matt adhesive tape is less obtrusive on wrapping paper.

Saucers and glass sheets Mix runny paints in saucers and spread thick paint on a sheet of glass for potato and rubber-stamp printing.

Acetate sheet Clear acetate is hard-wearing and easy to clean, making it ideal for stencils that will be used repeatedly; a 0.075 gauge is thin enough to cut easily.

Bone paper folder This bookbinding tool gives a crisp edge to a fold when it is run along the edge of loosely folded paper.

Mixing bowls These are useful for holding paints, glues, wallpaper paste etc and as moulds for papier-mâché.

Balloons When blown up, they make excellent globe moulds for papier-mâché. Lightly grease before using.

Wire mesh This can be formed into interestingly shaped frameworks for papier-mâché.

BASIC TECHNIQUES: PAPIER-MACHE

Papier-mâché is the art of modelling with torn or shredded paper bound together with glue, usually a water-based type. The techniques are quickly mastered and offer endless variation.

Almost any object can be used as a mould for papier-mâché, although round objects are easier to cover smoothly if the mould is to be removed later. Bowls and large dishes are excellent. Wire mesh shapes can be moulded to produce any number of interesting shapes, and structures made from cardboard, known as armatures, can also be covered.

You can use papier-mâché pulp to make bowls or to build up sculpted images. Just push it into shape with your hands or a stiff paintbrush. Drying may take several days.

To make your own paper pulp, tear five sheets of newspaper in to 2.5 cm (1 in) squares and place in a saucepan. Cover with water and simmer for 30 minutes. Spoon the paper and water into a blender and process to a pulp. Transfer the pulp to a lidded plastic box and store until required (it will keep for several weeks).When ready to use, add 2½ tablespoons PVA (white) glue and 1 tablespoon each wallpaper paste, plaster of Paris and linseed oil and stir vigorously.

TEARING NEWSPAPER

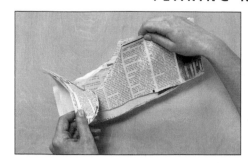 

1 Tearing rather than cutting newspaper creates less obvious joins between strips. Newspaper has a grain and will tear much more easily in one direction than the other. Generally, the grain runs from the top to the bottom of the newspaper. If you try to tear against the grain, it becomes impossible to control.

2 To make paper strips, grasp several folded sheets of newspaper in one hand. Begin to tear about 2.5 cm (1 in) from the edge, along the grain. Pull directly down, and the paper will tear into long, straight strips. Strips of almost any width can be produced this way.

PREPARING A MOULD

Before applying papier-mâché to a mould, the surface must be lightly greased with petroleum jelly to create a barrier between the glue and the mould, preventing the papier-mâché from sticking to it. It will then be easy to remove the papier-mâché when it has dried. Cling film (plastic wrap) can sometimes be used instead.

LAYERING

Cover large moulds with five to six layers of paper strips, 2.5 cm (1 in) wide. Spread the strips with PVA (white) glue on both sides and lay them individually in the greased mould from top to bottom. The strips should protrude slightly beyond the mould. Lay the second and third layers at right angles to the first. Smooth each strip with your fingers and press out any air bubbles.

REMOVING FROM A MOULD AND FINISHING

1 When the surface of the paper in the mould is dry, gently pull back the edge and, if it seems almost dry underneath, insert a blunt knife and gently prise (pry) the paper away from the mould. Leave the papier-mâché upside down to dry completely.

2 Trim the raw edge from the paper shape using scissors, following the indent of the edge of the mould to ensure an accurate curve. To prevent the layers of paper from coming apart, bind the edges of the shape using thin strips of newspaper.

DRYING FLAT OBJECTS

Papier-mâché objects such as picture frames and wall panels should be dried flat after sealing to prevent warping. Place the object on a wire cake rack or a sheet of thin plastic; the glue will stick to the plastic as it dries, but the plastic can easily be peeled away once the papier-mâché is dry.

MAKING A CARDBOARD FRAMEWORK

1 You can make a three-dimensional mould using heavy corrugated cardboard and covering it with papier-mâché. Measure each piece of the framework carefully, and glue and tape it in place to make it sturdy and durable. Brush the framework with diluted PVA (white) glue to seal the surface and leave to dry.

2 Cover the sealed framework with papier-mâché strips, applying each layer at right angles to the previous one. About five layers will disguise the corrugations and make a strong object. Place the framework on a wire cake rack in a warm place to dry naturally; speeding up the drying can cause the papier-mâché to warp.

USING A PLASTICINE SHAPE AS A MOULD

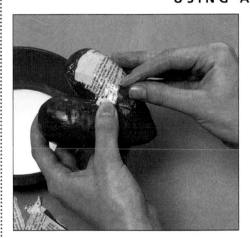
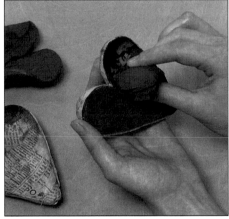
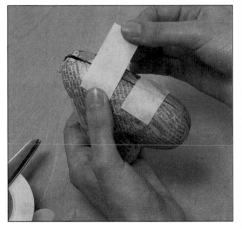

1 Form plasticine into the desired shape. Lightly grease it with petroleum jelly then cover with thin strips of newspaper dipped in diluted PVA (white) glue; five layers should be sufficient. Allow it to dry thoroughly.

2 Draw a cutting line all around the edge of the shape. Using a craft knife, cut slowly around the shape to divide it in half. Gently separate the plasticine from each paper shell.

3 Fit the paper halves together, matching the cut edges exactly. Join them using masking tape and cover the join with three layers of thin papier-mâché strips.

PAINTING PAPIER-MACHE

1 Before you paint papier-mâché, the surface should always be prepared properly, especially if it is made from newspaper. Smooth the surface with fine-grade sandpaper, disguising the edges of the paper strips. Wear a protective face mask when sanding.

2 Prime the papier-mâché with two coats of white paint, allowing it to dry between coats. This conceals the newsprint and provides a good ground for the decoration. Emulsion (latex), poster or powder paints all work well. If the decoration is to be acrylic paint, use this also for priming.

BASIC TECHNIQUES: DECOUPAGE

Decoupage is a way of decorating almost any object or surface with cut-out pieces of paper. The raw materials for decoupage are all around us: magazines, greetings cards, wrapping paper, postcards and illustrated catalogues are there waiting to be cut out.

Surfaces for decoupage need to be clean, dry and smooth. Clean metal with a solution of equal parts of water and vinegar; old metal items will need rubbing with wire (steel) wool first. Lightly sand wood surfaces, then wipe with white spirit (paint thinner). Wipe down glass and ceramics to remove grease and dirt. Porous surfaces should be sealed with matt emulsion (latex) paint.

SEALING

Before cutting out an image, it is a good idea to seal it with a coat of shellac. Gift wrap, colour or black-and-white photocopies or one-off (one of a kind) pictures all benefit from this treatment. Shellac also stiffens delicate images, making them easier to cut out and prevents discoloration.

CUTTING OUT

1 Exactly how you cut out will often depend on the shape and size of the selected images. Sometimes it is easier to first cut out shapes roughly using large scissors, leaving a generous margin around the image.

2 Cut around the edge of the image with a smaller pair of scissors. For delicate images, hold the paper in your hand and rotate it as you cut the curves. Always use a ruler to tear straight edges. To cut out internal unwanted paper and very intricate designs, you may prefer to use a craft knife with a cutting mat.

GLUING IMAGES IN POSITION

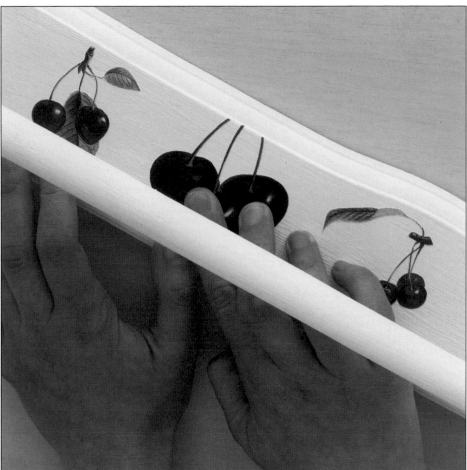

1 Arrange the cut-out images on the background surface. Using blobs of low-tack re-usable adhesive allows you to experiment with different arrangements without damaging or wasting the images.

2 When you are happy with the arrangement, glue the motifs on to the background using PVA (white) glue diluted with a little water. Some people prefer to use wallpaper paste, as it is slippery when wet, allowing the images to be easily slid into position.

3 Use a pair of tweezers to pick up delicate images. Place them in position, press down and rub over them with your fingers or a soft cloth to get rid of any air bubbles and excess glue. Wipe off any excess glue with a damp cloth. Allow to dry.

VARNISHING

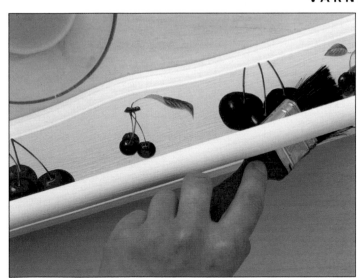

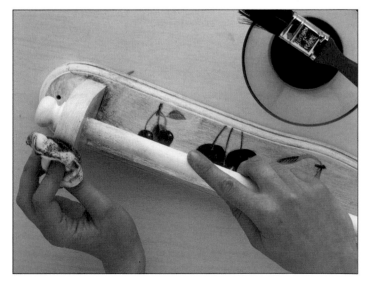

1 Varnish the finished decoupage to protect it. Apply up to 12 coats of clear varnish, lightly sanding between each coat once it has dried in a dust-free environment.

2 To age an object and to blend the colours, you can paint on a stained varnish such as antique pine or oak. To eliminate any brushstrokes, rub off the excess stain by lightly dabbing a clean cloth all over. Finally, apply a wax polish to give a deep satin finish.

BASIC TECHNIQUES: PAPER CUTTING AND COLLAGE

Paper cutting and collage are not complicated crafts, but some practice will improve your cutting and folding techniques. Essential pieces of equipment are a sharp pair of scissors or a craft knife with a supply of new blades. The number of times you fold paper will affect how many times a cut-out image is reproduced. Folding once produces a mirror image, twice gives four images and so on. To make a crisp edge by hand, fold the paper loosely, then run your nail along the crease.

FOLDING PAPER

1 Hold a metal ruler firmly on the paper, fold the paper up to its edge and run your thumbnail along it.

2 Alternatively, fold the paper loosely, then run the edge of a bone folder along it.

TRANSFERRING

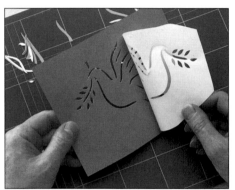

To transfer patterns, you can trace them directly on to the paper or use a photocopier. Alternatively, cut out a photocopy and stick it to the paper using spray adhesive, then carefully cut out the design.

SINGLE FOLDS

Fold the paper in half. Draw half of your pattern on the fold and cut it out. Open the paper out to reveal the perfectly symmetrical cut-out shape.

DOUBLE FOLDS

Fold the paper in half, then in half again. Cut a shape out of the middle of the square, without touching any fold or edge.

CUTTING PAPER

1 To start an internal cut, poke the pointed end of closed scissors into the centre of the paper that is to be removed. Withdraw the scissors, insert the lower blade through the hole and cut out the shape. Always turn the paper towards the blade, in the most comfortable position.

2 If you prefer to use a craft knife, hold it like a pencil and cut smoothly without pressing down hard. Always cut with a sharp blade. Use a cutting mat to protect your work surface and to prevent the paper slipping.

FINISHING OFF

The folds that you have made to reproduce the pattern of your papercut will still be visible after you unfold the finished work. You can flatten it by placing inside a book and applying pressure with a heavy weight for a day or two. Alternatively, cover the papercut with a sheet of paper and smooth the surface with a small metal ruler.

BASIC TECHNIQUES: STAMPING

Stamping is a quick and effective method of repeating a design on paper or card. Remember that motifs will be reversed when stamped. Use your stamp with an inkpad, applying light pressure, or with paint. Ready-made stamps in a multitude of designs are widely available, but they are also easy to make yourself using foam or sponge, lino (linoleum) blocks or even potatoes. Making a lino (linoleum) block stamp is fairly simple but the results can be surprisingly intricate. Simple potato prints are also amazingly effective.

USING HIGH- AND LOW-DENSITY SPONGES

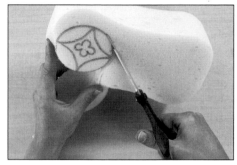

1 For detailed designs, first trace the motif, roughly cut around it and attach it to a high-density sponge using spray adhesive. Cut along the outline using a craft knife, then pinch the background and cut away.

2 A low-density sponge will give a softer image. Draw the design directly on to the sponge using a marker pen. Cut out the basic shapes using sharp scissors, then cut away the background.

USING A LINO (LINOLEUM) BLOCK

1 Make a tracing of the motif to fit the lino (linoleum) block. Slip a sheet of transfer paper, chalky side down, between the tracing and the lino (linoleum), then tape the edges in place with masking tape. Draw over the lines with a sharp pencil to transfer the design to the block.

2 Remove the paper and cut around the outline using a craft knife. Cut any fine detail or straight lines by making shallow, angular cuts from each side, then scoop out the V-shaped sections.

3 Cut the rest of the pattern using lino (linoleum) tools: a scoop for removing large areas of background and a gouge for cutting finer curves and pattern details. Hold the lino (linoleum) down firmly with your spare hand placed safely behind your cutting hand.

POTATO STAMPS

Cut a potato in half using a kitchen knife. Draw the motif on the potato using a fine felt-tipped pen. Using a craft knife, cut the outline, then undercut and scoop out the background. As potato stamps are short-lived, keep the tracing in case you need to cut another stamp.

COATING A STAMP WITH PAINT

1 Using a brush is a good way of applying thick water-based paint such as emulsion (latex) or artist's acrylic. One advantage is that you can use several colours on one stamp in a very controlled way.

2 Alternatively, use a roller. Place some paint on one side of a plate and run a small roller through it several times until it is covered evenly with colour. Test on scrap paper then run the roller over the stamp to transfer the paint.

BASIC TECHNIQUES: STENCILLING

Stencilling is not difficult but it is worth practising on scrap paper. Thick, dry paint is difficult to apply evenly and wet, runny paint will seep under the stencil, blurring the outline. Use very little paint and apply the colour with a dabbing and brushing movement and always use a fresh brush for each colour. You can stencil shapes with a single colour or build up a design using several colours applied one at a time. Varying the way the paint is applied will greatly affect the result and with practice you will be able to achieve quite different end results, varying from the subtle to the very bold.

CUTTING OUT STENCIL SHAPES

1 Trace the template with a pencil, then rub over the back with a soft pencil. Place the tracing right side up on stencil cardboard or clear acetate and draw over the original lines with a hard pencil. Alternatively, draw a design freehand, using a black felt-tipped pen for the acetate.

2 Tape the stencil on to a cutting mat and cut out the stencil using a craft knife. Cut towards you in a continuous line, with the blade on the line and lifting it from the stencil as little as possible. When working round awkward shapes, move the cutting board towards you and the knife.

BLOCK STENCILLING

Block stencilling usually consists of filling in large areas in a single solid colour. Do not apply the paint too heavily and blot off excess paint on blotting card before you begin. Two-colour blocking involves applying the first colour in some areas only, perhaps outlining those areas that are to receive the second colour.

ROTATING

Using a very dry brush with a tiny amount of paint, rotate the bristles in a circular motion to produce a lighter, softer look than block application. If you wish to add shading, apply the paint to one side of the stencil first then apply a slightly darker shade on the edges in the same way.

ROUGH STIPPLING

This method uses more paint and less pressure than rotating or flicking and gives a rougher look. Take a reasonable amount of paint on the bristles of the brush and place it down lightly. Do not go over the design too many times as this will spoil the effect. It is essential to dab most of the paint off the bristles before starting.

FLICKING

Here, the petals have been coloured by rotating using a very dry brush, but to achieve the flicking effect used on the leaves, use slightly more paint on the brush. Working from the centre, flick paint outwards once or twice. Do not overdo.

BRUSHING UP AND DOWN

This is similar to flicking. Using slightly more paint on your brush than for rotating, brush up and down, then from side to side. Keep the lines vertical and horizontal to give a lined effect.

DROP SHADOW

Apply the first colour, which should be a light shade, using a block effect. Move the stencil a few millimetres in one direction (here to the right), taking care not to move it up or down. Block again, using a darker colour to create the shadow effect.

BASIC TECHNIQUES: WORKING WITH CARDBOARD

The use of cardboard in a creative way has increased enormously over recent years, particularly as the awareness of the importance of recycling has grown. Generally made from about 60 per cent recycled pulp, cardboard's availability and cheapness make it a very appealing medium to work with. Moreover, cardboard is an easy material to handle and does not require many specialist skills nor does it involve the use of difficult equipment. The following simple techniques will help you handle cardboard successfully.

FOLDING FINE AND THICK CARDBOARD

1 To score fine cardboard, using a metal ruler, press the blade of a craft knife along the fold line, being careful not to cut too deeply. Gently fold the cardboard with the scored line inside the fold.

2 If the fold is to run along the flutes of thick corrugated cardboard, just run the edge of your thumb between the flutes firmly to make an indent, then fold. Do not use your nail as this may rip the surface.

JOINING CARDBOARD

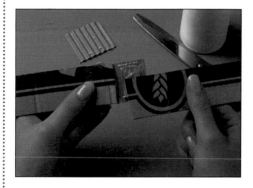

Cut away a small section of lining paper and fluting on the end of one strip, leaving just one layer of lining paper attached. Apply glue to this and stick the end of the other strip on top, butting up the ends.

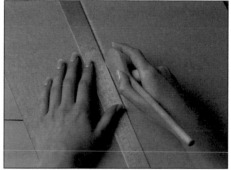

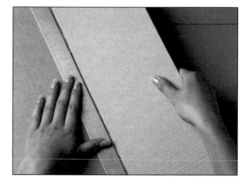

3 To get a neat fold across the flutes of thick corrugated cardboard, score it with a wooden spoon with a blunt point on it or a blunt pastry wheel. Run the point of the spoon along the fold line, using a ruler as a guide. Try not to rip the surface of the cardboard, just flatten the flutes.

4 To fold thick corrugated cardboard along the scored line, hold a ruler firmly to one side of the line. Carefully push the cardboard up along the other side of the line. Hold the cardboard with the flat of your hand so that it does not bend in the wrong place.

MAKING HOLES

Use a revolving hole punch to make neat holes in cardboard. Mark the position of the hole, select the required setting, then squeeze the punch together firmly on the mark, twisting it slightly to cut properly.

DRAWING CURVES

To make curved shapes, simply mark where the curve is to be and, choosing a paint can, cup or plate of the right size, draw around a section of it on to the cardboard.

STRENGTHENING

To strengthen corrugated cardboard further, sandwich several layers together with the flutes running vertically and horizontally to each other, maximizing the strength of each layer. Use a strong glue and leave to dry completely before cutting.

PAPIER-MACHE

Papier-mâché is one of the easiest and most satisfying of the
paper crafts. Not only does it make wonderful use of a major
waste material, it is ridiculously simple to produce. Although
almost any type of paper can be used to make papier-mâché,
perhaps the most commonly used type is newspaper. It is the
absorbency of newspaper that makes it ideal for soaking up the
glue and wallpaper paste that are the other two main ingredients
used. Papier-mâché can be fashioned into extremely sturdy
structures, useful articles for the home, or delicate, decorative
items. Some artists use it as a medium for sculptures, even quite
large ones. Papier-mâché is also easy to decorate,
using paint once the surface is sealed.

The projects illustrated on the following pages show how to
make and decorate a fascinating selection of useful and
decorative objects that you can use in your home or use as gifts.
They range from pretty, functional plates and bowls to
decorative wall sconces, from pomanders to scent your rooms
with to a waste bin for the office, from picture frames to
interesting boxes for hiding trinkets and keepsakes. There are
even suggestions for unusual jewellery and love tokens that any
recipient would cherish. As soon as you have mastered the two
main ways of making papier-mâché and practised some of the
projects shown here, there will be nothing to stop you
from creating any number of objects that your
imagination can conjure up.

BALLOON FRUIT BOWL

A balloon makes a satisfying mould for a papier-mâché bowl. Remove the balloon when the papier-mâché is dry by popping it with a pair of scissors. An elegant foot made from a ring of cardboard gives this bowl a stable base.

YOU WILL NEED
Materials
balloon
newspaper
wallpaper paste
stiff cardboard
masking tape
white emulsion (latex) paint
acrylic paints
acrylic spray varnish

Equipment
container for wallpaper paste
scissors
pencil
ruler
fine-grade sandpaper
small decorator's paintbrush
medium and fine artist's paintbrushes
paint-mixing container

1 Blow up the balloon fully to make a firm base for the papier-mâché. Tear newspaper into 2.5 cm (1 in) strips and soak in wallpaper paste. Cover the balloon in five layers of papier-mâché, leaving the area around the knot bare.

2 Leave the papier-mâché in a warm place until it is completely dry. Using scissors, burst the balloon and remove it. Trim the papier-mâché bowl to the desired height.

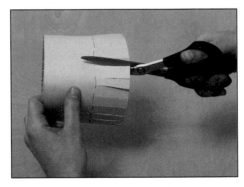

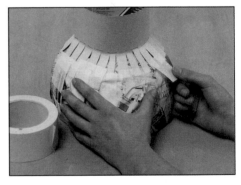

3 Cut a strip of cardboard about 13 cm (5 in) wide and mark a line 5 cm (2 in) from one long edge. Bend the strip into a ring and secure with masking tape. Cut 2 cm (¾ in) inside tabs all the way around up to the marked line.

4 Stand the bowl upright and centre the cardboard ring over it, bending the tabs outwards. Use masking tape to attach the foot to the bowl by all the tabs.

5 Cover the bowl and the foot in further layers of papier-mâché and leave in a warm place to dry completely. Roll up some sheets of newspaper and twist them tightly to make ropes long enough to go around the rim and foot of the bowl.

6 Using masking tape, attach the newspaper twists to the top and bottom of the foot and to the rim of the bowl. Cover with more layers of papier-mâché and leave to dry.

7 Lightly rub down with fine-grade sandpaper, then prime inside and out with two coats of white emulsion (latex) paint. Allow to dry. Decorate the bowl inside and out with acrylic paints and finish with a coat of acrylic varnish. Leave to dry.

FRAGRANT POMANDERS

Once believed to protect the wearer against infection and disease, sweet-smelling pomanders have been popular for centuries. These delicately coloured papier-mâché pomanders are made using rubber balls as moulds, and are filled with dried lavender to perfume a room with a lovely lingering fragrance.

YOU WILL NEED

Materials
small rubber balls
newspaper
powdered glue paste
reusable putty adhesive
PVA (white) glue
scrap wood
cork
emulsion (latex) paints: white and
 a variety of colours
dried lavender
narrow ribbon
pearl-headed pins

Equipment
petroleum jelly
container for glue paste
egg cups
pencil
craft knife
cutting mat
bradawl
medium artist's paintbrush
paper funnel

1 Smear a thin layer of petroleum jelly over the surface of each rubber ball so that it will be easy to remove the papier-mâché when dry.

2 Tear small, narrow strips of newspaper and coat them with glue paste. Cover each ball with six layers of strips, and stand in an egg cup to dry.

3 When the papier-mâché is dry, draw a line around each ball to divide it into two equal halves. Secure each ball on a cutting mat with a blob of reusable putty adhesive and cut carefully around the line, repositioning the ball as necessary. Separate the paper shells and leave them face-up to dry.

4 When the shells are dry, glue them back together with PVA (white) glue, aligning the cut edges precisely. Cover the joins (seams) with two layers of small, thin papier-mâché strips and leave them to dry.

5 Place each pomander on a piece of scrap wood and pierce holes in the top with a bradawl. Cut a thin section of cork into quarters. Make a small hole for the cork in the bottom of each pomander.

6 Prime the pomanders with a coat of white emulsion (latex) paint, then a coat of coloured paint, avoiding the holes. Using a paper funnel, fill each pomander with lavender and seal with the cork. Tie a ribbon bow around each pomander. Keep the ribbons in place with a blob of PVA (white) glue and pearl-headed pins.

FISH
PRINT
PLATE

This beautiful papier-mâché plate takes its shape from the dinner plate used as a mould. It is decorated with hand-printed decoupage, made with the lino (linoleum)-printing technique, and is finally embellished with some freehand painting.

YOU WILL NEED

Materials
white paper
lino (linoleum)
acrylic paints: sky blue and
   ultramarine
newspaper
wallpaper paste
white emulsion (latex) paint
all-purpose glue
acrylic spray varnish

Equipment
marker pen
tracing paper
hard and soft pencils
lino (linoleum)-cutting tool
paint-mixing containers
medium and fine artist's paintbrushes
scissors
dinner plate to use as mould
cling film (plastic wrap)
container for wallpaper paste
fine-grade sandpaper

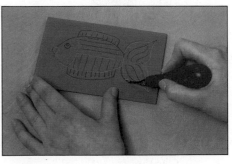

1 Work out the fish design on paper, using bold lines that will suit the lino (linoleum)-cutting technique. Trace the design and rub over the back of the tracing with a soft pencil. Transfer the drawing to a piece of lino (linoleum).

2 Using a lino (linoleum)-cutting tool, cut out the lines of the fish design. Take care not to gouge too deeply into the lino (linoleum).

3 Cover the lino (linoleum) with sky blue acrylic paint, using broad, light brush strokes. Don't overload the brush or allow the paint to flood into the grooves of the design.

4 Lay a sheet of paper carefully over the design and press down evenly. Repeat to make as many prints as you need to decorate your plate.

5 When the paint is dry, cut out all the fish prints using scissors and reserve them while you make the plate.

6 Cover the dinner plate with cling film (plastic wrap). Tear newspaper into 2.5 cm (1 in) strips and soak in wallpaper paste. Cover the plate with five layers of papier-mâché and leave in a warm place until dry.

7 Remove the papier-mâché carefully from the mould and peel away the cling film (plastic wrap). Trim the edges of the plate and finish them and the back neatly with another layer of papier-mâché.

8 When the plate is completely dry, smooth it with fine-grade sandpaper then paint both sides with two coats of white emulsion (latex). Leave to dry, then glue on the fish prints.

9 Using a fine brush and ultramarine acrylic paint, add a random pattern of spots all over the white areas of the plate. Allow the paint to dry, then spray the plate on both sides with a protective coat of acrylic varnish and leave to dry.

HANDMADE PAPER GLOBE

To make this elegant globe shade, you could use light tissue paper mixed with fibrous handmade paper scraps, layering dried flowers and leaves between them. Keep the same thickness across the top of the balloon mould, but allow it to taper off towards the tied end.

YOU WILL NEED
Materials
balloon
wallpaper paste
handmade paper scraps containing leaves and flower petals
cream or white tissue paper
gauze or mesh
cardboard ring the same size as the lamp fixture
all-purpose glue
pendant lamp fixture

Equipment
container for wallpaper paste
small decorator's paintbrush
pin
scissors

1 Blow up the balloon fully to make a firm base for the papier-mâché. Apply wallpaper paste to small pieces of paper, and stick them on to the balloon in a random overlapping arrangement, beginning at the top.

2 Cover the top two-thirds of the balloon with three layers of paper, tissue paper and gauze or mesh.

Leave until bone dry. This may take several days. Use a pin to pop the balloon and remove it from the shade.

3 Cut a small hole in the top of the shade. Use the lamp fixture as a guide.

4 Reinforce the hole by gluing a cardboard ring inside the shade. Screw the two halves of the lamp fixture together, one on each side of the shade, and ask an electrician to wire the fixture to a flex (cord).

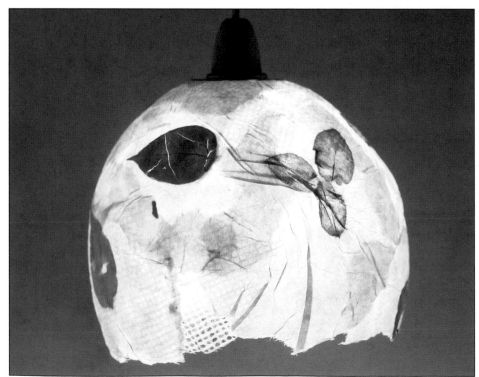

DECORATIVE PLATE AND BOWL

Formed from recycled paper, papier-mâché is inexpensive, easy to make, and produces surprisingly fine results. The pieces shown here would not be appropriate for serving a meal, but they are a delightfully decorative feature on the table, and could perhaps be given as party favours to each guest.

YOU WILL NEED

Materials
plenty of white packing paper
wallpaper paste
white matt emulsion (latex) paint

Equipment
plate and bowl to use as moulds
cling film (plastic wrap)
pastry brush or similar
small decorator's paintbrush

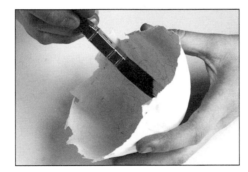

1 Tear the paper into strips. Cover the plate and bowl with sheets of cling film (plastic wrap) for protection. Apply paste to the cling film (plastic wrap) using a pastry brush.

2 Lay the paper strips on the cling film (plastic wrap) to cover it, then paste the paper. Apply another layer of paper. Allow to dry thoroughly. Repeat until the desired thickness is reached. Allow to dry thoroughly. This process may take a couple of days, depending on how thick you wish the papier-mâché to be.

3 Very carefully, remove the papier-mâché bowl and plate from their respective moulds, then paint them with an even coat of white matt emulsion (latex) paint, using the small decorator's paintbrush. Leave the bowl and plate in a safe place to dry thoroughly.

LOVE TOKEN BOWL

This bowl is made using a very simple papier-mâché technique, but the decorative design adds a special touch. It would make a delightful container for a Valentine's gift, such as chocolates or a small trinket.

YOU WILL NEED

Materials
newspaper
papier-mâché pulp
PVA (white) glue
white acrylic primer
masking tape
gouache or acrylic paints: blue,
    white, red, yellow and gold
clear gloss varnish

Equipment
bowl to use as mould
petroleum jelly
container for PVA glue
medium and fine artist's paintbrushes
tracing paper
pencil
scissors
paint-mixing container

1 Line the bowl with petroleum jelly, then with newspaper strips. Press a layer of papier-mâché pulp into the bowl and leave to dry. When dry, release the pulp from the bowl and cover with newspaper strips dipped in PVA (white) glue. Leave to dry.

2 Paint the papier-mâché bowl with white primer. Trace the template, enlarging it as required. Snip the edges so the template may be taped flat inside the bowl, then transfer the outline.

3 Paint the background pale blue, dabbing on lighter shades for a mottled effect.

4 Paint the design, mixing colours for greater subtlety. Paint the rim gold. When dry, apply a coat of varnish.

ORANGE BOWL

Save old magazines so that you can collect orange and yellow paper to make this papier-mâché bowl: it is designed to look like half an orange, plain outside and textured inside.

YOU WILL NEED

Materials
old newspaper, torn into strips
wallpaper paste
old magazine pages that are
*   predominantly orange and yellow*
plain orange wrapping paper
gloss varnish
gold paint

Equipment
large bowl to use as mould
petroleum jelly
container for wallpaper paste
scissors
medium and fine artist's paintbrushes

1 Coat the inside of the bowl with petroleum jelly. Soak the newspaper strips in wallpaper paste. Cover the inside of the bowl with at least ten layers of strips. Let the bowl dry out completely, then gently ease it from the mould.

2 Tear the old magazine pages into long, narrow triangles and paste them around the inside of the bowl so that they taper towards the bottom.

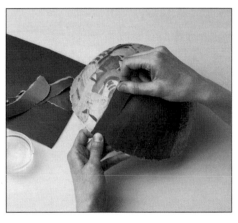

3 Cover the outside of the bowl with torn strips of plain orange wrapping paper, carefully overlapping the edges.

4 Let the bowl dry completely, then trim the top edge using scissors. Coat the bowl with a protective layer of varnish. Paint a thin line of gold paint along the top edge.

DECORATIVE FRAME

This frame is constructed around a cardboard base that is scored with a knife before being folded. Layers of papier-mâché are added and the frame is decorated using clay that hardens by itself, without firing. The colours used here are strong and bold: use softer colours if you prefer.

YOU WILL NEED
Materials
cardboard
masking tape
wire
wallpaper paste
newspaper
white emulsion (latex) paint
self-hardening clay
poster paints: royal blue, violet and
  yellow
clear varnish
PVA (white) glue

Equipment
pencil
tracing paper
ruler
craft knife
container for wallpaper paste
large and medium artist's
  paintbrushes
clay-modelling tool

1 Trace the template and cut out the frame from cardboard. Cut out the centre square and save it. This will be used later on to stick your picture on and make the backing for the frame. Score along the dotted lines using a craft knife. Be careful not to cut right through.

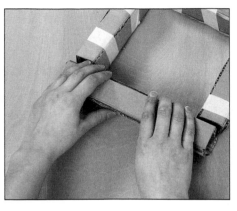

2 Fold each flap inwards along the scored edges and tape the frame together with masking tape.

3 Attach a piece of wire to the back, using masking tape. Mix up the wallpaper paste according to the manufacturer's instructions.

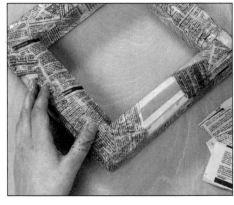

4 Tear the newspaper into pieces about 2.5 cm (1 in) square. Dip in the paste and stick on the frame until both front and back are covered.

5 Prime the frame with white emulsion (latex) and leave it to dry. Give the frame a second coat of emulsion (latex), to make sure that the surface is opaque. Leave this to dry.

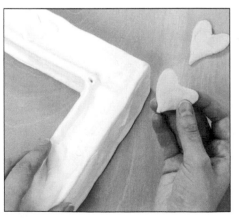

6 Decorate the front with self-hardening clay. Form heart shapes by hand and push these on to the frame. Hold them in place by smoothing down the sides of the hearts with a clay-modelling tool.

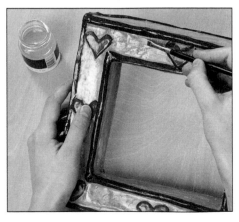

7 Paint the frame with poster paints and leave to dry. Apply a coat of varnish. Stick your painting or photograph on the backing card set aside in step 1 and attach it to the frame with glue or masking tape.

KEEPSAKE BOX

This box's sophisticated appearance belies its simple construction; it is straightforward to make, but must be precisely measured and cut. The delicate surface is achieved by painting with three colours, overlaid and rubbed back to create an aged effect. Subtle painted motifs and collaged scraps enhance the look.

YOU WILL NEED
Materials
A2 (16½ x 23 in) sheet of mounting
 board
PVA (white) glue
masking tape
newspaper
wallpaper paste
white emulsion (latex) paint
gouache paints: variety of colours
scraps of interesting paper
matt acrylic varnish
ornamental button

Equipment
metal ruler
set square
pencil
craft knife
cutting mat
containers for PVA (white) glue and
 wallpaper paste
brush for PVA (white) glue
medium and small artist's paintbrushes
fine-grade sandpaper
paint-mixing container

1 For the base of the box, cut two pieces of mounting board measuring 11.5 x 16.5 cm (4½ x 6½ in), and glue them together. Using a metal ruler and pencil, carefully measure and mark the positions of the box walls and compartments as follows. Draw a rectangle 1.5 cm (⅝ in) from the edges of the base. Draw a second rectangle 2 mm (1⁄16 in) smaller all round. Divide this rectangle into eight equal sections for the compartments.

2 Cut three strips of mounting board measuring 13.5 x 2.5 cm (5¼ x 1 in). Glue and tape one strip along the centre of the base. Glue and tape the other two strips along the edges of the inner rectangle. Cut two further strips of 2.5 cm (1 in) wide mounting board to make the walls for the ends of the inner rectangle. Glue and tape one of these strips into place.

3 Cut four strips of 3 cm (1⅛ in) wide board to make walls for the larger rectangle. Glue and tape three strips in position, as before. Measure and cut eight pieces of 2.5 cm (1 in) wide board to make the compartments, and glue and tape them in place inside the central rectangle. Glue the remaining two board strips in place at the side of the box.

4 Cut four 3 cm (1⅛ in) wide strips of board to make the outer walls of the base, and glue and tape them into position. Cut four strips of board to fit over the space between the compartments and the outer walls, and glue and tape them into place.

5 To make the lid, cut out two rectangles of mounting board 3 mm (⅛ in) smaller all round than the opening in the top of the box. Glue the rectangles together. Draw a line around the lid 2 mm (1⁄16 in) in from the edge. Cut four 3 mm (⅛ in) pieces of mounting board to fit inside the pencil line and glue them in place to make a lip for the lid.

6 Using a pencil and ruler, divide the top of the lid into four sections to find the central point. Cut a small rectangle of board to make a ledge for the button that forms the handle. Cut a small notch into the rectangle to contain the shank of the button.

7 Tear the news-
paper into pieces
about 2.5 cm (1 in)
square. Dip them in
the paste and stick
on the box, covering

the entire box and
lid. Paste two layers
smoothly over the
surface. Leave the
box and lid to dry
thoroughly.

8 Prime the box
and lid with
white emulsion
(latex) paint. When
dry, apply a coat of
turquoise paint,
mixed from gouache
and white emulsion
(latex). Follow this

with a coat of
lighter, blue-green
paint, then yellow
ochre. Apply the
colours with a dry
brush and leave to
dry. Lightly rub
down the surface
with sandpaper.

9 Paste the scraps
of paper on to
the surface of the
box and lid. Sketch
decorative motifs
faintly with a pencil,
then fill in using
gouache paints.

When the box and
lid are dry, seal
them with a coat
of acrylic varnish.
Finally, glue the
button to the top
of the lid to make
the handle.

CLASSICAL GREEK VASE

This stately vase demonstrates how papier-mâché can disguise and breathe new life into almost anything: it is based on a balloon and yogurt pots (containers). The final layer of natural-coloured recycled paper gives the vase a stone-like quality, complemented by the twine decoration.

YOU WILL NEED
Materials
balloon
newspaper
PVA (white) glue
tracing paper
heavy corrugated cardboard
thick cotton cord
1 large and 1 medium-sized yogurt
    pot (container)
masking tape
strong clear glue
decorative recycled paper
natural twine

Equipment
small bowl
container for PVA (white) glue
pencil
craft knife
cutting mat
small decorator's paintbrush
scissors
fine-grade sandpaper

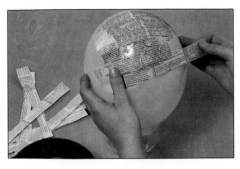

1 Blow up the balloon and rest it on a small bowl. Tear the newspaper into 2.5 cm (1 in) strips, coat them in diluted PVA (white) glue and cover the balloon with five layers of papier-mâché. Leave in a warm place to dry.

2 Trace the handle pattern and transfer it twice to the corrugated cardboard. Cut out the handles using a craft knife and cutting mat. Brush diluted PVA (white) glue over the handles to seal them. Leave to dry completely.

3 Cover the handles with four layers of papier-mâché, working the strips neatly over the edges to keep the shapes sharply defined. Leave them overnight in a warm place to dry.

4 Cut a length of cotton cord to fit around the top of each of the yogurt pots (containers). Use tape to hold the cord in place, to make a prominent lip on the neck and foot of the vase.

5 Using narrow strips of newspaper, apply five layers of papier-mâché to the yogurt pots (containers). Leave them overnight in a warm place to dry. When dry, cut the bases from the yogurt pots (containers).

6 Burst the balloon and pull it out of the papier-mâché. Position the larger yogurt pot (container) on top of the wider end of the balloon shape. Draw around the inside of the pot (container) and cut out.

7 Place the narrow end of the balloon shape on the smaller yogurt pot (container) and glue and tape in position. Attach the larger yogurt pot (container) to the top of the vase in the same way, then add the two handles.

8 Cover all the joins (seams) with three layers of papier-mâché. Leave overnight in a warm place to dry. Tear the recycled paper into small strips and coat them in diluted PVA (white) glue. Cover the vase completely with one layer of papier-mâché. Leave to dry.

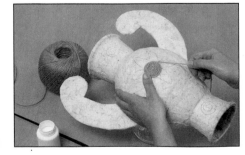

9 Smooth the surface slightly, using sandpaper. Draw guidelines for the twine decoration. Rest the vase on a small bowl. Paint undiluted PVA (white) glue over each area to be decorated and apply lengths of twine, coiling them over the guidelines.

STARRY DRAWER KNOBS

Decorative knobs can enliven the plainest door or drawer. These drawer knobs are made entirely from tissue paper pulp, but are very strong when dry. A machine screw fixes (attaches) them to the drawer. They are simply finished with spirals of household string, and a touch of gold paint to emphasize their shape.

YOU WILL NEED
Materials
tissue paper
PVA (white) glue
newspaper
white emulsion (latex) paint
hairy (rough) string
gold acrylic paint

Equipment
container for PVA glue
wire rack
scrap wood
bradawl
pencil
a 50 x 3 mm (2 x ⅛ in) machine screw and 3 nuts for each knob
fine-grade sandpaper
medium artist's paintbrush
scissors
clamp
hand drill

1 Loosely crumple a sheet of tissue paper into a ball and dip it into diluted PVA (white) glue until completely saturated.

2 Squeeze the excess glue from the paper and work it between your hands for a few seconds, so that it breaks down and becomes pulpy.

3 To make each knob, hold a ball of pulp between your thumbs and fingers and flatten it into a disc. Gently press the disc between your fingers until the paper is completely smooth. Place on a wire rack to dry slightly.

4 Tear small pieces of tissue paper and dip them into diluted PVA (white) glue. Squeeze and roll them between finger and thumb to make pointed shapes. Press the points firmly into the edges of each disc. Leave to dry thoroughly on a wire rack.

5 Cover the knobs with one layer of small papier-mâché strips. When dry, place on a piece of scrap wood and use a bradawl to make a hole in the centre. Widen each hole with a pencil until a machine screw will fit into it.

6 Insert a screw through the middle of each knob and secure it in place with a matching nut. Cover the head of each screw with two layers of papier-mâché strips and leave the knobs to dry.

7 Lightly sand each knob then prime with two coats of white emulsion (latex) paint, allowing the first coat to dry thoroughly before the second is added.

8 Spread a little undiluted PVA (white) glue in the middle of each knob and coil a length of string on to it to make a decorative centre.

9 Paint the tips of the knobs gold. Mark the centre of each drawer. Clamp the drawer firmly and drill a hole. Wind a nut on to the machine-screw shank. Push the end of the shank through the hole in the drawer and add another nut. Tighten all the nuts.

SWEET- HEART FRAMES

These frames are made from pulped sugar paper, which is moulded into shape then dried to make a surprisingly strong material. You can use coloured paper, as here, or white paper, ready to paint or decorate.

YOU WILL NEED

Materials
A2 (16½ x 23 in) sheet of coloured sugar paper for each heart
kitchen foil (tinfoil)
1 large and 1 small bottle cap for each heart
paper ribbon
all-purpose glue
adhesive tape
picture

Equipment
heat-resistant bowl
liquidizer (optional)
small heart-shaped cake tins
glue brush

1 For each heart tear the sugar paper into small pieces and place in a bowl. Pour on boiling water and leave to cool. Break up the paper with your hands or put in a liquidizer. Drain off the excess water.

2 Small cake tins make suitable moulds for the pulp hearts. Line each cake tin with kitchen foil (tinfoil).

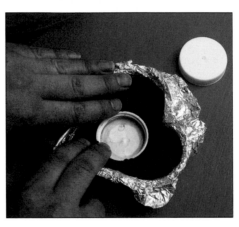

3 Place a small bottle cap in the centre of the tin mould and pack pulped paper around it. Press out as much water as possible then continue to pack in more pulp.

4 When the pulp is level with the top of the cap, put a larger cap centrally on top to form the rebate to the frame. Pack more pulp around the cap to the top of the tin, draining off the excess water.

5 Lift the foil out of the mould and carefully remove. Leave the pulp to dry in a warm place for 2–3 days, or in a warm oven. Remove the bottle caps.

6 Glue a loop of paper ribbon to the back of each frame for hanging. Tape a picture into the rebate.

CHECKED DOORS

You can turn dull bathroom or kitchen cabinets into striking items, using just a few layers of tissue and handmade paper. Seal with diluted varnish to make the paper highly practical and to create a translucent, interesting texture. Gather a collection of papers that match your existing decor, and experiment with different colours, shapes and designs.

YOU WILL NEED

Materials

water-based acrylic wood primer
white tissue paper
PVA (white) glue
handmade papers: yellow ochre
  and brown
sheet of Japanese tissue paper
thin corrugated cardboard
coloured tissue paper
matt oil varnish
white spirit (turpentine)

Equipment

fine-grade sandpaper
small and medium decorator's
  paintbrushes
container for PVA (white) glue
metal ruler
scissors
thin rubber gloves

1 Lightly sand the front and sides of each door. Apply a coat of acrylic wood primer and leave it to dry thoroughly.

2 Tear pieces of white tissue paper. Apply one layer to the front of the door, using diluted PVA (white) glue.

3 Measure the inner recess of the door. With the aid of a metal ruler, tear large squares of yellow ochre and brown handmade paper to fit the space. Reserve the brown squares.

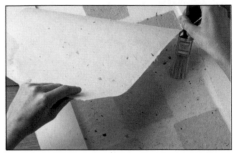

4 Using diluted PVA (white) glue and a brush, attach the yellow squares to the front of the door in a checked pattern. Tear a rectangle of Japanese tissue paper the same size as the inner panel, and glue it over the top of the yellow squares to subdue the colour.

5 Cut small squares from the cardboard and glue them around the door frame with undiluted PVA (white) glue to make a low-relief border.

6 Tear irregular-sized strips of coloured tissue paper and glue over the cardboard squares and the sides of the door, using diluted PVA (white) glue and a wide brush.

7 Tear tiny squares of brown and yellow handmade paper. Using diluted PVA (white) glue, stick them on to the centres of the cardboard squares, alternating the colours.

8 Glue the large brown paper squares between the yellow squares in the door recess. Tear narrow strips of the same paper and glue around the inside of the recess, covering the edges of the squares. Leave to dry. Wearing rubber gloves, and working in a well-ventilated area, dilute two parts varnish with one part white spirit (turpentine) and seal the door with two coats.

DECOUPAGE
WASTE BIN

Brown parcel wrapping paper is used for the top layer of papier-mâché on this sturdy bin and makes a perfect background for the gold gift wrap decoupage decoration. Vary the size and pattern of the decorations to give depth and an interesting texture to the bin.

YOU WILL NEED
Materials
heavy corrugated cardboard
gummed paper tape
PVA (white) glue
paper
wallpaper paste
brown wrapping paper
sheet of gold patterned gift wrap
acrylic spray varnish

Equipment
pair of compasses (compass)
pencil
metal ruler
craft knife
cutting mat
sponge
large decorator's paintbrush
containers for PVA (white) and
    wallpaper paste

1 Using a pair of compasses (compass), draw a circle with a radius of 13 cm (5 in) on the cardboard. Next divide the circumference into six sections. Reduce the radius of the compasses (compass) to 6 cm (2½ in) and mark off six intersecting arcs, so that the circle is divided into 12. Join the marks to give a 12-sided shape and cut out using the craft knife.

2 Cut out a sheet of corrugated cardboard 78 x 35 cm (30 x 14 in). (The corrugations should run vertically down the sides of the bin.) Divide it into 12 sections, 6 cm (2½ in) wide, and rule a line 5 cm (2 in) from the top edge. Score along all the lines.

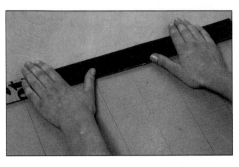

3 Fold over the 5 cm (2 in) strip across the top to make the border of the waste bin.

4 Cut 12 pieces of gummed tape and stick them to each edge of the bin base, moistening them with a damp sponge.

5 Turn the base over and use the gummed tape to attach the sides to the base, bending the sides along the scored lines.

6 Use gummed paper tape to join the side seam, taking the tape over the top edge and down inside the bin. Seal the cardboard with a coat of diluted PVA (white) glue.

7 Tear some paper into strips and soak in wallpaper paste. Apply four layers of papier-mâché to the bin, inside and out. Leave in a warm place to dry. Apply a final layer of papier-mâché using brown wrapping paper. Allow to dry. To decorate the bin, tear images from the gift wrap.

8 Paste the images with undiluted PVA (white) glue and arrange them all over the bin as you wish.

9 Tear some narrow strips of gift wrap and stick these to the rim of the bin and the line below the raised border. Protect the bin inside and out with a coat of acrylic spray varnish. Leave to dry.

LEAFY WALL PANELS

Papier-mâché panels and other architectural details were popular during the nineteenth century when elaborate imitations of plaster and stuccowork were produced. These panels are less ornate than their predecessors, but will add a touch of elegance around a door frame.

YOU WILL NEED
Materials
heavy corrugated cardboard
PVA (white) glue
thick cotton cord
masking tape
newspaper
emulsion (latex) paints: white
    and blue
petroleum jelly

Equipment
scissors
small decorator's paintbrushes
container for PVA (white) glue
sheet of plastic
metal ruler
pencil
hole punch
tracing paper
cutting mat
craft knife
fine-grade sandpaper
soft cloth

1 For the side and top of the door, cut three panels of cardboard to fit around your door. Brush both sides of each panel with a coat of diluted PVA (white) glue and lay flat on a sheet of plastic to dry.

2 Draw a line down the centre of each panel. Measure and mark a point every 15 cm (6 in) down the line.

3 Dab a spot of undiluted PVA (white) glue at each 15 cm (6 in) mark. Cut a length of cotton cord for each panel, and attach in a wavy line, curving it in and out between the dabs of glue. Use small pieces of masking tape to keep the cord in place. Line the panels up, end to end, to make sure that the ends of the cords form a continuous wavy pattern.

4 Make a tracing of the leaf template and transfer it four times to a piece of cardboard for each panel. Place the cardboard on a cutting mat and carefully cut out all the leaves, using a craft knife. Glue the leaves at equal distances down the length of each panel. Tear newspaper into 2.5 cm (1 in) strips, dip in diluted PVA (white) glue, and cover each panel with three layers. Lay flat on a sheet of plastic to dry.

5 Gently rub down each panel with fine-grade sandpaper. Prime the panels with two coats of white emulsion (latex) paint and leave to dry thoroughly.

6 Paint the front of each panel with a coat of blue emulsion (latex) paint. Leave them to dry thoroughly.

7 Using a soft cloth, apply a very thin coat of petroleum jelly over the front of each panel.

8 Paint each panel with two coats of white emulsion (latex) paint, completely covering the blue surface. Leave the panels to dry thoroughly.

9 Rub down the surface of each panel very lightly, using fine-grade sandpaper, so that specks of blue paint are revealed. Attach the panels around the door frame, using PVA (white) glue.

NAUTICAL WALL HANGING

This jaunty wallhanging provides safe storage for all those important little odds and ends that are always going astray. Hung in the bathroom, it makes the ideal place to keep nail varnish and cotton balls.

YOU WILL NEED

Materials
balloon
newspaper
wallpaper paste
heavy corrugated cardboard
PVA (white) glue
masking tape
white emulsion (latex) paint
acrylic paints
acrylic spray varnish
picture-hanging eyelet

Equipment
container for wallpaper paste
strong scissors
marker pen
ruler
small decorator's paintbrushes
fine-grade sandpaper
fine artist's paintbrush
paint-mixing container

1 Blow up the balloon fully to make a firm base for the papier-mâché. Tear newspaper into 2.5 cm (1 in) strips and soak in wallpaper paste. Cover the lower two-thirds of the balloon in five layers of papier-mâché.

2 Leave the papier-mâché in a warm place until completely dry. Burst the balloon and remove it. Using large, strong scissors, trim the top of the bowl evenly, then cut it in half.

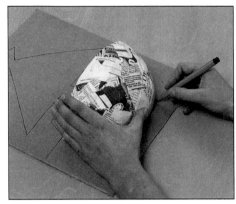

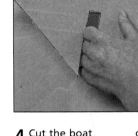

3 Using a marker pen, draw the mast, sails and cabin of the boat on the cardboard. Place the half-bowl in position and draw around it to complete the boat.

4 Cut the boat shape out of the cardboard using the scissors. Seal the cardboard with a coat of diluted PVA (white) glue and leave to dry.

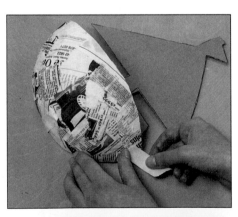

5 Using masking tape, attach the papier-mâché bowl shape to the cardboard shape. Cover the sails and the back of the boat with layers of papier-mâché and add another layer to the bowl. Leave in a warm place to dry completely.

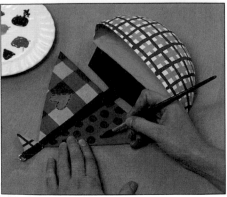

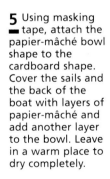

6 Rub down lightly with fine-grade sandpaper, then prime with two coats of white emulsion (latex). Allow to dry then decorate with acrylic paints. Leave to dry.

7 Attach an eyelet to the top of the mast. Spray the boat with varnish.

NIGHT AND DAY MOBILE

Golden suns and blue moons contrast with one another in this attractive mobile. Although mobiles are usually associated with children's rooms, this one is sophisticated enough to hang up as a decoration in any room in the house.

YOU WILL NEED
Materials
corrugated cardboard
newspaper
masking tape
wallpaper paste
small brass screw rings
epoxy resin glue
PVA (white) glue
white emulsion (latex) paint
gouache paints: blue, silver, orange,
     red and white
gloss and matt varnishes
gold enamel paint
small jewellery jump rings
picture-hanging wire

Equipment
pencil
craft knife
container for wallpaper paste
medium and fine artist's paintbrushes
paint-mixing container

1 Draw sun, star and moon shapes on the corrugated cardboard and cut them out with a sharp craft knife.

2 Bulk out the shapes by scrunching up pieces of newspaper. Wrap masking tape around the newspaper balls to secure them in place.

3 Cover the shapes in several layers of newspaper strips soaked in wallpaper paste. Allow to dry overnight, or longer if necessary.

4 Screw in the brass screw rings in the appropriate places for hanging, securing them with epoxy resin glue.

5 Coat the shapes with PVA (white) glue and allow to dry. Coat with white emulsion (latex) and leave to dry again.

6 Mix the gouache paints to make a range of bright colours and decorate the shapes.

7 Give the shapes several coats of gloss varnish, picking out some areas in matt varnish to contrast. Allow to dry. Add details in gold enamel, painted on with a fine paintbrush.

8 Assemble all the pieces, using the brass screw rings and jump rings to join them together. Suspend the mobile from a length of picture wire threaded through the ring in the topmost shape.

SUNBURST BOWL

Papier-mâché gives you the ability to make graceful vessels without the skill and equipment needed for making ceramics. This bowl is ideal for fruit, nuts or small display items, but you may well want to leave it empty to show it off. Use all your creativity to make the design as exuberant as possible.

YOU WILL NEED
Materials
petroleum jelly
newspaper
papier-mâché pulp
PVA (white) glue
white emulsion (latex) paint
gouache or acrylic paints: yellow, blue
    and red
gold "liquid leaf" paint or gold
    gouache paint
fixative spray
gloss varnish

Equipment
bowl for mould
container for PVA (white) glue
medium decorator's paintbrush
pair of compasses (compass)
pencil
fine artist's paintbrush
paint-mixing container

1 Apply a coat of petroleum jelly to the inside of the bowl you are using as a mould. Tear strips of newspaper and, after dipping them in water, lay them over the inside of the mould.

2 Press the papier-mâché pulp into the mould so it is about 1 cm (½ in) thick. Leave to dry in a warm place, such as an airing cupboard. This usually takes about five days.

3 Release the dried pulp from the mould. Dip strips of newspaper in PVA (white) glue and use these to cover the dried pulp bowl. Leave to dry.

4 Apply two coats of white emulsion (latex) paint to the bowl, allowing the first coat to dry completely before applying the second.

5 Use a pair of compasses (compass) to locate the sun shape accurately; first draw a small circle for the centre and then a larger one to contain the rays. Draw the rays freehand.

6 Paint the yellow and gold areas. Paint the rim in gold. Fill in the blue background, leaving a white band below the gold rim.

7 Finally, paint the red border and allow to dry. Seal the bowl with fixative spray. Protect it with a coat of varnish.

■ WALL SCONCE

Delicate touches of gold glint in the candlelight on this pretty sconce. The printed pages used for the papier-mâché have been left showing as part of the decoration so, instead of newspaper, use a few pages from an old book for the final layer.

YOU WILL NEED
Materials
heavy corrugated cardboard
masking tape
PVA (white) glue
galvanized wire
newspaper
wallpaper paste
old book
white emulsion (latex) paint
gold wax crayon
acrylic spray varnish
nightlight in metal container
strong clear glue
small mirror

Equipment
pencil
ruler
strong scissors
containers for PVA (white) glue and wallpaper paste
large, medium and fine artist's paintbrushes
pliers
paint-mixing container

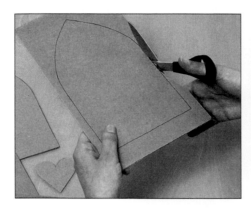

1 Using a photocopier, enlarge the templates and draw them on cardboard. The back and base of the wall sconce are each made from three layers of cardboard for extra strength. Cut out.

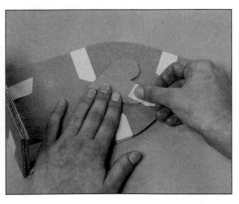

2 Tape the layers of the back and base together, then tape them at right angles to each other. Tape the heart shape to the upper back section, leaving room for the mirror. Seal with a coat of diluted PVA (white) glue.

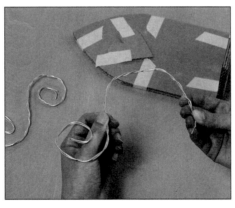

3 Twist two lengths of galvanized wire together, then bend them into a curly S-shape to fit between the back and the base. Twist a second pair of wires to match exactly.

4 Tape the wire supports firmly to the back and base. Tear newspaper into 2 cm (1 in) strips and soak in wallpaper paste. Cover the sconce in four layers of papier-mâché. Use pages from an old book for the final layer.

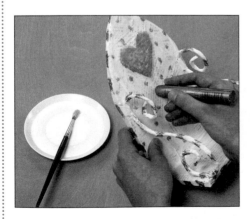

5 Leave the sconce in a warm place to dry completely, then paint it all over with a wash of diluted white emulsion (latex) paint. When dry, colour the heart gold and add an all-over pattern of spots, using a gold wax crayon.

6 Spray the sconce with acrylic varnish to protect the decoration. Apply a few coats to give a good finish.

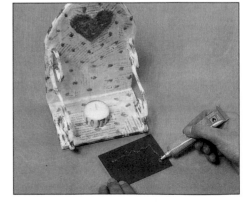

7 Decorate the nightlight container to match the sconce and glue it in the middle of the base, using strong clear glue. Glue a small mirror to the inside lower back of the sconce to reflect the flame.

CROWN BOX

This regal box would be perfect for holding cufflinks or earrings. Bigger boxes could, of course, be made for larger items – perhaps envelopes and writing paper, or paintbrushes.

YOU WILL NEED

Materials
heavy corrugated cardboard
strong clear glue
masking tape
newspaper
PVA (white) glue
white emulsion (latex) paint
poster or gouache paints
clear gloss varnish

Equipment
pencil
ruler
craft knife
cutting mat
container for PVA (white) glue
fine-grade sandpaper
medium and large artist's
  paintbrushes

1 Using a photocopier, enlarge the templates for the box pieces and transfer them to the cardboard. Cut out each piece with a craft knife. Glue the pieces together, and tape them in place to dry.

2 Tear the newspaper into strips about 2.5 cm (1 in) wide. Dip each newspaper strip into diluted PVA (white) glue and stick it down on to the box framework. Overlap each strip of paper slightly, to give added strength. Cover both parts of the box with four layers of papier-mâché, and leave to dry in a warm place.

3 When the box is dry, lightly smooth its surface with fine-grade sandpaper then prime it with two coats of white emulsion (latex) paint. Draw in the crown motifs.

4 Decorate the box with poster or gouache paints. You may wish to add definition to the design by painting the edges black.

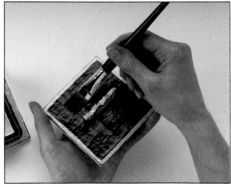

5 Allow the box to dry overnight, then seal it with two coats of clear gloss varnish. Leave to dry.

DISC NECKLACE

Papier-mâché is made by recycling paper, so why not carry on this ecological theme by decorating a papier-mâché necklace with daisies and insects? Alternatively, decorate the discs with other motifs of your choice.

YOU WILL NEED
Materials
corrugated cardboard
newspaper
PVA (white) glue
white emulsion (latex) paint
poster or gouache paints
clear gloss varnish
strong glue
eye pins
coloured cord

Equipment
large coin
pencil
scissors
container for PVA (white) glue
fine and medium artist's paintbrushes
darning needle

1 Place the coin on the cardboard. Draw around it to make 12 discs, and cut them out.

2 Tear the newspaper into 2.5 cm (1 in) strips and dip into diluted PVA (white) glue. Cover each disc with three layers of papier-mâché.

3 When completely dry, prime each disc with two coats of white paint. Leave to dry. Draw a daisy or ladybird (ladybug) on each disc. Fill in the design with paints.

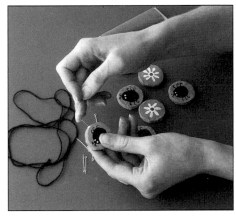

4 Seal each disc with two coats of gloss varnish. When dry, make a hole in the top of each disc with a darning needle. Dab a little strong glue over each hole and push in an eye pin.

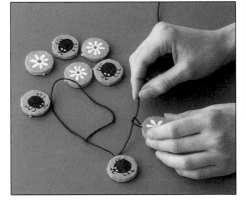

5 Cut a long length of cord. Pass the cord through the eye pin of each disc and tie it before adding the next.

CROWN
JEWELS
FRAME

This papier-mâché frame takes on a new sophistication with the addition of silver paint and foil-wrapped "jewels". You can make the frame as simple or as lavish as you wish by your choice of paint colours and accessories.

YOU WILL NEED
Materials
corrugated cardboard
cardboard
PVA (white) glue
newspaper
tissue paper
white acrylic primer
acrylic paints: purple and green
silver poster paint
assorted costume jewels
kitchen foil (tinfoil)
strong adhesive tape
mirror glass or picture

Equipment
tracing paper
soft pencil
scissors
container for PVA (white) glue
fine and medium artist's paintbrushes

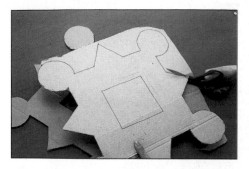

1 Trace the template and enlarge if necessary. Using strong scissors, cut out two frames from the corrugated cardboard. Cut out three squares or triangles of plain cardboard for each of the four sides of the frame.

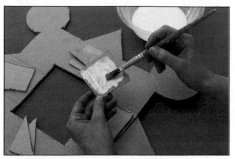

2 Using PVA (white) glue, stick a stack of three cardboard shapes to each side of the back of one frame. Place the second cardboard frame on top and glue it in position.

3 Tear strips of newspaper and dip in diluted PVA (white) glue. Start by laying strips over the gaps at the sides of the frame.

4 Build up the papier-mâché in layers all over the frame, painting the diluted glue on to the papier-mâché and covering it with dry strips of paper. Build up about six layers in this way.

5 Make two borders with tissue paper soaked in diluted glue and twisted into ropes. Lay one rope around the outer edge and one around the inner edge of the frame. Leave to dry.

6 Next, cover the whole frame with two sheets of tissue paper laid down individually and soaked with the diluted glue.

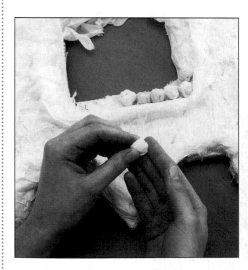

7 Make small balls of glue-soaked tissue paper and glue around the inside of the frame. Allow to dry thoroughly – this may take several days. Prime the frame all over with several coats of white acrylic primer.

8 Paint the frame with a base coat of acrylic paints in purple and green. Allow to dry, then lightly brush on silver poster paint, letting the base colours show through.

9 Wrap the edges of the jewels with foil torn into small squares. Dull the foil with a little of the purple acrylic paint. Glue the jewels on to the frame. Tape a piece of mirror glass or a picture to the back of the frame.

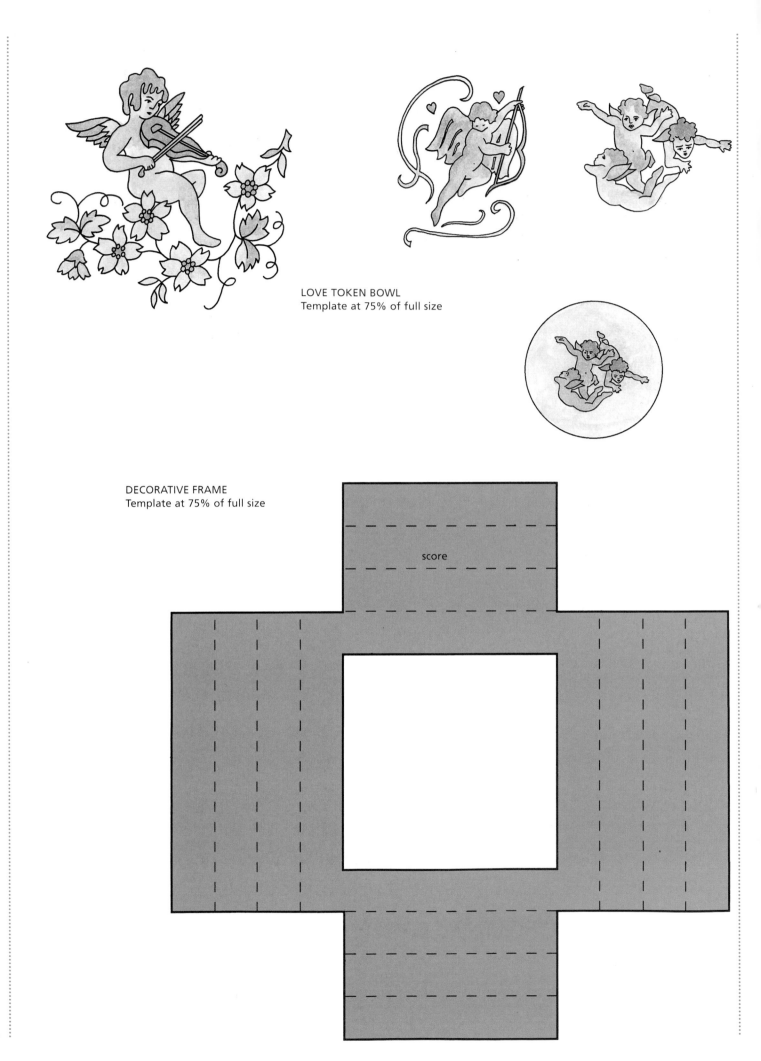

LOVE TOKEN BOWL
Template at 75% of full size

DECORATIVE FRAME
Template at 75% of full size

score

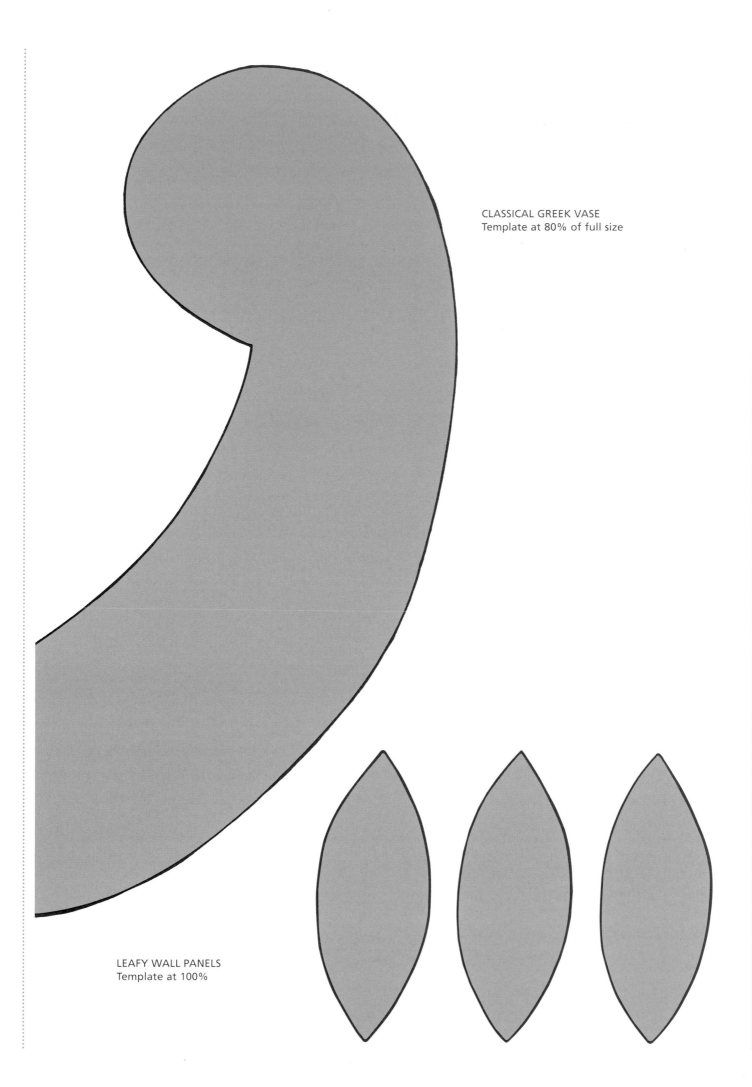

CLASSICAL GREEK VASE
Template at 80% of full size

LEAFY WALL PANELS
Template at 100%

WALL SCONCE
Template at 100%

CROWN BOX
Template at 100%

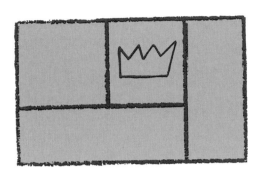

CROWN JEWELS FRAME
Template at 80% of full size

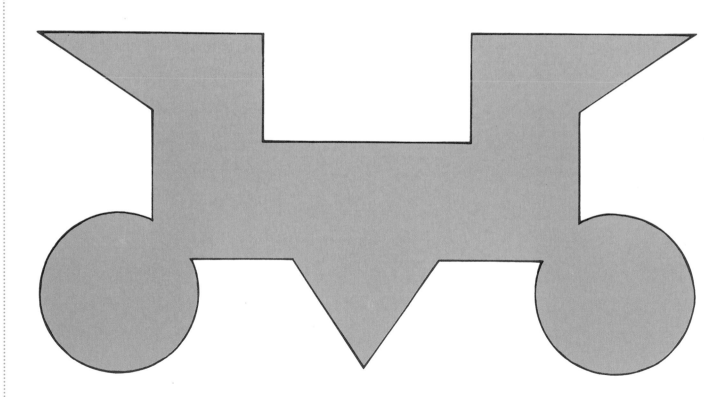

DECOUPAGE

Whilst it can be used to create some extremely stunning effects, the art of decoupage is really quite simple to master. It relies mainly on an ability to select interesting shapes and colours from material that is readily available all around us. Once you know how to cut out the shapes and stick them down on the chosen object, it is your personal creativity that comes into play. Designs can be as simple or as complicated as you like, but will always look good and you can use the technique to customize virtually any article in the home.

The projects that appear on the following pages show how anything from trays, boxes and lampshades to frames, coat racks and even clock faces can all be treated to turn a dull surface into a work of art. Even some types of furniture such as tables, cupboards and screens can be transformed. Interesting effects can also be created. Painting a crackle glaze over the surface, once the images are stuck down, will give them a cracked, antique look. Painting on a stained varnish will blend the colours and age the appearance.

The wide range of styles and applications shown here will inspire you to look at unwanted magazines, decorative paper scraps, wallpaper, postcards, old catalogues, even photocopies, in a new light. All these materials can be plundered and used to turn everyday objects into items of beauty.

"OLD MASTERS" BOX

This beautiful box can be used for keeping special photographs, letters and mementoes. Choose faces and lettering from wrapping paper or prints and combine them with a collage of handmade paper scraps in complementary colours. The finished box is colourwashed to give it an aged look.

YOU WILL NEED
Materials
wooden box
reproductions of "old master" drawings of faces, animals and lettering
handmade uncoloured Japanese paper
PVA (white) glue
photocopies of old parchment
watercolour paints
magazine pictures
burnt umber acrylic paint
clear oil-based matt varnish

Equipment
fine-grade sandpaper
tracing paper or carbon paper
pencil
small and medium decorator's paintbrushes
container for PVA (white) glue
fine and medium artist's paintbrushes
scissors
stencil cardboard
ruler
craft knife
cutting mat

1 Sand the box with fine-grade sandpaper to get a smooth surface, and clean the metal hinges and catches of the box.

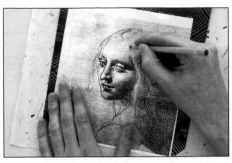

2 Photocopy reproductions of "old master" drawings. Trace over the images and transfer them on to pieces of handmade paper. Alternatively, place carbon paper face down on the handmade paper and draw over the image, as shown.

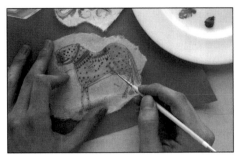

3 When you have traced a selection of images, tear them out roughly. Also tear up some plain handmade paper into irregular pieces. Arrange the images on the box.

4 Glue down the paper pieces, completely covering the surface of the box. Make coloured photocopies of different types of lettering. Glue photocopies of old parchment on to the box, too.

5 Handpaint some motifs of your own, to add touches of colour and interest. Leave to dry, then cut roughly or tear round these images and glue on to the box. Glue on any other details cut or photocopied from colour magazines.

6 Design and cut out a stencil pattern for the edges of the box from stencil cardboard, using a craft knife and cutting mat.

7 Use a sponge to stencil the border pattern on to handmade paper with watercolour paints.

8 Enhance the images on the box with touches of watercolour paint. Wash over the entire surface with an antiquing colour such as diluted burnt umber acrylic paint.

9 Finish with a coat of clear oil-based matt varnish to protect your work.

Bathroom cupboards need to be functional – a place to put all those odds and ends that seem to gather in quantity in the bathroom – but there is no reason why they cannot be pretty as well. The inside of this cupboard has been decorated with an attractive gift wrap, though wallpaper could be used instead. Choose a paper that is in scale with the cupboard for the best effect.

YOU WILL NEED

Materials

small pine cupboard
emulsion (latex) paints: cream and
* pale green*
gift wrap or wallpaper
wallpaper paste
wax crayon
matt varnish

Equipment

fine-grade sandpaper
soft cloth
small decorator's paintbrush
medium artist's paintbrush
scissors

1 Rub the surface of the cupboard with sandpaper to remove any polish or dirt before painting. Wipe off any dust with a dry cloth. Paint the exterior of the cupboard lightly with cream paint. Allow to dry. Rub down with fine-grade sandpaper, so that the grain of the wood is revealed in places.

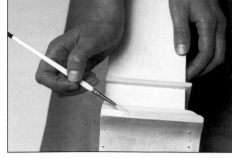

2 Pick out the moulding and the door frame in pale green, using an artist's paintbrush. Allow to dry and sand again, until you have achieved a slightly distressed appearance.

3 Cut the gift wrap or wallpaper to fit and attach it to the cupboard, using wallpaper paste.

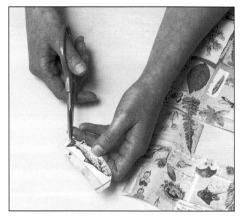

4 Choose a motif from the paper, in this instance the fish. Cut it out carefully and use to decorate the exterior of the cupboard. The pondweed behind the fish has been drawn in using a crayon. Paint inside and outside the cupboard with two coats of matt varnish to seal and protect the paper and the paint.

R O S E   E G G S

Reuse salvaged wrapping paper or look out for reproductions of brightly printed Victorian scrapbook rose motifs to make these densely patterned eggs.

YOU WILL NEED
Materials
*rose scrapbook motifs or rose-
    decorated wrapping paper*
PVA (white) glue
wooden or blown eggs
clear nail varnish (polish)

Equipment
small, sharp scissors
container for PVA (white) glue
fine artist's paintbrush

1 Cut out a selection of small rose motifs. You may find other motifs you can incorporate, such as butterflies or forget-me-nots. Look for interesting shapes and cut carefully around the outlines.

2 Using PVA (white) glue, stick the cut-out flowers to the eggs, overlapping the edges to make a densely patterned surface. Make sure that all the wood or shell is covered.

3 When the glue is dry, coat the eggs with three or four coats of clear nail varnish (polish), allowing each coat to dry completely before adding the next.

CUT-FLOWER FRAME

This delightful frame is constructed with a wide border to allow plenty of space for the decoration. Here, photocopied images are cut out and coloured with watercolour paints but you can use ready-coloured scraps to save time.

YOU WILL NEED

Materials
brown wrapping paper
6 mm (¼ in) medium-density
    fibreboard (MDF), three pieces cut
    to 20 x 22 cm (8 x 8½ in)
wood glue
white acrylic primer
white emulsion (latex) paint
selection of photocopied pictures
watercolour paints
glue stick
gloss varnish

Equipment
pen
ruler
scissors
drill
jigsaw
medium and large-sized surforms
fine-grade sandpaper
fine and medium artist's paintbrushes
small, sharp scissors
brush for varnish

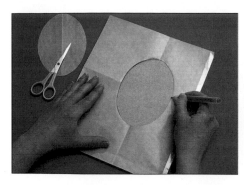

1 Cut a piece of brown wrapping paper 20 x 22 cm (8 x 8½ in) and fold it in quarters. Draw a shape in the middle for the frame opening and cut out. Open out the template and mark the opening, here an oval shape, on one piece of medium-density fibreboard (MDF).

2 From the other two pieces of MDF, cut out a rectangle, 11.5 x 15 cm (4½ x 6 in), to fit over the oval. Drill a hole in the corners of the rectangle and use a jigsaw to cut out the shape.

3 With a medium-sized surform, file down the edge of the opening to soften the curve.

4 Glue the three pieces of MDF together with wood glue and leave to dry.

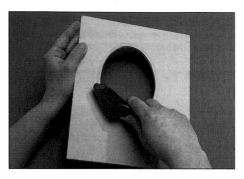

5 Use a large and a medium-sized surform to smooth the frame and to round the edges.

6 Finish all the edges with sandpaper to make them extra smooth. Prime the frame with white acrylic primer then apply a coat of white emulsion (latex) paint.

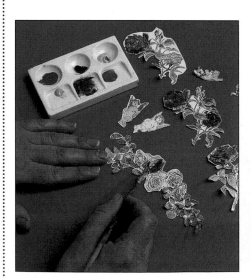

7 Cut out a selection of photocopied images using small, sharp scissors. Tint the cut-outs with watercolour paints.

8 Glue the cut-outs on to the frame using a glue stick. Gently smooth out the cut-outs with your fingers.

9 Use a gloss varnish on the frame to seal the images and to give the frame a shiny finish.

CANDLE SHADES

Delicate-looking shades, made from Japanese handmade paper and photocopies of real leaves and flowers, match the soft glow of candlelight. These are treated with fire-proofing spray, but do not leave them unattended when lit.

YOU WILL NEED
Materials
Japanese handmade paper
clear oil-based dead-flat varnish
cardboard
selection of fresh and dried flowers
    and leaves
masking tape
PVA (white) glue
decorative paper
fire-proofing spray
candle
candlestick

Equipment
small decorator's paintbrush
pair of compasses (compass)
ruler
pencil
scissors
craft knife
cutting mat
container for PVA (white) glue
medium artist's paintbrush

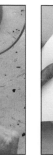

1 Varnish the handmade paper with clear oil-based dead-flat varnish and leave to dry.

2 Using a pair of compasses (compass), a ruler and a pencil, draw the shape of the shade on to cardboard, following the design shown in the photograph. Cut out to use as a template. It is a good idea to make a trial shade out of newspaper.

3 Draw around the cardboard template on to the handmade paper and cut out.

4 Make colour photocopies of the flowers and leaves. Carefully cut them out using a craft knife and cutting mat.

5 To plan your design, arrange the cut-outs on the handmade paper, securing them temporarily with masking tape. Glue them in place.

6 Cut out edging details from strips of decorative paper and glue them in place. Leave space at the joining edge. Once the shade is made up, you can add extra pieces to cover the join (seam). Cover the shade with a coat of clear varnish. Leave to dry, then glue the shade together.

7 Draw around the circumference on a piece of cardboard to make the shade support.

8 In the centre of the support, draw a smaller circle for the candle to fit through. Draw intersecting lines through this circle. Then mark four more holes to allow air to circulate. Cut out the support and the small circles.

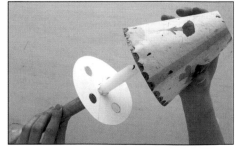

9 Spray the shade and cardboard with fire-proofing spray. Push the candle through the cardboard support on to the candlestick. Place the shade over the candle to rest on the support.

CRACKLE-GLAZED ANTIQUE PRINT

Antique prints are expensive, but with this technique you can create your own completely original design very cheaply. Use a photocopier to enlarge or reduce motifs and practise arranging them until you have a design that appeals.

YOU WILL NEED
Materials
selection of black-and-white prints
spray adhesive
cardboard
tea bags and instant coffee
PVA (white) glue
large piece of hardboard or cardboard, for backing
acrylic medium
clear acrylic gloss varnish
burnt umber acrylic paint

Equipment
scissors
large soft Chinese paintbrush
container for PVA (white) glue
decorator's paintbrush
fine artist's paintbrush
paint-mixing container

1 Cut out the prints and lightly coat them on the back with spray adhesive. Arrange the prints on cardboard until you are happy with the result. Using spray adhesive, you can reposition them as many times as you like. Photocopy the result.

2 Make a "cocktail" of one tea bag and three teaspoons of coffee and let it cool. Apply to the print with a Chinese paintbrush. You can experiment with brews of different strengths and apply the mixture several times, to create depth. Let it dry completely.

3 Mix equal parts PVA (white) glue and water and apply the mixture to the back of the print with a decorator's paintbrush. Smooth the print on to the hardboard or cardboard backing. (You can also apply the print directly to a wall or a piece of furniture.) Brush the PVA (white) glue mixture on top of the print and backing and leave to dry.

4 Cover the print and backing with acrylic medium in the same way. This may cause the paper to wrinkle, but don't worry: once dry, the wrinkles will vanish.

5 Coat with acrylic varnish to give a shiny finish and add an antique look.

6 Mix burnt umber acrylic paint into the varnish and paint cracks with a fine paintbrush. Add more shadows and blend them in softly. Finally, apply another coat of acrylic varnish and leave to dry.

DECORATIVE TRAY

A good tray will be strong enough to carry mugs and plates, and handsome enough to hang up as a decoration when not in use. This one has been decorated with a selection of old engraving tools, but you could use any design you choose.

YOU WILL NEED
Materials
tray
woodwash in corn yellow
photocopied motifs
wallpaper paste
clear satin varnish
crackle glaze (optional)
raw umber artist's oil paint

Equipment
decorator's paintbrush
fine-grade sandpaper
sharp-pointed scissors or craft knife
cutting mat
large artist's paintbrushes
soft cotton cloth

1 Prepare the tray by painting it with corn yellow woodwash as a base colour. When dry, rub the surface of the tray with fine-grade sandpaper.

2 Cut out the photocopied motifs carefully, moving the paper towards the scissors or around on the cutting surface.

3 Turn the cut-outs over and paste the backs with wallpaper paste, right up to all the edges, covering the entire area.

4 Place the cut-outs, glued side down, in position on the tray, making an attractive arrangement. Use a soft cloth or sponge to smooth out any bubbles. Leave to dry overnight.

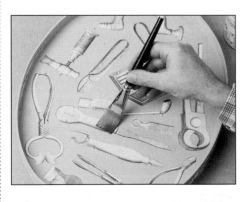

5 Using a clean new paintbrush, apply a sparing coat of varnish to the whole surface of the tray. When dry, rub lightly with sandpaper and repeat several times.

6 A further dimension has been added to this decoupage design by the application of a crackle glaze. It is best to follow the specific instructions for the product you use. Here the base varnish is being painted on to the tray.

7 When this coat is dry (after 20 minutes), apply an even coat of crackle glaze and leave it to dry for 20 minutes.

8 Rub a small amount of artist's oil paint into the cracks, using a soft cloth. Raw umber was used here, which gives a naturally aged effect, but any colour can be used.

9 When the cracks have been coloured, gently rub the excess paint from the surface, using a soft cloth. Give the tray at least two more coats of clear satin varnish; more, if time and patience allow.

TABLE-TOP DECORATION

These chilli peppers make a colourful decoration for a table with an easily achieved distressed paint finish. Experiment with different paint colours and decorate with your favourite vegetables.

YOU WILL NEED
Materials
wooden table
emulsion (latex) paints: white, green and yellow
wax
colour pictures of vegetables
PVA (white) glue
clear water-based acrylic satin varnish

Equipment
medium and small decorator's paintbrushes
soft cloth
fine-grade sandpaper
tape measure
craft knife
cutting mat
small, sharp scissors
plastic wrap

1 Paint the table with white emulsion (latex) paint. Leave to dry.

Next, paint with green emulsion (latex) paint and leave to dry.

2 Using a soft cloth, rub wax unevenly over the surface of the table. Leave to dry.

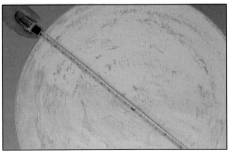

3 Paint the table with yellow emulsion (latex) and leave to dry completely before sandpapering.

4 Using fine-grade sandpaper, gently rub the surface of the table until you can see the green paint showing through. Sand the surface until the desired distressed look is achieved.

5 Measure the surface of the table so that you know by how much to enlarge the vegetables.

6 Photocopy the vegetable pictures. Start by cutting out the small inner areas of the vegetable design using a craft knife and cutting mat. Take care not to tear any of the delicate stems.

7 Cut out larger pieces with a small pair of scissors, again taking care not to break the delicate stems.

Arrange the vegetables and leaves on the table until you are happy with the design.

8 Pick up the cut-outs one at a time and turn upside down or lay them on a piece of plastic to apply the glue. Gently pick each cut-out up and lay it down on the table, taking care to smooth the surface gently and making sure there are no creases.

9 To finish, varnish with about four coats of clear satin varnish, leaving each coat to dry before applying the next.

MARINE TRAY

Here, an enchanting tray is created from a garden seed box and an old book of prints; images from old magazines would work just as well. The art is to choose a theme – fish, sea birds or shells – then paint the tray in an appropriate colour.

YOU WILL NEED
Materials
garden seed box
piece of hardboard
tacks
emulsion (latex) paints: aqua-blue, blue and brown
shell and fish images and paper
piece of wood
matt varnish
rope

Equipment
screwdriver
drill
pencil
saw
fine-grade sandpaper
glue gun and sticks
hammer
small decorator's paintbrushes
fine artist's paintbrush
scissors
masking tape

1 To remove the base of the box, insert a screwdriver between the side and the base and lever off.

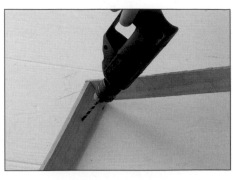

2 Drill two holes in each end of the tray for the string handles.

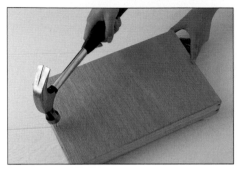

3 Mark a new base on the hardboard. Cut out the new hardboard base using a saw, and sand down the edges to make them smooth. Glue the base to the tray then hammer it securely in position.

4 Apply an even coat of aqua-blue emulsion (latex) paint to the tray, inside and out. Leave to dry thoroughly. Paint the whole tray roughly with blue paint, making sure that the aqua-blue shows through in places.

5 Roughly cut out a variety of shell and fish images. Enlarge the images on a photocopier if required. Lay the images on a piece of wood and secure in place with masking tape.

6 Brush a very watered-down wash of paint all over the images. Leave to dry thoroughly.

7 Remove the images from the wood and carefully cut them out.

8 Position and glue the paper motifs on the tray. Varnish over the motifs on the tray, giving it at least three coats, and allowing each coat to dry thoroughly before applying the next.

9 Cut two lengths of rope for the handles, and tape around the ends with masking tape. Push the rope through the holes in the tray. Knot the ends of the rope securely to hold the handles in place.

RABBIT
DUMMY
BOARD

Dummy boards originated as shop or inn signs; in the days when few people could read, a painted sign would indicate the trade being practised on the premises. The signs would either hang above the doorway or stand on a wooden block. You can give this oversized rabbit a support to make it stand up, or hang it on the wall.

YOU WILL NEED
Materials
paper
wallpaper paste
A2 (16 ½ x 23 in) sheet of marine
   plywood or similar
shellac
varnish: antique pine colour and
   clear matt
scrap wood for stand
PVA (white) glue

Equipment
container for wallpaper paste
small decorator's paintbrush
soft cloth
jigsaw
fine-grade sandpaper

1 Photocopy the rabbit template, enlarging it to the edges of an A4 (8¼ x 11½ in) sheet of paper. Cut the enlargement in half to give two A5 (5¾ x 8¼ in) sheets.

2 Enlarge both of these up to A3 (11½ x 16½ in) size. Depending on the machine, this process can be done in one step, or may take several enlargements.

3 Apply a coat of wallpaper paste to the plywood. This seals the surface and provides a key for the pasted paper.

4 Trim the "joining" edges of the photocopies right up to the rabbit, so that they can butt up against each other with no overlap. Apply a thin layer of wallpaper paste right up to the edges and stick the two halves together on the board. Smooth out any bubbles with a soft cloth and leave to dry overnight.

5 Use a jigsaw to cut out the shape, leaving a flat base. If you are unfamiliar with a jigsaw, you will need to practise to get the feel of it. Take your time, or ask someone with more experience to cut it for you.

6 Using fine-grade sandpaper, sand back the edges of the rabbit shape until smooth.

7 Seal the surface with a coat of shellac, which will give it a yellowish glow. Apply a coat of antique pine-coloured varnish, followed by several coats of clear varnish, allowing each coat to dry before applying the next.

8 Trace the pattern for the stand. Use it to cut out the wood stand. Rub down the edges with fine-grade sandpaper and glue in place.

OAK-LEAF BOX

Find one pretty motif and you can create lovely repeating patterns with it instantly, using a photocopier. Copies of old engravings are perfect for this technique: here they are delicately hand-coloured in autumnal shades.

YOU WILL NEED
Materials
wooden box
cream emulsion (latex) paint
black-and-white leaf motif
acrylic paints: yellow ochre and red oxide
PVA (white) glue
clear gloss acrylic varnish

Equipment
medium decorator's paintbrush
paint-mixing container
fine artist's paintbrush
scissors
craft knife
cutting mat
container for PVA (white) glue

1 Paint the box with two or three coats of cream emulsion (latex) paint. Make copies of the leaf motif in two sizes for the sides and lid. Hand-tint the copies with a thin wash of yellow ochre, then red oxide.

2 Use scissors to cut around the outside of the leaf shapes. Cut away any small spaces within the design with a craft knife.

3 Arrange the leaves on the lid and sides of the box. Glue them on with PVA (white) glue and leave to dry.

4 Protect the box with two or three coats of clear gloss acrylic varnish.

LEMON MIRROR FRAME

Hunt around for interesting printed material to combine with the lemon motif on this striking papier-mâché frame. You could use a photocopier to reproduce graphics from books, or you could produce an "ancient manuscript" of your own!

YOU WILL NEED
Materials
corrugated cardboard
mirror, 15 x 18 cm (6 x 7 in)
wallpaper paste
newspaper
acrylic paints: black, yellow
    and green
paperclip
acrylic gesso
lemon motif gift wrap
scraps of printed paper or manuscript
white tissue paper
matt acrylic varnish

Equipment
craft knife
metal ruler
cutting mat
container for wallpaper paste
medium artist's paintbrush
natural sponge

1 Cut two 16.5 x 20 cm (6½ x 8 in) rectangles from the cardboard. Lay the mirror in the centre of one piece and cut strips of cardboard to fit around it down two sides and across the bottom. Cut a window out of the centre of the other cardboard rectangle, leaving a 4 cm (1½ in) border.

2 Coat all the pieces of cardboard with wallpaper paste. Leave to dry. Tear the newspaper into strips and coat with paste. Cover the front of the frame. Paste the cardboard spacer strips in position on the sides and bottom of the back panel and cover with papier-mâché strips. Leave to dry. Apply a second layer.

3 When the papier-mâché is dry, paint the inside surfaces of the frame black to minimize any possible reflection they might give in the mirror.

4 Open out the paperclip and thread one end through the papier-mâché at the centre back of the frame. Paste strips of newspaper over the paperclip, leaving the top section showing to act as a hook.

5 Attach the front of the frame to the back with more strips of pasted newspaper. Paste folded strips over the top of the frame to either side of the opening for added strength. Once dry, paint the frame with acrylic gesso.

6 Sponge the entire frame with thin yellow paint, and allow to dry. Next, sponge the frame with green paint to create an all-over mottled effect.

7 Tear lemon motifs from the gift wrap in interesting shapes and then arrange over the frame. Fill the gaps between the lemons with small pieces of printed paper. Paste in position.

8 To soften the design, tear small pieces of white tissue paper and paste on to the frame, crinkling them slightly and overlapping the edges of some of the motifs. When the paste is dry, paint the frame with two coats of matt varnish and insert the mirror into the top slit.

SCREEN TEST

This screen is decorated with colour photocopies of flowers and leaves, and the scope for different colours and shapes is enormous. The combination of delicate gold tissue paper with pretty dried and photocopied flowers is very arresting.

YOU WILL NEED

Materials
unpainted screen
parchment-coloured matt emulsion
    (latex) paint
white tissue paper
gold spray paint
wallpaper paste or PVA (white) glue
fresh leaves and flowers
dried flowers and leaves
handmade paper
clear oil- or water-based satin varnish

Equipment
medium decorator's paintbrushes
pencil
tape measure
ruler
scissors
craft knife
cutting mat
stencil cardboard

1 Paint the screen with one coat of parchment-coloured paint, using a medium decorator's paintbrush. Leave to dry completely, then apply a second coat of paint.

2 The screen is decorated with squares of tissue paper, so mark vertical and horizontal guidelines over the screen using a pencil, tape measure and ruler.

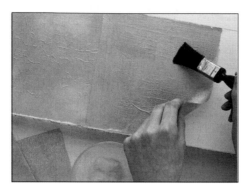

3 Spray the sheets of tissue paper with gold paint. Stick down squares of tissue on to the screen using a paintbrush and wallpaper paste or PVA (white) glue.

4 Cut pieces of tissue paper to fit the curved top edge of the screen and glue in place. Make colour photocopies of the fresh leaves and flowers. Carefully cut out the shapes using a craft knife and cutting mat.

5 Select some dried flowers and leaves to decorate the curved top panels of the screen.

6 Next, arrange the leaf and flower photocopies on the screen to your liking and glue in position.

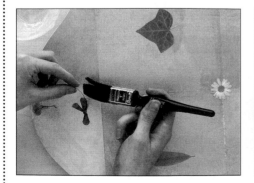

7 Arrange the dried flowers and leaves on the curved top sections and glue in place.

8 Make a tooth-edged pattern template out of stencil cardboard. Use this to cut out edging strips from handmade paper.

9 Glue the strips to the edges of the screen. When the glue is dry, cover the screen with two coats of satin varnish, leaving to dry between coats.

SHOES IN THE NEWS

Special shoes deserve a home of their own, and these sturdy wooden wine boxes can be made stylish enough to house anything from work shoes to glass slippers. The boxes are lined with different types of newsprint: put leather lace-ups in the pink financial pages, party shoes in comic strips and velvet pumps in the arts and literary review pages.

YOU WILL NEED
Materials
wooden wine crates
PVA (white) glue
variety of newsprint
clear matt varnish or shellac
*   button polish*

Equipment
sandpaper
container for PVA (white) glue
small decorator's paintbrushes
craft knife

1 Sand down each wine crate. Then mix PVA (white) glue with water in equal parts and apply a coat to the inside.

2 Apply another coat of the PVA (white) glue mixture, then smooth newsprint all over the inside. The glue will be absorbed by the paper. Apply undiluted PVA (white) glue along the top edges and smooth the paper over it. Leave to dry before applying more paper and glue to make a random all-over pattern.

3 Leave until completely dry, then trim the paper along the outside top edges with a craft knife.

4 Varnish the whole box with either clear matt varnish or, if you want an "aged" look, shellac button polish. Leave to dry, then apply one or more coats of varnish.

HATBOX

A traditional hatbox will store a variety of objects, and is also an attractive piece to display in your home. A simple form of decoupage using wrapping paper is shown here, but pictures from magazines, postcards and greetings cards can all be used.

YOU WILL NEED
Materials
cardboard hatbox
white matt emulsion (latex) paint
poster paint
wrapping paper
PVA (white) glue
coloured varnish

Equipment
large artist's paintbrushes
fine-grade sandpaper
natural sponge
rag
scissors
container for PVA (white) glue

1 Paint the hatbox with white emulsion (latex) paint. Rub down using fine-grade sandpaper. Using a natural sponge, add a wash of watery poster paint to age the box, removing some of the paint with a rag as you go.

2 Cut out the images from the wrapping paper that most appeal to you. Arrange them on the box ready to glue on.

3 Glue your images on to the box using diluted PVA (white) glue and leave to dry.

4 Varnish the box with a coloured varnish, again removing a lot of it with a rag to give the box warmth and to add to its antiqued look.

SHOE BOX

The pictures of shoes decorating this box have been dipped in cold tea to "antique" them. Different images could be used depending on the contents of the box: pictures of hats could adorn a circular hatbox, or jewels a trinket box. Good sources of illustrations are old clothing catalogues, greetings cards, and any Victorian or Edwardian technical manuals.

YOU WILL NEED

Materials
brown wrapping paper
cardboard shoe box
paper glue
old shoe catalogues
cold tea

Equipment
small, sharp scissors
small bowl
pinboard (corkboard) and pins

1 Cut out pieces of brown wrapping paper to fit the shoe box. Use to cover the box and lid completely and glue in place. Roughly cut out images from the catalogues.

2 Fill a small bowl with cold tea, and submerge each image for a few seconds so that the tea penetrates the paper. Pin up to dry. If the images hang vertically this should prevent them from wrinkling as they dry. If they do crease a little, press them quickly on the reverse side using a cool iron.

3 Cut around the pictures carefully and arrange them on the box and lid.

4 When you are happy with your design, glue each picture in position. Apply two coats of varnish to seal.

ARCHITECTURAL SCREEN

During the eighteenth century it was fashionable to create print rooms, with engravings cut out and attached to walls in formal designs. Here, black-and-white architectural drawings are used in the same way to create a stylish screen, painted an elegant duck-egg blue, a colour very popular in the late eighteenth century.

YOU WILL NEED
Materials
pre-cut three-panel screen
water-based wood undercoat
duck-egg blue emulsion (latex) paint
black-and-white images
PVA (white) glue
black acrylic paint
clear acrylic varnish
piano hinges and screws

Equipment
small and medium decorator's
    paintbrushes
fine-grade sandpaper
cutting mat
container for PVA (white) glue
craft knife
pencil
ruler
screwdriver

1 Paint the panels with undercoat. Lightly rub them down with sandpaper, then apply a coat of duck-egg blue paint.

2 Place your black-and-white images on a cutting mat and cut around them carefully using a craft knife.

3 Draw a 4 cm (1½ in) border around the top, bottom and outside edges of the side panels and at the top and bottom of the central panel. Divide the panels into equal sections and place side by side. Arrange the cut-outs on the panels and glue with diluted PVA (white) glue.

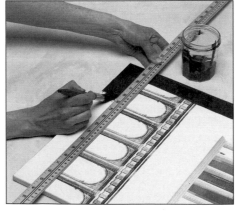

4 Split any continuous designs with a craft knife when the glue has dried. Paint the border with black acrylic paint using a straight edge as a guide. Let the panels dry thoroughly then seal with two coats of varnish. Hinge the panels together.

COAT RACK

Using images taken from books, magazines and posters, this contemporary design is perfect for children's rooms. Woodworking skills are needed to make the rack, although you could simply decorate a ready-made rack. Let each child create his or her own montage.

YOU WILL NEED

Materials
1 cm (½ in) thick medium-density fibreboard (MDF)
duck-egg blue emulsion (latex) paint
magazine pictures
plain coloured paper
PVA (white) glue
3 wooden knobs
silver acrylic paint
3 countersunk screws
clear matt water-based acrylic varnish
2 mirror plates and screws

Equipment
ruler
pencil
jigsaw and protective mask
small decorator's paintbrush
craft knife
cutting mat
medium artist's paintbrush
container for PVA (white) glue
drill and wood drill bits
screwdriver

1 Following the template, draw out the shape of the coat rack on fibreboard (MDF) with a ruler and pencil. Cut out using a jigsaw and wear a protective mask.

2 Paint the coat rack with two coats of duck-egg blue emulsion (latex), leaving the paint to dry completely between coats.

3 Cut out pictures from magazines using a craft knife and cutting mat.

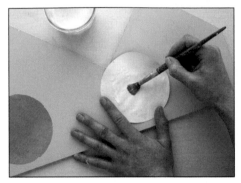

4 Cut three 10 cm (4 in) diameter circles of plain paper. Glue the backs and position along the base of the rack, below each point.

5 Arrange the motifs on the rack and stick them down. Start with your favourite images and arrange the rest to complement these.

6 Paint the wooden knobs with silver acrylic paint and leave to dry.

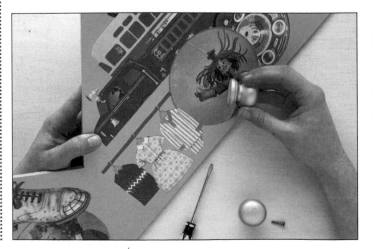

7 Drill three holes in the rack, one through the centre of each paper circle. Countersink the holes on the back of the rack. Use countersunk screws to attach the knobs to the rack. Varnish the whole rack and leave to dry.

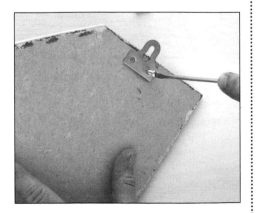

8 Attach a mirror plate to each end of the back of the coat rack.

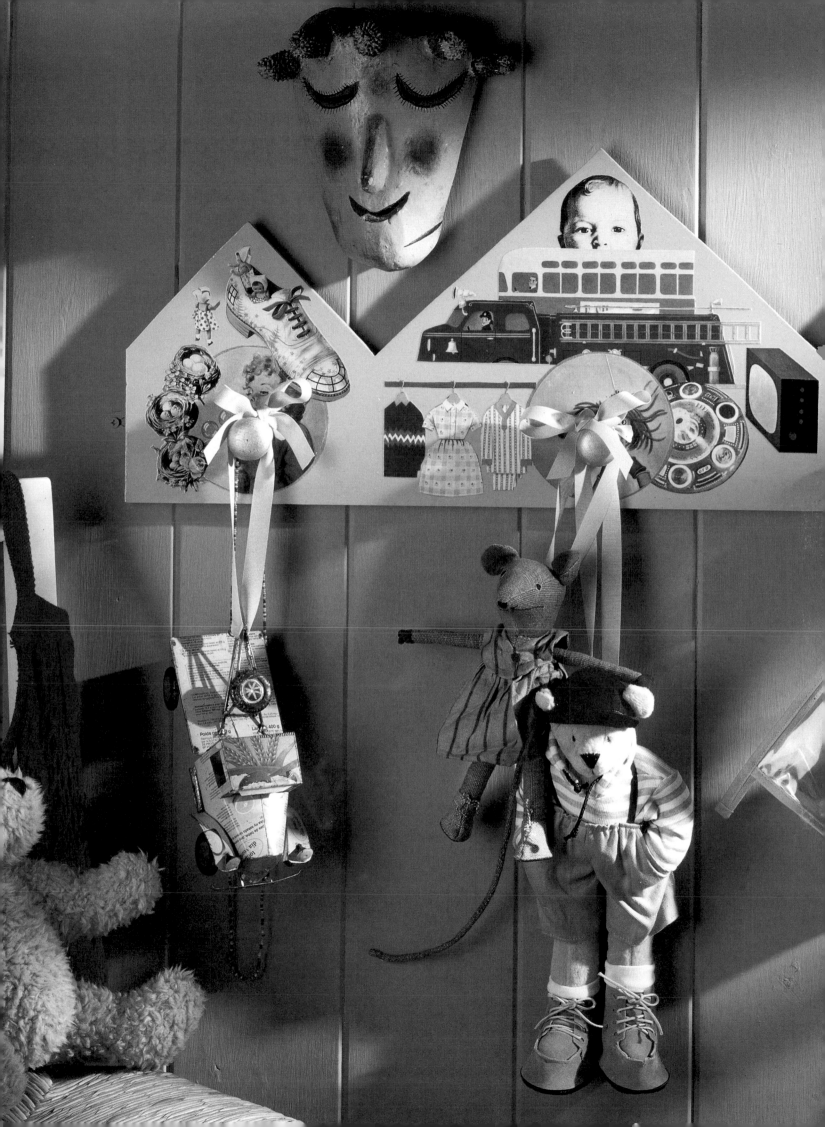

HAND-TINTED FRAME

To decorate this frame black-and-white pictures are hand-tinted to match the background colour. However, a different effect can be achieved by tinting the pictures with a colour that contrasts with the frame. Alternatively, you can dip the pictures in cold tea to give the paper a pleasing "aged" effect similar to old photos, or you can colour them with paints.

YOU WILL NEED
Materials
painted picture frame
assorted black-and-white pictures
paint to match the frame
PVA (white) glue
clear gloss varnish

Equipment
fine-grade sandpaper
small, sharp scissors
paint-mixing container
container for PVA (white) glue
medium artist's paintbrushes

1 Remove the glass and backing from the picture frame. Lightly rub down the paint with fine-grade sandpaper to give a patchy, antiqued effect.

2 Carefully trim the pictures, leaving a slight border around the edges.

3 Make a thin solution of paint, and dip each cut-out briefly into it until the paper is stained. Lay the cuttings out flat and leave to dry.

4 Arrange the dried cut-outs around the frame. When you are pleased with the composition, stick them in place with PVA (white) glue.

5 Protect your design by sealing the frame with three or four coats of clear gloss varnish. Leave to dry.

6 Once dry, select a picture to go in the frame. Fit your picture inside the frame and replace the glass and backing.

FLOWER CLOCK

Purchasing a basic clock movement allows you to create a clock face to your own design. Here, simple yet effective materials are used to fashion a pretty clock in the shape of a decoupage flower.

YOU WILL NEED

Materials
white cardboard
gold paper
flower and leaf images
PVA (white) glue
clear acrylic varnish
clock movement and hands

Equipment
large plate
pen
cup or small bowl
craft knife
bradawl
scissors
container for PVA (white) glue
medium artist's paintbrush
damp cloth
small decorator's paintbrush

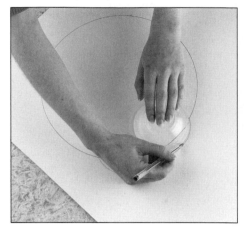

1 Draw round a large plate on to white cardboard, leaving enough cardboard around the plate to make cup-sized petals. Draw round a cup or small bowl to make semi-circular petals all the way round the rim of the large circle.

2 Using a craft knife, cut out the flower shape and pierce the centre with a bradawl to make the hole for the clock spindle.

3 Use the flower shape as a template to draw on to the back of the gold paper. Cut out the gold paper flower with scissors.

4 Cut out flowers and leaves from wrapping paper or magazine cuttings. Stick the gold paper flower on to the cardboard base using PVA (white) glue.

5 Arrange the flowers and leaves on the gold background and stick them down using PVA (white) glue. Wipe off any excess glue using a damp cloth.

6 Apply a coat of clear acrylic varnish, and leave to dry. Attach the clock movement and hands.

STILL LIFE

Classic Dutch tulips captured in a still life have a timeless appeal. Create your own decoupage flower arrangement and preserve it forever on a small box, a table top or a tray. The design is quite simple but some care is needed to apply the pieces accurately.

YOU WILL NEED
Materials

small cardboard box with lid
emulsion (latex) paints: white and
   yellow
reproduction of an old flower print
PVA (white) glue
green paper
clear water-based acrylic
   satin varnish

Equipment

medium and small decorator's
   paintbrushes
small, sharp scissors
container for PVA (white) glue
medium artist's paintbrush
craft knife
ruler
cutting mat

1 Paint the box and lid with white emulsion (latex) and leave to dry. Next, paint with two coats of yellow emulsion (latex).

2 Make colour photocopies of the print and carefully cut out the flowers using a pair of small, sharp scissors.

3 Arrange the flowers on the lid. Keep the stems close together to form a bunch. Glue them down using a small brush to apply the PVA (white) glue.

4 Cut out a rectangle of green paper. Fold it in half lengthways and then in half again. Cut three small triangles from the folded edge. Open out the paper and glue in place on the lid to form a vase.

5 To match up the flowers on the edge of the lid and the sides of the box, hold each flower against the lid and press to make a crease.

6 Cut along the crease with a craft knife and cutting mat, using a ruler as a guide.

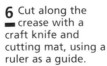

7 Glue the flower on to the edge of the lid, then line up the flower on the box side and glue in place. Add more flowers around the box.

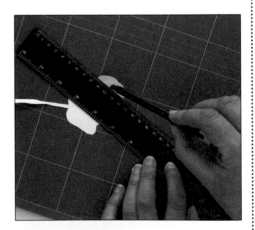

8 Varnish the finished box with three or four coats of clear satin varnish, leaving to dry completely between coats.

ASTROLOGICAL CLOCK

The passing of time is the basis of astrology. As the stars make their regular journeys around the heavens, you can reflect on time's importance with the help of this stylish clock. Battery-operated clock mechanisms are now readily available; all you have to supply is the clock face.

YOU WILL NEED
Materials
thick white cardboard
set of zodiac signs
PVA (white) glue
black acrylic paint
clear acrylic varnish
clock movement and hands

Equipment
scissors
pair of compasses (compass)
pencil
craft knife
container for PVA (white) glue
fine artist's paintbrush
small decorator's paintbrush

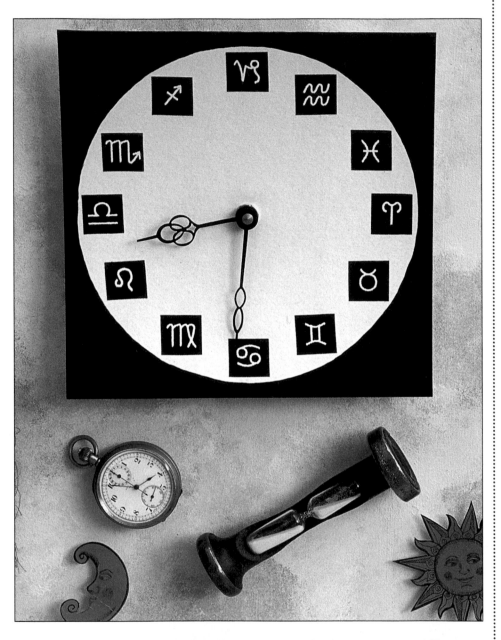

1 Cut a 20 cm (8 in) square of cardboard. Using a pair of compasses (compass), draw a circle slightly smaller than the square. Cut out a small circle in the centre where the hands meet. Photocopy the zodiac symbols, or use the templates. Cut them out.

2 Arrange the 12 star signs around the clock face, in the correct order (as shown in the picture). Position those corresponding to 12, 3, 6 and 9 o'clock first, then space the rest equally. Stick down with PVA (white) glue.

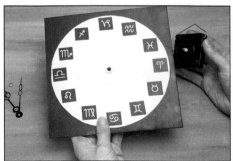

3 Using a decorator's paintbrush, paint the area around the clock face black. Allow the paint to dry, then seal the whole clock with two coats of varnish. Attach the clock mechanism and the hands.

TOY BOX

Colourful shapes and images can be used to transform old or uninspiring nursery (play room) furniture. Here, a dull toy box is given a new lease of life with a splash of paint and fun cut-outs. A layer of varnish means the paper shapes will not rub off and the finished decoration is very hardwearing.

YOU WILL NEED
Materials
wooden toy box
emulsion (latex) paints in five bright
  colours
children's gift wrap
PVA (white) glue
clear acrylic satin varnish

Equipment
fine-grade sandpaper
small decorator's paintbrush
scissors
medium artist's paintbrush

1 First, sand down the toy box. Paint the box with emulsion (latex) paint, using a different colour for each side. Leave the paint to dry then apply a second coat.

2 When the paint is dry, cut out shapes from the gift wrap.

3 Arrange the paper shapes on the box to make a good design. Using the PVA (white) glue, paste them in place.

4 When the glue is dry, varnish the box and fill with toys.

GREEK-STYLE GIFT WRAP

This wrapping paper features a simple repeating pattern, but you could also use a mixture of different images, letter forms and numbers to make your own personalized paper.

YOU WILL NEED
Materials
black-and-white image
paper glue
white paper, large and small
red moiré satin ribbon

Equipment
scissors
coloured felt-tipped pen

1 Once you have chosen an image to reproduce, make three photocopies of it. Cut them out and stick them in a line on a sheet of paper. Make at least ten photocopies of this sheet.

2 You now have 30 images to cut out and arrange on a larger sheet of white paper.

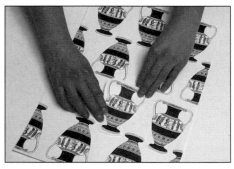

3 The first arrangement leaves a balancing white space as a background with the urns spaced widely and inverted on the second row, moving up into the space left by the row above.

4 This arrangement allows less background space, and the urns are used base to base and top to top. Cut some urns in half to fill the paper right to the edges.

5 Photocopy your artwork on to the larger sheet of paper. You can also make reductions at this stage, returning to the smaller size for a small gift. Experiment with colour, using a felt-tipped pen.

6 Black-and-white paper contrasts brilliantly with this red moiré satin ribbon, set off with a generous bow.

RABBIT DUMMY BOX
Template at 75% of full size

RABBIT DUMMY STAND
Template at 70% of full size

COAT RACK
Template at 100%

ASTROLOGICAL CLOCK
Template at 75% of full size

PAPER CUTTING AND COLLAGE

Paper lends itself especially well to the delicate art of cutting, allowing some amazingly intricate designs to be cut out of a square that will still hold together. Designs can be as simple or as complicated as you like, and they can be in almost any style. Paper cuts are particularly appropriate for making valentines and love tokens, but they can also be put to any number of other decorative uses. Here, you will find appropriate papercuts for wrapping paper and gift tags, jam pot covers, cards and bookmarks. In addition, such diverse objects as boxes, room dividers, screens and even a firescreen have all been decorated with paper cuts.

As it relies on fairly intricate designs, most paper cutting requires a little practice to master the techniques as well as safely handling the sharp tools: a very sharp pair of good quality scissors and an equally sharp craft knife or scalpel are essential. To save your work surface from scratches and to protect your cutting blades, always work on a protective surface such as a self-healing cutting mat.

The word collage comes from the French verb, "coller", meaning to stick, and is a good way of using up odd scraps of paper. Experiment with textured papers to create objects that can be as simple or intricate as you desire.

SNOWFLAKES

There is an infinite number of patterns that you can make by combining simple cuts in folded paper, and by using shiny reflective papers you can make decorations that look like large sparkling snowflakes. The patterns at the end of this chapter will help you to reproduce these snowflakes, and will no doubt lead you to create your own designs.

YOU WILL NEED

Materials
selection of reflective silver, gold and
*   sparkling papers*
gold thread

Equipment
pair of compasses (compass)
pencil
scissors: small, sharp pair and a
*   larger pair*
tracing paper
craft knife
cutting mat

1 Using a pair of compasses (compass), draw a circle on the back of the reflective paper and cut it out.

2 Fold the circle of paper in half three times, taking care to match edges.

3 Photocopy the snowflake patterns, enlarging them to the size you want. Have some larger than others. Trace one of the segments.

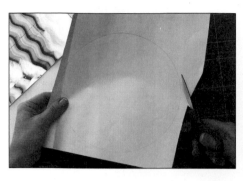

4 Transfer the tracing on to the folded reflective paper.

5 Use the small, sharp scissors to snip out the traced pattern shapes. Unfold the circle and flatten.

6 Do the same with the other papers and patterns, using a craft knife and cutting mat to make small, internal cuts.

7 For the curved pattern, fold the circle in the usual way and cut the first part of the pattern with scissors.

8 Now unfold once and fold in half the other way, then cut out triangular notches along the fold line.

9 Attach lengths of gold thread to hang up the snowflakes.

DECORATED EGGS

In Switzerland, intricate symmetrical designs, depicting the natural world and village life, are cut from folded black paper. This can be adapted and applied to the surface of an egg as the papercut is very flexible.

YOU WILL NEED
Materials
black craft paper
white hens' eggs, blown
wallpaper paste
acrylic varnish

Equipment
scissors: small, sharp pair and a
    larger pair
pinking shears
container for wallpaper paste
artist's paintbrush
paperclip

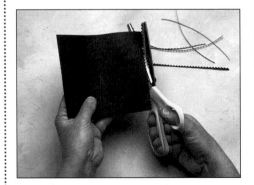

1 Using large scissors, cut a strip of black paper 3 mm (⅛ in) wide. Using the pinking shears, cut two strips 3 mm (⅛ in) wide and long enough to fit around the egg lengthways.

2 Smear wallpaper paste round the long side of the egg and on to the paper strips. Stick the strips to the egg as shown above. Trace the template.

3 Cut a 10 cm (4 in) square of paper and fold it in half. Place the straight side of the template against the fold and secure it with a paperclip. Using small scissors, cut around the template and remove.

4 Smear wallpaper paste on one side of the egg and the back of the paper cut-out. Place it centrally on the egg and smooth it out carefully. Repeat with the other side. Leave to dry before coating the egg with acrylic varnish.

EIGHTEENTH-CENTURY ITALIAN PAPERCUT

This most intricate Italian design is made from a single sheet of thin black paper, folded in half and cut out with a craft knife. It is very delicate and should be mounted on paper and framed.

YOU WILL NEED

Materials
white paper
thin black paper

Equipment
spray adhesive
craft knife
cutting mat
tracing paper
metal spoon

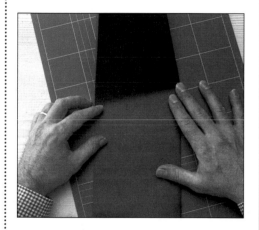

1 Photocopy the pattern on to a piece of white paper. Fold the piece of black paper in half.

2 Using spray adhesive, stick the photocopied pattern on to the folded paper.

3 Cut out the design carefully, using a craft knife and working from the middle out towards the edges.

4 Gently remove the pattern. Press the papercut flat by covering it with a sheet of tracing paper and rubbing with the back of a spoon.

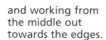

■ S I L H O U E T T E S

This project uses modern technology by starting with a photograph, but the end result has the authentic look of an old silhouette portrait. To take the photograph, pose your subject with a bright light behind, either in front of a sunlit window, or a back-lit sheet of white paper. This should eliminate foreground detail and give a dark silhouette shape.

YOU WILL NEED
Materials
photograph of subject
thin black paper
mounting paper
all-purpose glue
frame

Equipment
masking tape
tracing paper
hard pencil
craft knife or small, very sharp
  needlework scissors
cutting mat (optional)

1 Stick a strip of masking tape across the back of the photograph, so that the tape overlaps each side.

2 Place a sheet of tracing paper over the top; the tape will hold the tracing paper still. Carefully draw around the profile.

3 Rub the reverse side of the tracing with a pencil.

4 Secure the tracing on the black paper using masking tape. Use a hard, sharp pencil to go over your traced lines.

5 Cut out the silhouette with a sharp craft knife, beginning at the back of the head. Move the paper to help you get clean lines, and hold the knife upright so that you only cut with the point. Alternatively, you can use small, very sharp needlework scissors to cut out the silhouette, moving the paper as you cut.

6 Cut out the facial features and separate the image from the background. Glue the black silhouette on to a sheet of mounting paper and display it in a frame.

TRADITIONAL VALENTINES

The tradition of making papercut Valentines goes back at least two hundred years. Both men and women used to cut elaborate love tokens decorated with hearts, ribbons, birds, flowers and stars. This project uses rough-textured handmade paper for the cards, with red and silver papercuts added.

YOU WILL NEED

Materials
red fibrous handmade paper (flecked with petals or leaves)
plain white paper
silver-coated wrapping paper
natural-coloured handmade paper
spray adhesive
textured silver foil paper (not cooking foil (tinfoil)

Equipment
tracing paper
pencil
craft knife
cutting mat
metal ruler
pinking shears

PAPER CUTTING AND COLLAGE

1 Fold the red paper in half, then fold the sheet of white paper around it. This will make it easier to cut.

2 Trace one of the patterns on to the white paper.

3 Using a craft knife and cutting mat, make the internal cuts first, then those along the fold.

4 Turn the paper around so that you always cut at the most comfortable angle.

5 Fold the sheet of silver-coated wrapping paper in half and slide it into the fold of the papercut. Draw a half-heart shape around the outside of the papercut.

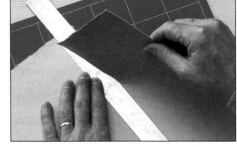

6 Using a metal ruler, tear a piece of natural-coloured handmade paper a little bigger than the height of the silver heart, for the backing.

7 Using spray adhesive, gently place the heart and papercut on to the backing paper.

8 Make the second card by folding the silver foil paper in half inside another sheet of plain white paper. Trace the second pattern, then cut out with pinking shears.

9 Cut a pattern along the fold, then open out and stick the foil cut-out on to another torn backing sheet. Cut out small heart shapes to add further depth to the design.

122

LOVE TOKENS

The cut and folded paper love token originated in Switzerland and Germany, where it was elevated into a skilled craft, creating beautiful symmetrical compositions. These "scherenschnitte" were cut from rag paper and were sometimes pierced and tinted with watercolours before being mounted on a contrasting colour, usually black.

YOU WILL NEED
Materials
plain paper
thin black paper
spray adhesive
mounting paper
frame

Equipment
pencil
craft knife
ruler
cutting mat

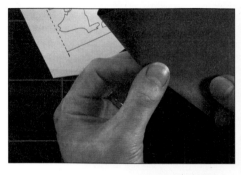

1 Enlarge the pattern to the size you require and draw it on plain paper. Fold the piece of thin black paper in half.

2 Cut along the centre edge of the design, using a craft knife and ruler.

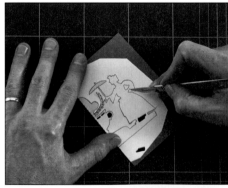

3 Give the reverse side the lightest coating of spray adhesive and stick it to the back of the black paper. Cut out the shapes very carefully, using just the sharp tip of the craft knife. Move the paper around when you cut, so that you are always cutting at the easiest angle.

4 Separate the black paper from the design. Take great care when you do this as the papercut is fragile and easily torn.

5 Unfold your "scherenschnitte" and display it on mounting paper in a frame.

PAPER LANTERNS

These delicate handmade paper shades cast exquisite patterns of light through their Matisse-style cut-out designs. In the case of the triangular lantern, the shapes are only partly cut out so that the glow of the candle is cast upwards against the shade, creating a lovely play of light and shadow.

YOU WILL NEED
Materials
pastel-coloured handmade paper
double-sided tape

Equipment
tracing paper
pencil
craft knife
cutting mat
ruler
kitchen knife

1 For the cylindrical lantern, enlarge the template so that it fits the sheet of handmade paper approximately 20 x 30 cm (8 x 12 in). Transfer the motifs on to the handmade paper using tracing paper and a pencil.

2 Using a sharp craft knife and a cutting mat, carefully cut around the traced outlines.

3 Place a strip of double-sided tape along one short side of the lantern and peel away the backing paper.

4 Curve the lantern to form a cylinder and press the overlap firmly together.

5 For the triangular lantern, enlarge the template as before and trace the design lines on to a sheet of handmade paper. Using a craft knife and cutting mat, cut along the solid outlines only.

6 Lightly crease each motif along the dotted line so that the shapes protrude a little from the lantern.

7 On the reverse side of the paper, score along the vertical dotted fold lines using a ruler and the back of a kitchen knife.

8 Crease along the scored lines and bend the lantern into a triangular shape, fixing the overlap with a strip of double-sided tape.

PIERCED AND CUT LAMPSHADE

This project uses a ready-made paper lampshade suitable for a table lamp, and although it is not difficult to cut the pattern, you should be extremely careful when using a sharp-bladed craft knife. Never be tempted to place your fingers behind the paper as you cut.

YOU WILL NEED
Materials
stiff paper lampshade
low-tack masking tape

Equipment
tracing paper
pencil
hatpin or similar instrument
craft knife
sharp-pointed thick needle

1 Enlarge the pineapple motif. Next using tracing paper and a pencil trace the pineapple motif and stick the tracing to the lampshade, using masking tape to hold it taut.

2 Prick out the design with the hatpin, marking the edges of the scallop shapes and the leaves.

3 Cut the scallops using your pinpricks as a guide. Insert the craft knife at one pinprick and form an arc to the next. Hold the lampshade steady with your spare hand, and keep your fingers clear of the blade.

4 Cut each end of the leaf shapes, leaving a "bridge" in the middle. Take your time when cutting because the bridge is vital to the design, and a slip of the knife will spoil the effect.

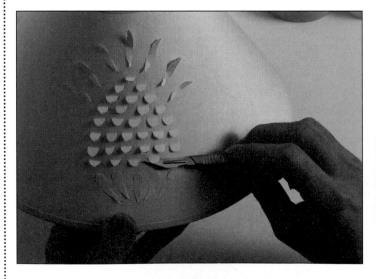

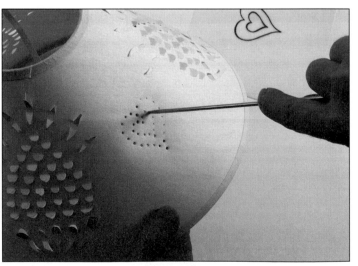

5 Use the blunt edge of the craft knife to ease the shapes away from the background to roughly 45 degrees, which will allow them to settle at 30 degrees. Do not despair if the first pineapple is not perfect – let that be the one that faces the wall.

6 Cut two more pineapples around the lampshade, and then tape a tracing of the hearts in the spaces between them. Use a thick needle to prick out the hearts. Hold the lampshade firmly, keeping your fingers away from the point of the needle.

PAPER CUTTING AND COLLAGE

PAPERCUT SCREEN

This screen is inspired by traditional Polish papercuts, which are made at certain times of the year, such as Easter, to decorate farmhouse walls. Cool Scandinavian colours are used here instead of the more exuberant Polish colours.

YOU WILL NEED

Materials
pre-cut three-panel screen
water-based wood primer
blue-grey satin finish wood paint
thin paper: white, red, yellow
    and blue
wallpaper paste
thin cardboard
bulldog clips
two piano hinges and screws

Equipment
small decorator's paintbrushes
scissors
pencil
ruler
pair of compasses (compass)
pinking shears
hole punch
container for wallpaper paste
tracing paper
screwdriver

1 Paint the screen panels with primer, then apply two coats of blue-grey paint. Also paint the edges of each panel.

2 Cut two long and two short strips of white paper to fit around the edges of each panel. Draw a line 1 cm (½ in) from the edge. Using a pair of compasses (compass), draw semi-circles along the length of each strip to make a scalloped edge.

3 Cut around the curved edges of each strip using pinking shears. Punch decorative holes in the centre of each semi-circle and along the straight edges.

4 Draw a 1 cm (½ in) border around the edges of each panel. Mix the wallpaper paste to a fairly thin consistency and glue the scalloped strips along the drawn lines as shown.

5 Trace the flowerpot template and cut from thin cardboard. Fold a sheet of white paper in half and place the straight edge of the template along the fold, holding it in place with bulldog clips. Draw around the template twice for each panel and cut out.

6 Carefully position the papercuts on the panels and glue in place with wallpaper paste.

7 Draw and then cut out circles of red, yellow and purple paper in graduated sizes. Fold the red and yellow circles into quarters and cut notches into the curves to make the flowerheads. Glue the red flowers in place, then glue a yellow flower and a purple dot on top.

8 Using pinking shears, cut bands of purple paper and glue them to the flowerpots as decoration. Hinge the panels together.

JAM POT COVERS

Pretty paper circles like these are perfect for dressing up your homemade jams and chutneys to give as presents or to sell on a produce stall. They make an assortment of unmatching recycled jars into a set that will stand out from all the rest with their imitation lace edgings.

YOU WILL NEED
Materials
handmade paper
ribbon

Equipment
scissors: small, sharp pair and a larger pair
jam jars
pencil
cutting mat or piece of wood
small hole punch
small hammer

1 For each cover, cut out a circle of paper that is roughly twice the diameter of the jar lid.

2 Fold the circle of paper in half four times, taking care to match the edges exactly each time.

3 Lightly pencil in half-hearts on the edges and carefully cut them out. Mark dotted hearts – one in the middle and two halves on either side along the folded edges.

4 Place the folded paper on a hard surface and use the hole punch and hammer to tap out the dotted holes.

5 Using the small scissors, cut a scalloped edge by snipping out triangles between the hearts.

6 Unfold and flatten the cover. Place it over the jam jar and secure it with ribbon tied in a bow.

■ ZANY GIFT TAG

Tissue paper and coloured newspaper make perfect wrappings, especially when accessorized with brightly coloured homemade cards and eye-catching ric-rac ties.

YOU WILL NEED
Materials
coloured cardboard
tissue paper or coloured newspaper
contrasting ric-rac braid or string

Equipment
scissors
pencil
hole punch
craft knife
cutting mat

1 Cut a gift tag from coloured cardboard. Draw a leaf shape on to the card.

2 Punch a hole in the corner of the card.

3 Using a craft knife and cutting mat, cut out most of the leaf shape then push it out from the background. Wrap the gift in tissue paper or newspaper and bind with ric-rac or string. Thread the card on to the ric-rac or string and tie to secure.

GEMINI PAPER CUT-OUTS

Gemini – the twins – is the chosen motif for this attractive card: the two halves of the card are identical in design, yet one is the negative image of the other. Cut-outs are traditional in Poland, where they are usually deftly cut freehand using just a pair of scissors.

YOU WILL NEED
Materials
thin cardboard or paper in two colours, plus a large sheet for backing
all-purpose glue

Equipment
tracing paper
pencil
craft knife
cutting mat
scissors

1 Trace the design from the template and enlarge if necessary. Glue the tracing to the rough side of one piece of coloured cardboard.

2 Using a craft knife, carefully cut out through the template and reserve all the shapes.

3 Remove the tracing paper and then turn the card over, and back it with the contrasting colour. Cut the backing cardboard twice the size of the cut-out card. Fold it down the centre.

4 Stick a piece of the contrasting cardboard or paper to one side and arrange cut-out pieces on it to match the original design. Stick the cut-out card on the opposite side.

BOOKMARKS

The idea for these unusual bookmarks comes from a collection of American folk art. Children were kept amused for hours with just a pair of scissors and paper, such as old ledgers, letters and household account books, recycled as play material.

YOU WILL NEED
Materials
coloured paper
old documents or ledgers
spray adhesive

Equipment
craft knife
ruler
cutting mat

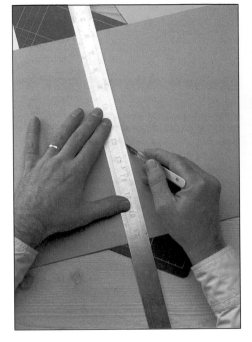

1 Trim the coloured paper to A4 (8¼ x 11½ in) size so that it will fit in the photocopier.

2 Select the best part of your calligraphy and photocopy on to the coloured paper.

3 Select the most suitable parts of your photocopied papers. Trim them to double the pattern size and fold in half.

4 Next, make photocopies of the templates and cut them out.

5 Cut each pattern in half, spray the backs of the patterns lightly with spray adhesive and carefully stick them along the folds of the coloured papers.

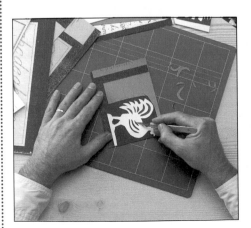

6 Using a sharp craft knife, carefully make all the inside cuts first.

7 To finish the cutting, cut around the outside edges of the pattern.

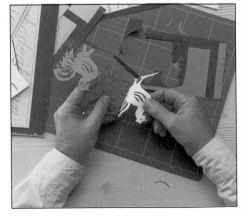

8 Carefully peel off the pattern from the paper and open out the papercut bookmarks.

CYCLIST COLLAGE

The inspiration for this project comes from the Polish tradition of making brightly coloured papercut pictures full of wonderful lively images. Coloured paper is sold in packs of different coloured squares that are pre-gummed, but here glue is also used to stick on the fragile pieces.

YOU WILL NEED
Materials
coloured gummed paper squares,
*   including grey, yellow and green*
PVA (white) glue
background paper

Equipment
tracing paper
pencil
small, sharp scissors
craft knife
cutting mat
fine artist's paintbrush
container for PVA (white) glue

1 Using tracing paper, make tracings of all the pattern pieces, except for the wheels. Transfer the tracings on to the coloured paper squares.

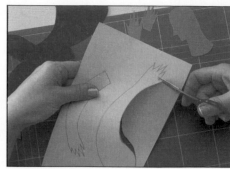

2 Cut out all the pieces of the cyclist using small, sharp scissors.

3 Cut out the parts of the bicycle, using small, sharp scissors.

4 Fold a piece of grey paper in half and cut out the chain.

5 Draw two circles for the wheels, then fold in half three times.

6 Trace and transfer a section of each wheel pattern from the end of this chapter. Cut out the pattern. Unfold and flatten.

7 Draw and cut out the fine detailing for the cyclist's arms and legs. Fold up small circles of yellow paper and one green one, then cut out notches to make the wheel centres, bike light and cap badge.

8 Start to assemble the collage by sticking the detail pattern on to the cyclist's clothes, using PVA glue. Then decorate the wheel spokes.

9 Arrange all the pieces on the background paper without sticking them down. When you are happy with the look of your picture, you can systematically stick each piece down. The left foot should be stuck down on top of the bicycle chain, last of all.

LETTER FILE

Important and treasured letters should be saved, and a letter file is the perfect container. As they are so easy to make, you can create as many as you like to sort your correspondence. Decorate them with colourful cut-outs for a stylish effect, perhaps to reflect the nature of the contents.

YOU WILL NEED

Materials
heavy coloured paper: red, blue, yellow and orange
paper glue
scraps of thin coloured paper

Equipment
ruler
pencil
scissors

1 Measure and draw a rectangle 47 x 32 cm (18½ x 12½ in) on the heavy coloured paper. Cut it out.

2 Following the diagram, mark up the rectangle to form the file. Cut away the excess paper and stick the side panels together in the centre. Stick the base flap over the bottom of the side panels.

3 Cut out a hand motif from red paper. Cut an asymmetrical rectangle from blue paper to represent an envelope. Cut the stamp from yellow and orange scraps.

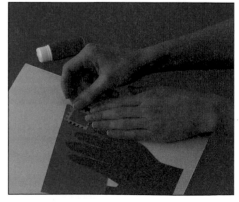

4 Carefully stick the cut-outs to the front of the letter file. You can make additional files in the same way decorated with your own designs.

OCTOPUS GARDEN

Easily made from brightly coloured paper, this friendly octopus and other sea creatures will delight children and brighten up a bedroom or bathroom. This is an inexpensive and easy way to make a mobile – the paper is simply torn and stuck together to form the bold sea creatures.

YOU WILL NEED
Materials
thin cardboard
papers, brightly coloured on one side
PVA (white) glue
thread

Equipment
scissors
pencil
hole punch

1 Cut out two identical octopus shapes from cardboard using the template. Cut eight simple fish, squid and starfish shapes in varying sizes to your own design.

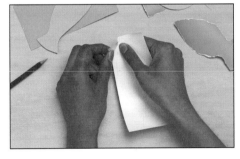

2 Fold the paper so that the coloured side is innermost. Draw around each of the cardboard shapes. Tear out each shape, slightly outside the pencil outline. Two copies will be produced from each folded piece of paper.

3 Glue the paper on to both sides of each cardboard shape. Using contrasting colours, tear out eyes, fins, tails and scales. Glue them into position.

4 Cut a slot in each of the octopus shapes, one to halfway down from the top of the head and the other to halfway up from the bottom of the body. Punch a hole in the end of each octopus arm and two holes in each head piece. Punch a hole at the top edge of each sea creature.

5 Slot together the two octopus pieces. Use thread to hang the sea creatures from the octopus's arms. Tie thread to the top of the octopus's head for hanging.

GREETINGS CARDS AND GIFT TAGS

Homemade greetings cards are to be kept and treasured and make a lovely gift. These stylish cards and gift tags make good use of the natural look of fine corrugated cardboard, with thin manila cardboard and natural raffia adding the finishing touches. Choose one of these motifs or design your own for an even more personal approach.

YOU WILL NEED

Materials
plain paper
very fine single-faced corrugated
    cardboard
natural raffia
manila and natural-coloured
    cardboard
high-tack glue

Equipment
tracing paper
pencil
scissors
revolving hole punch
large darning needle

1 Trace the templates, enlarging to the required size, and transfer on to plain paper. Cut out the shapes and punch holes where indicated with the revolving hole punch, using the smallest hole size setting.

2 Place the cut-out paper shapes on to the smooth side of the corrugated cardboard and carefully draw around them with a pencil. Mark the positions of all the holes making sure that the template does not move.

3 Cut out the shapes from the corrugated cardboard with scissors. Punch holes where indicated, again using the hole punch on its smallest setting.

4 Cut a length of raffia and thread it through the darning needle. Stitch the shapes with the raffia using the photograph as a guide. Finish off the stitching with a small knot on the back of each shape.

5 Cut out large rectangles of manila and natural-coloured cardboard, fold them in half and stick the embroidered motifs in the centre. Cut out smaller square rectangles of cardboard and punch a small hole in each one for the gift tags. Stick more embroidered motifs on to them.

6 For each gift tag, cut a length of raffia and fold in half to make a loop. Thread the loop through the hole, pass the ends through the loop and pull.

GOLD AND SILVER VALENTINE CARD

A handmade valentine card really conveys your feelings. This card captures the spirit of elaborate Victorian valentine cards, with its combination of gold and silver lace, soft, velvety pink background and central cupid motif, yet it is very easy to make using paper doilies, which instantly give a delicate, antique look.

YOU WILL NEED
Materials
all-purpose glue
15 cm (6 in) square dark pink paper
20 cm (8 in) square gold cardboard
decorative gold cake band
paper doilies: silver and white
paper scraps: lilac and dark green
Victorian-style cupid motif

Equipment
small, sharp scissors

1 Glue the pink paper to the gold cardboard, leaving an equal margin all around. Trim the edges with narrow strips of gold foil lace, cut from the cake band. Cut out a small flower for each corner from the silver doilies:

2 Cut out four petals and two flowers from a white doily and back with lilac paper. Choose a larger rectangular shape for the centre and back it with dark green paper. Stick the backed shapes on to the background.

3 Cut out silver flowers and white leaves and glue them around the edges of the main shape, in an interesting pattern.

4 Finish by gluing the cupid to the centre and adding a few more cut-out gold motifs.

PAPER CUTTING AND COLLAGE

144

PRESSED FLOWER
GIFT TAGS

These labels combine the natural textures of handmade paper, raffia and twine with familiar office stationery – paper fasteners and reinforcement rings. They are easily assembled and then decorated with printed scraps and pressed flowers.

YOU WILL NEED
Materials
2 sheets of handmade papers in different colours
brass paper fasteners
printed scraps
reinforcement rings
raffia

Equipment
ruler
craft knife
cutting mat
hole punch

1 Tear a rectangle measuring about 7.5 x 9 cm (3 x 3½ in) from the darker paper. To do this, hold a ruler down on the paper and pull the paper against the ruler. This will give a soft deckle edge to the tag but will ensure a reasonably square shape.

2 With a sharp craft knife, cut a second rectangle, 1 cm (½ in) smaller all round than the first.

3 Attach the two pieces of paper together with brass paper fasteners in three of the corners, as shown. Stick a small printed scrap, or cut-out picture, in the fourth corner.

4 Make a hole in one corner with a hole punch and stick a reinforcement ring on the back. Make a tie from a short length of raffia and loop it through the hole.

CHRISTMAS GIFT WRAP AND TAGS

This Christmas delight friends and family by designing your own gift wrap and tags. With some brightly coloured scraps of paper, some paint and a little imagination, you'll be surprised by what you can create.

YOU WILL NEED
Materials
white cartridge paper
watercolour inks
stencil paints: gold and black
foreign language newspaper
all-purpose glue
plain gold gift wrap

Equipment
tracing paper
pencil
stencil cardboard
craft knife
cutting mat
fine artist's paintbrush
stencil brush
scissors
corrugated cardboard
cellulose kitchen sponge

1 Transfer the Christmas tree template to a piece of stencil cardboard and cut out, using a craft knife and cutting mat. Paint white cartridge paper in different coloured inks. Next, stencil the paper in black and gold.

2 Paint sections of the newspaper in bright watercolour inks. Cut a triangular Christmas tree shape out of kitchen sponge and stick it to a piece of corrugated cardboard. Stamp some of the coloured newsprint with gold trees.

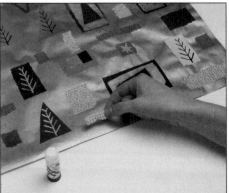

3 Tear strips, rectangles and simple tree shapes from the coloured newsprint. Tear around the stamped and stencilled motifs, and cut some out with scissors to give a different texture. Arrange the motifs on the gold gift wrap and glue them in place.

COLLAGE FIRESCREEN

Use old sepia photographs, sheet music and other printed ephemera to create a nostalgic firescreen full of family memories and mementoes. For a personal touch, dried flowers from your garden will add a subtle glow of faded colour. This screen is for decoration only, and should never be placed near a lighted fire.

YOU WILL NEED
Materials
pre-cut firescreen
water-based wood undercoat
white satin-finish wood paint
newspapers, sheet music and
*   photographs*
PVA (white) glue
gold paper
epoxy resin glue
corn stalks (husks)
dried rose petals
masking tape
clear polyurethane varnish

Equipment
small decorator's paintbrushes
artist's paintbrush and container
*   for PVA (white) glue*

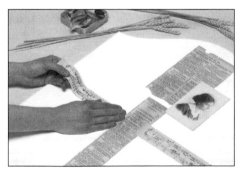

1 Paint the firescreen and feet with two coats of undercoat then paint white. Tear pieces of newspaper and sheet music into strips and glue to the screen with PVA (white) glue.

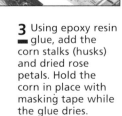

2 Lay photographs on the screen and arrange them until you are happy with the overall design. Glue some images to rectangles of gold paper. Glue everything in position.

3 Using epoxy resin glue, add the corn stalks (husks) and dried rose petals. Hold the corn in place with masking tape while the glue dries.

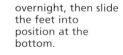

4 Seal the design with a coat of varnish. Leave the firescreen to dry overnight, then slide the feet into position at the bottom.

This colourful divider is made by layering simple tissue paper shapes to create a translucent, kaleidoscope effect. Each section is formed as a separate square, then stitched to a background of Japanese handmade paper, which is sheer but incredibly strong. Seen against daylight, the effect of the translucent tissue paper is heightened, and the colours glow with a vivid intensity.

YOU WILL NEED

Materials

bleedproof tissue paper: white and a variety of colours
PVA (white) glue
handmade Japanese paper
matching sewing thread
length of dowel

Equipment

pinking shears or large scissors
sheet of plastic
medium decorator's paintbrush
container for PVA (white) glue
cutting mat
craft knife
metal ruler
dressmaker's pins
sewing machine

1 Cut the required number of backing squares measuring 35 x 35 cm (14 x 14 in) from white tissue paper. Cut a range of coloured tissue paper shapes.

2 Place a white square on a sheet of plastic. Lay the coloured shapes on top according to the design. Brush diluted PVA (white) glue over the square and apply the first layer of shapes. Build up the design, adding layers. Leave the square to dry. Repeat with the other white backing squares.

3 When the squares are thoroughly dry, gently peel them from the plastic. Place each one on a cutting mat and carefully trim the edges, using a craft knife and metal ruler.

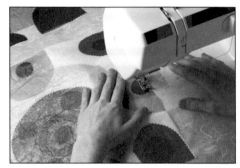

4 Place the paper squares in position on the sheets of handmade paper, making sure that they are evenly spaced. Pin the squares to the paper and machine stitch them in place, removing the pins before you get to them.

5 Trim the handmade paper to size if necessary, then glue the sheets together using undiluted PVA (white) glue to make the screen as wide and long as necessary.

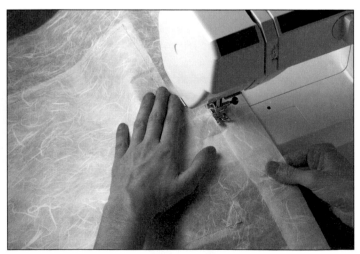

6 Fold over 2.5 cm (1 in) of paper to the back of the screen and crease it into place. Stitch along the edge of the fold to make a casing for a length of dowel, so that the screen can be suspended.

GILDED PATCHWORK LAMPSHADES

Give two plain lampshades a glittering new look by covering them in paper patchwork in two different styles. Although the arrangement and techniques for each shade differ slightly, they have enough in common to be used as a stunning pair.

YOU WILL NEED

Materials

interesting paper materials for the cut-paper patchwork: corrugated cardboard, coloured scrim ribbon, brown wrapping paper, handmade papers, paper mesh

2 plain cream fabric or paper lampshades

wallpaper paste or PVA (white) glue

gold size

Dutch metal leaf

interesting paper materials for the torn-paper patchwork: photocopied typescript, paper mesh, brown wrapping paper, handmade fibre paper, tracing paper

shellac

denatured alcohol

water-based stain in a natural wood shade

Equipment

scissors

small decorator's paintbrushes

fine artist's paintbrush

container for wallpaper paste or glue

firm-bristled brush

soft cloth

1 For the cut-paper patchwork, cut out "squares" from the different materials. Make them roughly equally sized, but trim them at an angle on both sides to taper slightly to fit the shade's conical shape.

2 Try out various combinations of texture and colour until you are happy with the arrangement. Apply a coat of wallpaper paste or PVA (white) glue to the back of the shapes, and stick them in place on the shade. Butt them against each other to form a solid patchwork.

3 Paint bold "stitches" of gold size to link the squares together. Make the lines vertical on the top and bottom of the squares and horizontal on the sides.

4 Cut the Dutch metal leaf into strips, with the backing sheet still in place. Gently press the leaf on to the tacky gold size "stitches".

5 Use a firm-bristled brush to clean away all the excess leaf, leaving just the stitches. Burnish with a soft clean cloth.

6 For the torn-paper patchwork, tear the different papers into similarly sized shapes, leaving the edges ragged and uneven.

7 Tint one-third of the shapes with shellac. It is fast-drying and will make the papers stiffer and also slightly transparent. The brush will need cleaning with denatured alcohol. Tint another third of the paper shapes using water-based stain and allow them to dry.

8 Arrange the shapes on the shade, overlapping them in places and making a feature of the ragged edges. Apply wallpaper paste or PVA (white) glue to the backs of the shapes, and stick them on to the shade, using the stained shapes first. Space them wide apart to begin with, slowly building it up. Fill in gaps with the untinted papers.

9 Paint a 1 cm (½ in) border line around the top and bottom of the shade with gold size. Cut the sheets of Dutch metal leaf into strips, with the backing sheet still in place.

10 Press the strips against the tacky gold size. Overlap them when you need to. The leaf will only stick to the sized sections. Rub off any excess leaf, and burnish with a soft cloth.

SEASHORE CARDS

Receiving a card that has been made for you is so special that it makes the card a gift in itself. In this project the card is used as the base in which to frame pretty shells found on a seaside stroll. The envelope completes the gift, stitched together with raffia and held closed by a feather threaded through a weathered limpet shell.

YOU WILL NEED
Materials
assorted handmade papers
raffia
PVA (white) glue
seaweed
assorted shells
fine-grade sandpaper
double-sided sticky tape
weathered limpet shell with hole
feather

Equipment
darning needle
scissors
container for PVA (white) glue

1 Fold a sheet of paper in half to make a card. Tear two squares from paper in contrasting colours, one smaller than the other.

2 Thread a darning needle with raffia and sew the larger square on to the card with a rough running stitch around the edge.

3 Glue the smaller square into the centre with PVA (white) glue. Glue on some seaweed and a shell.

4 Back a piece of fine-grade sandpaper with double-sided sticky tape. Cut out starfish shapes from the sandpaper, remove the backing paper from the tape and stick one starfish in each corner. Glue a small shell in the centre of each starfish.

5 Cut a rectangle of paper with a triangular flap at one end – the rectangle should be large enough when folded to hold the card. Fold the envelope and stitch the sides together. Start stitching at the bottom and continue to the point of the flap, leaving a loose end of raffia.

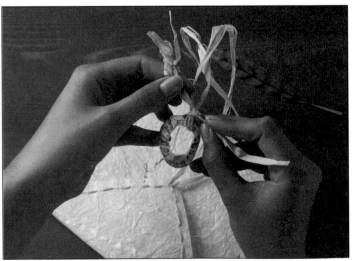

6 Tie a limpet shell on to the end of the two loose strands of raffia. Wrap the raffia around the envelope and thread the feather through the raffia under the limpet to hold the envelope closed.

DANCING BEES BOX

The bees encircling this painted box have been cut out of folded paper like a row of dancing dolls. Measure the lid before you begin and enlarge or reduce the template so that the ring of bees will fit well. This box would make a wonderful gift filled with pots of honey or beeswax cosmetics.

YOU WILL NEED
Materials
circular painted box
black paper
yellow acrylic paint
all-purpose glue
clear acrylic varnish

Equipment
tracing paper
pencil
white marker pencil
small, sharp scissors
medium artist's paintbrush
paint-mixing container
small decorator's paintbrush

1 Trace the bee template and adjust the size as necessary to fit your box. Fold a sheet of black paper in half, then in half again. Position the template across the folded corner so that the tips of the wings are touching the folds, and draw round it with the white pencil.

2 Cut out, making sure that the bees are joined by their wings. Unfold the bees carefully. Make two sets of bees. Draw the bees' stripes on each circle and paint their stripes and wings in yellow acrylic paint.

3 Glue one circle of bees to the lid of the box. Cut the second set of bees in half and stick them on the sides of the box. Protect the box with a coat of varnish.

FLOWER COLLAGE

A collage is a good way of using up all sorts of scrap paper. Before you start, choose a theme – the subject here is a vase of flowers. Scissors are used to make the sharp edges, contrasting with pieces of torn paper for a varied effect.

YOU WILL NEED
Materials
selection of coloured papers
strong clear glue
white cardboard

Equipment
small, sharp scissors

1 Using scissors, cut up coloured paper for all the sharp edges such as the table top and vase. Tear lots of paper into plant-like shapes such as leaves and flowers.

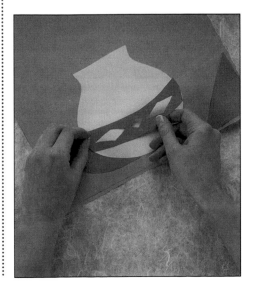

2 Place the pieces representing the table top and vase on a large sheet of paper. Stick them down in sequence with glue.

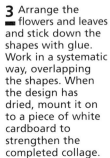

3 Arrange the flowers and leaves and stick down the shapes with glue. Work in a systematic way, overlapping the shapes. When the design has dried, mount it on to a piece of white cardboard to strengthen the completed collage.

PARCHMENT PAPER ART

There is such an interesting variety of textured and coloured papers available that it is easy to find the right basic ingredients to make some simple but extremely effective pictures, without being skilled at painting. These woven contrasting papers don't need to be clean-cut; tearing their edges actually enhances the finished look.

YOU WILL NEED
Materials
parchment paper
coloured papers
plain white paper

Equipment
pencil
metal ruler
craft knife
cutting mat
drawing pins

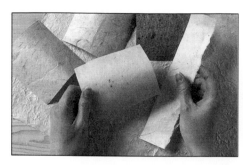

1 Decide on the most interesting combination of papers.

2 Use plain white paper to plan your design. Draw lines where you want the slits to be.

3 Cut these slits carefully with a craft knife and cutting mat.

4 Thread strips of coloured paper through the slits. When the design is ready, re-work using parchment instead of the plain white paper.

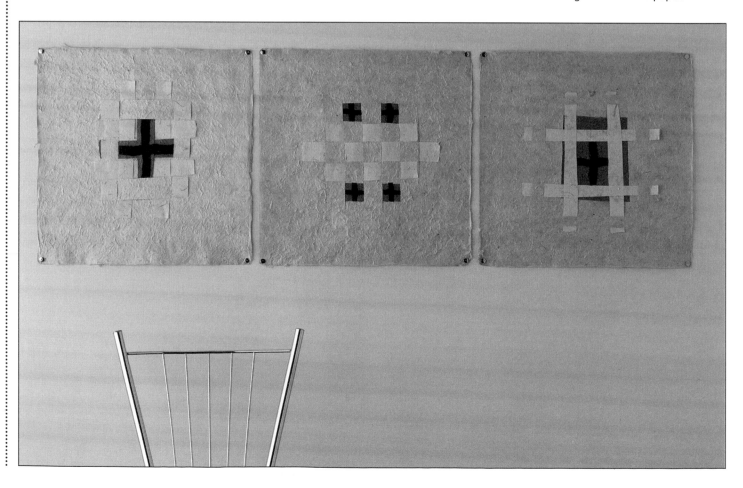

SNOWFLAKES
Template at 75% of full size

DECORATED EGGS
Template at 50% of full size

TRADITIONAL VALENTINES
Template at 75% of full size

EIGHTEENTH CENTURY ITALIAN PAPERCUT
Template at 60% of full size

LOVE TOKENS
Template at 60% of full size

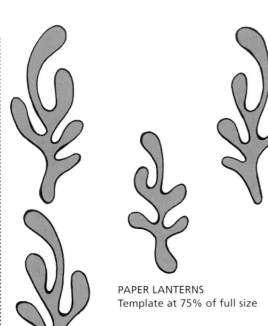

PAPER LANTERNS
Template at 75% of full size

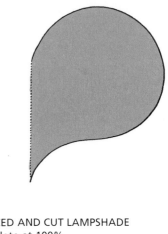

PIERCED AND CUT LAMPSHADE
Template at 100%

PAPERCUT SCREEN
Template at 75% of full size

Place on fold

GEMINI PAPER CUT-OUTS
Template at 75% of full size

LETTER FILE
Template at 50% of full size

BOOKMARKS
Template at 75% of full size

CYCLIST COLLAGE
Template at 70% of full size

CHRISTMAS GIFT WRAP
AND TAG
Template at 100%

OCTOPUS GARDEN
Template at 75% of full size

x2

GREETINGS CARDS AND GIFT WRAP
Template at 75% of full size

DANCING BEES BOX
Template at 100%

DECORATING PAPER

Plain paper can be simply decorated in a number of ways to turn it into an attractive commodity in its own right. Three of the most common ways to decorate paper are to paint, stencil or stamp designs directly on to it. Stencils can be bought or made at home using stencil cardboard. Stamps can be bought from craft shops then used to make up interesting patterns or images, but you can also cut stamps yourself from a potato or lino block. The advantage of making your own stamps and stencils is that the design will be exactly what you want.

This section of the book shows just a selection of the infinite designs that can be used to decorate paper as well as illustrating all the different techniques to get the best results. The ideas shown can be used to create unusual gift wrap, unique sets of personal stationery and colourful cards or to customize paper goods such as notebooks. You will even learn how to make your own handprinted wallpaper and friezes. Following these projects will give you the confidence to use your new skills to create unique designs that you will never find in a shop, and you can make these as simple or as complicated as you like.

In addition to ordinary flat paper, you can, of course, apply any design to other types of paper goods. For instance, paper or cardboard boxes and lampshades can be entirely transformed into beautiful objects to be admired.

CHECKED POTATO PRINT GIFT WRAP

A potato has been cut in half to make this chequerboard pattern. One half is simply cut into a square, the other is given the same treatment, then a cross shape is made by cutting out four triangular sections and squaring off the ends.

YOU WILL NEED
Materials
potato
acrylic paints: cadmium yellow and
  cobalt blue
kitchen paper (paper towels)
plain wrapping paper
adhesive tape
narrow blue satin ribbon
florist's wire

Equipment
chopping (cutting) board
sharp knife or craft knife
2 saucers
scissors

1 On the chopping (cutting) board, cut the potato in half with one smooth movement. Cut the sides off one half to make a square.

2 Cut the other half into a square, then cut out a cross shape by removing triangular sections around the edge and squaring off the ends of the cross.

3 Put the paints in separate saucers and have kitchen paper (paper towels) handy. Print the yellow squares first, starting in one corner and working down and across the sheet of wrapping paper.

4 Print the blue crosses in the white squares. Leave to dry.

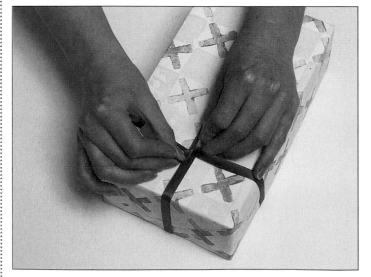

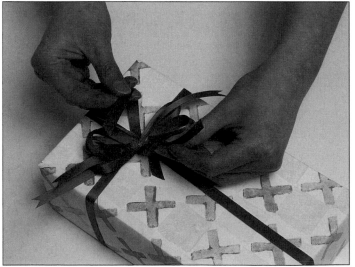

5 Wrap the gift, and use the blue satin ribbon, set off-centre, as a trimming.

6 For a more elaborate effect, make a separate bow, securing loops of ribbon with florist's wire.

GIFT WRAP IDEAS

The presentation of a gift adds the finishing touch which can transform a very simple and modest item into something extravagant and exciting.

FOR THE GIFT TAGS YOU WILL NEED
Materials
paper glue
pressed petals and leaves
coloured cardboard
handmade rough-textured paper: pale colour or white (optional)
raffia or fine string

Equipment
hole punch

FOR THE GIFT BOX YOU WILL NEED
Materials
cardboard box
plain white paper
all-purpose glue
metallic stars and crescents
ribbon in contrasting colour
tiny posy (bouquet) of roses

Equipment
scissors

1 Using paper glue, carefully stick the flowers and leaves in a design on coloured cardboard or, for a layered effect, use a paler or white piece of paper as shown here. To create a rough "torn" edge, wet the paper until it is moist but not soaked and gently tear the shape you require.

2 Punch a hole in the cardboard and thread through a piece of raffia or fine string for tying to the parcel.

3 For the gift box, cover the box with white paper, gluing it securely in place and trimming the corners neatly. Dab dots of glue all over the top and sides of the box and scatter metallic stars and crescents over it. Shake off the loose shapes and save them.

4 Cut a piece of contrasting ribbon to length and tie around the box, knotting it in the centre of the lid.

5 Attach a tiny posy (bouquet) of roses to the knot with more of the same ribbon. Finish off by tying the remainder of the ribbon in a bow.

SPRING MEADOW STENCIL

Stencilling is an extremely versatile way of decorating wrapping paper. There are many pre-cut stencils now available, mostly for home decorating.

YOU WILL NEED

Materials
plain-coloured handmade wrapping
    paper
sepia watercolour paint
kitchen paper (paper towels)
adhesive tape
ribbon

Equipment
pre-cut stencil
saucer
small natural sponge (a make-up
    sponge is ideal)
scissors

1 Position the stencil in one corner of the paper, lining up the edges. Dilute the paint slightly with a little water in the saucer and soak it up with the sponge. Dab the sponge on to kitchen paper (paper towels) to remove any excess paint, then begin to apply the stencil pattern, pressing lightly through the stencil.

2 Repeat the pattern across the paper, then position the stencil on the row below, between two above. This way the pattern will not divide up into blocks, but give an all-over effect.

3 If there are any obvious blank spaces, fill them with random floral sprigs and butterflies.

4 Choose a complementary ribbon and finish the gift off with a simple bow.

FRUIT AND FOLIAGE GIFT WRAP

Even basic brown parcel wrapping paper can take on a very special look. Use a gilded skeletonized leaf and gold twine, or a decoration of leaves and dried fruit slices.

YOU WILL NEED
Materials
picture framer's gilt wax
large skeletonized leaf
brown parcel wrapping paper
adhesive tape
gold twine
seagrass string
dried fruit slices
preserved leaves

Equipment
glue gun and glue sticks

1 Rub gilt wax into the large skeletonized leaf. This takes a little time, as it has to be worked well in.

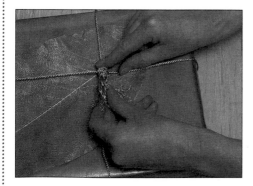

2 Wrap the parcel in the brown paper and rub gilt wax on to the corners. Tie the parcel with gold twine, bringing the two ends together and tying a knot. Fray the ends to create a tassel effect. Slip the leaf under the twine, securing it with glue at each end if necessary.

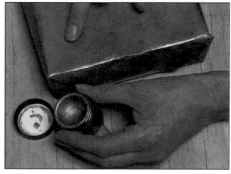

3 Alternatively, wrap the parcel with brown paper and rub in gilt wax, paying special attention to the corners.

4 Tie the parcel with seagrass string, and then glue a different dried fruit or leaf to each quarter.

CHRISTMAS STRIPES

Christmas wrapping paper is produced in many thousands of variations, yet sometimes the most stylishly wrapped presents are relatively plain. This project is a good example of how stripes of strong colour can be used on ordinary parcel wrap for a really dramatic effect.

YOU WILL NEED

Materials
brown parcel wrapping paper
scrap paper
emulsion (latex) paints: white and dark green
double-sided adhesive tape
wide red moiré satin ribbon
florist's wire

Equipment
ruler
7.5 cm (3 in) small paint rollers and tray
scissors

1 Lay a sheet of wrapping paper on scrap paper. Use a roller to paint a white stripe, just in from the edge. Allow a roller's width plus 2 cm (¾ in), then paint the next white stripe. Repeat and leave to dry.

2 Use a fresh roller for the dark green paint. Begin painting the dark green stripe about 1.5 cm (⅝ in) away from the first white stripe, so that a small stripe of brown paper shows through. Repeat as many times as necessary to complete the striped paper, and leave to dry.

3 Using the gift as a measuring guide, trim off any excess paper. Wrap the gift, securing the edges invisibly with double-sided tape.

4 Cut a long length of red moiré ribbon and tie around the gift.

5 Make the bow by looping the ribbon over three times on each side and securing it with florist's wire.

6 Attach the bow to the parcel with an extra piece of ribbon. If desired, the ribbon and bow can be placed off centre.

ARIES GIFT WRAP

Personalize a special birthday gift by creating original gift wrap stencilled with the relevant star sign. Deep red and black have been used here. When stencilling, do not overload the brush; blot any excess paint on kitchen paper (paper towels) before you begin.

YOU WILL NEED
Materials
plain deep red wrapping paper
masking tape
kitchen paper (paper towels)
black acrylic paint

Equipment
pencil
thin cardboard or paper
sheet of acetate
black marker pen
craft knife
cutting mat
stencil brush

1 Draw a template following the finished picture on to cardboard or paper. Place the acetate over the template and trace the outline with a black pen.

2 Carefully cut out the stencil using a craft knife. It is advisable to work on a cutting mat.

3 Decide on the positioning of the motifs on the paper, marking lightly with a pencil if necessary. Position the stencil and use a little masking tape to hold it in place. Stipple the design with the black paint, using a stencil brush. Lift the stencil off carefully and repeat. If paint seeps under the edges of the stencil, wipe it off carefully before repositioning the acetate.

BUTTERFLY GIFT WRAP

Original, hand-printed wrapping paper can make an ordinary present into something very special. Once you've tried stencilling your own paper, you may never want to buy printed gift wrap again.

YOU WILL NEED
Materials
coloured paper
masking tape
acrylic paints: red and black

Equipment
tracing paper
pencil
sheet of acetate
black marker pen
craft knife
cutting mat
stiff artist's paintbrush

1 Trace the butterfly template and enlarge it as necessary. Place a piece of acetate over it and use a marker pen to draw the wings for the first stencil. Use a second piece of acetate to make a stencil of the body and wing markings.

2 Cut out both stencils carefully using a craft knife. Secure the first stencil lightly to the coloured paper with masking tape and stipple on the red paint. Do not overload the brush. Reposition the acetate and repeat to cover the paper.

3 When the red paint is dry, secure the second stencil in place with masking tape. As the acetate is clear it is easy to position the stencil accurately. Stipple on the black paint and repeat to complete the butterflies.

CUPID WRAPPING PAPER

This delightful wrapping paper design, with its dropped-shadow image, can be achieved either by stencilling or stamping. Homemade gift wrap would be the perfect finishing touch for a Saint Valentine's Day present: choose appropriate colours for the occasion.

YOU WILL NEED
Materials
plain wrapping paper
acrylic paints: red oxide and gold

Equipment
cupid motif
sheet of acetate
black marker pen
craft knife
cutting mat
stencil brush
tile
small paint roller
cupid rubber stamp

1 If you are using the stencil method, place a cupid motif (or a freehand sketch) under a sheet of acetate. Draw the image on the acetate with a black marker pen. Cut it out with the craft knife to create the stencil.

2 Stencil the cupid on to the wrapping paper, using red oxide paint and a stencil brush. Leave to dry. Using gold paint, stencil the cupid slightly off-centre for a shadow effect.

3 If you are using the rubber stamp method, put some red oxide paint on the tile and use the roller to coat the stamp. Stamp the images, then overprint using the stamp and the gold paint as before.

ANTIQUE MANUSCRIPT GIFT WRAP

The ancient and modern are combined to make this unusual gift wrap. A page from an old manuscript has been enlarged many times on a photocopier to make a random pattern of white spaces and black shapes.

YOU WILL NEED
Materials
piece of old manuscript
plain white paper
watercolour paints: yellow ochre and pink
adhesive tape
ribbon

Equipment
containers for paints
broad artist's paintbrush
scissors

1 Photocopy a section of your chosen manuscript on to plain paper. Enlarge the copy by 200% and then make a copy of it on to larger paper.

2 Use diluted watercolours to tint the paper with streaks of yellow ochre and pink, giving it an antiqued effect. Leave to dry.

3 To wrap a round box, place it in the middle of the paper and begin pulling up the edges, sticking each section down with tape as you go. Cut a paper disc, slightly smaller than the box top and glue this on top to cover the gathered edges.

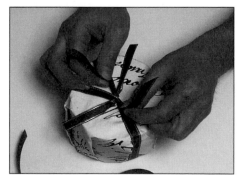

4 Cut three equal lengths of ribbon and tie them in simple knots on top of the box. Trim the ends of the ribbon to the same length.

HERALDIC STATIONERY

This project demonstrates the variety of ways in which a single stamp can be used to produce different effects. The resulting stationery is based on a common theme but with plenty of individual flourishes. Experiment with your favourite colour combinations, and try all-over or border patterns to add even more variety. Many craft stores sell special embossing powders that can be heated to produce a raised print.

YOU WILL NEED

Materials
dark blue watercolour paint
brown parcel wrapping paper
small notebook, folder, postcards and
    textured and plain notepaper
gold paint
dark blue paper
PVA (white) glue

Equipment
plates
small paint rollers
diamond, fleur-de-lys and crown
    stamps
craft knife
cutting mat
ruler
set (T) square
fine artist's paintbrush
container for PVA (white) glue

1 Spread some dark blue watercolour paint on to a plate and run a paint roller through it until it is evenly coated. Ink the diamond stamp and print one motif on to a small piece of the brown wrapping paper.

2 Cut out the diamond shape with a craft knife on a cutting mat. Try not to overcut the corners because the shape will be used as a stencil and the paint may bleed through.

3 Position the paper stencil in the middle of the notebook cover and use the roller to apply dark blue watercolour paint through it. Allow to dry.

4 Spread some gold paint on to a plate and run another paint roller through it. Ink the diamond stamp and stamp a gold print directly over the solid blue diamond, lining up the edges.

5 Cut a rectangle the size of the fleur-de-lys stamp block out of dark blue paper. Measure and divide it in half lengthways. Cut away one side with a craft knife, leaving a narrow border around the edge to make a window.

6 Using a ruler and set (T) square to position the stamp, print a dark blue fleur-de-lys in the centre of the folder. Glue the blue paper over the print so that half the fleur-de-lys shows through the window.

7 Ink the fleur-de-lys stamp with gold paint. Cover the cut-out side of the design with a straight-edged piece of brown wrapping paper. Stamp a gold fleur-de-lys to align with the sides of the blue print. Remove the piece of wrapping paper.

8 Stamp a blue fleur-de-lys on the notebook cover or a postcard. Cover one half with a straight-edged piece of brown wrapping paper and overprint in gold to make a two-colour print.

9 Fold a piece of textured notepaper to make a card. Stamp a blue fleur-de-lys on the front. Add flourishes of gold paint using a fine artist's paintbrush. Stamp a gold crown at the top of plain white sheets of notepaper.

PRIVATE CORRESPONDENCE

This project shows you how to make your own rubber stamp from an eraser. Choose one or two images that express something about your character to use on your writing paper. For a raised image, stamp the motifs with embossing powder.

YOU WILL NEED
Materials
drawings of motifs
plain paper
liquid lighter fuel
stamp inkpad
embossing ink and powder (optional)

Equipment
craft knife
new eraser
lino (linoleum)-cutting tool
scalpel

1 Cut out and arrange your chosen motifs on a piece of paper so they will fit on to the eraser.

2 Photocopy the motifs and cut out with a craft knife the shape to fit the eraser. Place this squarely on the eraser, with the drawing face-down.

3 Spread about three drops of lighter fuel over the back of the paper. Make sure the paper does not slide across the eraser as you do this.

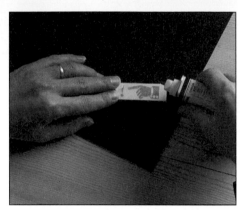

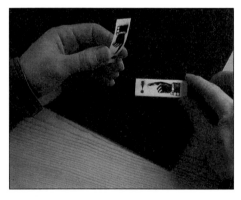

4 Remove the paper to reveal the transferred design. This will be reversed, but the stamping process will reverse it again.

5 Use a fine lino (linoleum)-cutting tool and a scalpel to cut around the outline and the pattern details carefully. Scoop out any excess to leave the design raised above the eraser.

6 Press the eraser stamp into a coloured stamp inkpad and print your stationery.

7 Buy embossing kits from rubber stamp suppliers. To use, stamp your motif using embossing ink.

8 Sprinkle some embossing powder over the ink (which will still be wet) and tap off the excess.

9 Follow the manufacturer's instructions to apply heat to the paper. This will produce a raised, glossy image.

BUNCH OF GRAPES STATIONERY

Have fun experimenting with stamp designs and create your own range of stationery at the same time. The stamps can be used alone or in combination with each other to make a whole range of patterns linked by the use of colour to form a set.

YOU WILL NEED
Materials
sepia acrylic paint
PVA (white) glue
scrap paper
notebooks
brown parcel wrapping paper
off-white acrylic or latex paint
folder
small file
handmade paper folded into cards
natural brown envelopes

Equipment
plates
small paint rollers
grape, tendril and leaf stamps
craft knife
cutting mat
medium artist's paintbrush

1 Spread some sepia paint on to a plate. Add PVA (white) glue and mix together.

2 Run a roller through the paint until it is evenly coated and ink the grape stamp. Make several test prints on scrap paper to gauge the way the paper absorbs the paint and how much paint you will need to apply to the stamp to achieve the desired effect.

3 Stamp a bunch of grapes in the middle of a notebook cover. Ink the tendril stamp and surround the grapes with tendril motifs. The pattern can be repeated on the back cover of the notebook.

4 Stamp a bunch of grapes on to a small piece of brown wrapping paper. Carefully cut around the outline with a craft knife on a cutting mat to make a stencil.

5 Spread some off-white paint on to a plate and run a roller through it until it is evenly coated. Position the stencil on a notebook cover and run the roller over the stencil to make a solid grape shape. Leave to dry.

6 Ink the grape stamp with sepia and overprint the stencilled shape to add the detail.

7 Cut a window from a sheet of scrap paper the same size as the folder cover to make a paper frame. Lay the frame on the cover. Ink the leaf stamp with sepia and stamp leaves all over the cover, overlapping the frame. Leave to dry, then remove the paper frame to reveal a plain border around the leaf pattern.

8 Mix some off-white paint into the sepia to make a lighter brown. Using a brush, apply the lighter brown paint to one side of the grape stamp and sepia to the other.

9 Stamp one bunch of grapes on to the cover of a small file. The shape will be shaded on one side, creating a three-dimensional effect.

10 Place the folded cards of handmade paper on sheets of scrap paper. Stamp an all-over pattern of sepia tendrils, overlapping the edges so that the cards look as if they have been cut from a larger sheet of stamped paper. The texture of the paper will show through in places.

Brown parcel wrapping paper is perfect book-covering material – it is strong, folds crisply and costs very little. Pattern making with potato stamps is great fun, and the elements used here can be used in different combinations to make a variety of designs. These papers would make ideal covers for a row of cookbooks on a kitchen shelf.

YOU WILL NEED

Materials

2 potatoes
PVA (white) glue
watercolour paints: brick-red, brown and yellow-ochre
brown parcel wrapping paper

Equipment

knife
container for PVA (white) glue
paintbrush
plate
craft knife

1 Cut the potatoes in half, then trim the edges to give them all the same square shape.

2 Combine PVA (white) glue and water in equal amounts, then add a drop of brick-red watercolour paint. The texture should be thick and sticky.

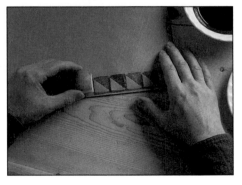

3 Spread an even coating of the paint mixture on to a plate, then dip a potato into it – this will make it easier to see the design as you cut it out. Leave a square border around the edge, then divide the rest of the surface diagonally. Scoop out one triangular section with a sharp craft knife.

4 Print a row of this pattern along the bottom edge of the paper. Brown paper usually has a shiny side and a matt side, with the matt side being more absorbent to paint.

5 Stamp the next row with the same stamp the other way up. Add variety to the design by rotating the stamp for each new row, to form different patterns.

6 To make a chequerboard pattern, leave a gap between the prints. Dip a small piece of potato into the paint and stamp dots in the middle of the blank squares. Experiment with your own combinations. Repeat with the other print colours.

FLOWERPOT FRIEZE

This witty frieze has a 1950s feel and creates an eye-catching feature above a half-boarded wall. Use scraps of left-over wallpaper or sheets of wrapping paper for the pots, and stamp an exuberant display of flowers around your kitchen.

YOU WILL NEED

Materials

matt emulsion (latex) paints: pale blue and white
wallpaper or gift wrap in different designs
PVA (white) glue
green acrylic paint
stamp inkpads in a variety of colours
scrap paper

Equipment

small and medium decorator's paintbrushes
cloth
pencil
scissors
container for PVA (white) glue
fine artist's paintbrush
large and small daisy rubber stamps
cottonwool buds (balls)

1 Paint tongue-and-groove boarding or the lower half of the wall with pale blue emulsion (latex) paint and leave to dry.

2 Using a dry paintbrush, lightly brush white emulsion (latex) over the flat colour. For a softer effect, rub the paint in with a cloth.

3 To make the frieze, draw flowerpot shapes on to scraps of different wallpapers or gift wrap. Cut them out. Cut scalloped strips of paper and glue one along the top of each pot, using PVA (white) glue.

4 Glue the flowerpots along the wall, at evenly spaced intervals.

5 Using acrylic paint and a fine artist's paintbrush, paint green stems coming out of each pot. Leave the paint to dry before beginning to print the flowers.

6 Use coloured inkpads to ink the daisy stamps, using the lighter colours first. To ink the flower centre in a different colour, remove the first colour from the centre using a cottonwool bud (ball). Use a small inkpad to dab on the second colour.

7 Test a stamp on a sheet of scrap paper before applying the image to the wall.

8 Print the lighter-coloured flowers on the ends of some of the stems, using large and small daisy stamps. Allow the ink to dry.

9 Print the darker flowers on the remaining stems. Allow the flowers to overlap to create full, blossoming pots.

▮ NOAH'S ARK FRIEZE

Rather than just stencilling a repeat pattern, why not depict a favourite tale on a frieze? This one depicts the animals fleeing to Noah's Ark to escape the rising flood waters, but you need only a little imagination to recreate any story you like.

YOU WILL NEED
Materials
thin coloured cardboard
paint in a variety of colours
paper glue (optional)

Equipment
ruler
pencil
scissors
waxed stencil cardboard
craft knife
cutting mat
saucer
squares of household sponge

1 Measure and cut out a length of thin coloured cardboard 25 x 90 cm (10 x 36 in) or two pieces 25 x 46 cm (10 x 18 in).

2 Draw various animal shapes such as an ark, clouds and water on rectangles of waxed stencil cardboard.

3 Cut out each stencil using a craft knife and a cutting mat.

4 Place the stencils in position on the coloured cardboard strips. Place a small amount of paint on to a saucer. Using a square of sponge, gently dab paint over the area exposed by the first stencil. Carefully lift the stencil from the cardboard.

5 Continue blocking each stencil using appropriately coloured paint. Add a row of clouds at the top of the frieze, and water beneath the animals.

6 Allow the finished frieze to dry thoroughly, and glue it together if more than one sheet of cardboard has been used.

HANDPRINTED SUN WALLPAPER

Unlike most rubber stamping projects, this one needs a certain amount of pre-planning and a long, clear work surface. Measure the walls to be covered, adding approximately 2 m (2 yd) to allow for pattern matching. Lining paper, which comes in a natural off-white colour, is used here. The paint is emulsion (latex), which is fast-drying, but care must still be taken not to smudge the pattern as you move along the paper.

YOU WILL NEED

Materials
lining paper
paper strip the width of the wallpaper
turquoise-green emulsion (latex)
  paint
wallpaper paste

Equipment
ruler or straight edge
felt-tipped pen
sun motif rubber stamp
pencil
small roller tray
small rubber roller
pasting brush

1 Use a ruler or straight edge to draw lines that butt up against the extremities of the sun stamp. Extend these around the sides of the stamp, so that the exact position of the shape is visibly marked.

2 Make a measuring guide with a strip of paper. Mark out the width of six stamps along the paper strip.

3 Place the measuring guide along the bottom edge of the wallpaper. Coat the stamp with paint using the roller. Make a test print to ensure that the stamp is not overloaded.

4 Make the first stamp print in the second section, the next in the fourth and the last in the sixth, lining them up along the measuring strip.

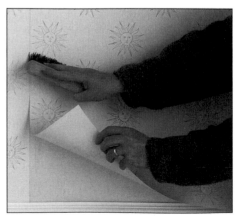

5 Place the paper measuring guide along the side edge of the wallpaper, making light pencil marks as a guide.

6 Reposition the measuring strip horizontally and print the next row of motifs in the first, third and fifth sections. Move the stamp up using the vertical pencil marks as a guide and print the third row in the same positions as the first. Continue in this way until the wallpaper is completed.

7 Hang the wallpaper to form a continuous pattern, matching up the rows of suns with a final row resting on the dado (chair) rail.

GILDED LAMPSHADE

A simple parchment lampshade makes an ideal base for gilding. This stencilled design on a shellac base coat gives the shade an antique appearance. Remember always to use a low-wattage bulb with this shade to avoid tarnishing.

YOU WILL NEED
Materials
plain parchment lampshade
amber shellac varnish
gold stencil paint
masking tape

Equipment
stencil brushes
tracing paper
pencil
stencil cardboard
craft knife
cutting mat

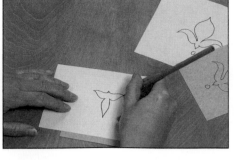

1 Using a large round stencil brush, stipple an even but blotchy coat of amber shellac varnish over the surface of the lampshade and leave to dry for 30 minutes to one hour.

2 Trace the templates and transfer on to stencil cardboard.

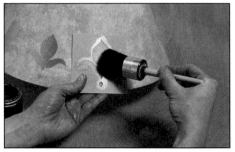

3 Cut out the stencils with a craft knife on a cutting mat. It is easier if you move the stencil towards the blade when cutting.

4 Mark the positions for the stencils around the lampshade. Secure the first stencil at the bottom of the shade with masking tape. Stir the gold paint well, then stipple through the stencil. Do not load the brush with too much paint or it will bleed. Remove the stencil carefully before repositioning for the next one.

5 When you have completed the bottom row, secure the second stencil at the top of the shade with masking tape. Stencil the top row in the same way as before and leave the shade to dry for at least one hour before using.

INCA BIRD LAMPSHADE

Make an impression on a tall conical lampshade by stamping it all over with a strong printed pattern. The shade used here is made of thin, mottled card that resembles vellum in appearance and casts a warm glow when the lamp is lit.

YOU WILL NEED
Materials
white paper
spray adhesive
PVA (white) glue
wallpaper paste
ready-mixed watercolour paints in
*   droppered bottle: golden brown*
*   and darker brown*
conical paper lampshade

Equipment
high-density foam rubber block
craft knife
spoon
flat plate
small paint roller

1 Photocopy the motif of the Inca bird. Spray the back lightly with adhesive and stick it on to the foam block. Carefully cut around the shape with a craft knife and scoop away the background so that the bird motif stands out clearly.

2 Put a spoonful of PVA (white) glue on the plate. Add a similar amount of wallpaper paste and a few drops of golden brown paint and mix well. Run the roller through the mixture to coat it evenly and use it to coat the stamp.

3 Print the bird motif on the lampshade in several places by pressing the stamp on to the surface and then removing it directly. The wallpaper paste makes the paint gelatinous, leaving an interesting texture when you lift the stamp.

4 Add a few drops of the darker paint to the mixture and stamp more motifs on the shade.

BARONIAL WASTEPAPER BASKET

Create a grand look in your sitting-room or study with an elegant wastepaper basket. Containers ready for painting can be bought at speciality craft stores, or you could use any appropriate container.

YOU WILL NEED

Materials
5 mm (¼ in) thick foamcore or corrugated cardboard
wastepaper basket
glue stick
cotton piping cord
acrylic gesso
thin cardboard
acrylic paints: red, yellow and dark green
shoe polish: brown, black and neutral
kitchen paper (paper towels)
gold size
Dutch gold leaf
polyurethane varnish

Equipment
paper
pencil
scissors
craft knife
cutting mat
glue gun and glue sticks
decorator's paintbrushes
fine artist's paintbrush

1 Scale up the templates for the shield and cross motifs and cut out of paper. Draw the shield motif four times on the foamcore or cardboard and cut out with a craft knife. Stick the shields on to the sides of the basket. Cut lengths of piping cord to go around the shields and tie at the bottom in a bow. Stick them on with a glue gun. Paint the whole piece, inside and out, with two coats of acrylic gesso.

2 Paint a piece of thin card with gesso and, when dry, draw around the cross template four times on this. Mix the acrylic paints to resemble red oxide primer and paint the shields and the top edge of the basket. Using a large brush in a random sweeping motion, apply patches of brown and black shoe polish, each mixed with neutral to tone them down, over the gesso, including the string and the cross motifs. Wipe the polish off with kitchen paper as you go, to build up the desired antiqued effect.

3 Cut out the crosses. Paint a thin layer of gold size on the red oxide areas and when it is nearly dry gently apply the gold leaf and rub it down through the backing paper with your thumbnail. Rub harder in some areas to reveal the red oxide beneath. Put a spot of gold leaf in the centre of each cross motif. Stick a cross to the centre of each shield with the glue stick. Coat inside and out with polyurethane varnish.

LEAF
PICTURE

Delicate skeletonized leaves come in such breathtakingly exquisite forms that they deserve to be shown off. Mount them on handmade papers and frame them to make simple yet stunning natural collages.

YOU WILL NEED
Materials
wooden picture frame
paint
backing paper
skeletonized leaf
picture framer's gilt wax
handmade paper
PVA (white) glue

Equipment
fine-grade sandpaper
medium decorator's paintbrush
pencil
scissors

1 Take the frame apart and sand it down to provide a key before painting. Paint the frame with the paint of your choice.

2 Allow the paint to dry, then sand the paint back to the wooden frame to leave a veil of colour on the surface with shading in the mouldings.

3 Use the hardboard back of the frame as a template for the backing paper. Draw around it with a pencil to form a cutting line.

4 Cut the backing paper out with scissors and stick on to the frame back.

5 Prepare the leaf by rubbing with picture framer's gilt wax. It will take a little time to work it in well.

6 Glue the hand-made paper in the centre of the backing paper and then attach the leaf on top. Finally, put the frame back together.

RUSTIC
SHOE BOX

Shoe boxes make perfect containers. This one is intriguingly covered with brown parcel wrapping paper that is rolled and twisted, then unravelled.

YOU WILL NEED
Materials
shoe box
cream emulsion (latex) paint
brown parcel wrapping paper
wallpaper paste
PVA (white) glue
thick white paper
wood stain (such as antique pine)
thick, coarse string
10 x 10 cm (4 x 4 in) square of calico
clips or pegs (clothes pins)

Equipment
small decorator's paintbrush
large artist's paintbrushes
scissors
container for PVA (white) glue
glue gun and glue sticks (or all-purpose glue)

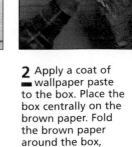

1 Paint the shoe box with cream paint until all of the lettering is covered. Leave to dry. Roll up some brown paper, crumpling it. Fold up, then twist it as small as possible. Untwist and open it out.

2 Apply a coat of wallpaper paste to the box. Place the box centrally on the brown paper. Fold the brown paper around the box, pressing it into the pasted surface, but not smoothing it too much. Inch the paper along the edges of the box and cut along these. Fold the end flaps inside, sticking them in place with wallpaper paste.

3 Fold the brown paper around the sides of the box, one end at a time, pasting one on top of the other to create two large triangular shapes.

4 Fold the triangular shapes up over the sides and paste them against the inside of the box.

5 Neaten the insides by cutting a piece of brown paper to fit the base exactly. Paste it over the paper edges.

6 Using a dry brush, paint a streaky coat of undiluted PVA (white) glue on to the white paper. Leave some areas of the white paper unpainted. Leave to dry completely. Brush wood stain on top, creating a bark-like effect.

7 Tear the paper into rough triangular shapes. If you tear at a slight angle, the paper will rip in such a way that it makes the edges white and thin. Paint these white edges with wood stain so that they blend in.

8 Roll up the paper triangles, beginning with the widest part and rolling toward the point. Bundle the strips together with string and tie a reef knot. Separate the strands of string so that they bush out from the knot.

9 Fray the edges of the calico, then scrunch it up in the middle, using clips or pegs (clothes pins) to hold the shape. Heat the glue gun and apply glue to the scrunched folds. Press the calico on to the centre of the box lid.

10 Remove the clips or pegs (clothes pins) from the calico and apply more hot glue. Press the "bark" bundle on top of the calico.

ROSE PETAL CONFETTI BOX

This sweet little paper box makes a much prettier holder for confetti than a commercially made one, and can be kept after a wedding as a reminder of the special day.

YOU WILL NEED

Materials
cardboard or stiff paper
pink paint
gold ink
double-sided adhesive tape
ribbon
rose petal confetti

Equipment
tracing paper
pencil
scissors
fine artist's paintbrush
metal ruler
blunt knife
cutting mat
craft knife

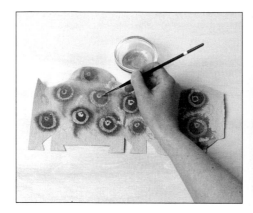

1 Trace the template for the confetti box and enlarge. Lay the template on the cardboard, draw around it and cut it out. Wet the cardboard and paint round pink shapes, so that the colour bleeds out. Leave to dry. With gold ink, paint circles and leaf shapes. Leave to dry.

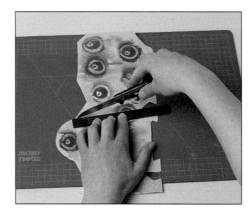

2 Lay the cardboard on a cutting mat. With a ruler and blunt knife, score the fold lines.

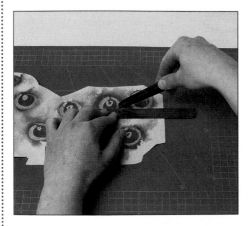

3 With a sharp craft knife, carefully score the slits for the ribbon.

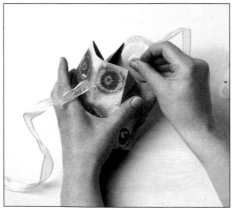

4 Cut a piece of double-sided tape and stick it to one side of the tab. Peel off the backing, overlap the tab and stick in place. Fold under the bottom edge and thread the ribbon through the slits. Fill with confetti then tie the ribbon in a bow.

CONTEMPLATIVE CUPID CARD

This elaborate card isn't difficult to make and will tell someone special that they are in your thoughts. Some ordinary pencils are water-soluble, so try what you have to hand before making a special trip to a shop.

YOU WILL NEED
Materials
masking tape
heavy watercolour paper
thin cardboard
water-soluble pencils: dark green, light green, dark blue, light blue, red, pink and grey
watercolour or drawing inks: pink and orange
all-purpose glue
glitter glue

Equipment
tracing paper
pencil
cutting mat
craft knife
scissors
fine artist's paintbrush
brush for glue

1 Trace the templates for the background and the cupid and enlarge them, if necessary. Tape them to the heavy watercolour paper and carefully go over the outlines with pencil, leaving an indentation on the paper. Fold along the fold lines.

2 Transfer the design for the frame on to the thin cardboard in the same way. Cut out the card and frame and fold them.

3 Colour in the background and cupid, using the water-soluble pencils, and carefully cut out the cupid. On spare pieces of watercolour paper, draw and colour in some simple flowers and stems. Go over the pencil work with a wet paintbrush, to blend the colours.

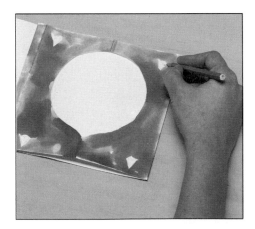

4 Decorate the outside of the card with the watercolour or drawing inks, mixing the colours for a patchy effect.

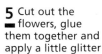

5 Cut out the flowers, glue them together and apply a little glitter glue to the centres. Apply glitter glue to the wings of the cupid.

6 Line up the edges of the cupid with the edges of the background at points A and C. Glue on some flowers.

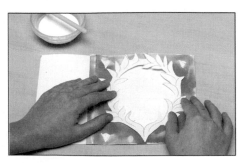

7 Glue the frame to the front of the card at point D. Attach a few more flowers to the inside of the frame.

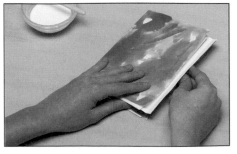

8 Finally, glue the background and cupid into the card, taking care to line up points B. Stick flap A to join the card together and fold up the card. Press it under a book before sending.

CRAZY SNAP CARDS

A game of snap is always good fun – why not make your family their own set of cards? Each stencil can be used several times if allowed to dry thoroughly between colours.

YOU WILL NEED

Materials
heavy paper in four different colours
paint in four different colours
paper glue
medium-weight coloured cardboard

Equipment
ruler
pencil
stencil cardboard
scissors
craft knife
cutting mat
small squares of household sponge
palette or saucers for paints

1 Measure and cut four pieces of stencil cardboard measuring approximately 6 x 9 cm (2½ x 3½ in).

2 Draw a different symbol on each card. Cut out with a craft knife and cutting mat.

3 Cut rectangles of coloured paper measuring 6 x 9 cm (2½ x 3½ in). Place the first stencil on one of the rectangles. With a sponge square, dab paint over the stencil until the cut-out is covered. Carefully remove the stencil, taking care not to smudge the paint. Repeat with all the stencils until you have made enough cards. Stick each stencilled rectangle on to a slightly larger piece of medium-weight cardboard. Allow the glue to dry thoroughly.

ELEGANT EMBOSSED CARDS

Embossed paper has a very subtle, expensive and specialist look about it, but in fact it is not at all difficult to make. There are several different methods, but the simplest way is to place the paper over a stencil on a flat surface, and simply rub the back of the paper.

YOU WILL NEED
Materials
coloured paper, cardboard and envelopes
PVA (white) glue

Equipment
ready-cut stencil, or cardboard cut-out
embossing tool
scissors
brush for glue

1 Place the stencil or cut-out on a flat work surface and cover it with the paper.

2 Holding down firmly, rub the embossing tool gently over the cut-out area to define the shape. Increase the pressure until the shape shows up as a clear indentation.

3 Trim the paper to shape and stick it on to a cardboard background. Pair it with a contrasting envelope or, if you prefer, punch a hole in it, thread with ribbon and use it as a gift tag.

STRING PRINTING

String can be fixed to a cardboard block in any number of designs and then used to print repeat patterns on paper. String printing can literally be child's play if youngsters are encouraged to use this technique.

YOU WILL NEED
Materials
cardboard
PVA (white) glue
string
coloured paints
coloured paper

Equipment
scissors
marker pen
brush for glue
containers for glue and paint
large artist's paintbrush

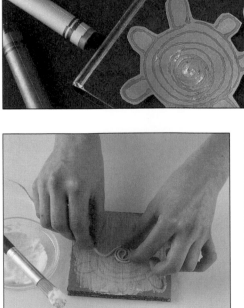

1 Cut out a few squares of cardboard with a pair of scissors and stick the pieces together with PVA (white) glue to make a thick block.

2 Draw a design on the cardboard with a marker pen.

3 Cover the cardboard with glue and stick the string around the outline of the design. Leave to dry.

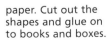

4 Dab paint on to the block with a paintbrush. Press down on to the paper. Cut out the shapes and glue on to books and boxes.

PAINTED POSTCARDS

Be original and make your own postcards. This ingenious method of applying and scratching off paint gives very professional-looking results.

YOU WILL NEED

Materials
heavy coloured paper in different colours
gold paper
paints in a variety of colours
paper glue

Equipment
ruler
soft pencil
scissors
medium artist's paintbrush

1 Measure and cut out rectangles of coloured paper measuring 10 x 12 cm (4 x 4³/₄ in).

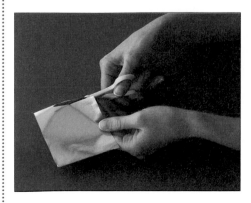

2 Cut smaller rectangles of gold paper and apply a coat of paint to the gold paper.

3 While the paint is still wet, draw a design in the paint with a soft pencil. Allow the paint to dry thoroughly.

4 Cut around the scratched images leaving a small border. Stick each one to a rectangle of coloured paper with paper glue and allow to dry.

BUTTERFLY GIFT WRAP
Template at 100%

INCA BIRD LAMPSHADE
Template at 75% of full size

GILDED LAMPSHADE
Template at 100%

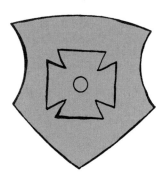

BARONIAL WASTEPAPER BASKET
Template at 100%

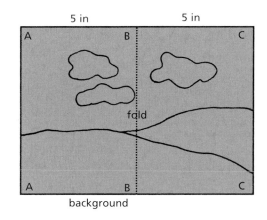

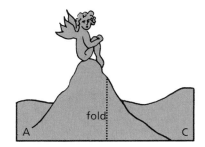

A   fold   C

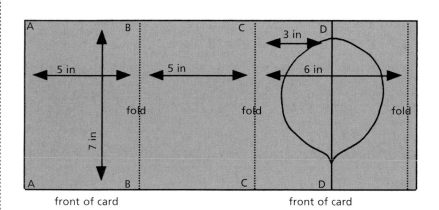

front of card   front of card

background

CONTEMPLATIVE
CUPID BOX
Template at 100%

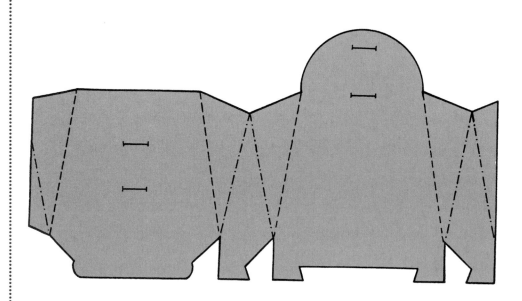

ROSE PETAL CONFETTI BOX
Template at 100%

PAPER CONSTRUCTION

The Japanese are renowned for their ingenious use of paper for constructing all manner of items, ranging from little boxes to the walls of houses. Between these two extremes, there is any number of delightful goods that can be made entirely from paper or its near cousin, thin corrugated cardboard. Once constructed, the items can be painted or varnished to give them a durable and attractive finish.

The following pages contain many projects which create useful everyday objects from what at first sight appears to be an unlikely basic material. Storage boxes of all shapes and sizes are an obvious product, but the principles of paper construction can be extended to dozens of others goods. You will learn how to make a range of items, including decorative cards, trays, bags, satchels, folders for the safekeeping of stationery, lamp bases, lanterns, sculptures, mobiles, screens, a doll's house and even a tiny chest of drawers for storage.

Once you have learnt the basic principles of folding, joining and strengthening cardboard and paper, you will be able to adapt the ideas shown on these pages to suit your own creativity and requirements. Some furniture makers have even constructed tables and chairs from corrugated cardboard, so there is nothing to stop you from attempting ever more ambitious projects.

DOLL'S HOUSE

This quirky doll's house is made by slotting together thick grey chipboard. The cardboard pillars distinguish it from the traditional doll's house design. The house could be painted with water-based paints and decorated inside with gift wrap or scraps of fabric.

YOU WILL NEED

Materials
thick unlined grey chipboard
high-tack glue
single-faced corrugated packing cardboard
strong glue
metal hinges and screws

Equipment
paper
pencil
craft knife
cutting mat
metal ruler
scissors
glue gun and glue sticks (optional)

1 Using the diagrams, make templates for the front and the back of the doll's house. Next, transfer them on to the chipboard. Mark the position of the window on the front piece and cut out, then cut the piece in half. Mark the positions of the slits in the back piece and carefully cut them out using a sharp craft knife, cutting mat and metal ruler. Take care to be accurate with all measuring.

2 Draw the two side pieces for the house on to chipboard. Cut them out, cutting carefully round the tabs. Cut out the windows and the slits where marked.

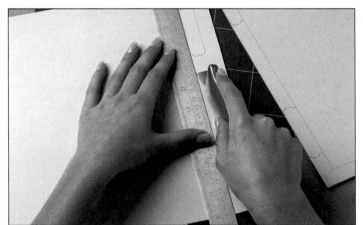

3 Draw the two floor pieces on to the chipboard and carefully cut them out. You may need to change the blade frequently to ensure that the craft knife is always sharp.

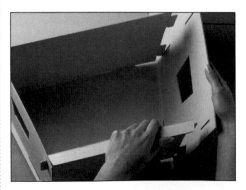

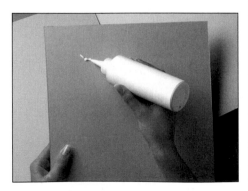

4 Score along the flap at the front of the floor piece and gently fold it over. Lay the back piece on the surface and slot the two floor pieces into this. Slot the side pieces into the back and floor pieces, easing them in gently by carefully bending the chipboard.

5 For the roof, cut out a 64 x 33 cm (25 x 13 in) rectangle from the chipboard. Mark a line down the middle of the length. Score along the line lightly. Cut two extra pieces measuring 29 x 28 cm (11½ x 11 in).

6 Glue the two pieces of chipboard on to each half of the roof piece a few millimetres from the central score line. Carefully bend the roof so that it folds along the score line. Apply glue along the top of the two side walls and the back of the house, then stick the roof in place, butting up the panels inside the roof to the glued edges. For extra strength, glue a triangle of cardboard inside the roof.

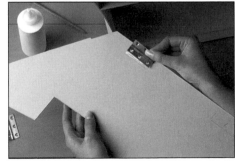

7 Using the diagram as a guide, draw the tile pieces on to the back of the corrugated cardboard. Cut out with scissors. Starting from the bottom, glue the tiles on to the roof, overlapping them slightly, until the whole roof is covered. Cut a strip of cardboard along the corrugated ridges and glue to the ridge of the roof.

8 Cut out rectangles of corrugated cardboard for the pillars, 6 x 33 cm (2½ x 13 in) and 6 x 30 cm (2½ x 12 in). Bend them over slightly and glue them on to each front piece. Make scrolls out of strips of cardboard, securing them with glue. Cut out the awnings using the templates at the end of this chapter and stick along the roof edge of the fronts. Cut strips of corrugated cardboard to edge the windows and door, and glue in position.

9 Hold each front piece against the house in the required position and make two marks inside on the front panel and side wall for the hinges. Glue the hinges in place using strong glue and a glue gun if necessary. Glue a strip of corrugated cardboard along the edges of the front of the roof. Cut out curtain shapes and brick shapes and glue in place.

ORIGAMI BOXES

This little box is a suitable project for a complete beginner, but it may take a couple of practice attempts before it suddenly "clicks". You can make the boxes any size you like, and use any paper that is not too flimsy. Parcel wrap creases well and is both cheap and strong, so practise on that to begin with.

YOU WILL NEED

Materials
sheet of paper, for each box
double-sided adhesive tape

Equipment
scissors

1 Fold and trim a sheet of paper to make a perfect square. Fold the square corner to corner and open it out again so you can see the lines of four equal triangles folded on the paper.

2 Turn the paper over, then fold into four square quarters. Unfold again so you can see eight equal triangles folded on the paper. The centre of the paper is Point A.

3 Hold the model in the air and push all the sides together so that the corners meet in the middle.

4 Flatten the model. Point A is now a corner of the flattened model. Keep it facing you.

5 Fold the point opposite Point A over to meet it. Crease it along the mid-line.

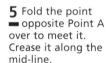

6 Now fold it back up to the mid-line and crease the fold. Unfold it again.

7 Fold the same point up to the last crease, then fold it over again, up to the mid-line. Turn the model over and repeat steps 5–7.

8 With point A still facing you, take the top layer of the left-hand corner and fold it over on to the right-hand corner. You are now faced with a square. Fold the left-hand corner and the top layer of the right-hand corner into the centre point, and crease. Bring the right-hand top layer over on to the left. Turn over and repeat.

9 Point A now forms the base of a smaller triangle. Fold this up at the point where it meets the sides. Crease well, then fold it in the other direction and crease again. Unfold.

10 Insert your hand through the open end. Splay out your fingers while pushing up the bottom of the model, Point A. The box shape will appear with two folded edge sides and two taller pointed sides.

11 Fold the two pointed sides down to be level with the others and tuck the ends under the box. These ends can be secured with a small piece of double-sided tape.

TWISTING MOBILE

This crisp, geometric mobile is formed by simply scoring and cutting a single piece of two-coloured cardboard. The twisted squares demonstrate that stunning mobiles can be made from the simplest of materials.

YOU WILL NEED

Materials
medium-weight cardboard, white on one side and coloured on the other
cord or thread

Equipment
pencil
metal ruler
craft knife
cutting mat
eraser
hole punch

1 Cut a square of cardboard 18 x 18 cm (7 x 7 in). Draw two 90-degree "V" shapes as shown. Note that one is closer to the edge of the cardboard.

2 Draw another pair of "V"s inside the first on the second diagonal. Draw a third pair of "V"s on the first diagonal.

3 Draw a final pair of "V"s on the second diagonal. If there is space, continue to fill the cardboard.

4 Carefully cut along the "V"s with a craft knife. Erase the pencil lines and punch a hole in one corner of the shape.

5 With the cardboard still flat, score short lines between the ends of the "V"s where you will fold the cardboard. Do this by turning the craft knife blade upside down and carefully running it along the edge of the ruler.

6 Fold the cardboard along the scored lines and pull out to form a series of twisted square shapes positioned within each other. Thread cord or thread through the punched hole for hanging. If desired, make a second twist-out and suspend it from the first.

PAPER QUILLS

The old-fashioned paper craft known as quilling is used to make this distinctive card. You can design a picture using the same technique.

YOU WILL NEED
Materials
assorted coloured paper
strong clear glue
cardboard in a contrasting colour

Equipment
scissors
ruler
pencil ·

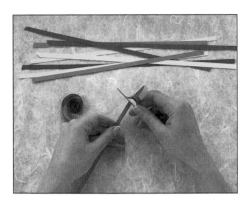

1 Cut long narrow strips of various shades of coloured paper. First curl one end of each strip with the blunt edge of a pair of scissors, then, starting at this end, roll the strip into a tight coil.

2 Release the coil slightly and glue the end. Hold this in position until the glue is dry. Pinch the outside of the coils between your fingers to form different shapes such as a pear, scroll or eye.

3 Measure and cut a rectangular piece of cardboard and fold in half. Arrange the shaped quills on the front of the cardboard and stick down, spreading the glue on the bottom edge of each quill.

PAPER
WINDMILL

This pretty windmill spins round in a breeze, and makes a delightful decoration for a child's bedroom.

YOU WILL NEED
Materials
coloured paper in 3 colours
PVA (white) glue
paperclip
25 cm (10 in) dowel
cork

Equipment
scissors
brush for glue
ruler
pencil
eraser
fine-grade sandpaper
drill

1 Cut out two 15 cm (6 in) squares from paper, each in a different colour. Glue together.

2 Using a ruler and pencil, draw a diagonal line across the centre of the square in both directions. Measure 7 cm (2¾ in) from each corner and mark with a dot. Cut up to the dots, then erase the pencil lines.

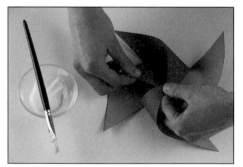

3 Gently bend every other point into the centre of the square. Using a brush, glue the points together, holding the paper in place until the glue hardens.

4 Cut out a small circle from the third colour of paper. Straighten out a paperclip, bend one end into a coil and glue on to the centre of the circle.

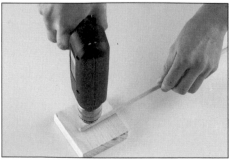

5 Gently push the other end of the paperclip through the centre of the windmill. Sand the ends of the dowel then drill a small hole 3 cm (1¼ in) from one end.

6 Push the sharp end of the paperclip through the dowel. Glue the end of the paperclip and push it into a piece of cork for safety.

PAPER SCULPTURE BIRDS

These colourful birds have a bright, crisp modern feel, with a touch of folk art in the painting. Several of them strung on nylon thread make a fabulous mobile.

YOU WILL NEED

Materials
stiff coloured papers
paints
fine cord

Equipment
pencil
tracing paper
scissors
ruler
stapler
hole punch
saucers
fine artist's paintbrush

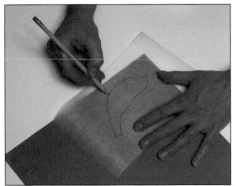

1 Trace the bird templates, then transfer to the coloured papers.

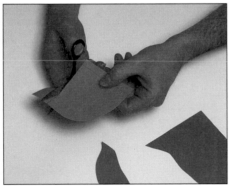

2 Using small, sharp scissors, cut out the body and wing shapes.

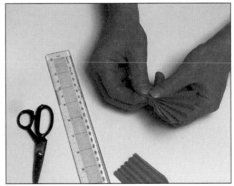

3 Use the blunt edge of the scissors to score fold lines at 6 mm (¼ in) intervals across the wings, then pleat them.

4 Staple a wing to each half of the bird and fan the wings out. Punch a small hole through both sides for the bird's eyes.

5 Paint spots on the underside of the bird's body and when dry add a small contrasting spot in the middle. Leave to dry.

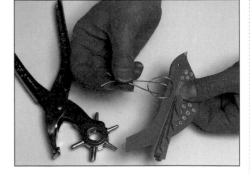

6 Punch a hole through the top of the bird, about halfway along, and thread it through with fine cord.

JAPANESE PAPER LANTERNS

The subtle textural variations of handmade Japanese paper are shown to perfection in these two beautiful paper lanterns. Put small candles inside glass jars and place inside the lanterns for a gentle, muted light.

YOU WILL NEED
Materials
paper
sheets of handmade Japanese paper
masking tape
thin willow twig
double-sided adhesive tape
natural pine strip (used in basket-making) or thin cardboard

Equipment
pencil
scissors
bradawl
craft knife
cutting mat

1 For the simple shade, scale up the template and draw the lantern shape on the handmade Japanese paper. Make faint pencil marks to indicate the positions of the holes for the fastener. Cut out the shade.

2 Place a small tab of masking tape on the back of the paper at each hole position, to act as a reinforcement.

3 Using a bradawl, pierce small holes where indicated on the template.

4 Cut a short length of willow twig to act as a fastener, then bend the lantern into a cylinder and match up the holes. Insert the twig to hold the lantern in shape.

5 For the petal shade, scale up the template at the end of this chapter and draw the shapes on the Japanese paper. Cut out the two pattern pieces, indicating the overlap and fastener slits faintly with a pencil. Reinforce the back of each slit position with a tab of masking tape, then lay the two pieces flat, overlapping where indicated. Attach the pieces together with a strip of double-sided tape.

6 Make small slits where indicated on the template using a craft knife and cutting mat.

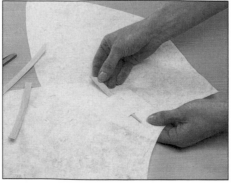

7 Cut an elongated triangular fastener from pine strip or thin cardboard and insert into the slits.

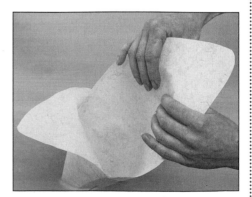

8 Bend the lantern into a cylinder and attach the overlap with double-sided tape. Gently bend over the top of each petal shape.

GIFT BOXES

With little more than some coloured cardboard, the most basic of tools and some imagination, it is simple to transform a flat sheet of thin cardboard into an attractive gift box.

YOU WILL NEED
Materials
thin coloured cardboard
stamp inkpad
double-sided tape

Equipment
ruler
pencil
craft knife
cutting mat
rubber stamp
set (T) square
blunt knife

1 Draw the box, following the diagram. Increase or decrease the measurements as required, but keep the proportions the same.

2 Cut out the box, using a craft knife and ruler to make neat, accurate lines.

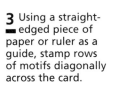

3 Using a straight-edged piece of paper or ruler as a guide, stamp rows of motifs diagonally across the card.

4 It is important to extend the pattern over the edges, so stamp partial motifs at the ends of each alternate row.

5 On the wrong side of the cardboard, hold a set (T) square or ruler against the fold lines and score along them with a blunt knife. Do not break the surface of the cardboard.

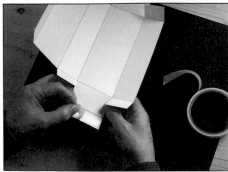

6 Fold along the score lines, making sure the corners are square. Apply double-sided tape to the joining edges, then peel off the backing paper and press the sides together. Accuracy is important at this stage, as double-sided tape cannot be repositioned.

7 Continue folding and sticking the cardboard in this way, ensuring the edges fit together neatly. Fold in the end pieces.

CORRUGATED PAPER FOLDER

This handmade corrugated paper folder is a cross between a box and an envelope. It is a perfect way to gift wrap a silk scarf or lacy underwear.

YOU WILL NEED
Materials
tissue paper
adhesive tape
corrugated paper
thick coloured paper
4 eyelets or brass paper fasteners
fine string

Equipment
scissors
eyelet punch (optional)

1 Wrap your gift in tissue paper and secure with adhesive tape. Measure the shape and cut a length of corrugated paper, just long enough to wrap around it. Secure with a small piece of tape.

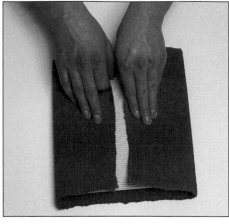

2 Turn the shape over and fold a second measured sheet around it to cover the open ends. There should be a small gap between the ends. A rough or deckled edge to the paper will give added interest.

3 Cut four 2 cm (¾ in) diameter discs and four contrasting 1.5 cm (⅝ in) discs from thick coloured paper. Attach them to the edges as shown, using eyelets or brass paper fasteners.

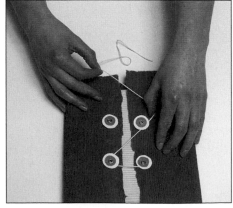

4 Wrap a piece of string around the discs, crossing over in the middle. Pull together firmly and knot to secure the folder.

PAPER ROSES GIFT BOX

To make a gift seem extra special, present it in this prettily decorated box. The romantic roses make this a perfect wedding present.

YOU WILL NEED

Materials
single- and double-sided crêpe paper
   in soft colours
adhesive tape
round cardboard box, with lid
wire-edged ribbon

Equipment
scissors
ruler
pencil
glue gun and glue sticks

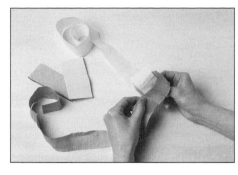

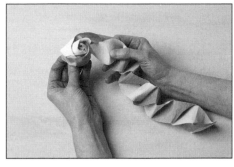

1 To make the roses, cut through the folded crêpe paper to make strips about 5 cm (2 in) wide. Tape two strips at right angles to each other. Fold one over the other, to make an accordion shape.

2 Holding the ends, stretch the accordion to its fullest extent and wind it up, twisting to get a rose shape. Tape the ends of the strips into a "stalk". Make several roses in different colours and sizes.

3 Cover the box and lid with crêpe paper, neatly pleating the fullness and sticking it down so it is as flat as possible in the centre of the lid.

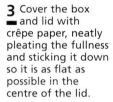

4 Glue the roses on top. Finish with wire-edged ribbon shaped in a generous bow.

FUN PAPER BAGS

Tiny paper bags are very easy to make and they can be used for all sorts of fun occasions. They are ideal for handing out at children's parties, or to hold a slice of cake.

FOR THE CARRIER BAGS YOU WILL NEED
Materials
stiff coloured paper
double-sided adhesive tape
cord or ribbon

Equipment
tracing paper
pencil
ruler
scissors
hole punch

FOR THE CREPE-PAPER BAGS YOU WILL NEED
Materials
crêpe paper
contrasting thread
metallic stick-on stars
silver or gold cord

Equipment
pinking shears
sewing machine with zigzag attachment
scissors

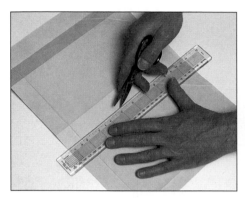

1 Enlarge the carrier bag template to the required size and transfer it on to stiff paper. The dotted lines indicate mountain folds and the dashed lines are valley folds and need to be folded in the opposite direction. Use scissors and a ruler to score along the fold lines.

2 Cut out the shape. Stick the bag together using double-sided adhesive tape along the seams. Using a hole punch, make two sets of holes opposite each other on the top seam.

3 Place a square of double-sided adhesive tape below each hole inside the top seam. Thread the cord or ribbon through the holes, peel the backing off the tape and press together to hold the handles in position between the bag and the overlapping seam.

4 For the crêpe-paper bag, cut out a pair of rectangles, using pinking shears.

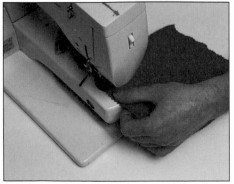

5 Set a sewing machine to a large zigzag stitch and use contrasting thread to sew along three edges.

6 Place the stick-on stars randomly over the bag, then fill with your gifts and tie with silver or gold cord.

HOUSEWARMING GIFT

This project transforms a cardboard box into a novelty gift container in the shape of a house.

YOU WILL NEED

Materials
strong cardboard box
sheet of rough-textured, natural-coloured handmade paper
PVA (white) glue
sheet of corrugated cardboard
doll's house roof-tile paper
narrow gingham ribbon

Equipment
pencil
scissors
ruler

1 Find the centre point of the longest side flap of the box and draw lines to the sides, at least 7.5 cm (3 in) down from the top. Cut this triangular section away, and do the same to the other side. This gives you the pitch of the roof.

2 Measure all around the box and cut the textured paper to fit. If your sheet is long enough you will be able to cut it out in one piece. Use the box itself as a pattern, turning it to draw all the sides. Cut the paper out.

3 Spread the back of the textured paper with PVA (white) glue, right up to the edges, then smooth it in place over the box.

4 Measure the length of the roof along the line of the pitch, allowing a slight overlap at both sides. Cut the corrugated cardboard and roof-tile paper to the correct length and width and glue the two together.

5 Cut the roof section in half, then glue each half to a side flap. The idea is to part the roof to open the box, so make sure that the two halves meet in the middle to form the apex of the pitched roof. Cut a strip of corrugated cardboard roughly 4 cm (1½ in) wide and score it down the middle. Trim it to fit along the top of the roof, and cover with tile paper. It will sit on top of the roof and hold the two sides together, being held in place itself by the ribbon.

6 Pass a long length of gingham ribbon over the top of the roof, cross it over underneath the box and then pull it tight and tie it in a bow on top of the pitched roof.

CHEST OF DRAWERS

This chest of drawers is made from children's shoe boxes painted in lovely bright colours, so it will appeal to children of any age. It can be made bigger using larger shoe boxes and is ideal for storing stationery, sewing tools and odds and ends as well as children's things.

YOU WILL NEED
Materials
9 shoe boxes
polyboard
wood glue
dressmaker's pins
water-based paints in 3 colours
9 wooden knobs and screws
single-wall corrugated packing
*   cardboard*

Equipment
metal ruler
pencil
craft knife
cutting mat
small decorator's paintbrush
bradawl
screwdriver

1 Measure the height and width of one box and multiply both measurements by three, then measure the length of one box. Add 1 cm (½ in) to each of these three measurements. Cut eight pieces out of the polyboard: two for the top and base, which are the length by the width plus the thickness of four pieces of polyboard; two for the horizontal struts, which are the length by width plus the thickness of two pieces of polyboard; and four for the vertical struts, which are the length by the height plus the thickness of two widths of polyboard. Cut slits wide enough to take the thickness of one piece of polyboard a third and two-thirds of the way along two of the horizontal struts and two of the vertical struts. Slot the pieces of polyboard together at right angles as shown. Put to one side.

2 Lay one of the pieces of polyboard you cut for the top and base on the work surface. This will be the base. Glue the two remaining vertical struts at right angles at either end of the base. Pin them in place to secure. When the glue has dried, glue the top pieces, pinning them in place. Leave to dry.

3 Lay the open box shape on the work surface. Apply glue to all the ends of the polyboard grid and place it inside the box. Pin from the outside through the polyboard so that it is securely fixed together. Cut a piece of polyboard the width and height of the whole box and glue and pin it to the back of the frame.

4 Paint the shoe boxes with one of the water-based paints. Paint the lid as well. The inside could be painted with a co-ordinating paint or lined with patterned gift wrap. You may need to give them two coats of paint for an even coverage. Paint the chest in another colour and leave to dry.

5 Paint the wooden knobs with the same colour paint as the chest. When the paint on the boxes and the handles is dry make a hole with a bradawl in the front of each box. Fix a knob to each box front.

6 Cut a long piece of corrugated cardboard the width of the chest and long enough to make a scroll shape for the feet. Roll it up from both ends until the rolls are the required size and equal to each other. Glue in place.

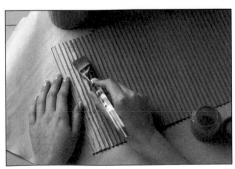

7 Cut another strip of corrugated cardboard the same width and long enough to cover the top of the chest in a wavy shape. Paint the long strip and the rolls with the third paint colour.

8 Stick the long strip up the side of the chest, turning the edge under the bottom, and glue in three waves across the top. Glue down the other side and leave to dry. Pin in place down the sides.

9 Apply glue to the top of each roll and centre the chest on top. Leave to dry.

CORRUGATED
LAMP BASE

Corrugated packing cardboard has sculptural qualities that elevate it from a mere packaging material. Its construction, with one smooth and one ridged side, means that it can be rolled into even, tubular shapes to make lamp bases. Corrugated cardboard is very lightweight so place the lamp where it is unlikely to be knocked over.

YOU WILL NEED
Materials
roll of corrugated packing cardboard
bottle-adaptor lamp fixture

Equipment
tape measure
craft knife
cutting mat
glue gun with all-purpose glue sticks
pencil

1 Cut a 52 x 35 cm (20¾ x 14 in) rectangle of cardboard and roll it lengthwise, leaving the centre hollow for the lamp fixture. Glue the loose edge.

2 Cut a 135 x 4 cm (54 x 1½ in) strip from the cardboard. Measure 18.5 cm (7¼ in) from the top left corner, draw a line between this point and the bottom right corner and cut along this line. Apply glue to the square end and line it up with the column base. Wrap the cardboard strip around the base, gluing to hold the layers together. Keep the base flat.

3 Cut a 52 x 4 cm (20½ x 1½ in) strip. Then glue and wrap it around the base to add extra stability.

4 Cut another 135 x 4 cm (53 x 1½ in) strip. Then glue and wrap this around the top of the column. Keep the top flat. Ask an electrician to install the bottle-adaptor lamp fixture to the column and to wire it to a flex (cord).

THREE-DIMENSIONAL PAPER FRAMES

Paper and cardboard are easy to use for making frames. Layers of cardboard glued together produce a wonderful three-dimensional effect. For best results, make sure the cardboard is accurately and squarely cut, and that all the edges are aligned.

FOR THE CLASSICAL COLUMNS YOU WILL NEED

Materials
mounting board
rubber solution adhesive
double-sided adhesive tape

Equipment
tracing paper
pencil
cutting mat
45° mat cutter
craft knife
metal ruler

FOR THE PUNCHED-PAPER YOU WILL NEED

Materials
6 mm (¼ in) thick polyboard
thick watercolour paper
double-sided adhesive tape

Equipment
pencil
craft knife
cutting mat
towel or cloth

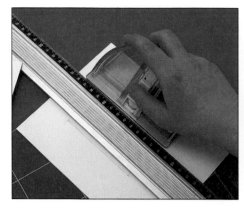

1 Trace the classical column templates at the end of this chapter and enlarge if necessary. Cut out the basic frame shape from mounting board, using a cutting mat and a 45° mat cutter.

2 Using a craft knife, cut four strips for each column and the steps, and four triangles for the roof, from another piece of mounting board.

3 Glue down the steps with rubber solution adhesive (any excess can be rubbed off when dry). Line up the cardboard strips with the frame base.

4 Glue the roof in place with the rubber solution adhesive. Leave to dry. Glue on the two columns, cutting the length of the strips to fit if necessary.

5 Insert your picture using double-sided tape and attach a piece of mounting board to the back as a stand.

6 For the punched-paper frame, draw the basic frame shape on the polyboard and cut out using a craft knife. Cut 6 mm (¼ in) wide strips of watercolour paper and glue to the inside and outside edges of the frame. Let the glue dry completely.

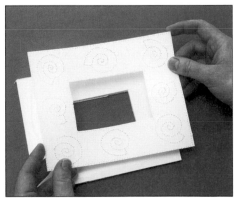

7 Cut out a piece of watercolour paper to the same size as the frame front and, using the template at the end of this chapter, draw the design on the back.

8 Lay the paper on a towel or cloth and, following the design, pierce a line of dots through the drawing with a darning needle.

9 When finished, glue the pierced paper to the front of the frame. Make a simple stand from polyboard and attach it to the back of the frame with double-side tape.

GREETINGS CARD

Inexpensive scraps of paper take on a sophisticated air when delicately bound together by a length of jute twine to form a unique handmade card.

YOU WILL NEED
Materials
olive oil
essential oil (optional)
kitchen paper (paper towels)
calligraphy paper
green sugar paper
paper glue
watercolour paper
high-tack PVA (white) glue
fine jute twine

Equipment
scissors
pencil
craft knife
cutting mat
metal ruler
bodkin

1 Scent some olive oil with a little essential oil, if desired. Working on a protected surface, use kitchen paper (paper towels) to rub the olive oil over a sheet of calligraphy paper until translucent. Leave to dry.

2 Cut a piece of green sugar paper to form the front of the card. With a pencil, draw an oak leaf shape approximately one-third of the way down from the top.

3 Cut out the leaf shape with a craft knife on a cutting mat. Put the leaf shape to one side.

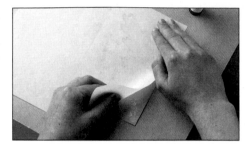

4 Glue the oiled paper on top of the sugar paper. The oil will cause uneven sticking, which gives the finished card a pleasingly mottled appearance. Leave until completely dry under a pile of books. Protect the books with several layers of kitchen paper (paper towels).

5 Score down the centre of the watercolour paper using the back of a craft knife and a metal ruler, and fold to make the greetings card. Tear away most of the paper to one side of the fold to produce a deckled edge.

6 Cut the oiled paper to the same size as the green paper. Apply glue to the top two-thirds of the torn side of the folded watercolour paper. Glue the layered green paper and oiled paper in place to form the front of the greetings card.

7 Tear across the front of the greetings card just below where the glue ends and remove the bottom third.

8 Cut a piece of green paper and a piece of oiled paper to the width of the greetings card, about half the height of the gap left below the oiled and green paper. Tear across the top. Glue the green paper to the inside of the card along the bottom and glue the oiled paper to the torn edge.

9 Make holes in the front of the card with a bodkin and thread through twine to join the upper and lower parts. Tie a simple knot at each end. For the gift tag, make a hole in the leaf shape. Attach a length of twine. Score a curving vein along the leaf using the back of the craft knife.

WOVEN PAPER CARDS

Paper weaving is a fun way to achieve exciting effects from a very simple process. You can use the weaving as a design on its own, or mount it behind shaped frames to make unusual greetings cards.

YOU WILL NEED

Materials
medium-weight cardboard: green, orange and red
paper glue

Equipment
ruler
pencil
scissors

1 Draw a rectangle measuring 16 x 24 cm (6¼ x 9½ in) on medium-weight green cardboard and cut it out.

Draw a line down the centre of the rectangle and gently score along it with scissors to form a fold.

2 Draw a 9 cm (3½ in) square on the front of the cardboard and cut it out to form a window.

3 Cut a piece of red cardboard measuring 10 x 10 cm (4 x 4 in). Make vertical cuts every 1 cm (½ in) down the cardboard, from just below the top edge almost to the bottom, but do not cut all the way.

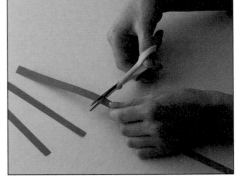

4 Cut several strips of orange paper approximately 1 cm (½ in) wide.

5 Weave the orange strips through the red cardboard to make a checked pattern.

Trim and attach the orange strips at each side of the card with paper glue.

6 Stick the woven square to the inside front of the green card so that it shows through the window.

CORRUGATED CARDBOARD TRAY

Gluing together layers of single-wall corrugated cardboard makes a sturdy tray, although one that is more for decoration than everyday use. The tray could be varnished to make it more robust, or it could be painted or decorated with collage or decoupage and then varnished.

YOU WILL NEED
Materials
single-wall corrugated cardboard
two large metal paper fasteners
high-tack PVA (white) glue

Equipment
pencil
metal ruler
craft knife
cutting mat

1 On the corrugated cardboard draw out ten rectangles 38 x 50 cm (15 x 20 in). Cut them out on the cutting mat using the metal ruler and craft knife. Draw the pencil lines on the wrong side of the cardboard (not the side that will show).

2 Draw a line 5 cm (2 in) from the edge on six pieces of the cardboard, and cut out the centre rectangle on each one. Put the spare pieces aside to use for the handles.

3 Take one of the large pieces of cardboard and again measure 5 cm (2 in) from the edge all the way round. Draw an equilateral triangle measuring 3 cm (1⅛ in) on a piece of spare cardboard. Cut it out. Starting at the centre and working towards the corners, place the triangle template along the inner side of one of the pencil lines and draw around it, again on the wrong side of the cardboard.

4 Continue along all four sides, finishing with a square at each corner. Cut out around the triangles, cutting from the pencil line to the point of the triangles.

5 On two of the remaining complete pieces of cardboard, draw lines 7.5 cm (3 in) from the edges all the way round. Cut out the inner rectangles and discard.

6 On the back of one of the first pieces, measure two points 10 cm (4 in) apart on either side of the centre of each short side. Make slits with a knife. Insert a paper fastener into each slit from the wrong side. Cut cardboard pieces 3 x 5 cm (1⅛ x 2 in) peel the back off and wrap them round the paper fasteners. Glue in position.

7 Following the diagram at the end of this chapter, make a template for the handle. Cut out a cardboard triangle and cut holes as indicated. Peel off one side of the cardboard.

PAPER CONSTRUCTION

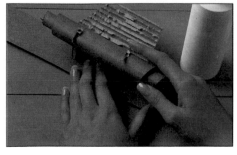

8 Roll up the triangle of cardboard quite tightly and hold it firmly in position. Push the roll on to the paper fasteners.

It should slot on to the fasteners quite easily. If it does not, then push firmly so that the fasteners push through the cardboard.

9 Push the roll down on to the cardboard stems. Spread glue on the underside of the

loose flap of cardboard and press in place. Hold firmly until the glue is dry.

10 Lay the remaining complete piece of cardboard right side up. Glue the back of each piece. Glue on the two pieces with rectangles cut out,

then the piece with the triangular edge. Finally glue the six rectangular frames on top of each other, finishing with the handles.

Heavy corrugated cardboard can be woven into very sturdy panels to make an excellent screen. The cardboard is light enough for the screen to be moved easily from room to room. It is painted with dazzling vertical stripes which, when woven, look like traditional wattle panels updated for the twentieth-century.

YOU WILL NEED

Materials
corrugated cardboard boxes of single-
  wall construction
water-based paints: white and
  assorted colours
strong, coloured nylon cord
wooden batten
large clips
scrap wood

Equipment
scissors
small paint roller
paint tray
stapler
bradawl
large darning needle
small saw
drill
small sponge

1 Cut panels of cardboard from the boxes, making sure that they are as flat and smooth as possible. Paint one side of each panel white, then add a pattern of multi-coloured stripes with the paint roller. Paint the other side in the same way, so that the finished screen is reversible.

2 Cut the cardboard into 10 cm (4 in) wide strips, cutting across the corrugations. Place six strips side by side, folding under 2 cm (¾ in) at both ends of each strip. Weave through a horizontal strip and staple the ends of the vertical strips to it.

3 Continue to weave in horizontal strips until you reach the desired height. Turn under the sides of the horizontals and staple to the verticals as you work.

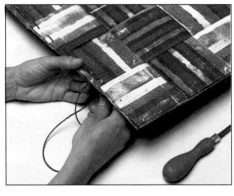

4 Using a bradawl, pierce holes in the top and bottom edges of each screen panel. Sew a line of decorative stitching through the holes, using the nylon cord and darning needle.

5 Cut four lengths of batten the same length as the sides of the screen panels. Drill a hole every 4 cm (1½ in). Sponge each piece with paint. Clip the battens to the edges of the screen panels. Place the edge of each panel on some scrap wood and pierce through the drilled holes to the cardboard, using a bradawl.

6 Sew the battens to the edges of the panels with nylon cord.

7 Place the panels together, matching the edges carefully. Lash them with cord, passing the needle underneath the top strip of batten, over the join (seam) to the back, and under the second strip.

CORRUGATED PAPER DECORATION

Corrugated paper is a much-maligned material that can look absolutely stunning if used innovatively. It can be used to make borders for windows and doors, and you can complete the look with decorative holders for candles, picture frames and book covers. Experiment with different shapes to see which looks most pleasing.

YOU WILL NEED
Materials
roll of uncoloured corrugated paper
thin cardboard
spray adhesive
masking tape (optional)
candles
white emulsion (latex) paint
string
fine corrugated paper in different
    colours
paper glue

Equipment
tape measure
scissors
ruler
pencil
craft knife
cutting mat
small decorator's paintbrush
glue gun and glue sticks

1 To make a window border, measure the width of the sill and cut the uncoloured corrugated paper to fit, plus the required drop. Flatten the ridges with a ruler.

2 Draw a design on to cardboard and cut out to use as a template. Draw the shape on the corrugated paper, using the template. Cut it out with a craft knife on a cutting mat.

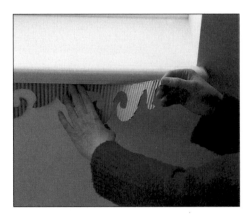

3 Spray the back of the corrugated paper with spray adhesive and fix in position. If you want to remove the decoration later, stick masking tape under the windowsill and glue the decoration to the tape. You can peel off the tape without harming the wall.

4 To make the candle-wrappers, cut strips of corrugated paper to the right size and paint them with white (latex) emulsion. Slit the corrugations with scissors.

5 Cut a wider strip and glue it to the back of the white strip. Wrap the decoration round the candles. Cut string long enough to wrap several times round the candles.

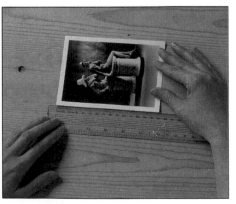

6 To make the picture frame, measure the image that will be framed and decide on the size and shape required.

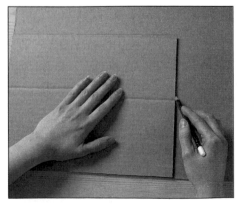

7 Draw the frame backing on to corrugated paper and cut it out with the craft knife and ruler.

8 Use the backing as a template to draw and cut out the front of the frame from coloured corrugated paper. Cut out the central frame area.

9 Stick the image in position with paper glue so the backing colour shows through in a thin border all round.

10 Make a stand for the frame, with a piece of corrugated paper cut to the shape shown. Decorate the frame with twisted strips of coloured paper if desired.

CHINESE LANTERN

This stick-and-cardboard lantern has a natural look by day, but lights up like a skyscraper at night. Sheets of corrugated cardboard can be bought in a range of colours from natural to fluorescent, and the wooden skewers can also be painted.

YOU WILL NEED
Materials
35 x 26 cm (14 x 10 ¼ in) sheet of corrugated cardboard
scrap paper
gold spray paint
wooden skewers

Equipment
metal ruler, approximately 3 cm (1¼ in) wide
pen or pencil
craft knife
cutting mat

1 Using the width of the ruler as a spacer, draw vertical lines across the length of the cardboard.

2 Cut slits across the width of alternate columns, starting one in from the edge. Moving the ruler down a width at a time, continue cutting slits to the bottom of the cardboard.

3 Cut through the uncut rows in the same way, but starting with the ruler a half-drop down, so that the slits fall halfway between the first ones. Continue until the sheet is covered with a "brickwork" pattern of slits.

4 Protect your work surface with scrap paper, then spray the smooth side of the cardboard with gold paint.

5 Turn the cardboard over and weave all but one skewer in and out of the slits. Allow about 2.5 cm (1 in) to protrude on one edge to give the lantern legs to stand on.

6 Trim the last column to within 1 cm (½ in) of the slits, so that the join (seam) will not be too bulky.

7 Hold the two edges so that they overlap (with the smooth gold side inside), then weave the last skewer through the double thickness to join the lantern edges together.

WOOD AND PAPER SCREEN

This elegant modern firescreen is ideally suited to a contemporary minimalist setting. The paper strips are cut from rolled sheets, and the natural curl keeps the paper in position between the bands of dowel. The combined effect of the natural wood and paper and the clean, simple design is peaceful and very easy on the eye. As the paper panels are not attached, they can be replaced with different colours.

YOU WILL NEED

Materials
six 90 cm (36 in) lengths of
    5 x 2.5 cm (2 x 1 in) softwood,
    such as pine
eighteen 30 cm (12 in) lengths of
    6 mm (¼ in) wooden dowel
white emulsion (latex) paint
clear acrylic varnish
wood glue
2 pairs of butterfly hinges and screws
white, heavy, textured watercolour
    paper

Equipment
fine-grade sandpaper or fine wire
    (steel) wool
small decorator's paintbrushes
pencil
clamps
drill
wooden mallet
screwdriver
craft knife
metal ruler
cutting mat

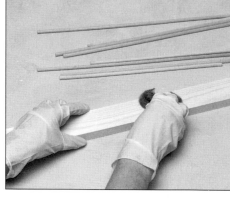

1 Lightly rub down all the pieces of wood with sandpaper or wire (steel) wool. Apply a thin, patchy coat of diluted white paint to all the wood and leave it to dry. Seal the surface of each piece with a coat of varnish.

2 Mark the positions of the dowels on the inside edges of each upright. Clamp the wood firmly and carefully drill a hole about halfway through the wood at each point.

3 Glue the dowels into one half of each pair of uprights. Squeeze a little glue into the holes in the second upright of each pair and attach the two together, matching corresponding holes. Gently tap the frame halves together, using a mallet.

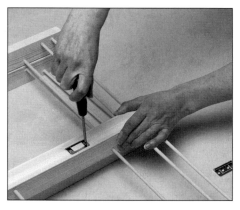

4 Place the frames side by side and mark the positions of the hinges. Make pilot holes for the screws to avoid splitting the wood, then screw the hinges in place.

5 Cut six 12 x 90 cm (4¾ x 36 in) lengths of watercolour paper using a craft knife, metal ruler and cutting mat. Roll it so that it is gently curled.

6 Weave the strips of paper in and out of the screen, experimenting to achieve the best effect.

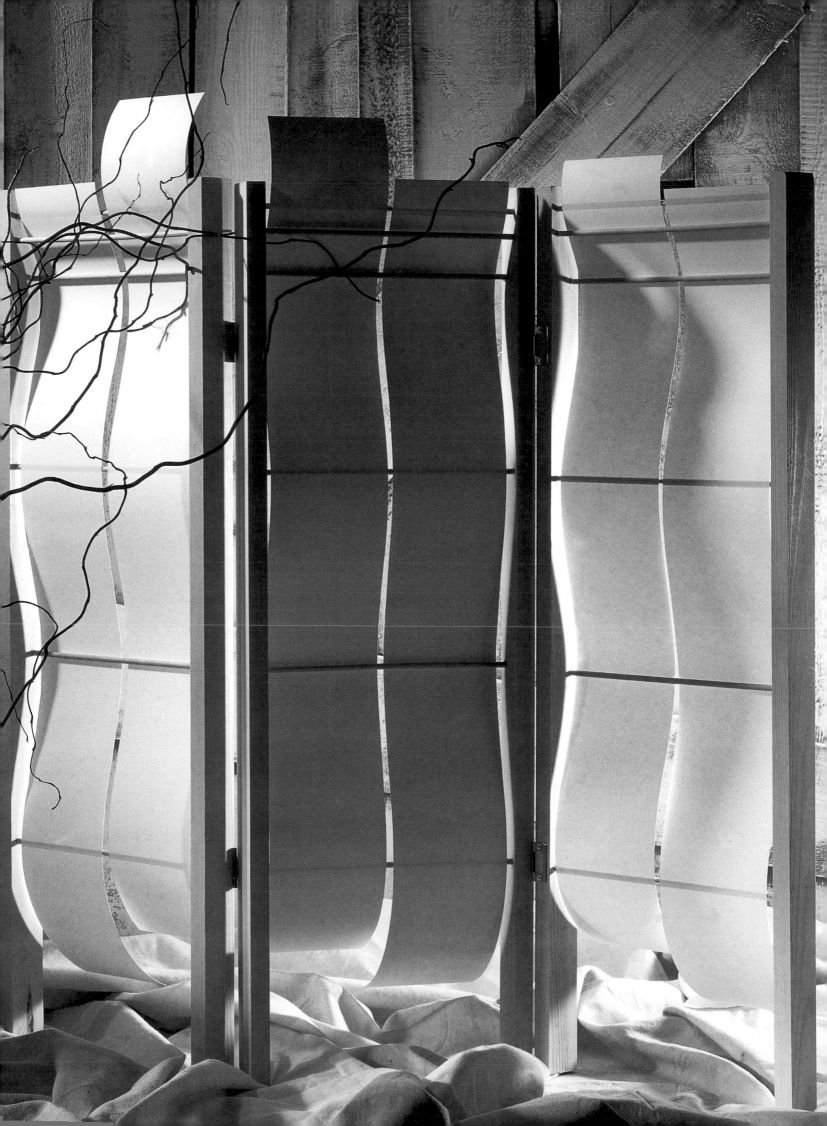

CARDBOARD SATCHEL

This satchel hardly looks like cardboard at all. It makes clever use of the wax used to waterproof clothing, which makes the bag more practical and adds a lovely mottled patina. The bag can be lined with wallpaper, as here, or with patterned fabric.

YOU WILL NEED
Materials
spray adhesive
wallpaper
small-flute single-wall corrugated cardboard
wax for waterproof clothing
eyelets
paper string
plastic piping
metal fasteners
washers

Equipment
soft cloth
hairdryer
tracing paper
pencil
craft knife
metal ruler
cutting mat
wooden spoon
hole punch
revolving hole punch

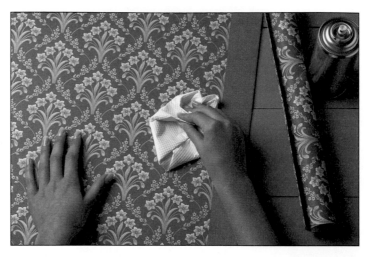

1 Spray adhesive on to the back of the wallpaper and stick on to one side of the cardboard. Starting from one edge, gently wipe over the wallpaper to remove air bubbles. Using a soft cloth, apply an even coat of wax all over the other side. Melt the wax with a hairdryer so it soaks in.

2 Using the diagram at the end of this chapter, cut out piece A, which is the back and front flap. Score the lines with the blunt point of a wooden spoon. Cut small holes for the eyelets and insert. Cut out the oval holes for the fastenings on the front flap. Punch holes all around the outside, 1.5 cm (⅝ in) apart.

3 Cut out the outside front (B), two side pieces for the pocket (D), two side pieces for the satchel pocket (C) and the pocket front (E) from the wallpapered cardboard. Also cut out the inside pocket divider (F), and paper on both sides. Punch holes 1.5 cm (⅝ in) apart along three sides, leaving the top edge free.

4 Score the unprepared side of the side piece for the pocket (D) along the fold lines, then fold. Centre the pocket (E) on the satchel front (B) and mark the position. Put the pocket (E) to one side. Position the pocket side (D) along the marked line, then punch matching holes in the two layers of cardboard and stitch on to the front of the satchel by threading paper string through the holes, starting and ending with a knot on the papered side. Fold over 2 cm (¾ in) along the straight edge of the pocket front (E) and attach to the pocket side (D).

5 Score along all the fold lines on the two side pieces (C) and bend along all the lines. Stitch one of them around the back satchel piece (A) and continue threading the string through all the holes on the flap. Lay the inside pocket divider (F) on top of this and lay the second side piece (D) on top. Stitch through all the layers.

6 Hold the front of the satchel (B) in place against the side strip (C). Stitch in place with the string, finishing by threading the string back through the previous hole and tying a knot inside.

7 Cut out a handle (G) and fold along the lines as indicated. Punch holes 1.5 cm (⅝ in) apart along the longest sides. Thread a double thickness of string through both of the eyelet holes and tie with a knot. Wrap the cardboard handle around the string and stitch together. (It is a good idea to use a piece of plastic piping to reinforce the handle.)

8 Hold the front flap flat against the satchel. Using a pencil, mark the positions for the backs of the fastenings on the pocket front. Carefully push the back of the metal fasteners through the cardboard. Bolt the other parts of the fasteners in the position marked. Use washers to stop them cutting through the cardboard.

BANDBOX

These brightly coloured oval pasteboard boxes were the early nineteenth-century equivalent of modern hand luggage. A bandbox is easy to create, and much more satisfying to make than to buy. Look for decorator's sample books of wallpapers, or try printing your own paper using stencils.

YOU WILL NEED
Materials
2 sheets of corrugated cardboard 38 x 38 cm (15 x 15 in)
drawing pins
cotton thread
2 sheets of thin cardboard 38 x 38 cm (15 x 15 in)
paperclip
strong matt-finish adhesive tape
PVA (white) glue
wallpaper paste
wallpaper
braid
gift wrap

Equipment
ruler
pen
craft knife
cutting mat
small decorator's paintbrush
scissors
clothes pegs (pins)

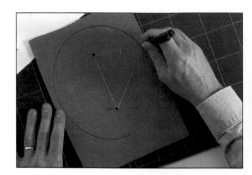

1 To draw an oval box base on one cardboard piece, draw a central line then place two drawing pins 10 cm (4 in) apart along the middle section of the line. Measure a 30 cm (12 in) length of cotton thread and join the ends. Loop this around both the pins and hold the cotton thread taut to one side by placing a pen within the loop. Draw with the pen, clockwise, holding the cotton thread taut all the time. Cut out the oval shape with a craft knife.

2 Place the base on to the other corrugated cardboard sheet and draw around it. Cut around the outside of the line, making a slightly bigger oval for the lid.

3 Wrap the thin cardboard around the base to form the oval box and secure the shape with a paper clip. Sticking strips of adhesive tape around the base, join the two sections. Make each strip at least 7.5 cm (3 in) long and space them around the base to give a firm join. Glue down the side seam.

4 Apply wallpaper paste to the box and roll the wallpaper on to it, smoothing out air bubbles as you go. Allow 1.5 cm (⅝ in) overlap at the top but at least 2.5 cm (1 in) at the base. Snip the overlap, glue and turn it in at the top, holding it in place with clothes pegs (pins) until it dries.

5 Place the lid on the second piece of thin cardboard and cut around it allowing a 2.5 cm (1 in) overlap. Make the lid as you made the box, but use a strip of card 4 cm (1½ in) deep, secured to the top with tape. Glue the side seam, then paste the wallpaper to the lid. Snip wedges out of the overlapping paper and glue the edges. Repeat for the base.

6 Glue the braid to the edge of the sides of the lid and secure it with a clothes peg (pin) until it dries. If you prefer, you can cut another strip of matching paper for this. The box can then be lined. Gift wrap was used here, measured and stuck on in the same way as the outer paper.

GOLDEN CLOCK

This sunburst clock with its gentle radiating curves is made by scoring and folding thin chipboard. Gilt cream gives a matt gold finish that is different from the finish of metallic paint. Applying this over deep red paint gives the gold a deeper, antique look.

YOU WILL NEED
Materials
tracing paper
thin unlined chipboard
deep red water-based paint
gilt cream
clock parts

Equipment
pencil
craft knife
metal ruler
cutting mat
paintbrush
soft cloth
bradawl
glue

1 Trace the templates from the end of this chapter and enlarge to your required size. Draw the main clock shape on to the chipboard. Cut out the inner shape and the two hands with a craft knife and metal ruler. Do the same on the main clock shape, but cut the curved part out freehand with the craft knife.

2 Score along all the pencil lines gently on the front of the clock face with the craft knife, being careful not to cut the chipboard. Do the same on the inner piece. Score along the lines on the hands.

3 Turn the chipboard over, draw lines on the back, and score, as before. Turn the inner piece over and score along the lines on that as well.

4 Gently fold along all the score lines ensuring that the chipboard does not crease. Concertina the fold lines together to make the folds. Do the same with the centre piece. Paint all the pieces with the red paint and leave to dry.

5 Using a soft cloth, wipe the gilt cream all over the clock slightly unevenly so that some of the red paint just shows through. Leave to dry completely.

6 Using a bradawl, cut holes into the middle of the back and front pieces of the clock and push through the clock mechanism. Screw on the metal screw. Glue the cardboard hands on to the plastic ones and push on to the clock.

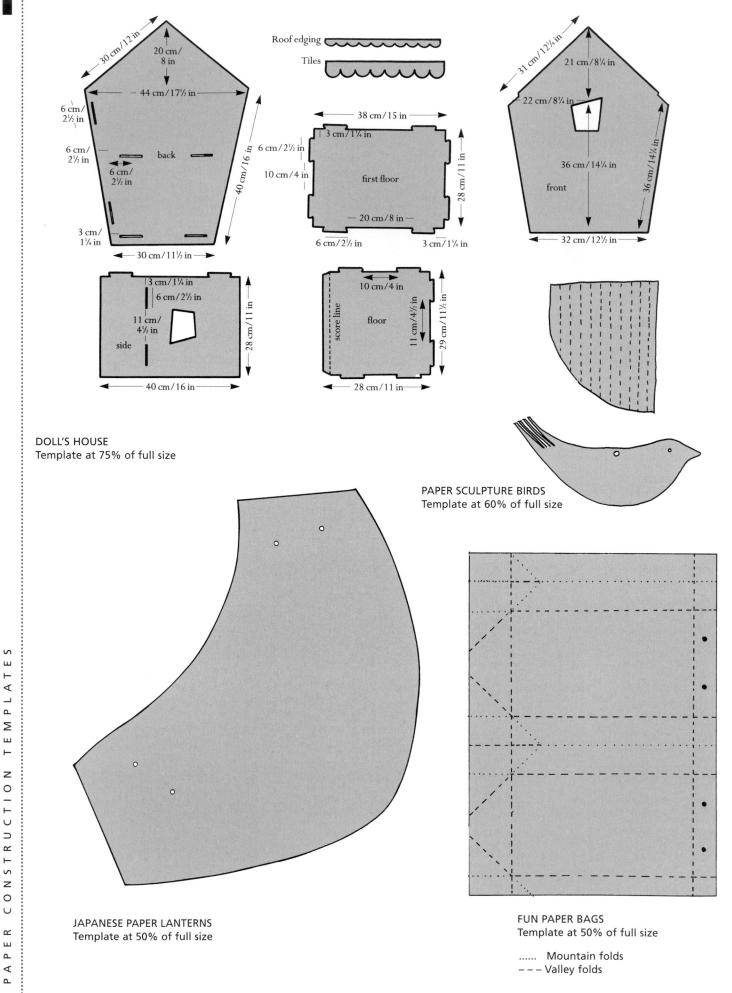

Roof edging

Tiles

back

30 cm / 12 in

20 cm / 8 in

44 cm / 17½ in

40 cm / 16 in

6 cm / 2½ in

6 cm / 2½ in

6 cm / 2½ in

3 cm / 1¼ in

30 cm / 11½ in

first floor

38 cm / 15 in

3 cm / 1¼ in

6 cm / 2½ in

10 cm / 4 in

28 cm / 11 in

20 cm / 8 in

6 cm / 2½ in

3 cm / 1¼ in

front

31 cm / 12¼ in

21 cm / 8¼ in

22 cm / 8¾ in

36 cm / 14¼ in

36 cm / 14¼ in

32 cm / 12½ in

side

3 cm / 1¼ in

6 cm / 2½ in

11 cm / 4½ in

28 cm / 11 in

40 cm / 16 in

floor

10 cm / 4 in

score line

11 cm / 4½ in

29 cm / 11½ in

28 cm / 11 in

DOLL'S HOUSE
Template at 75% of full size

PAPER SCULPTURE BIRDS
Template at 60% of full size

JAPANESE PAPER LANTERNS
Template at 50% of full size

FUN PAPER BAGS
Template at 50% of full size

...... Mountain folds
– – – Valley folds

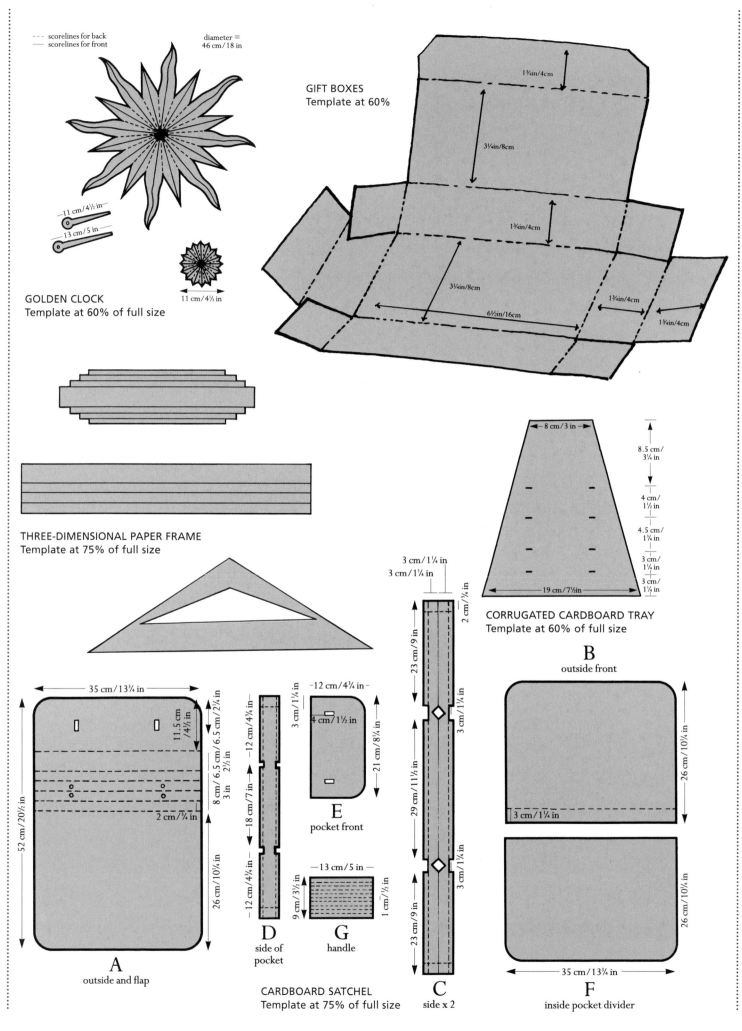

scorelines for back
scorelines for front

diameter = 46 cm/18 in

GIFT BOXES
Template at 60%

1¼in/4cm

3¼in/8cm

1¾in/4cm

3¼in/8cm

1¾in/4cm

6½in/16cm

1¾in/4cm

GOLDEN CLOCK
Template at 60% of full size

—11 cm/4½ in—

13 cm/5 in

11 cm/4½ in

THREE-DIMENSIONAL PAPER FRAME
Template at 75% of full size

8 cm/3 in

8.5 cm/ 3¼ in

4 cm/ 1½ in

4.5 cm/ 1¼ in

3 cm/ 1¼ in

3 cm/ 1¼ in

19 cm/7½ in

CORRUGATED CARDBOARD TRAY
Template at 60% of full size

B

outside front

3 cm/1¼ in
3 cm/1¼ in

2 cm/¾ in

23 cm/9 in

4 cm/1½ in

3 cm/1¼ in

29 cm/11½ in

3 cm/1¼ in

23 cm/9 in

26 cm/10¼ in

3 cm/1¼ in

35 cm/13¾ in

11.5 cm /4½ in

8 cm / 6.5 cm / 6.5 cm /2¼ in
3 in   2½ in

2 cm/¾ in

52 cm/20½ in

26 cm/10¼ in

A

outside and flap

—3 cm/1¼ in

—12 cm/4¾ in—

—12 cm/4¾ in—

—18 cm/7 in—

—12 cm/4¾ in—

D

side of
pocket

—12 cm/4¾ in—

4 cm/1½ in

21 cm/8¼ in

E

pocket front

—13 cm/5 in—

9 cm/3½ in

1 cm/½ in

G

handle

CARDBOARD SATCHEL
Template at 75% of full size

C

side x 2

26 cm/10¼ in

26 cm/10¼ in

35 cm/13¾ in

F

inside pocket divider

Origami

From its origins in ancient Japan, creative origami has become a universal pastime enjoyed by many the world over. Although it looks impenetrably complicated, creating a geometric figure from something as simple as a piece of paper can be easily learnt with a little patience and a good memory for sequence. The folding sequences can be anything from simple at one end of the scale to extremely complex at the other, but anyone who folds successfully will experience a great sense of achievement and satisfaction. All the projects shown in this book are satisfyingly within attainment for most people. There is a wide range of subjects to be made here, including many different animals, a sampan, a building, vases and decorative shapes.

The projects are divided into three groups according to their level of difficulty. By working through them from the beginning to the end, the novice will build up a degree of expertise that can be used either for personal satisfaction or to impress onlookers. Practice will make perfect, so why not get started now. All you need is a perfectly square piece of paper and a hard surface to fold against. Take care when creasing. Read the instructions carefully, then crease slowly, firmly and accurately. The early creases are probably the most important as if these are wrong in any way, subsequent creases will be difficult to place accurately and will look messy.

INTRODUCTION

It is not difficult to understand why origami is the most popular of all papercrafts: the art is very inexpensive, can be done anywhere at anytime and requires no equipment or facilities other than a sheet of paper and a firm surface to work on. Moreover, the transformation of an ordinary piece of paper into a pleasing origami design is a kind of alchemy, perhaps even more so in today's increasingly push-button, computer-controlled, battery-operated culture, than ever before.

The history of origami is rather obscure, but clearly cannot pre-date the invention of paper in China about two thousand years ago. The word 'origami' is not Chinese but Japanese, and is used worldwide out of respect for the ancestral home of the art. When China invaded Japan in AD 610, the secret of papermaking travelled with them and was immediately assimilated into Japanese culture, not just as origami, but more practically as screens, mats, bags, umbrellas, woven clothes and many other objects. As an indication of the importance of paper to the Japanese, the word 'origami' is formed from 'ori' (to fold) and 'kami'

meaning paper and also God ('kami' becomes 'gami' when combined with 'ori'). Indeed, many of the early origami designs were created for symbolic or ceremonial purposes, not for recreation.

The growth of creative origami in the West began in the 1950s, though it was a minor Spanish tradition and practised by the occasional creative individual before that time. Curiously, since that same decade, the art has also undergone a major creative revival in Japan, so much so that there are now several hundred Japanese language books currently in print, most containing new creative work. A great amount of new work is also coming from the West, in all manner of styles ranging from the charmingly simple to the astonishingly complex and from the expressive to the geometric.

If you are new to origami the next few pages will introduce the basics. Readers who have folded before will find these pages a useful refresher. The designs which follow have been graded according to their level of difficulty and you are encouraged not to be too ambitious too soon.

ORIGAMI PAPER

Although origami is defined as 'the art of *paper* folding', most paper folders spend little time thinking about paper, preferring to get straight down to the business of folding, frequently with whatever paper happens to be to hand, however inappropriate it may be. A little consideration for paper, though, can significantly improve the look of what you make and increase your pleasure in folding it.

The easiest and cheapest source of good quality practice paper is photocopy (Xerox) paper. The photocopy and quick print shops now found in most shopping centres sell reams (packets of 500 sheets) of white or coloured photocopy paper, either A4 size or American Letter Size (both about the same size as a page in this book). The shop will trim a ream to square on a power guillotine for a nominal sum. Two or three reams can usually be purchased for a very

reasonable price. Part-reams may also be purchased.

For two-tone models, origami paper bought in packets is ideal. However, it can be difficult to find and is relatively expensive. Also, the bright colours can make some designs look rather childish, so it should be used with care. Patterned gift-wrap paper is a good alternative if origami paper cannot be found. Other good practice papers include computer paper, typing paper, writing paper and even brown wrapping paper.

For displaying origami, perhaps at home or at a place of work, quality papers appropriate to the design should be used. A surprising range of interesting papers can be found in art, craft and graphic equipment supplies shops. It is also worth starting a collection of unusual papers such as old posters, discarded wrapping paper, wallpaper and telephone note blocks.

In many ways, nothing could be more basic than folding a sheet of paper. Yet, despite this wonderful simplicity, there are a few guidelines to follow that will make the process of folding easier and very satisfying. Please follow them.

- Check that the paper you are folding is *exactly* square. The best method for making a square is described in the following pages. Nothing is more frustrating than trying to fold paper which is not quite square!

- Do not fold against a soft surface, such as a carpet, your lap or bedsheets. Fold against a hard surface such as a large hardback book or a table.

- Crease slowly, firmly and accurately. Form the early creases with particular care – if they are incorrectly placed, all the later, smaller creases will be difficult to place accurately and will look messy.

- Read the instructions and follow the symbols on each step. Many a mistake is made by ignoring written instructions or by not following all the written instructions on a step, particularly during complex manoeuvres.

- The instructions and symbols on one step will create a shape which looks like the next step but stripped of its symbols. So, you must always *look ahead* to the next step to see what shape you are trying to make. Never look at steps in isolation, but see them as being interconnected, like links in a chain.

If you would like to know more about origami, here are addresses for two well-organized societies. Both accept overseas members and welcome beginners. Also, both publish regular magazines, hold conventions and regional meetings, sell a wide variety of books and paper, and publish booklets on specialist origami topics. The British Origami Society has a postal library service.

British Origami Society,
253 Park Lane,
Poynton,
Stockport,
Cheshire,
SK12 1RH,
England.

The Friends of the Origami Centre of America,
15 West 77th Street,
New York,
NY 10024,
USA.

The Japanese Paper Place,
966 Queen Street West,
Toronto M6J 1G8,
Canada.

The Australian Origami Society,
2/5 Broome Street,
Highgate,
Perth 6000,
Australia.

The New Zealand Origami Society,
79 Dunbar Road,
Christchurch 3,
New Zealand.

■ HOW TO MAKE A SQUARE

Most papers are bought as rectangular sheets that need to be trimmed square before being folded. Here, then, is a quick and simple way to accurately trim a large sheet to a smaller square, ensuring that the edges are kept straight and clean.

1 Fold over an edge of the sheet, lining up the edges at the sides to ensure square corners.

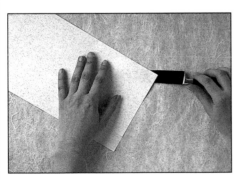

2 Carefully cut along the crease with a series of large, smooth slicing movements, made with a non-serrated kitchen knife (one with a 15 cm [6 in] blade is best). Set aside the unwanted portion of the sheet.

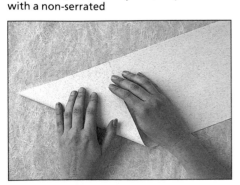

3 Fold over the short edge to make a triangle.

4 Bend the sheet backwards and make a crease underneath the bottom edge of the triangle.

5 Cut along the crease.

6 Unfold the triangle.

7 The square complete.

OTHER METHODS

Scissors
Duplicate the method shown in the photographs, but use scissors instead of a non-serrated knife. Be careful to control the cutting to ensure a straight edge.

Craft knife
Duplicate the method shown in the photographs, but unfold each crease and cut along them with a craft knife held against a metal rule. Before cutting, place thick card beneath the paper so that the knife does not damage your work surface.

Guillotine
Paper bought in bulk from photocopy print shops and cut on the premises on a power guillotine will be perfectly square, but paper cut by hand on a manually-operated guillotine has the annoying habit of never quite being square, whatever safeguards are taken. So, hand guillotining is not recommended if it is important that your paper is perfectly proportioned.

Tearing
Tearing is not recommended, but is acceptable if there is no other way to trim paper. Before tearing, crease the folded edge backwards and forwards several times, pressing firmly. This will weaken the crease and make tearing easier and neater.

▮ SYMBOLS

No sequence of origami diagrams can be followed without an understanding of the symbols they use. The meaning of most symbols is obvious and it is not necessary to learn them all now, but it would be very helpful to at least learn the difference between the mountain and valley fold symbols. The other symbols can be learnt as they appear by referring back to this page.

The same symbols can be found in most origami books, whatever language they are written in, be it English, Spanish or even Japanese. This standardization means that the language of origami is truly universal, and that enthusiasts can fold from almost any book, East or West.

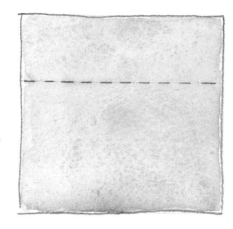
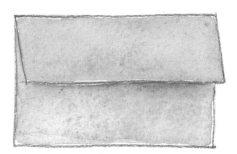

▮ valley

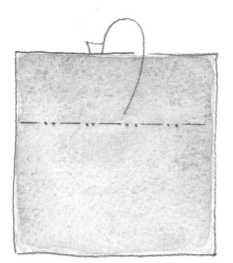

▮ mountain

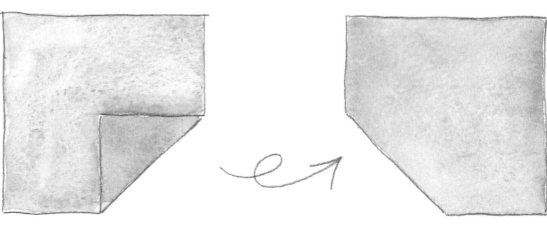

▮ existing creases

▮ turn over

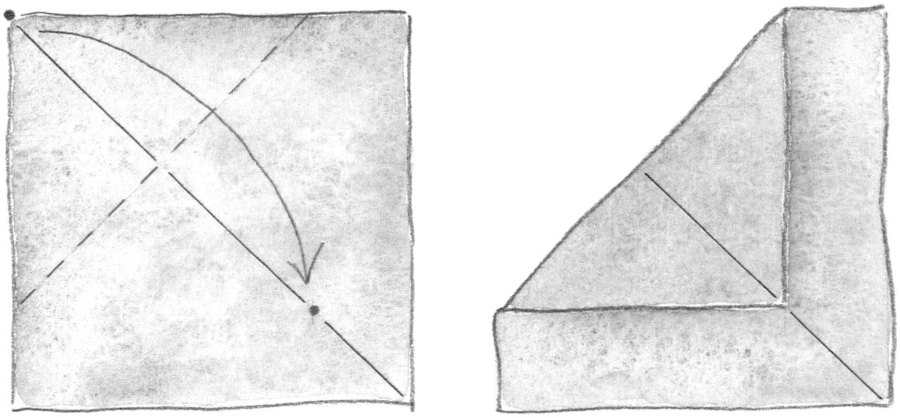

■ fold dot to dot

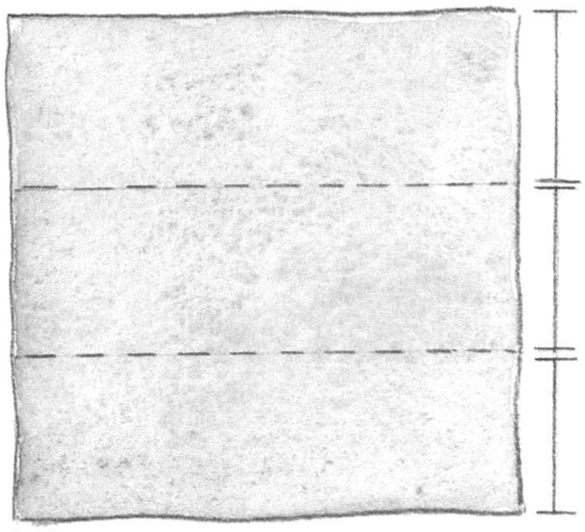

■ these distances are
equal

■ unfold or pull out

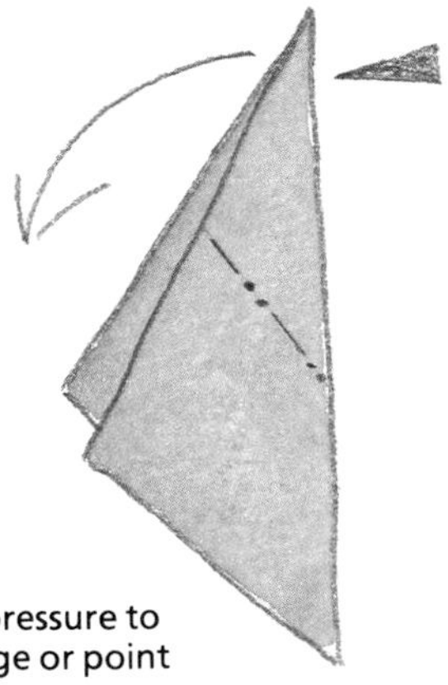

■ apply pressure to
this edge or point

■ inflate

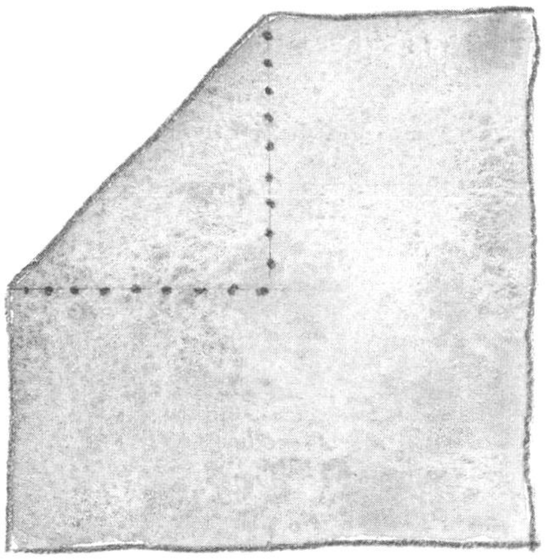

■ x-ray view

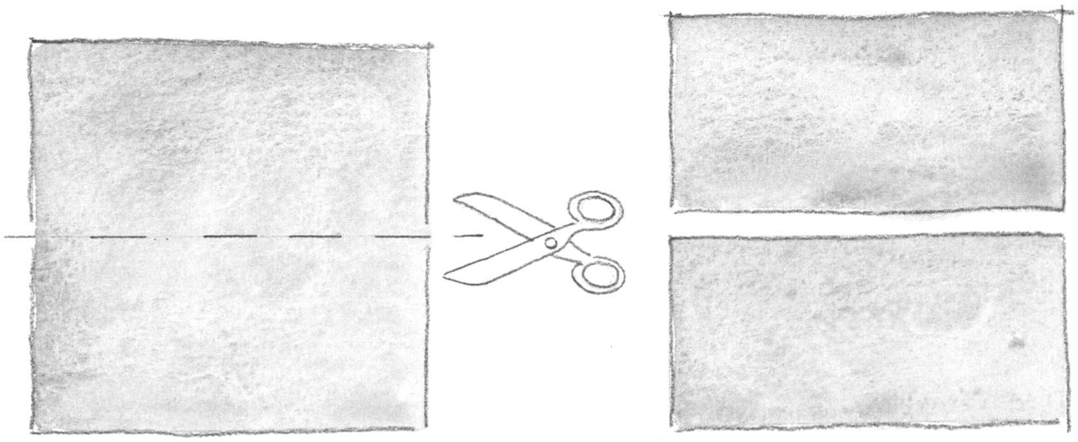

■ cut

Apart from the basic mountain and valley creases from which all origami designs are folded, there are four advanced techniques found in the designs that follow. These techniques are used in combination and are: the squash fold, the sink fold and the inside and outside reverse folds. However, not all designs use these advanced techniques, and only the Elephant uses them all together.

Squash and sink folds are the least common. To save space, a detailed explanation of each is given once in the book within a particular design. For an explanation of the squash fold see the Multiform House, Steps 4–6 for an explanation of the sink fold see the Star, Steps 8–12. When you come across a squash or sink fold in another design, refer to these designs for a step-by-step guide.

Inside and outside reverse folds are not more complex than squash or sink folds, but are more common and come in a greater variety. So, to simplify cross referencing, here are the basic forms of each. Refer to this page whenever you need to be reminded how to make them.

INSIDE REVERSE

Pull-through version

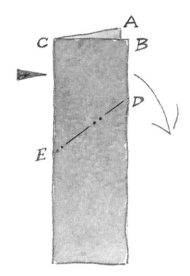

1 This is how the manoeuvre is illustrated in the book.

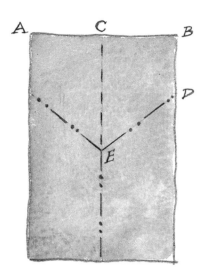

2 This is the crease pattern.

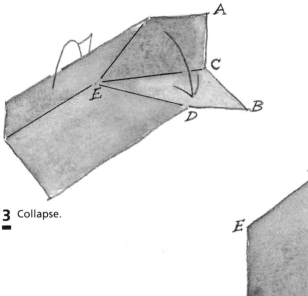

3 Collapse.

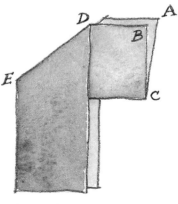

4 Complete.

Push-in version

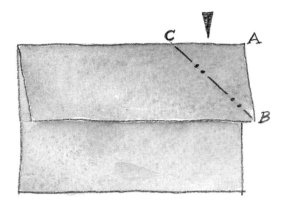

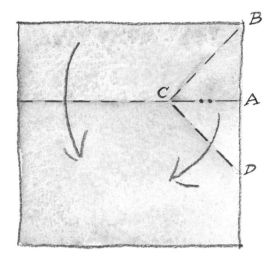

1 This is how the manoeuvre is illustrated in the book.

2 This is the crease pattern.

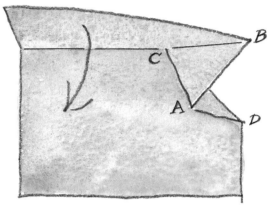

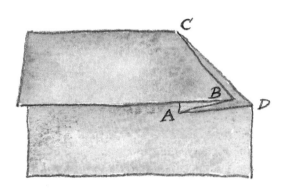

3 Collapse.

4 Complete.

OUTSIDE REVERSE

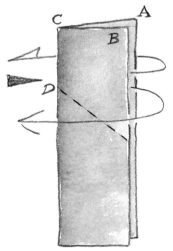

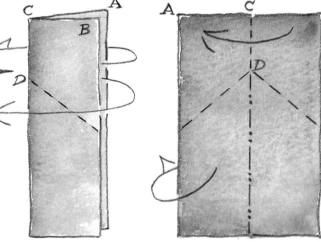

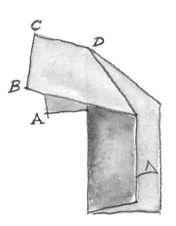

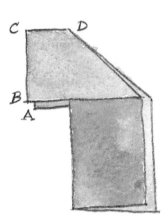

1 This is how the manoeuvre is illustrated in the book.

2 This is the crease pattern.

3 Collapse.

4 Complete.

SIMPLE PROJECTS

GLIDER

This design is one of a number of similar gliders of Chinese origin, all of which fly extremely well. The secret of good paper plane making is to fold with great accuracy and to practise a variety of launching actions – a carefully-made plane will not fly well if launched wrongly. Use an A4 or American Letter Size sheet of paper.

Traditional design.

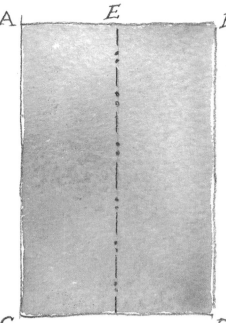

1 Fold the sheet in half down the middle, as a mountain fold (it is easier to make a valley fold, then to turn the sheet over). Unfold.

2 Fold in corners A & B to the centre crease.

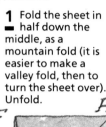

3 Fold down E along crease FG. Note that FG is a little below the level of AB.

4 Fold in corners F & G, leaving E exposed.

5 Fold up E over F & G.

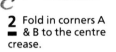

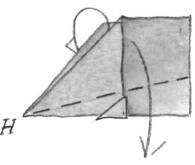

6 Mountain fold D to C.

7 Before creasing, press flat the existing creases. Then, make the wing creases from the nose tip at H.

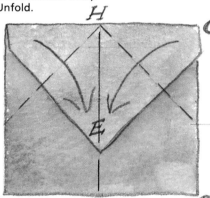

8 The Glider complete. Hold as shown at the point of balance, the wings forming a slight 'V' shape. Release smoothly but firmly.

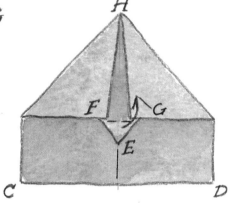

CANDY BAG

If folded from greaseproof paper, this practical design will hold fries and other oily or sticky foods. For extra strength, fold two squares together. For sweets or candies, use any paper, not too thin. Use a 15–25 cm (6–10 in) square. If using origami paper, start coloured side up.

Designed by Paul Jackson.

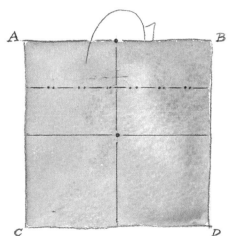

1 Fold and unfold the paper in half horizontally and vertically. Mountain fold edge AB to the centre crease.

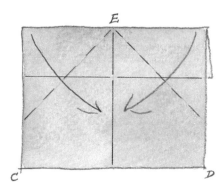

2 Fold in the top corners to the centre crease.

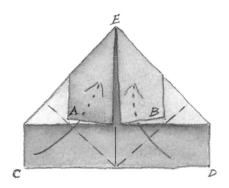

3 Similarly, fold in bottom corners C & D, but tucking them beneath A & B, to lock them flat.

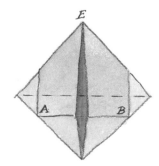

4 Valley fold in half across the middle, then . . .

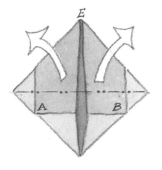

5 . . . mountain fold in half, to create a flexible crease. Open out the bag.

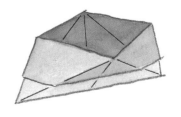

6 The Candy Bag complete.

BUTTERFLY

There are a great many origami butterflies in all manner of styles, some very complex. This is one of the simplest. It is important to use origami paper, so that white triangles appear at the edges between the coloured wings, to visually separate them. Cut a square of origami paper in half to create a 2 × 1 rectangle. Start coloured side up.

Designed by Paul Jackson.

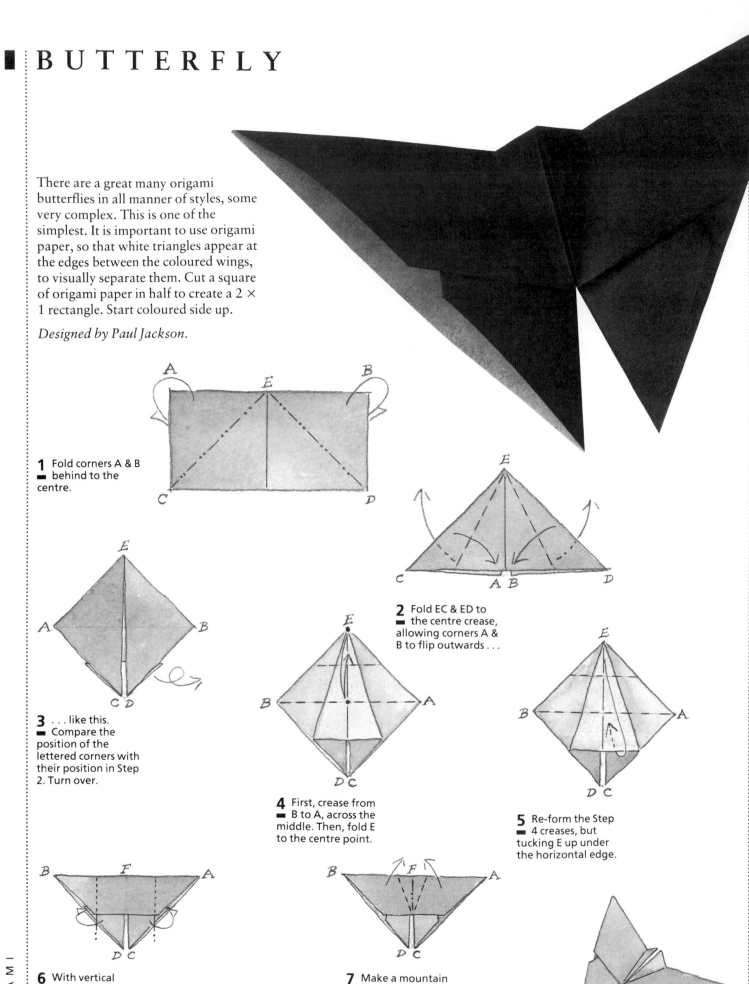

1 Fold corners A & B behind to the centre.

2 Fold EC & ED to the centre crease, allowing corners A & B to flip outwards . . .

3 . . . like this. Compare the position of the lettered corners with their position in Step 2. Turn over.

4 First, crease from B to A, across the middle. Then, fold E to the centre point.

5 Re-form the Step 4 creases, but tucking E up under the horizontal edge.

6 With vertical creases that run inside up to edge BA, mountain fold the loose corners behind as far as they will go.

7 Make a mountain and two valley creases where shown, to create the body and to swivel D & C apart.

8 The Butterfly complete.

■ SAMPAN

This is a simplified version of a sampan with a canopy over each end of the boat. Both designs feature an extraordinary move, here shown in Steps 7–9, in which the entire shape is turned inside out. With a little extra folding, one end of the sampan can be blunted to create a rowing boat. Use a square of paper. If using origami paper, start coloured side up.

Traditional design.

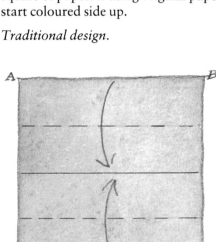

1 Crease and
■ unfold across the centre. Fold the top and bottom edges to the crease.

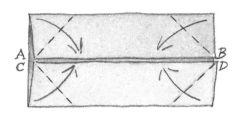

2 Fold in the
■ corners.

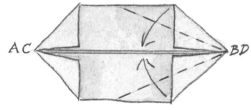

3 Narrow the
■ corner at the right, as though making the familiar paper dart.

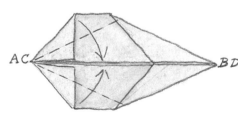

4 Repeat at the left,
■ overlapping the Step 4 creases.

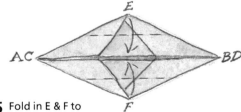

5 Fold in E & F to
■ the centre crease. The paper is thick, so press firmly.

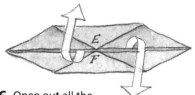

6 Open out all the
■ layers revealing the coloured base

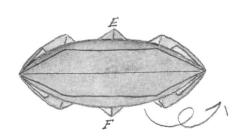

7 . . . like this, to
■ form a loose boat shape. Turn over.

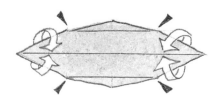

8 To lock the
■ sampan, push down on the four arrowed corners, so that the whole of the structure inverts and turns inside out!

9 The Sampan
■ complete.

▮ NAPKIN FOLDS

Napkin folds always create a point of interest on a dining table. The Duck Step is a basic form from which other varieties of napkin fold can be made. The Cable Buffet server allows guests at a buffet or picnic to help themselves to food, a napkin and cutlery all at once, while the Bishop's elegant curves and free-standing structure create a strong impact on any table.

Designed by Paul Jackson.

DUCK STEP

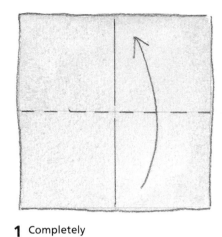

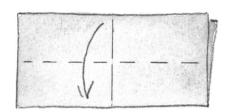

1 Completely unfold a napkin, then fold the bottom edge up to the top.

2 Fold the top edge down to the crease.

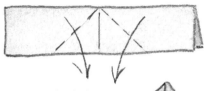

3 Fold each half of the top edge down the centre crease . . .

4 . . . like this. Turn the napkin over.

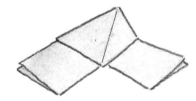

5 Mountain fold the right side behind the left.

6 Valley fold the front square up over the triangle. Repeat behind.

7 The Duck Step napkin complete.

CABLE BUFFET

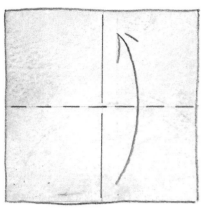

1 Completely unfold a napkin, then fold the bottom edge up to the top.

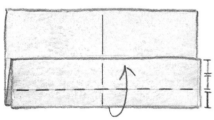

2 Fold the top layer down to the crease.

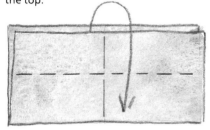

3 Fold the top layer back up a little way . . .

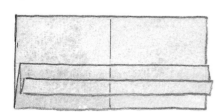

4 . . . like this. Turn the napkin over.

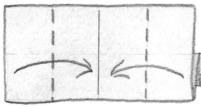

5 Fold the sides to the middle.

6 Tuck one half deep into the other, locking the napkin flat.

7 The Cable Buffet server complete. Insert cutlery into the pocket ready for the meal.

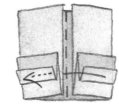

(Continued . . .)

BISHOP

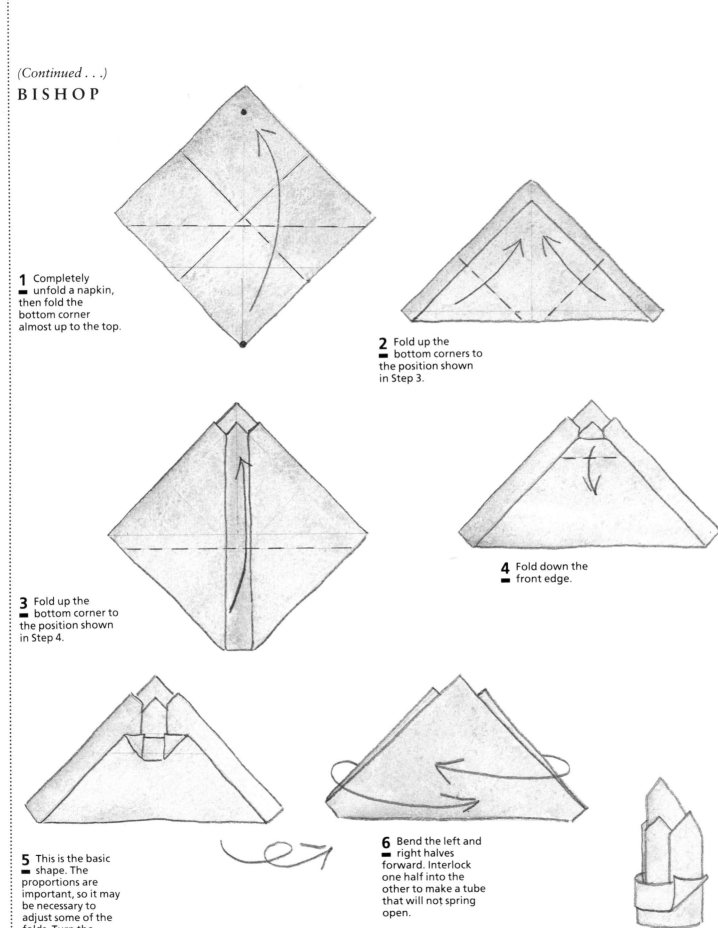

1 Completely unfold a napkin, then fold the bottom corner almost up to the top.

2 Fold up the bottom corners to the position shown in Step 3.

3 Fold up the bottom corner to the position shown in Step 4.

4 Fold down the front edge.

5 This is the basic shape. The proportions are important, so it may be necessary to adjust some of the folds. Turn the napkin over.

6 Bend the left and right halves forward. Interlock one half into the other to make a tube that will not spring open.

7 The Bishop napkin complete.

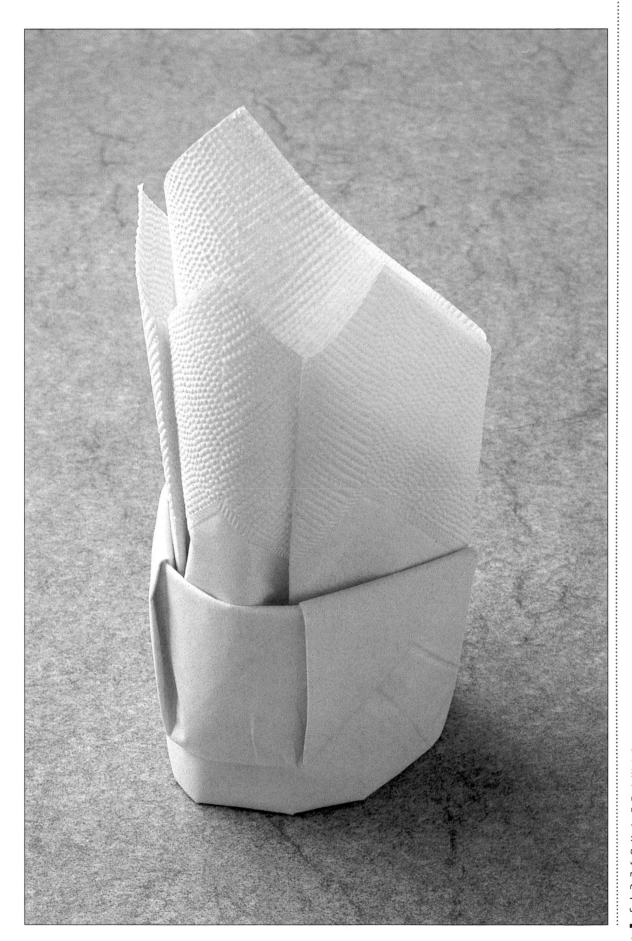

FISH

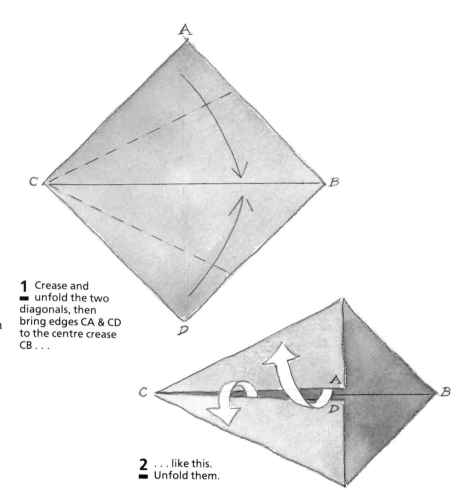

The creator of this fish is known for designs which are pre-creased and collapsed into shape. When pre-creasing, it is important to fold accurately (here, up to Step 5), otherwise the creases will not fall into place to achieve Step 6. For extra flatness, a speck of glue inside the mouth will close the layers. Use a square of origami paper, coloured side up, or a square with the same colour on both sides.

Designed by Jeff Beynon, UK.

1 Crease and unfold the two diagonals, then bring edges CA & CD to the centre crease CB . . .

2 . . . like this. Unfold them.

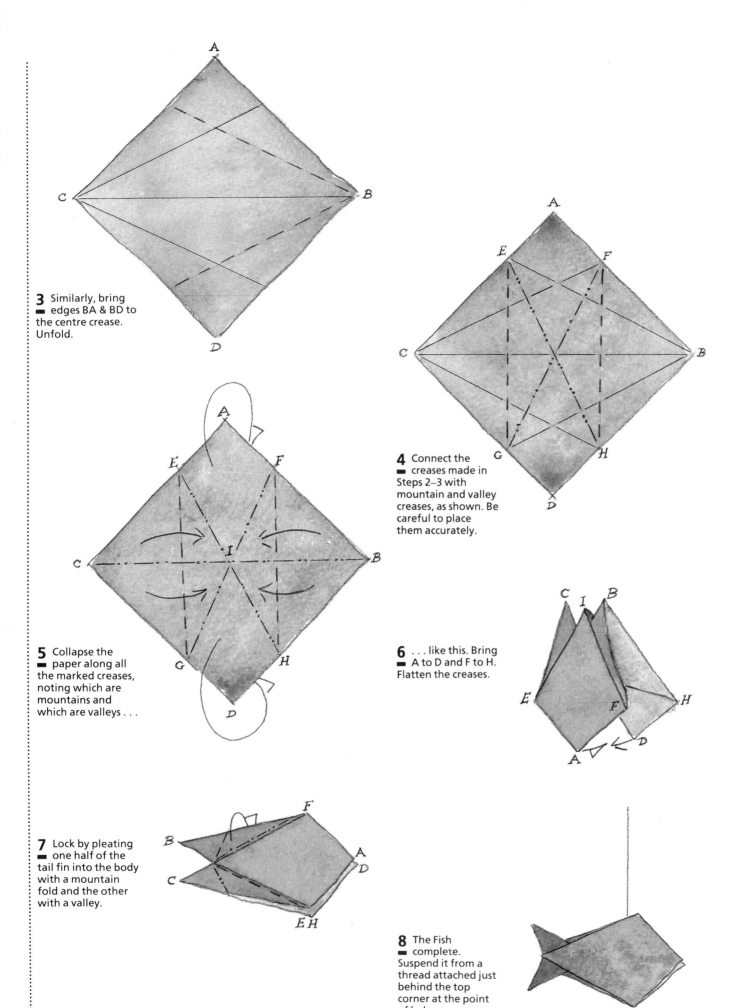

3 Similarly, bring edges BA & BD to the centre crease. Unfold.

4 Connect the creases made in Steps 2–3 with mountain and valley creases, as shown. Be careful to place them accurately.

5 Collapse the paper along all the marked creases, noting which are mountains and which are valleys . . .

6 . . . like this. Bring A to D and F to H. Flatten the creases.

7 Lock by pleating one half of the tail fin into the body with a mountain fold and the other with a valley.

8 The Fish complete. Suspend it from a thread attached just behind the top corner at the point of balance.

S L E E P Y   D O G

The design is simple to make, but it is important to place C accurately in Steps 1 & 2. Once Step 3 has been achieved, the remaining folds fall naturally into place. Note the way in which the eyes are suggested. Use a square of origami paper, coloured side up.

Designed by Paul Jackson.

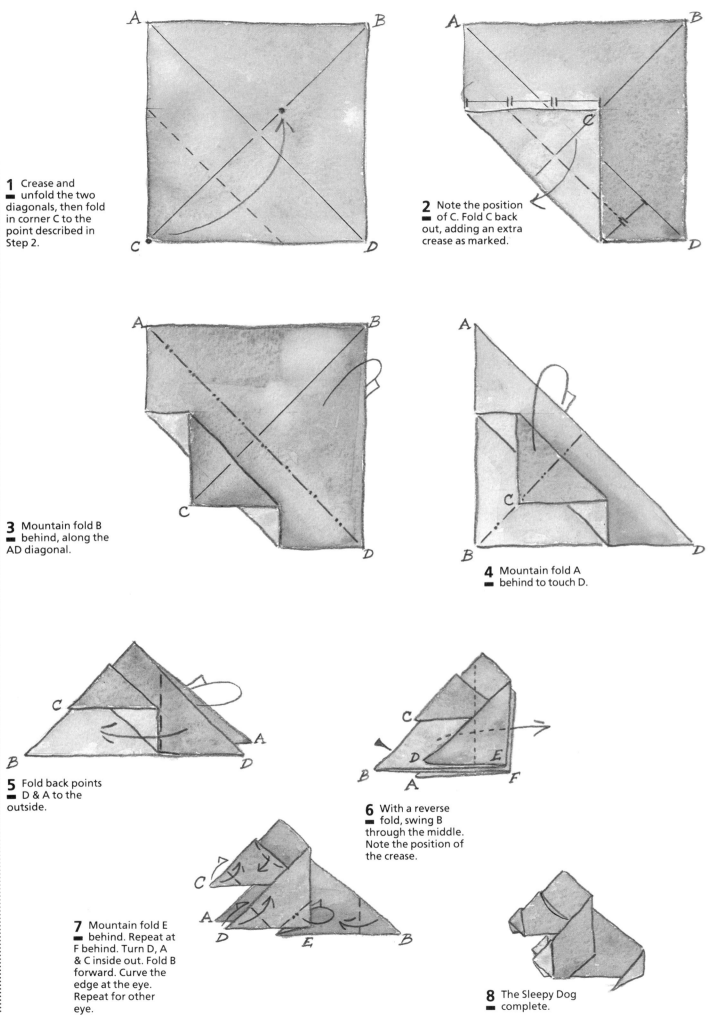

1 Crease and unfold the two diagonals, then fold in corner C to the point described in Step 2.

2 Note the position of C. Fold C back out, adding an extra crease as marked.

3 Mountain fold B behind, along the AD diagonal.

4 Mountain fold A behind to touch D.

5 Fold back points D & A to the outside.

6 With a reverse fold, swing B through the middle. Note the position of the crease.

7 Mountain fold E behind. Repeat at F behind. Turn D, A & C inside out. Fold B forward. Curve the edge at the eye. Repeat for other eye.

8 The Sleepy Dog complete.

MODULAR DECORATION I

A modular design is one in which a number of identical units are folded, then locked together without glue to create a decoration or geometric form. Other modular designs are included and appear later. In recent years, it has become a very popular branch of origami, East and West. Method 1 begins with a rectangle, Method 2 with a small square.

Designed by Paul Jackson.

METHOD 1

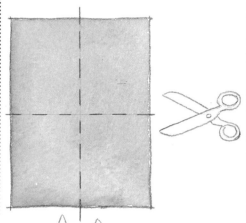

1 Cut an A4 or American Letter Size sheet of paper into quarters. For a colour change effect with four modules, cut two sheets of different colours.

2 Take one quarter sheet of paper and fold diagonal BC.

3 Fold A behind and D to the front.

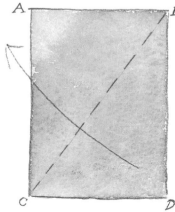

4 Unfold a little, but do not flatten the sheet.

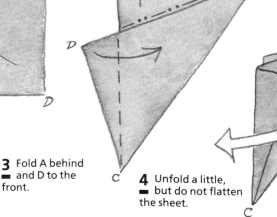

5 The Module complete. Make four: two of one colour and two of another.

METHOD 2

1 With a small square, mountain fold down the diagonal.

2 Fold in edges AB & CD to the crease.

3 Fold in short edges AE & DF to the centre.

4 Mountain fold from A to D.

5 Unfold a little.

6 The Module complete. Make four: two of one colour and two of another.

ASSEMBLY

1 The method of assembly is the same for Methods 1 & 2. Edge A1,F1 on the right-hand module is tucked behind edge AH on the left-hand module. At the same time, edge DE on the left-hand module is tucked behind edge D1,G1 on the right-hand module. Note that A1 touches A, G1 touches H and D1 touches D.

2 This is the result. The lock is not strong, but when two other modules are locked in, so that the fourth locks into the first to close the circle, the complete structure will lock well.

3 The Modular Decoration complete.

COLOUR-CHANGE BIRD

This design is included because it is a particular favourite. The simple shape of the completed bird and the effectiveness of the colour contrasts are achieved by a fluent and concise sequence of folds. Perhaps it is too stylized for some readers, but less can sometimes be more. Use a square of origami paper, white side up.

Designed by Paul Jackson.

1 Crease and unfold the two diagonals, then fold corner A to the centre point.

2 Roll the triangle downwards, along crease CB.

3 Fold C & B dot to dot, as shown.

4 Unfold C & B.

5 Turn over.

6 Fold dot to dot, aligning edges DC & DB with the tops of the creases made in Step 3.

7 Pull out corner A.

8 Fold down A, level with the folded edge.

9 Fold B behind.

10 Fold up B & C along existing internal (hidden) creases made in Step 3.

11 Reverse fold D to create the head. Fold out the feet to create a stable base for the bird.

12 The Colour Change Bird complete.

The basic modules are very simple to make, but some thought must be given to assembling them correctly. Once locked, they will hold together very well. For re-use – perhaps from one Christmas to the next – the decoration may be flattened for easy storage. Use two 10–15 cm (4–6 in) squares of paper. If using origami paper, start with the white side up.

Designed by Paul Jackson.

METHOD

1 Crease and fold a vertical diagonal, then fold D up to A.

2 Fold edge AD,B forward to the vertical crease (valley fold) and edge AD,C behind to that crease (mountain fold).

3 This is the completed module. Make another.

ASSEMBLY

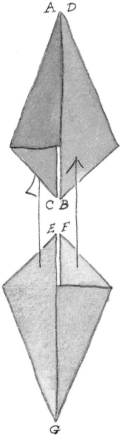

1 Take careful note of the lettered corners. Bring the two modules together, so that F is on top of B, and C is on top of E . . .

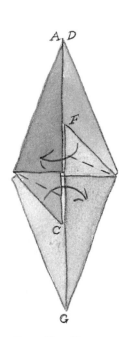

2 . . . like this. Fold F across to the horizontal. Repeat with C, then with E & B behind.

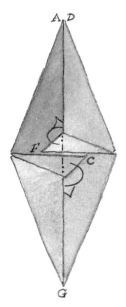

3 Lock the modules together by tucking F & C behind the vertical edges. Repeat behind with E & B.

4 Separate the modules by twisting one away from the other, so that they lie perpendicular to each other.

5 The Modular Decoration complete. Suspend from a thread.

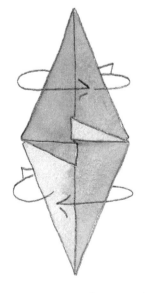

▌M U L T I F O R M

Here is a remarkable sequence of designs which are all made from the same basic shape, the House. The designs shown here are not the full set: it is also possible to fold a dustpan, purse, fox puppet, crown . . . and very probably many others! Experiment by folding the paper this way and that to see what you can discover. Use a square of origami paper, white side up.

Traditional design.

H O U S E

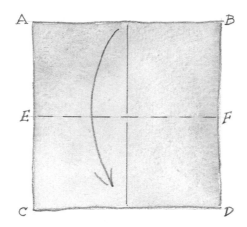 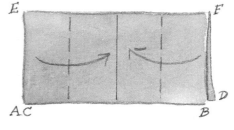

1 Crease and unfold down the middle of a square, then fold AB down to CD.

2 Fold the edges to the centre.

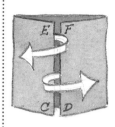

3 Unfold.

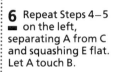

4 Lift up the edge BD,F. Separate B from D, applying pressure on the edges below F . . .

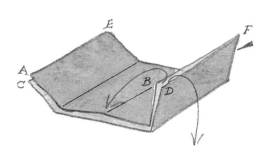

5 . . . like this. Pull B & D right apart and squash F flat.

6 Repeat Steps 4–5 on the left, separating A from C and squashing E flat. Let A touch B.

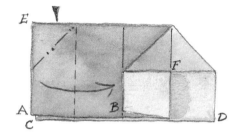

7 The House complete. Children like to draw windows and a door to finish the design.

3D HOUSE

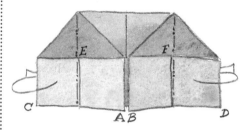

1 Begin with Step 6 of the House. Fold C & D behind.

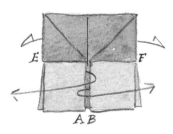

2 Unfold AC & BD.

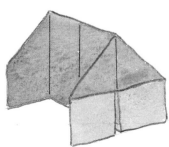

3 The 3D House complete.

(Continued . . .)

SEAT

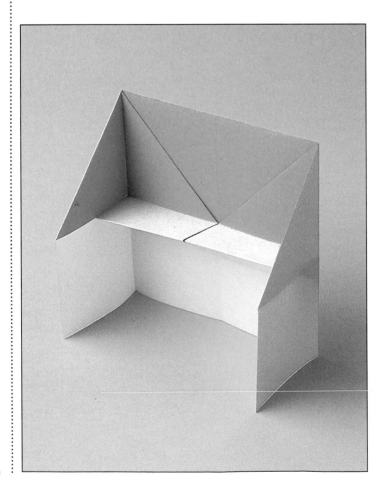

1 Begin with Step 6 of the House. Fold AB up to the top edge.

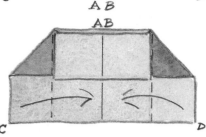

2 Fold in C & D.

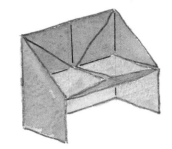

3 Swing open C & D and pull down AB.

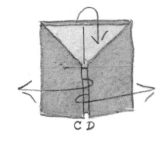

4 The Seat complete.

ORGAN

1 Begin with Step 2 of the Seat. Fold edge AB back down to the folded edge across the middle of the paper.

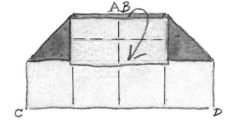

2 Fold in C & D.

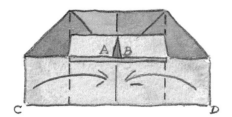

3 Swing open C & D and pull down the ledge.

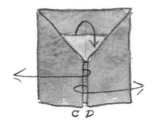

4 The Organ complete.

G.I. CAP

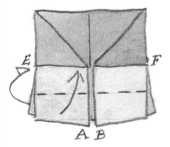

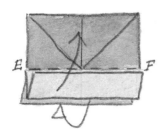

1 Begin with Step 2 of the 3D House. Fold AB up to EF. Repeat behind.

2 Fold up the bottom section along crease EF. Repeat behind.

3 Open out the cap.

4 The G.I. Cap complete. To make a full-sized cap, use a square trimmed from a large format newspaper.

■ STAR

The shape made in Step 7 is known in origami as the Preliminary Base, so called because other, more advanced bases can be developed from it, including the Bird and Frog bases and their stretched variants. Use a square of paper or perhaps paper-backed foil, coloured side up.

Designed by Florence Temko, USA.

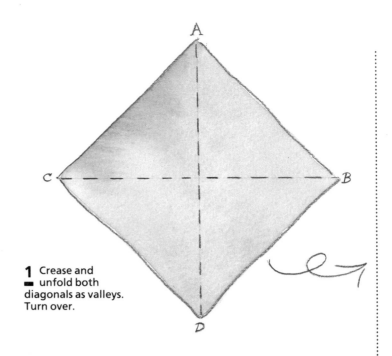

1 Crease and unfold both diagonals as valleys. Turn over.

2 Check that the diagonals are now mountain creases.

3 Fold and unfold in half down the middle, then . . .

4 . . . fold in half across the middle.

5 Hold as shown. If the mountain and valley creases have been placed correctly, a 3D diamond shape will emerge when the hands are swung towards each other . . .

6 . . . like this. Flatten G against E and F against H.

7 Fold the single layer corner C up to I, then unfold.

(Continued . . .)

8 Fold I down to the centre point. Unfold. Open the paper a little.

9 The crease formed in Step 8 makes a square. Crease the four sides of the square as mountains . . .

10 . . . like this. Flatten the centre square, then push it downwards into the paper . . .

11 . . . like this. Re-form the Step 8 shape, but with I now sunk inside the paper.

12 Fold up C again.

13 Swing C down to corner G, whilst also bringing corner F across to touch G. Note that the crease from G is a mountain, not a valley.

14 Halfway.

15 Complete. Note how F,C,G & E lie one behind the other.

16 Similarly, fold up D along line FH . . .

17 . . . and swing towards corner F, bringing H across to touch corner F. Repeat this sequence with A then B, turning the paper over and around each time, to keep the same number of layers on each side of the paper. Fan out the points in a symmetrical pattern.

18 The Star complete. Suspend from a thread.

INTERMEDIATE PROJECTS

WATERBOMB

Many people – particularly mischievous children – have learnt how to make a waterbomb, but without practice, it is very easy to forget how to lock it. Without a good lock, it cannot contain the water it is designed to hold! More peaceably, it makes an excellent Christmas decoration if folded from a patterned paper. Use a square of paper. If using origami paper, start with the white side uppermost.

Traditional design.

1 Mountain fold horizontally and vertically across the paper. Unfold each time.

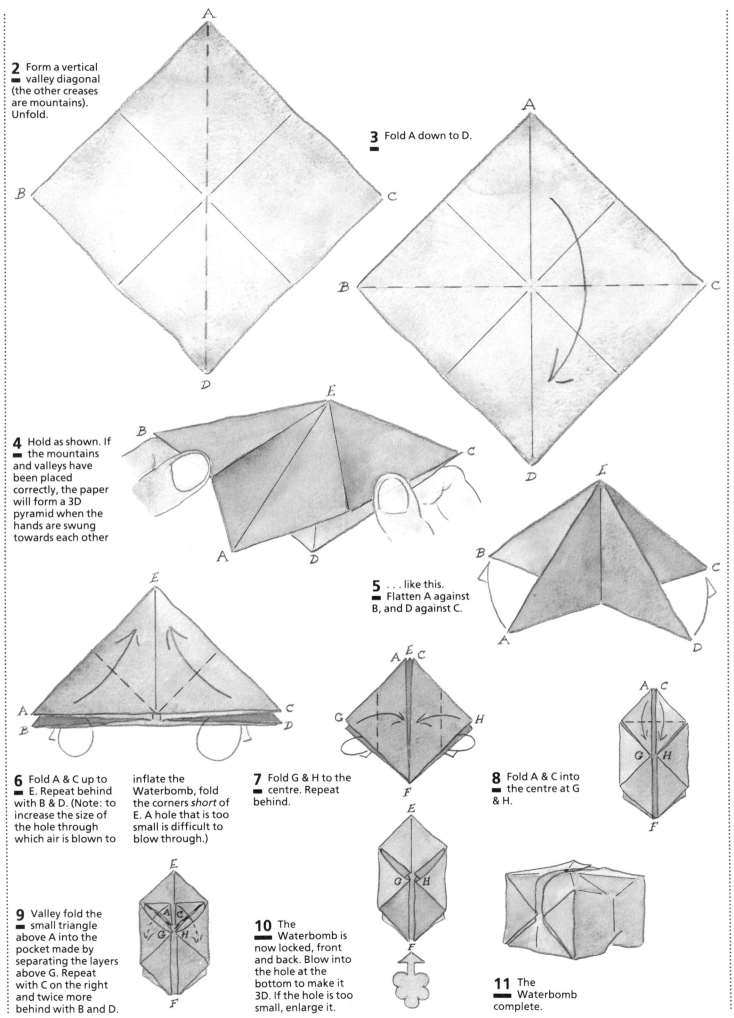

2 Form a vertical valley diagonal (the other creases are mountains). Unfold.

3 Fold A down to D.

4 Hold as shown. If the mountains and valleys have been placed correctly, the paper will form a 3D pyramid when the hands are swung towards each other

5 . . . like this. Flatten A against B, and D against C.

6 Fold A & C up to E. Repeat behind with B & D. (Note: to increase the size of the hole through which air is blown to inflate the Waterbomb, fold the corners *short* of E. A hole that is too small is difficult to blow through.)

7 Fold G & H to the centre. Repeat behind.

8 Fold A & C into the centre at G & H.

9 Valley fold the small triangle above A into the pocket made by separating the layers above G. Repeat with C on the right and twice more behind with B and D.

10 The Waterbomb is now locked, front and back. Blow into the hole at the bottom to make it 3D. If the hole is too small, enlarge it.

11 The Waterbomb complete.

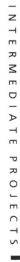

This is perhaps *the* classic origami box. It is quick and simple to make, and locks strongly. A box made from a slightly larger square will form a lid. In Step 3, if the creases are not placed at the quarter points, but elsewhere, taller or squatter boxes can be made. Use a square of strong paper. If using origami paper, start white side up.

Traditional design.

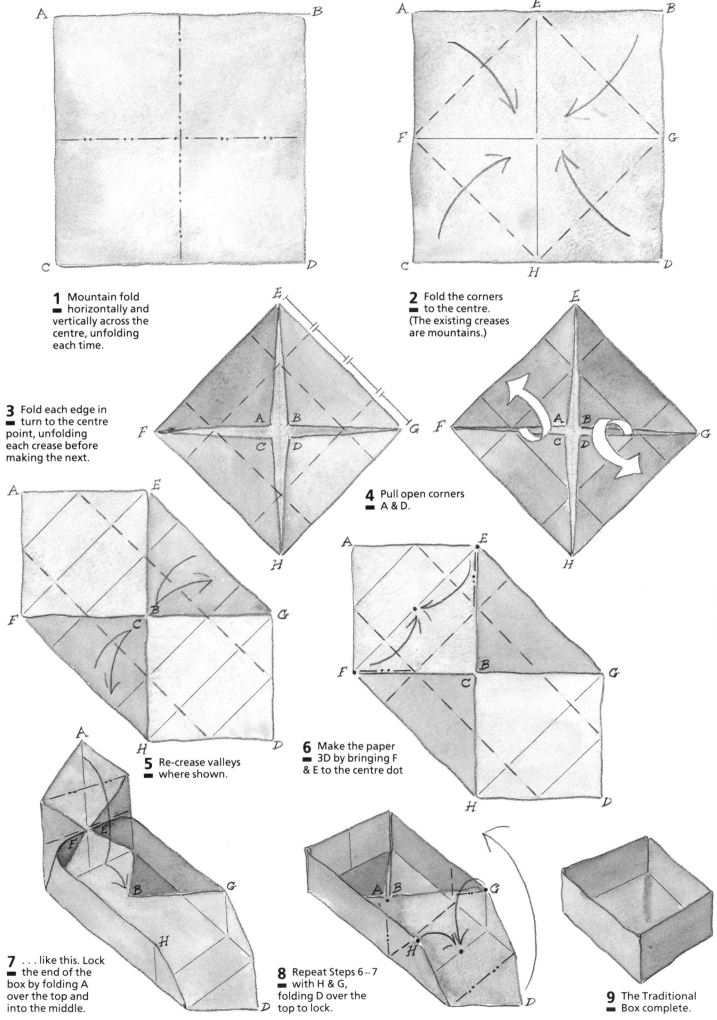

1 Mountain fold horizontally and vertically across the centre, unfolding each time.

2 Fold the corners to the centre. (The existing creases are mountains.)

3 Fold each edge in turn to the centre point, unfolding each crease before making the next.

4 Pull open corners A & D.

5 Re-crease valleys where shown.

6 Make the paper 3D by bringing F & E to the centre dot

7 . . . like this. Lock the end of the box by folding A over the top and into the middle.

8 Repeat Steps 6–7 with H & G, folding D over the top to lock.

9 The Traditional Box complete.

NESTING BIRD

The design features a peculiar and little-used manoeuvre at Steps 4–5, when one spike is pulled out from inside another that envelops it. The move is very satisfying! What was a closed and rather unpromising shape in Step 4 becomes much more useful by Step 6, yet no new creases are made. Begin with a square of paper, same colour both sides.

Designed by Paul Jackson.

1 Crease and unfold a vertical diagonal, then fold D up to A.

2 Fold edges AD,B and AD,C to the centre crease.

3 Fold out corners B & C.

4 Note the shape of the paper. Pull out D from inside A

5 . . . like this. Flatten D on top of A.

6 Turn over.

7 Collapse the paper as shown, separating A from D and bringing C to touch B.

8 Lift up corner C, squashing the paper flat at the left.

9 Fold B behind.

10 Reverse fold D. Fold out the bottom corners to stay away from the wings and so create a stable base for the bird to balance on.

11 The Nesting Bird complete.

BEAK

This is a variation on a well-known origami 'action' theme. The mechanism will be familiar to knowledgeable paper folders, but here the eyes are made differently. It is important to use origami paper, to achieve a contrast of colour for the eyes and the inside of the mouth. The colour should be on the outside in Step 1.

Designed by Paul Jackson.

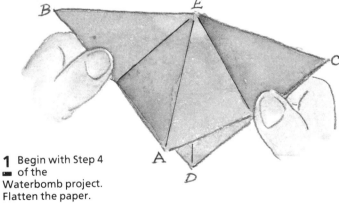

1 Begin with Step 4 of the Waterbomb project. Flatten the paper.

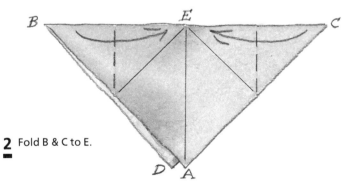

2 Fold B & C to E.

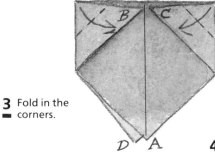

3 Fold in the corners.

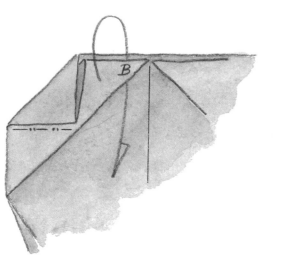

4 (The instructions now refer to B only, but repeat all Steps with C.) Swivel B behind and downwards . . .

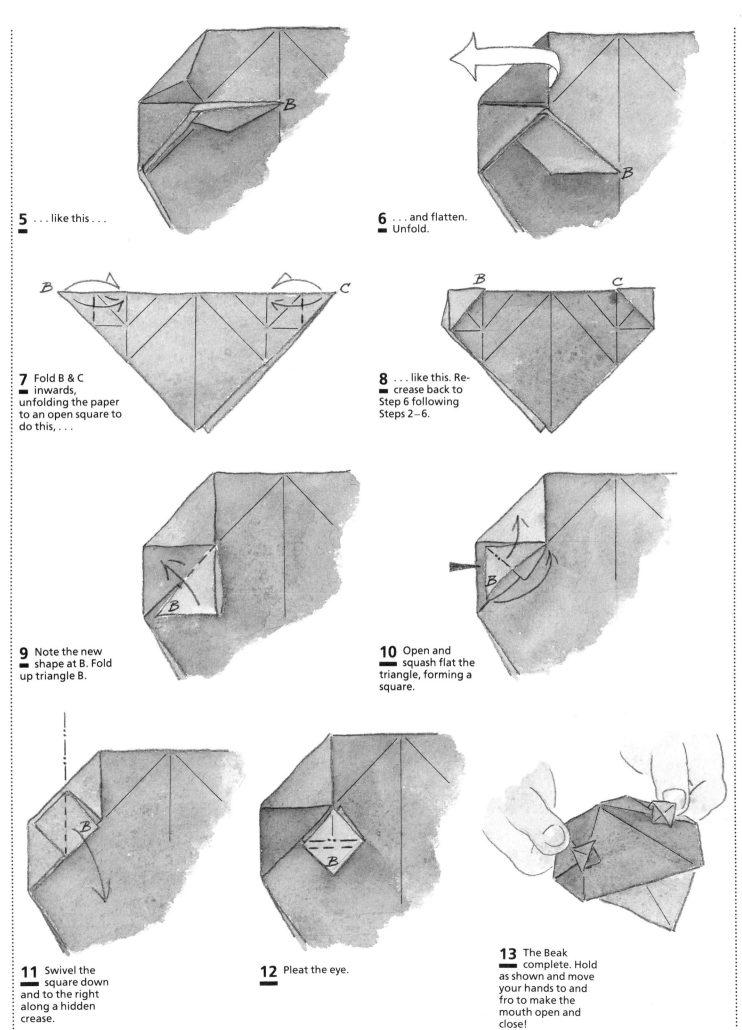

5 . . . like this . . .

6 . . . and flatten. Unfold.

7 Fold B & C inwards, unfolding the paper to an open square to do this, . . .

8 . . . like this. Re-crease back to Step 6 following Steps 2–6.

9 Note the new shape at B. Fold up triangle B.

10 Open and squash flat the triangle, forming a square.

11 Swivel the square down and to the right along a hidden crease.

12 Pleat the eye.

13 The Beak complete. Hold as shown and move your hands to and fro to make the mouth open and close!

LIGHTHEARTED

Original concepts are rare in origami. Most designs, however good, are created within relatively predictable themes, so it is pleasing to occasionally find a fresh approach. In this design, the final shape is unimpressive, but reveals a translucent heart when held against the light! Fold the paper carefully, particularly at Steps 2–3, or the heart will be poorly proportioned. Use a square of thin paper; thicker papers will not reveal the heart.

Designed by Wayne Brown, UK.

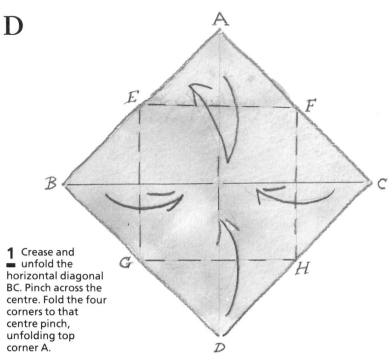

1 Crease and unfold the horizontal diagonal BC. Pinch across the centre. Fold the four corners to that centre pinch, unfolding top corner A.

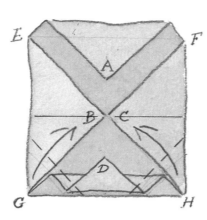

2 Fold down corner
A as shown. Pleat
triangle DGH as
shown.

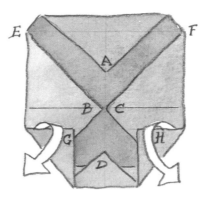

3 Fold in corners G
& H. Note the
very small intrusion
of the crease into
the D triangle. This is
important, as it
affects the
proportion of the
heart.

4 Unfold Step 3.

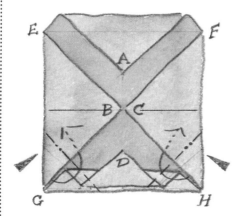

5 Re-crease Step 3,
but reverse
folding the top part
of each crease to
push G under B, and
H under C.

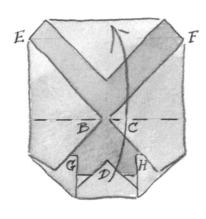

6 Fold in half.

7 Fold in E & F just a
little way.

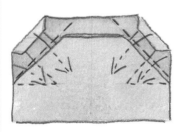

8 Fold over as
shown, locking
the edges into the
pockets made in
Step 5.

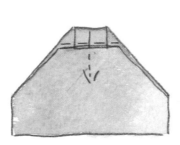

9 Fold the excess
paper into the
top pocket.

10 Note that the
shape is locked
flat.

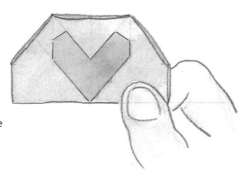

11 To see the
heart, hold the
paper up to a
window or other
diffuse light source
(but not the sun).

STAR BOX

This is one of the simpler decorative origami boxes. It is relatively easy to make a square, straight-sided box, such as the Traditional Box project, but the technical complexities increase as the final shape becomes less plain. Here though, the design is pleasingly bold. Use a square of origami paper, with the coloured side outwards.

Traditional design.

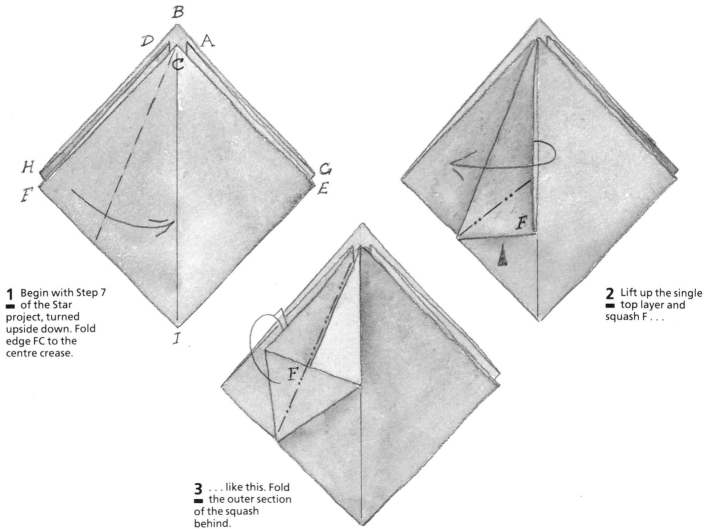

1 Begin with Step 7 of the Star project, turned upside down. Fold edge FC to the centre crease.

2 Lift up the single top layer and squash F . . .

3 . . . like this. Fold the outer section of the squash behind.

ORIGAMI

4 Repeat Steps 2–3 with E.

5 Turn over.

6 Repeat Steps 2–4 with G & H.

7 Crease and unfold across the full width of the paper. To help Step 9, the valley can be further creased as a mountain.

8 Fold down B as far as it will go. Repeat with A,C & D.

9 Open out the box, flattening the bottom along the Step 7 creases.

10 The Star Box complete.

There are many origami jumping frogs, most – like this one – made by creating a frog shape, then pleating across the body to create the spring. This version is a particularly athletic jumper. Use a 20 cm (8 in) square of paper. A 2 × 1 rectangle of thick paper may also be used, starting at Step 2.

Traditional design.

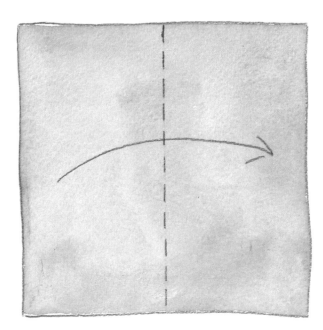

1 Fold a square in half down the middle.

2 The paper is now two layers thick, but will be referred to as though it was a single layer. Collapse AB to make the shape seen in Step 6 of the Waterbomb project.

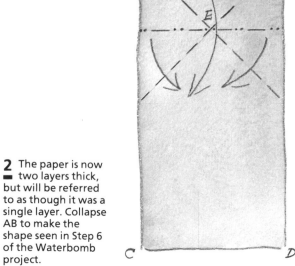

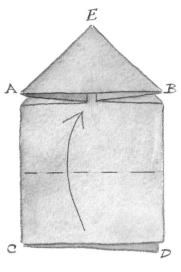

3 Fold up edge CD to AB.

4 Swing out A & B. Note that they do not touch E, but protrude to the side.

5 Fold in the sides.

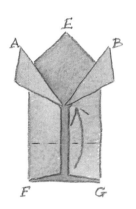

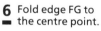

6 Fold edge FG to the centre point.

7 Fold down corners F & G . . .

8 . . . like this.

9 Hold tightly as shown. Slide F & G away from H . . .

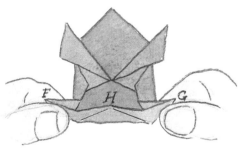

10 . . . like this, keeping firm hold of F & G. When F & G have been pulled out as far to the side as they will go, flatten the paper . . .

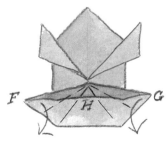

11 . . . like this. Fold down F & G.

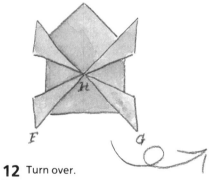

12 Turn over.

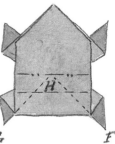

13 Make a pleat, with the mountain crease passing through H. The paper is very thick, so use considerable pressure.

14 The Jumping Frog complete.

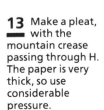

15 To make it jump, put your finger on its back. Flatten the pleat and slide your finger off! With practice, it will jump quite a distance.

BIRD

This design is straightforward until Step 9, when the difficult 3D crimp transforms an ordinary flat bird into a 3D bird with a pleasingly rounded shape. Some origami creators argue that such '3D-ing' at the end of the folding sequence is a cheat, and that a *truly* 3D design is folded as such from the start. Use a 15–20 cm (6–8 in) square of paper, coloured the same on both sides.

Designed by Paul Jackson.

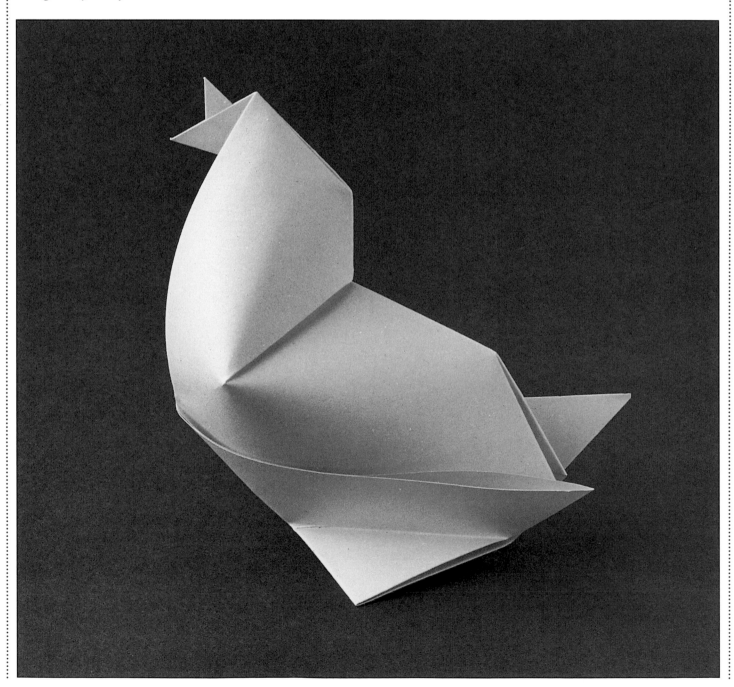

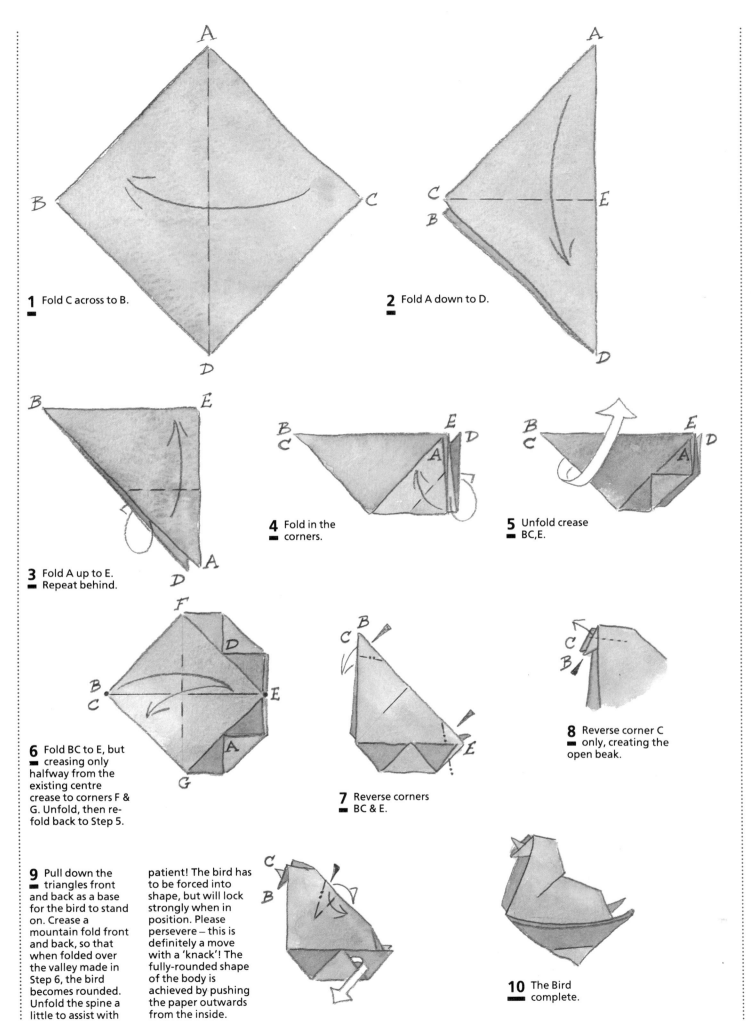

1 Fold C across to B.

2 Fold A down to D.

3 Fold A up to E. Repeat behind.

4 Fold in the corners.

5 Unfold crease BC,E.

6 Fold BC to E, but creasing only halfway from the existing centre crease to corners F & G. Unfold, then re-fold back to Step 5.

7 Reverse corners BC & E.

8 Reverse corner C only, creating the open beak.

9 Pull down the triangles front and back as a base for the bird to stand on. Crease a mountain fold front and back, so that when folded over the valley made in Step 6, the bird becomes rounded. Unfold the spine a little to assist with this crimp. Be patient! The bird has to be forced into shape, but will lock strongly when in position. Please persevere – this is definitely a move with a 'knack'! The fully-rounded shape of the body is achieved by pushing the paper outwards from the inside.

10 The Bird complete.

■ BUILDING

The design is included in the book to show how the rectangles and triangles that are created naturally by folding a square along halves and quarters, can be articulated to create a form such as this semi-abstract building, complete with colour-change roofs. Often, allowing the paper to do what it wants to do without contrivance is the best way to create. Use a square of origami paper, white side up.

Designed by Paul Jackson.

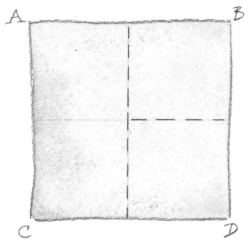

1 Crease as shown.
▬ Note the short
crease at the right.

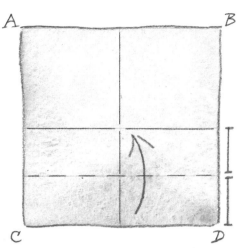

2 Fold edge CD up
▬ to the centre
crease, then fold in
half down the
middle.

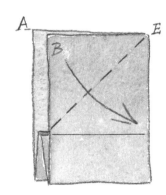

3 Fold down corner
▬ B.

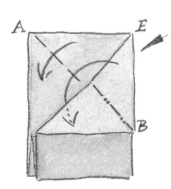

4 Reverse fold
▬ corner E behind B.

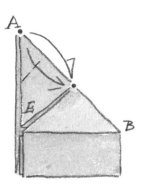

5 Fold corner A as
▬ shown, opening
the paper to do this.

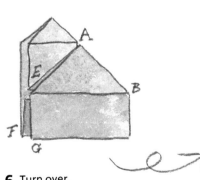

6 Turn over.
▬

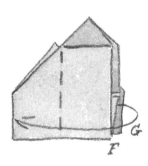

7 Swing F over to
▬ the left.

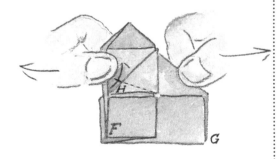

8 Hold as shown
▬ and move your
hands apart. Corner
H will lift. Crease and
flatten H as shown . . .

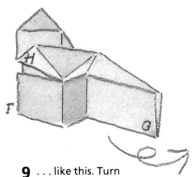

9 . . . like this. Turn
▬ over.

10 The Building
▬ complete.

PIG

The Pig, although a fairly complex project, is rewarding to construct, especially as the finished animal emerges in the final steps. Take time over the snout folds – they may appear complicated but do give a realistic result. Choose a 'pig'-coloured paper and use a 2 × 1 rectangle, the same colour on both sides. It is easy to create a whole 'family' of origami pigs: simply vary the size of the initial 2 × 1 rectangle.

Designed by Paul Jackson.

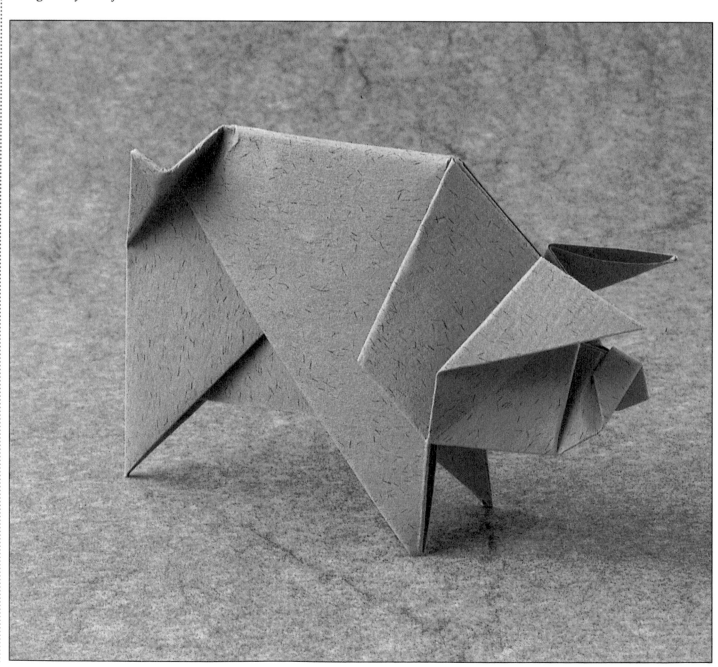

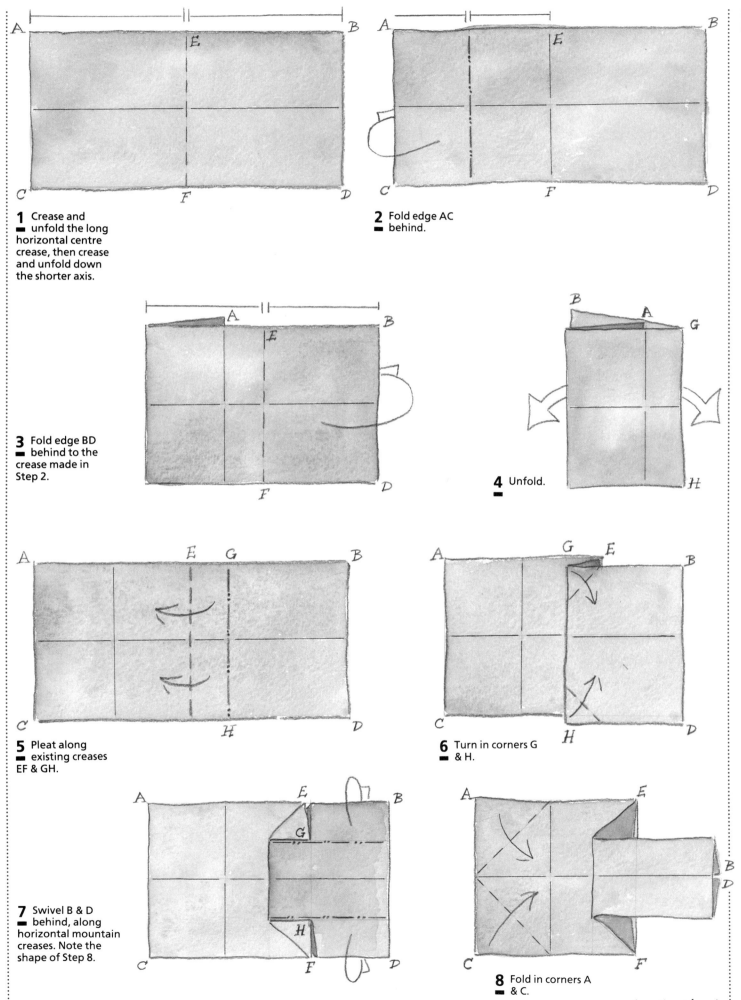

1 Crease and unfold the long horizontal centre crease, then crease and unfold down the shorter axis.

2 Fold edge AC behind.

3 Fold edge BD behind to the crease made in Step 2.

4 Unfold.

5 Pleat along existing creases EF & GH.

6 Turn in corners G & H.

7 Swivel B & D behind, along horizontal mountain creases. Note the shape of Step 8.

8 Fold in corners A & C.

(continued . . .)

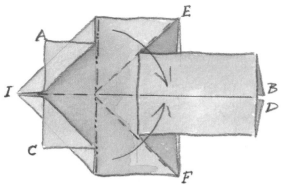

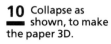

9 Fold A & C back out, the creases tapering towards I.

10 Collapse as shown, to make the paper 3D.

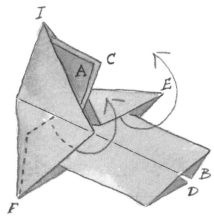

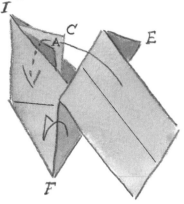

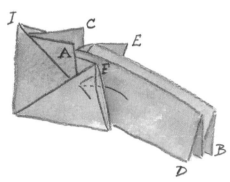

11 Pull out the hidden ledge . . .

12 . . . and feed it back into the pig between A & C . . .

13 . . . like this, bringing F & E back together again.

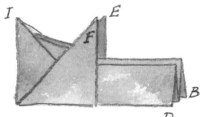

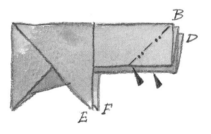

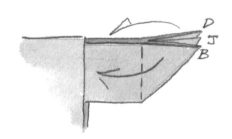

14 The manoeuvre is complete – its purpose is to stop the pig from splaying its front legs. Turn the paper the right way up.

15 Reverse fold at B & D.

16 Fold B & D towards the neck.

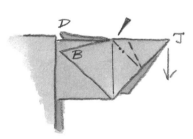

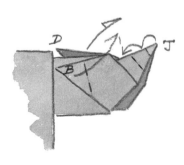

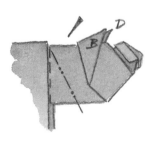

17 Create two reverse folds near the snout, forming a crimp.

18 Fold the snout over and over. Fold the ears forward.

19 Crimp the neck, lowering the head.

20 Pleat the tail.

21 The Pig complete.

STANDING HEART

Hearts are a favourite origami theme, particularly when combined with another element, such as a heart pierced by an arrow, twin hearts or a heart on a finger ring. Here is a conventional single heart, but one which could make an attractive standing ornament for a mantelpiece or desk top. Use a square of red/white origami paper, red side up.

Designed by Paul Jackson.

(Continued . . .)

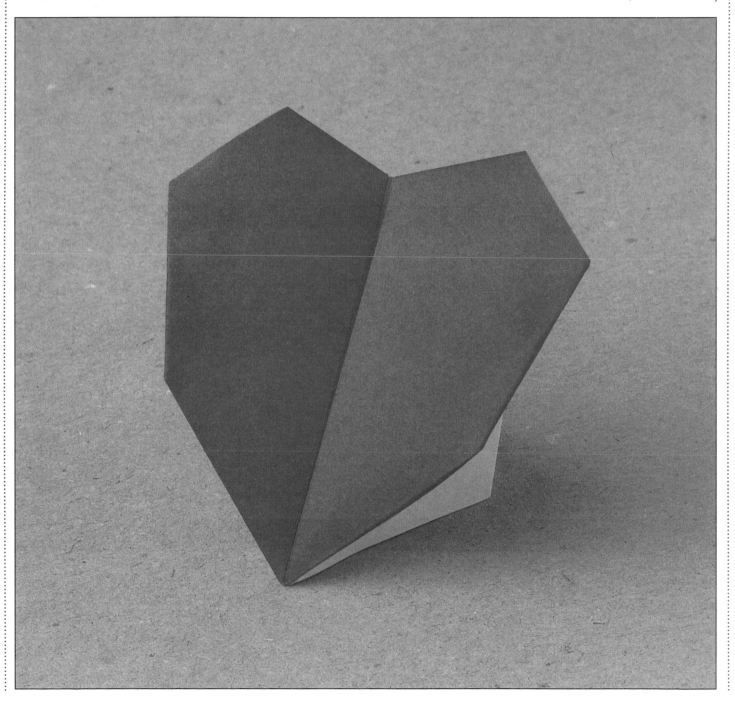

STANDING HEART

(continued)

1 Crease and unfold across the middle, then fold AC across to BD.

2 Mountain fold corners C & D inside.

3 Squash fold corner E.

4 Fold the outer section of the squash fold behind.

5 Open the paper between G & H. Turn over to see . . .

6 . . . a pyramid. Corner I is the apex (the corner nearest to you). Push on I so that it inverts and the paper pops inside out. Corner I is now the furthest point from you, not the nearest.

7 This is the shape. Note I.

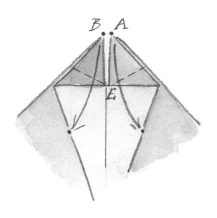

8 Fold down B & A, dot to dot.

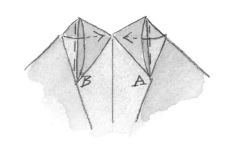

9 Tuck the excess paper into the pockets at B & A.

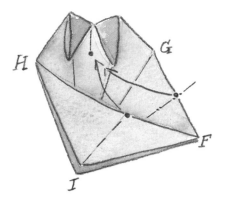

10 Collapse as shown, folding the two outer dots onto the inner one.

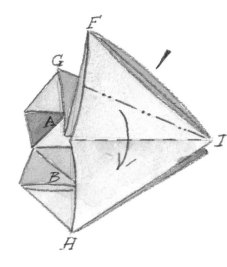

11 Squash F, presently standing upright.

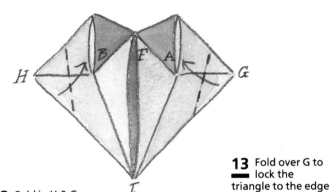

12 Fold in H & G.

13 Fold over G to lock the triangle to the edge behind.

14 Open out the pocket between F & I . . .

15 . . . like this, flattening the paper.

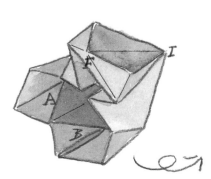

16 Partly close the pocket again. Turn over.

17 The Standing Heart complete.

FIGHTER JET

There are purists who may cry 'cheat' at this design, because it is made from two pieces of paper. A near-identical one-piece version from a 3 × 2 rectangle post-dated this original design, but is messy to make and lacks the simplicity of the original. Use two identical squares of paper of the same size and colour, coloured the same on both sides.

Designed by Paul Jackson.

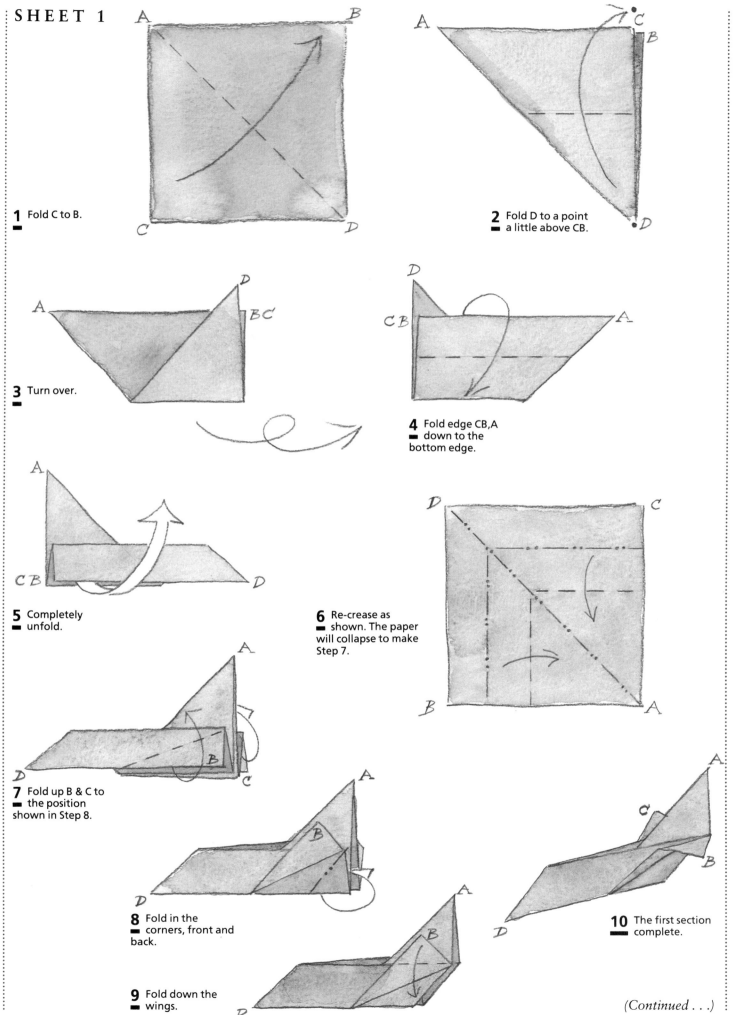

1 Fold C to B.

2 Fold D to a point a little above CB.

3 Turn over.

4 Fold edge CB,A down to the bottom edge.

5 Completely unfold.

6 Re-crease as shown. The paper will collapse to make Step 7.

7 Fold up B & C to the position shown in Step 8.

8 Fold in the corners, front and back.

9 Fold down the wings.

10 The first section complete.

(Continued . . .)

SHEET 2

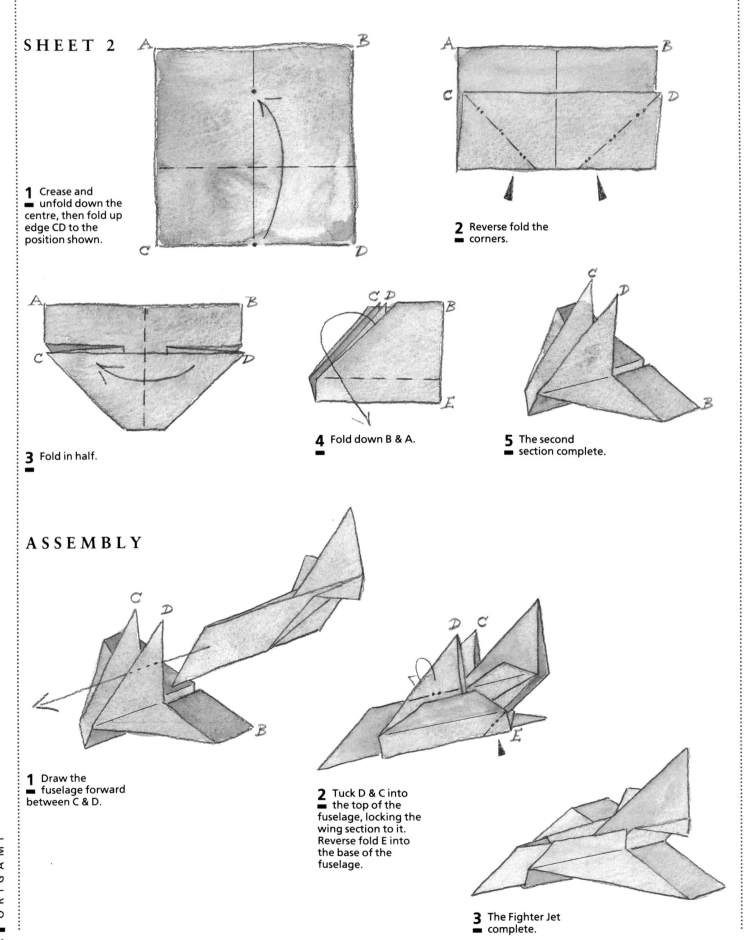

1 Crease and unfold down the centre, then fold up edge CD to the position shown.

2 Reverse fold the corners.

3 Fold in half.

4 Fold down B & A.

5 The second section complete.

ASSEMBLY

1 Draw the fuselage forward between C & D.

2 Tuck D & C into the top of the fuselage, locking the wing section to it. Reverse fold E into the base of the fuselage.

3 The Fighter Jet complete.

ADVANCED PROJECTS

CAMEL

The shape formed in Step 5 is commonly known in origami as the Fish base, and for obvious reasons. Apart from fishes (and a camel), the base at Step 6 is ideally shaped to create many different birds – the blunt points make wings and the sharp points form a head and tail. Use a 15–20 cm (6–8 in) square of paper, same colour both sides.

Designed by Paul Jackson.

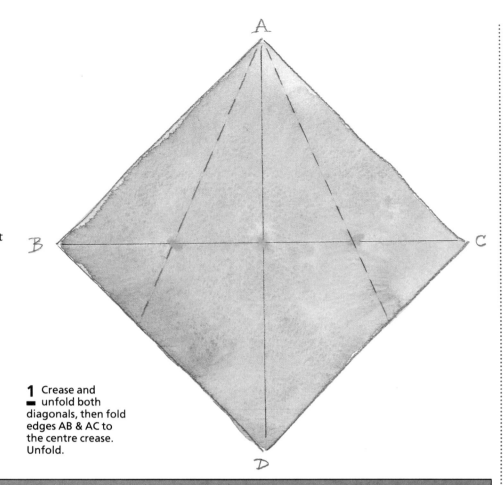

1 Crease and unfold both diagonals, then fold edges AB & AC to the centre crease. Unfold.

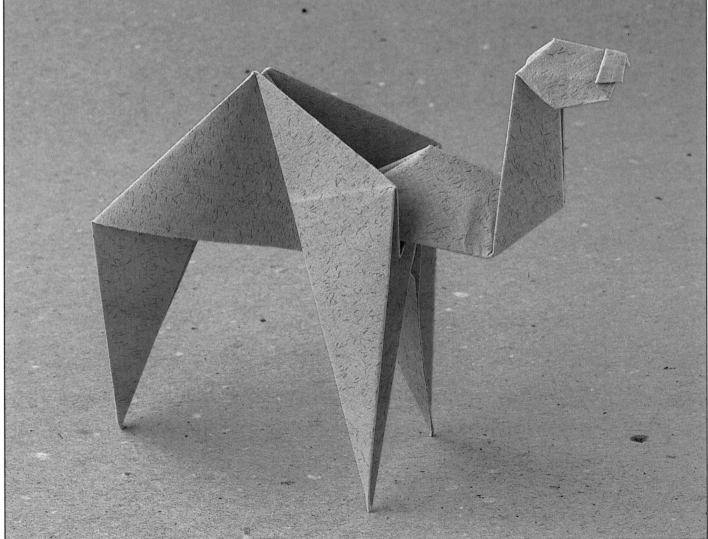

2 Similarly, fold edges DB & DC to the centre crease. Unfold.

3 Collapse the paper as shown, making it 3D.

4 Mountain fold across the middle, so that D swings up and back to lie behind A . . .

5 . . . like this. Fold in half.

6 Reverse fold A out to the left.

(Continued . . .)

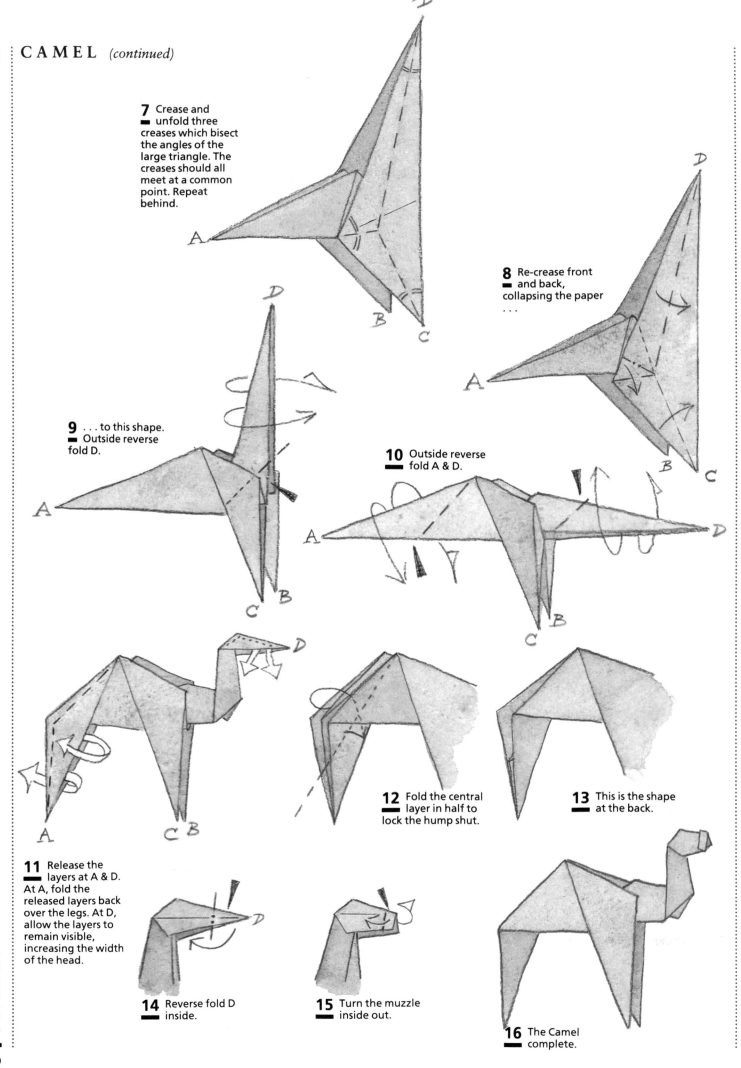

7 Crease and unfold three creases which bisect the angles of the large triangle. The creases should all meet at a common point. Repeat behind.

8 Re-crease front and back, collapsing the paper . . .

9 . . . to this shape. Outside reverse fold D.

10 Outside reverse fold A & D.

11 Release the layers at A & D. At A, fold the released layers back over the legs. At D, allow the layers to remain visible, increasing the width of the head.

12 Fold the central layer in half to lock the hump shut.

13 This is the shape at the back.

14 Reverse fold D inside.

15 Turn the muzzle inside out.

16 The Camel complete.

CHINESE VASE

This wonderful design was first
introduced to the West by Dr Philip
Shen (whose bowl appears earlier) and
popularized in the USA by the late
Verdi Adams. It has a beautifully direct
sequence of folds, climaxed by the
extraordinary opening out from 2D to
3D. Use a square of paper, not too
small. If using origami paper, start
white side up.

Traditional design.

(Continued . . .)

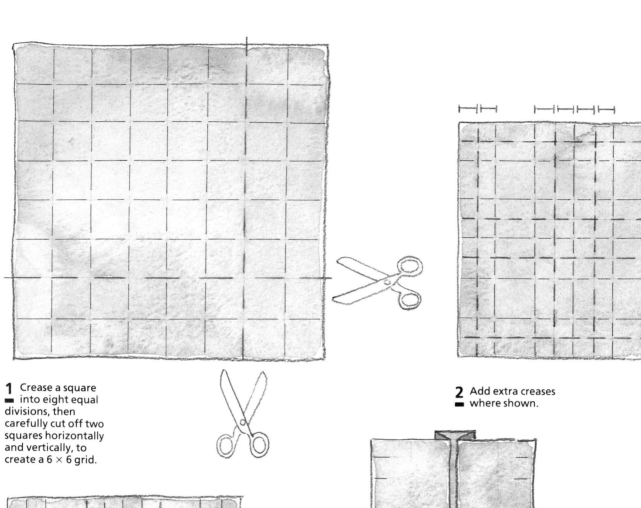

1 Crease a square into eight equal divisions, then carefully cut off two squares horizontally and vertically, to create a 6 × 6 grid.

2 Add extra creases where shown.

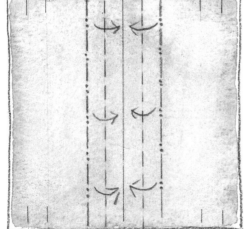

3 Pleat the paper as shown.

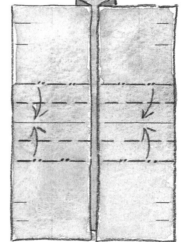

4 Similarly, pleat horizontally.

5 This is the shape of the paper. Turn over.

6 This is the shape.

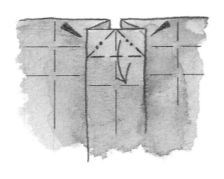

7 Lift and squash the end of each pleat . . .

8 . . . like this.

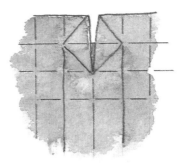

9 Repeat along each edge.

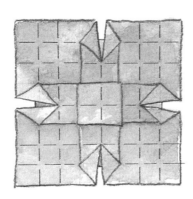

10 Here are the squashed pleats. Turn over.

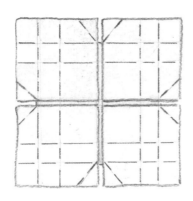

11 Crease and unfold each loose corner at the pleats. This is to prepare for Step 14.

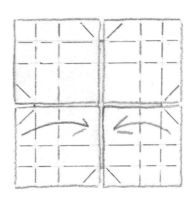

12 Fold the sides to the middle.

13 Fold the top and bottom edges to the middle, tucking the corners deep into the pockets.

14 Fold the loose corners inside, to create a square opening . . .

15 . . . like this. Turn over.

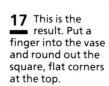

16 This is the fun part! Carefully tease out the trapped layers inside the pleats to make the vase 3D. Do this by rotating the paper frequently, so that all four sides are developed equally.

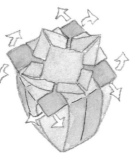

17 This is the result. Put a finger into the vase and round out the square, flat corners at the top.

18 The Chinese Vase complete.

SEATED FIGURE

One of the delights of origami is its ability to conjure complex subjects from relatively simple folds, to create not a detailed representation, but a stylized abstraction. When successful, the result is poetic, both in concept and form. Use a square of origami paper, coloured side up.

Designed by Paul Jackson.

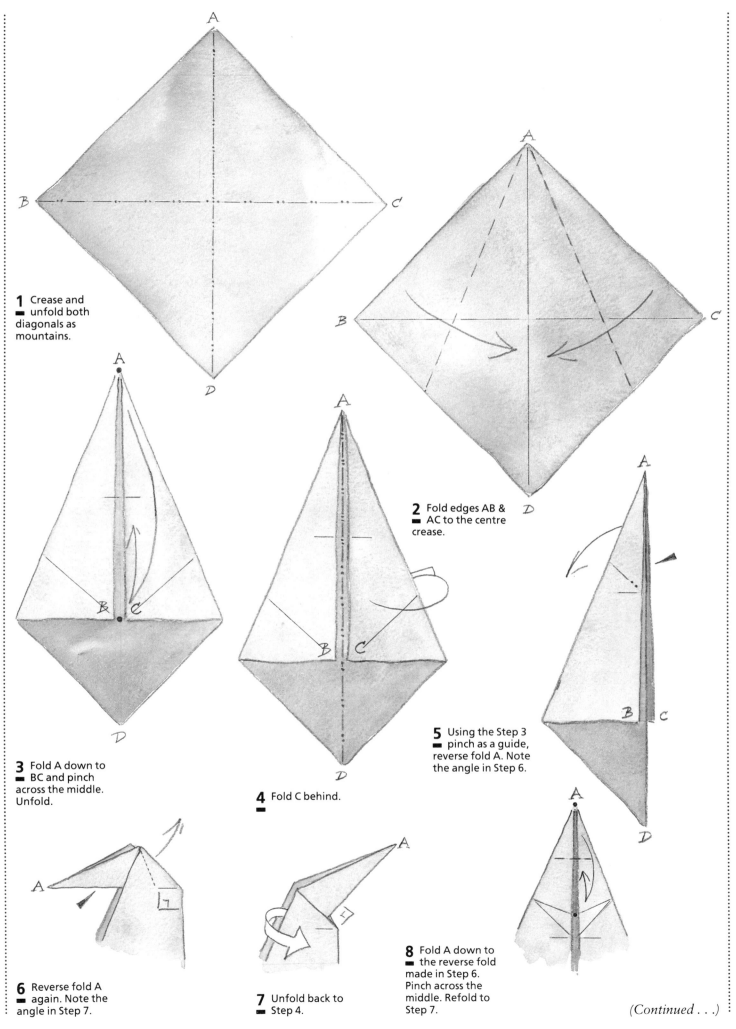

1 Crease and unfold both diagonals as mountains.

2 Fold edges AB & AC to the centre crease.

3 Fold A down to BC and pinch across the middle. Unfold.

4 Fold C behind.

5 Using the Step 3 pinch as a guide, reverse fold A. Note the angle in Step 6.

6 Reverse fold A again. Note the angle in Step 7.

7 Unfold back to Step 4.

8 Fold A down to the reverse fold made in Step 6. Pinch across the middle. Refold to Step 7.

(Continued . . .)

9 Reverse fold A, using the Step 8 pinch as a guide. Note the angle in Step 10.

10 Reverse fold A again. Note the angle in Step 11.

11 Completely unfold.

12 Mountain fold D behind.

13 Collapse as shown. Note that the reverse folds made in Steps 6 & 7 are here reformed through both layers, but the latter pair of reverse folds are not formed at all.

14 Fold back B & C.

15 Open the head.

16 Fold back the tip.

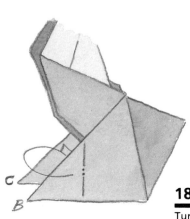

17 Fold in B & C.

18 Tuck C into B to lock the chair. Turn over.

19 The Seated Figure complete.

ELECTRA

An appeal of modular folding is that spectacular structures can be made from simple units, so that the whole is very much more than the sum of its parts. Thirty modules are needed for this design, which will take about an hour to make. Fold them all very carefully, then slot them together, with diligent regard for the '5 and 3' (pentagons and triangles) interlocking pattern. The result is a pierced structure of great beauty and strength. Use 30 10 cm (4 in) squares. If using origami paper, start with the coloured side up.

Designed by David Mitchell, UK.

(Continued . . .)

M E T H O D

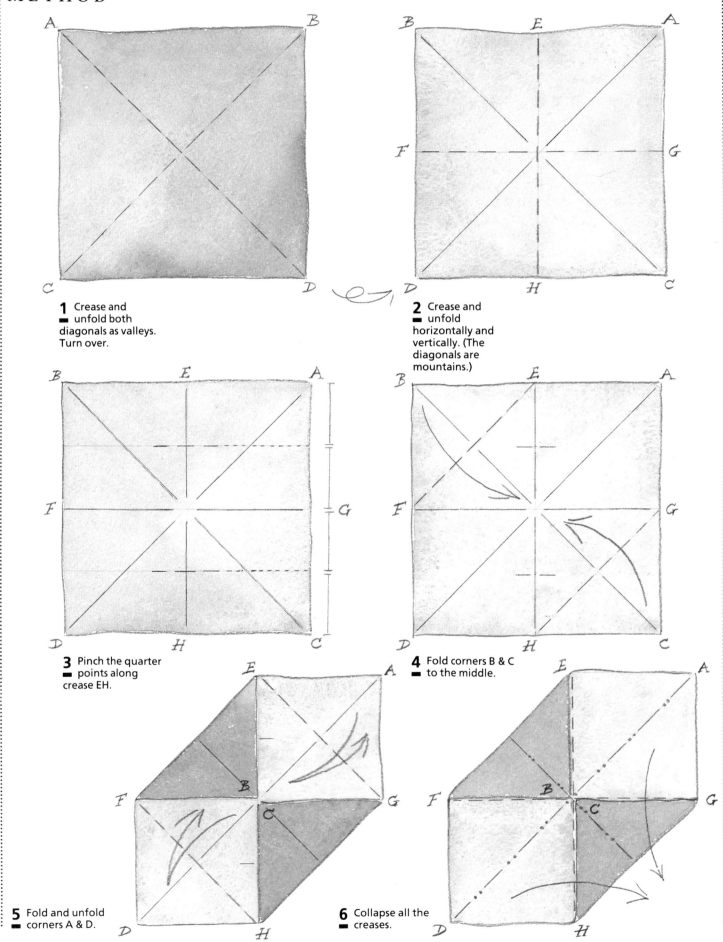

1 Crease and unfold both diagonals as valleys. Turn over.

2 Crease and unfold horizontally and vertically. (The diagonals are mountains.)

3 Pinch the quarter points along crease EH.

4 Fold corners B & C to the middle.

5 Fold and unfold corners A & D.

6 Collapse all the creases.

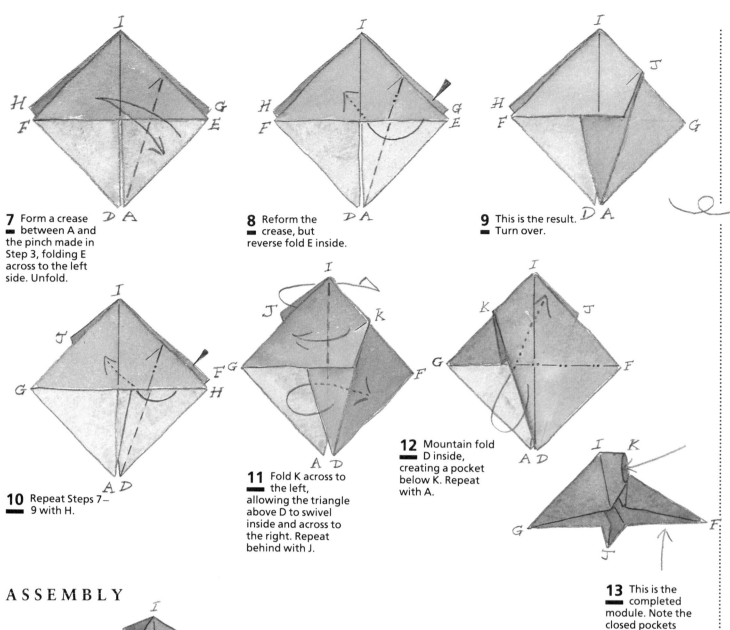

7 Form a crease between A and the pinch made in Step 3, folding E across to the left side. Unfold.

8 Reform the crease, but reverse fold E inside.

9 This is the result. Turn over.

10 Repeat Steps 7–9 with H.

11 Fold K across to the left, allowing the triangle above D to swivel inside and across to the right. Repeat behind with J.

12 Mountain fold D inside, creating a pocket below K. Repeat with A.

13 This is the completed module. Note the closed pockets below J & K and the extended flaps at F & G.

ASSEMBLY

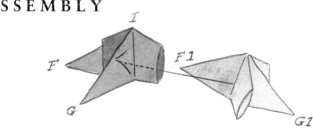

1 Tuck the extended flap on one module (F1), deep inside the pocket of another. To lock them together, fold F or G (depending on which one flap F1 has been tucked into) towards G1.

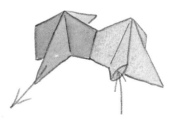

2 Repeat with the nearside flaps and pockets.

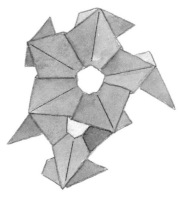

3 Lock 5 modules together, leaving no excess flaps in the centre of the pentagon. A sixth module is shown at the very bottom of the drawing connecting two neighbouring pentagon modules, thereby creating a triangle with no loose flaps in its centre. The completed Electra is thus a combination of pentagons and triangles. Interlock the remaining modules following this pattern.

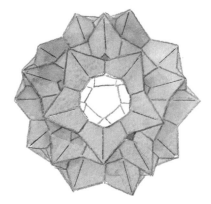

4 The completed Electra.

SEAL ON A ROCK

So called 'double subjects' or 'combination folds' are common in complex origami, where two subjects or objects are folded from a single sheet. Examples might include a mother pushing a pram, a man playing an instrument or, as in this case, a seal basking on a rock. Some creative folders have combined even more subjects, such as several birds in a nest. Use a square of origami paper coloured side up, or for a better effect, two differently coloured or textured sheets folded back to back.

Designed by Dr Martin Wall, UK.

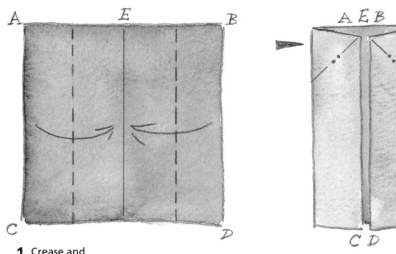

1 Crease and unfold down the centre, then fold the sides to the middle.

2 Reverse fold the top two corners.

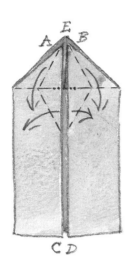

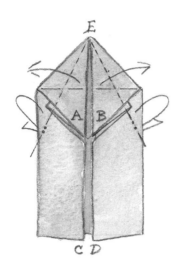

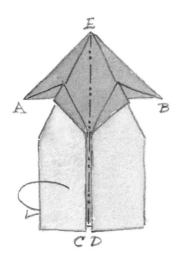

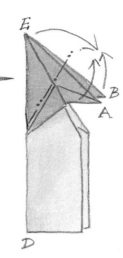

3 Collapse, folding A & B downwards and adding the reverse folds.

4 Fold as shown, allowing A & B to swivel outwards.

5 Mountain fold A behind.

6 Reverse fold E, allowing A & B to pivot upwards to touch E.

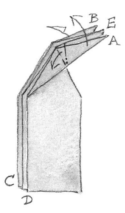

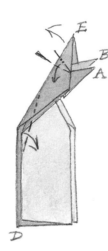

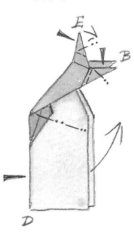

7 Narrow the paper with two reverse folds.

8 Pleat A & B.

9 Turn E inside out, lowering A & B.

10 Crimp the neck upwards. Release paper for the tail. Repeat behind.

11 Crimp the head. Squash the flippers. Reverse fold the rock.

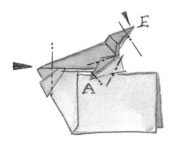

12 Reverse fold the snout. Round off the flippers. Sink the excess paper inside at the tail.

13 Crimp the rock to make it 3D.

14 The Seal on a Rock complete.

BOWL

Dr Shen is renowned for his geometric and abstract forms which collapse dramatically into shape from an apparently unpromising pattern of pre-creases. In this example, note how the soft, cushion-like base makes an effective contrast to the straight-sided walls. The locking mechanism in Steps 13–14 is also pleasing. Use a square of origami paper, white side up, or paper the same colour both sides.

Designed by Dr Philip Shen, Hong Kong.

1 Crease mountains and valleys as shown.

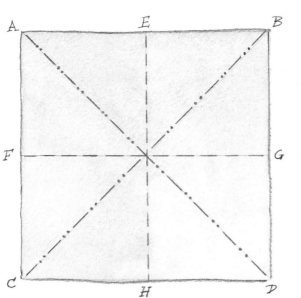

2 Lightly lay corner B onto crease HE, in such a position that if the paper were flattened to make a crease, the crease would run exactly to corner A. However, flatten to make a crease *only* in the two short sections shown. Be precise.

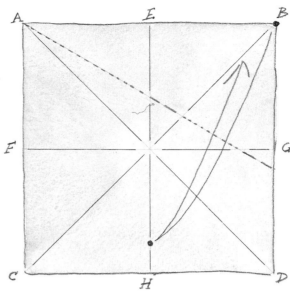

3 Repeat, laying corner C onto crease GF.

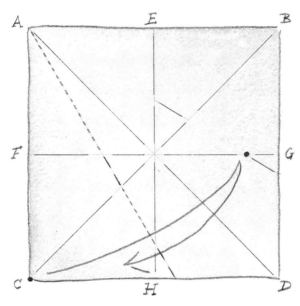

4 Note the crease pattern, both pairs of creases pointing to corner A. Repeat the pattern, so that pairs of creases point to corners B,C, & D.

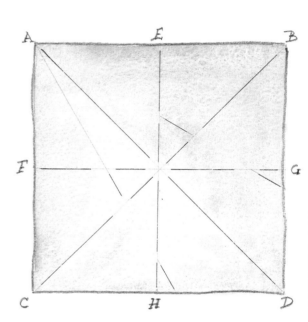

5 Note the octagon of creases in the centre and the 'V's' at E,F,G, & H. Fold B to point I, but crease only where shown. Similarly, fold C to J. Note that if extended, both creases would meet at corner A.

6 This is the crease pattern. Repeat Step 5, creating creases which if extended, would meet at corners B,C, & D.

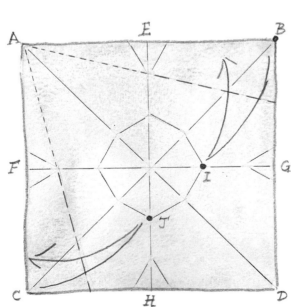

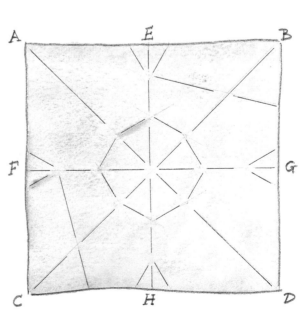

(Continued . . .)

BOWL

(continued)

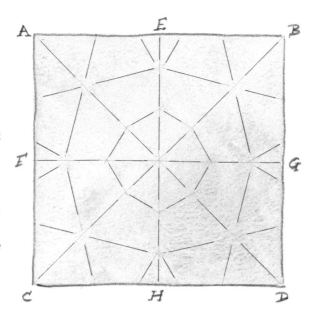

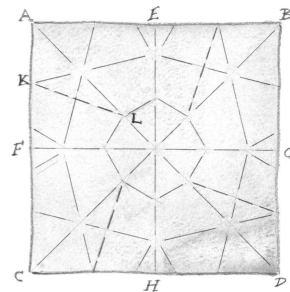

7 This is the present crease pattern.

8 Form crease KL to the left of corner A, then repeat with similar creases to the left of each corner, rotating the square 90° each time.

9 Form a pleat along AL & KL, making the paper 3D. Note that L is concave, not convex.

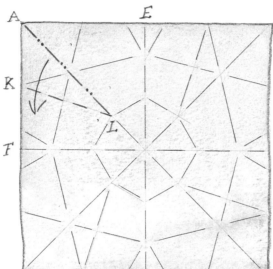

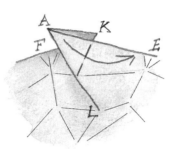

10 Fold A to the right along existing creases. Repeat with B, C & D, folding them also to the right.

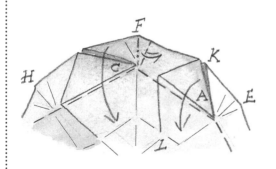

11 Collapse all the way round the bowl. Note the pleat at F, repeated at E,G & H.

12 This is the bowl at present – a loose, badly-locked and rather lumpy form. Turn it upside down.

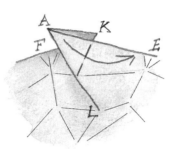

13 Form a mountain as shown . . .

14 . . . to create a flat-bottomed bowl standing on four squat, flat triangles. These flat triangles trap the K corners inside their layers, so neatening the inside of the bowl. Turn over.

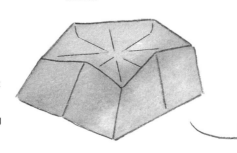

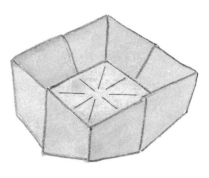

15 The Bowl complete. Note the soft, cushion-like form of the bottom.

ELEPHANT

This final design in the advanced origami section is appropriately the most difficult. Step 7 contains a fiendish closed sink, which will have even the most experienced folders fumbling a little. The Step 11 half-closed sink is little better. It is puzzling to wonder why a design which looks so little like a real elephant should be so immediately recognizable as one! Use a square of paper, same colour both sides. If using origami paper, the coloured side should be outside at Step 1.

Designed by Paul Jackson.

(Continued . . .)

1 Begin with Step 6 of the Waterbomb project. Fold A across to the right.

2 Fold A & D across to edge EC . . .

3 . . . like this, so that when the crease is made, it is precisely horizontal. Unfold it.

4 Unfold A & D, then swivel B upwards to create the Step 5 shape.

5 Squash, separating F from G.

6 Fold G behind.

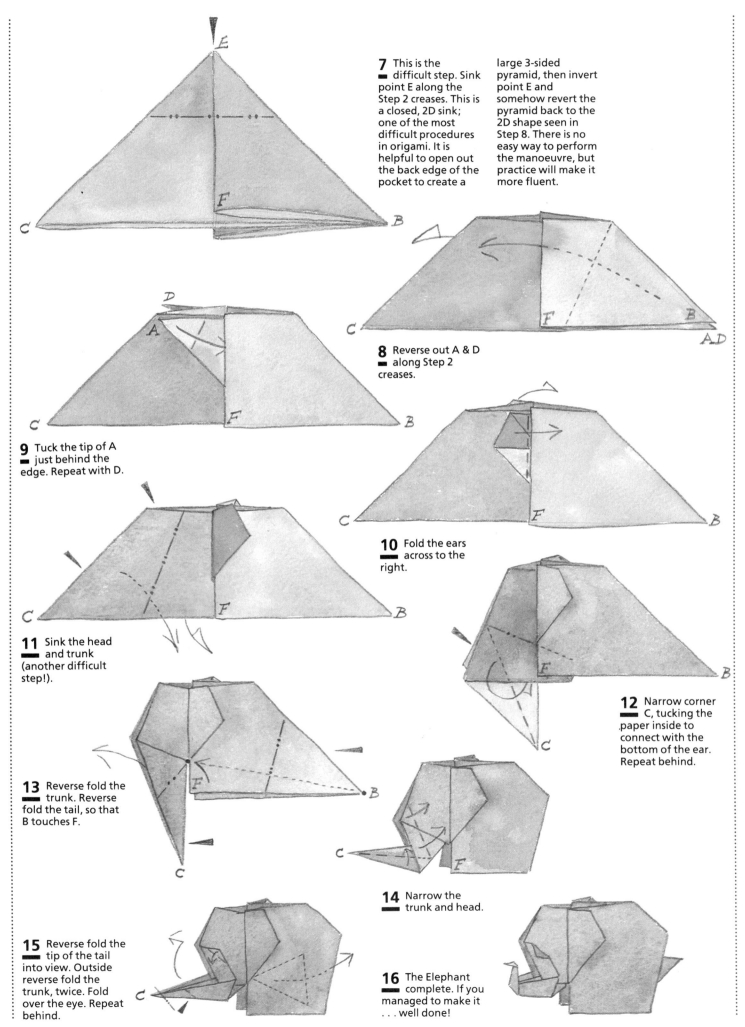

7 This is the difficult step. Sink point E along the Step 2 creases. This is a closed, 2D sink; one of the most difficult procedures in origami. It is helpful to open out the back edge of the pocket to create a large 3-sided pyramid, then invert point E and somehow revert the pyramid back to the 2D shape seen in Step 8. There is no easy way to perform the manoeuvre, but practice will make it more fluent.

8 Reverse out A & D along Step 2 creases.

9 Tuck the tip of A just behind the edge. Repeat with D.

10 Fold the ears across to the right.

11 Sink the head and trunk (another difficult step!).

12 Narrow corner C, tucking the paper inside to connect with the bottom of the ear. Repeat behind.

13 Reverse fold the trunk. Reverse fold the tail, so that B touches F.

14 Narrow the trunk and head.

15 Reverse fold the tip of the tail into view. Outside reverse fold the trunk, twice. Fold over the eye. Repeat behind.

16 The Elephant complete. If you managed to make it . . . well done!

Decorative papercrafts

This chapter is a delightful miscellany of decorative ideas for paper and paper goods around the home. Browsing through it you will find all sorts of fun ideas for livening up a wide range of items ranging from napkins to writing paper, wrapping paper, gift tags and boxes to name but a few.

Many different decorative techniques are shown, most of which are amazingly simple in both concept and execution, but which are highly effective. A number of stunning paint techniques are also illustrated, any of which can be used to completely transform an originally plain item. These include block printing, stencilling, batik effects, sponging, marbling, speckling, combing and feathering and are all used to create some wonderful results. In addition, you will learn how to make individual boxes, with curved or straight sides, decorative stationery and envelopes, pop-ups, napkin rings, a desk tidy, a notelet holder, party hats, place name cards, doilies, crackers and sweet cones. You will learn how to decorate paper with thread and ribbon in novel ways. There is even a project to show you how to make your own paper, including suggestions for intrinsic decoration and perfume.

Even if you do not follow all of the many projects in this section, reading through them will provide you with plenty of great ideas for decorating paper in your own individual style.

∎ NATTY NAPKINS

Here is a very quick way to add your own style to ordinary napkins and add a sparkle to the tone of your meal! Even a squiggle, a dot, or a circle can transform the napkin. Try experimenting with different shapes, and perhaps give everybody their own design.

YOU WILL NEED
Plain coloured paper napkins
Pen
Gold and silver metallic pens

1 For a Christmas feel use a plain red napkin and lightly mark out a holly leaf and berry sprig in pen.

2 Then take a silver metallic pen with a medium nib and carefully trace over the pen lines.

3 For a Hallowe'en evening take a black napkin and draw gold stars and half moons with a gold pen.

TWO-TONE GIFTWRAP

Here is another way to make your own wrapping paper, this time using two layers of co-ordinating crêpe paper.

YOU WILL NEED
Crêpe paper in two contrasting colours
Glue

1 First work out how much paper you will need in order to cover the gift. Now cut a piece of paper to this size in each of your two chosen colours. Decide which colour will be on top and pleat it lengthwise.

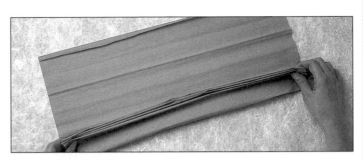

2 Now cut circles out through all the layers along both sides of the pleat.

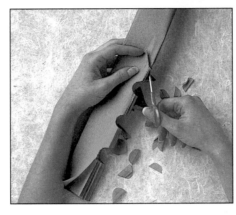

3 Open up the top paper and glue it onto the bottom. It is exciting to see how the colour of the bottom layer shows through. If you want a really elaborate design, add cut-out pieces in a further colour, leaving openings large enough to reveal the colours beneath. Now wrap your gift up in the two-tone dotty paper.

BAROQUE BAUBLES

We have used a polystyrene ball for this decoration. They can be found, in a range of sizes, in craft shops and are used for making dolls' heads.

YOU WILL NEED
Polystyrene ball
Gouache paint
Gold doily
Glue
Brass paper fastener
Gold thread

1 First of all, paint the bauble with some gouache in a suitable colour.

2 When the paint has dried, cut out pieces from a doily. Decide how they are to be arranged on the bauble and glue them into position.

3 Cut out a further motif from the doily and take a brass paper fastener and push it through the centre. Now push this into the top of the ball.

4 Taking some gold thread, wrap it around the brass fastener so that it is ready to be hung on the Christmas tree.

ORIENTAL FAN

Here is an easy way to make a beautiful fan to cool yourself on a hot summer's day. This fan is loosely designed on a Japanese fan and so we have made it with Japanese rice paper.

YOU WILL NEED
Thin card
Craft knife
Glue
Double-sided tape
Rice paper or tissue paper

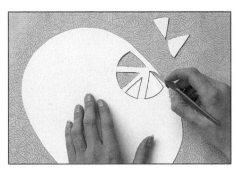

1 Cut out an oval piece of thin card. Make sure that the card is not too thick so that it is flexible for fanning. Cut out the bottom area of the fan with a craft knife.

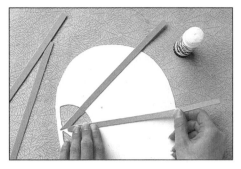

2 Next cut thin strips of card and lining them up at the base, stick them on both sides of the fan so that they follow the cut out lines.

3 To make the handle, cut out two strips of thicker card measuring 14 × 1½ cm (5½ × ½ in). Taper the ends and stick double-sided tape onto both pieces. Attach them to either side of the base part of the fan.

4 Now cover the fan in rice paper by gluing round the edge and along the struts. We have used a different colour paper on either side for variety. If you cannot find rice paper, use tissue paper instead. Trim the edges with scissors.

5 Cover the handle by wrapping it with a long strip of rice paper and gluing it at the bottom.

WELL-DRESSED NAPKIN

Here is a quick and simple way to dress up a napkin using coloured card. You can make the holder in contrasting or a toning coloured card to suit the setting.

YOU WILL NEED
Paper napkins
Thin card in two contrasting colours
Glue

1 First cut a square of card to the same size as the folded napkin.

2 Fold the card diagonally with the front fold half-way up. Cut a triangle in contrasting coloured card slightly smaller than the front triangle. Cut out a zigzag edge along two sides.

3 Now fold the napkin in half and place it into the napkin holder. Why not experiment with different designs on the front, or leave it plain and glue on a cut out motif from a magazine.

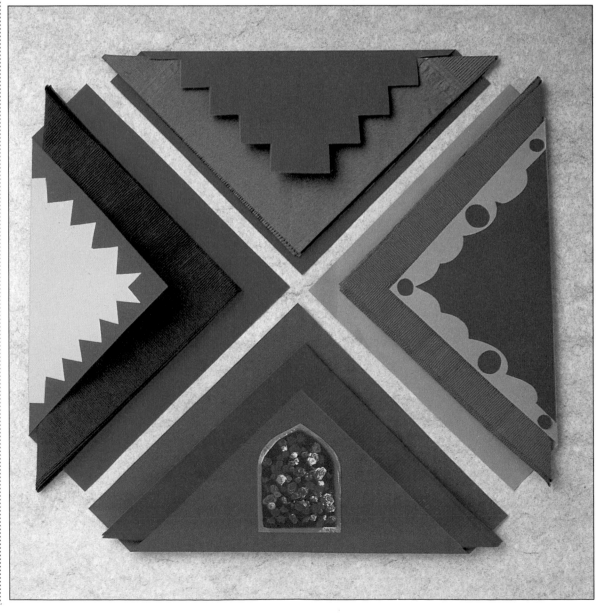

GIFT BOX

Here is an easy and stylish way to present an awkwardly-shaped gift. It also makes a lovely box to use afterwards to keep things in.

YOU WILL NEED
Empty shoe box with lid
Patterned and plain wrapping paper
Glue
Tissue paper

1 Wrap the outside of the box in the patterned paper.

2 Now line the inside of the box with plain paper.

3 Cover the lid of the box on the top and inside in the plain paper. Take some tissue paper in a co-ordinating colour, softly scrunch it up and arrange it in the bottom of the box. Place the gift inside and put the lid on.

4 As a further decoration, enhance the top by attaching paper strips cut from the patterned paper to suggest ribbons.

CLASSIC LINES

If you want to write a letter in a hurry, but still want it to be stylish, here are a couple of quick ways to make some beautiful writing paper. You will need some lightly coloured wrapping paper in a classical design.

YOU WILL NEED
Pale wrapping paper
Tracing paper
Glue
Sheet of white paper

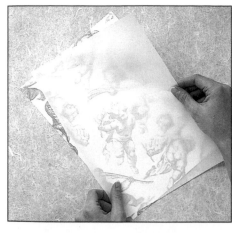

1 Cut out a rectangle of wrapping paper to the size of writing paper, and cut a piece of tracing paper to the same size. Stick the tracing paper on top of the wrapping paper, smoothing out any bubbles. Use a black felt-tip pen to write your letter so that it shows up clearly.

2 If you have a bit more time you could select one particular motif from the paper and cut this out.

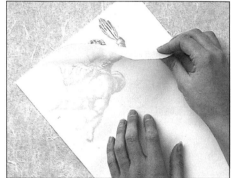

3 Glue the motif to a sheet of white paper.

4 As before, glue a sheet of tracing paper on top to give an elegant double layer. You could make a collection of writing paper by cutting out different motifs from one sheet of wrapping paper.

■ PAINT AND PAPER

Have fun turning an ordinary piece of black paper into bright and jazzy wrapping paper. You could of course vary the colour of the paper and paints.

YOU WILL NEED
Plain paper
Paints

2 Add more colours as you wish until the paper is brightly decorated.

1 Take a piece of black paper large enough to cover your present. Now choose the paint colours you are going to use. This example uses fuchsia pink, orange and gold paints to contrast with the black background. After preparing the paint on a saucer, decorate the paper with random 'blobs', working with one colour at a time.

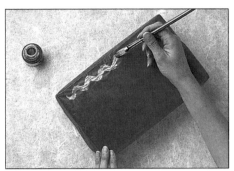

3 For a more regular painted pattern, the present can be wrapped first and then, following the shape of the gift, painted with wavy lines.

TWELFTH KNIGHT

Whether entertaining the Knights of
the Round Table or just arranging a
boys' party, these heraldic place mats
will certainly set the tone.

YOU WILL NEED
Silver, purple and orange card
Glue

1 Place mat
▬ To make this
heraldic place mat,
trace out a shield
shape onto silver
card and cut it out. It
should have a width
and length of about
25 cm (10 in). Cut six
strips of purple card
measuring 2 × 27 cm
(¾ × 11 in). Glue
and place two strips
to form a cross on
the shield and trim
at the edges.

2 Cut out eight
▬ wavy lines in
orange card and
five dots in purple
card. Using the
template, scaled to
the size required,
draw and cut out the
fleur-de-lys shape.

3 Following the
▬ design in the
photograph,
arrange all the
shapes onto your
card and glue them
into place one by
one.

4 Napkin holder
▬ Take a piece of
purple card 22 × 5
cm (9 × 2 in). Join
the short ends
together and glue.
Cut out a small silver
shield in card and an
orange fleur-de-lys.
Glue together and
then glue onto the
napkin holder.

5 Name place card
▬ To complete the
heraldic theme,
make up a name
place. Cut a piece of
silver card 9 × 10 cm
(3½ × 4 in) and fold
it lengthways down
the centre. Cut out a
smaller fleur-de-lys
shape 4 cm (1½ in)
high in purple card
and glue it onto the
silver card. Add the
orange band.

ELEGANT ENVELOPES

Finding the right size and style of
envelope to match your home-made
stationery can be a problem, so why
not make your own?

YOU WILL NEED
Coloured card
Glue
Contrasting coloured card

1 Measure out the
size that you
require by placing
your card onto a
piece of coloured
card. It must be
twice as long plus 3
cm (1 in), and as
wide plus 6 cm (2 in).
For a pointed flap
you will need an
extra 10 cm (4 in) on
the length.

2 Cut off the excess
corners and then
fold up the bottom
and sides and stick
them down.

3 Cut out a motif to
stick on the back
flap in a different
colour. If the
envelope has a
pointed flap you

might like to make
this a contrasting
colour by cutting out
a triangle to the
same size and gluing
it to the back flap.

IT'S A CRACKER

Sometimes a gift has such an obvious shape that even when it has been wrapped up it is immediately recognizable. Here is a fun way to disguise the shape by dressing it up as a cracker.

YOU WILL NEED
Cardboard tube
Wrapping paper
Double-sided tape
Ribbon

1 Place your gift inside the cardboard tube and cut a piece of wrapping paper so that it extends about 10 cm (4 in) at either end. Roll the paper around and secure it with tape. For a really professional look double-sided tape should be used.

2 Now cut two lengths of ribbon and tie at each end of the tube. Trim the ribbon ends. For a more colourful effect you could use several colours of ribbon.

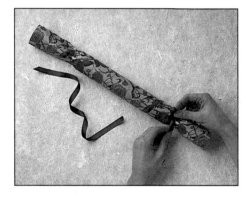

3 Holding the cracker in one hand, cut a zigzag design at the end and then turn around and repeat with the other end.

STENCILLING

Stencilling is a very popular craft and a huge variety of effects can be achieved. Stencilled patterns can be combined with other decorative techniques such as speckling or batik effects using wax crayons. Either a stencilling brush or a sponge can be used to apply the paint through the stencil; a brush will give a stippled effect, and a sponge a solid, denser result.

YOU WILL NEED
Stencilling card
Craft knife
Paper
Assortment of paints
Piece of sponge
Stencil brush

1 Draw a design onto the stencilling card and cut it out carefully using a craft knife.

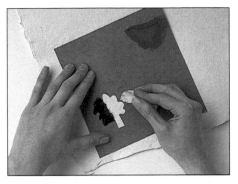

2 Lay a piece of paper onto a flat surface and place the stencil on top over the intended position of the design. Mix the paint until it is quite sticky in consistency; take up a fair amount of paint using the sponge and carefully dab it over the pattern in the stencilling card. Take care not to let the paint become too thin as it will seep under the edges of the stencil, giving a blurred design.

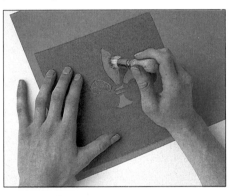

3 To use a stencil brush, lay a sheet of paper down on a flat surface and place the stencil on top. Load the brush with fairly thick paint and press it gently over the stencil, covering the paper beneath. Again, make sure the paint is not too thin. Dab paint over the stencil so that a mottled effect is achieved.

RIBBON PLAITS AND CURLS

There are many different effects that can be achieved by mixing and matching coloured ribbons. They can be plaited or twisted and grouped into colours to cascade down a wrapped present.

YOU WILL NEED
Assortment of ribbons
Double-sided tape
Felt-tip pens
Gold metallic pen

1 One of the most straightforward ways to use ribbon is to curl it. This effect is achieved by pulling the ribbon through closed scissors to make it twist and fall into natural ringlets. Try doing this to different lengths and colours of ribbons and then attach a bunch of curls to your present.

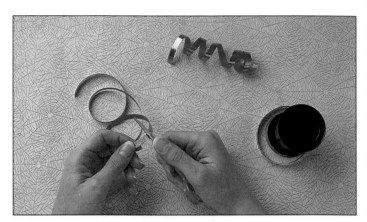

2 Another effective way to use ribbon is to plait it, using at least three different colours. Tape the ribbon ends together and plait to the required length. Secure and cut the ribbon ends.

3 In this example a whole medley of ribbons in different colours and widths is plaited together in order to create a riot of colour. Tape and cut ribbon ends.

4 To give ribbon an individual look, decorate it by drawing a design taken from the wrapping paper with a felt-tip or metallic pen.

TAG TIME

Make your own gift tags for a personal touch as well as to save money. Used greetings cards can often be cut down and made into brand new gift tags. Another idea is to take a motif from the wrapping paper used to cover your present.

YOU WILL NEED
Wrapping paper or greetings cards
Glue
Thin card
Ribbon

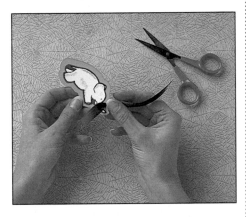

1 When you have wrapped the present, cut out a suitable motif from the spare paper. Glue the motif onto some thin card in a co-ordinating colour.

2 Following the shape of the motif cut around the design so that the card forms a border.

3 Now punch a hole in the card with a scissor blade and thread a ribbon through the hole. Write a message on the tag and attach it to the present.

STRAIGHT-SIDED BOX

This pretty box is made in two parts; each half can be in a different colour to create a contrast effect. It is assembled using a clever interlocking action.

YOU WILL NEED
Thin card in two different colours
Craft knife
Glue

1 Both halves are made in the same way. Scale up the template for the two halves of the box to the size required and transfer to the coloured card. Cut out the pieces with a craft knife. Fold in and glue the side tabs.

2 To assemble the box, interlock the two halves by first tucking each tongue beneath the shallow edge on all sides of the box. Push the halves together to close the box.

BATIK
EFFECTS

Lovely batik-like effects can be
achieved on paper with wax crayons
and thin paint. Designers' inks, which
have very intense colours, can be used
for striking results.

YOU WILL NEED
White and coloured paper
Wax crayons
Assorted poster or gouache paints, or
*   designers' inks*
Clear wax candle

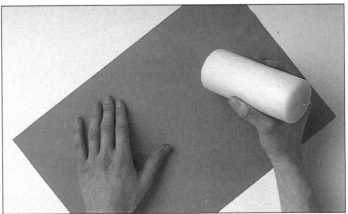

1 Draw a design
onto white paper
with wax crayons,
using either a single
colour or a variety.
Load a paint brush
with thin paint or
diluted ink and
brush it over the
wax. Two coats of
paint can be applied
to achieve a stronger
colour layer where
required.

2 To create a multi-
coloured effect
where the base
colour of the paper
will show through,
use a clear wax
candle to draw the
design onto
coloured paper.
Paint over the wax
marks with one
colour and leave to
dry. Next, make
more wax marks and
paint over the paper
again with a second
colour so that the
second set of designs
will take on the
colour of the first
layer of paint.

ABSTRACT STATIONERY

Every piece of writing paper will be different using this technique of tearing and gluing paper to create an abstract design.

YOU WILL NEED
Craft knife
Writing paper
Card in two contrasting colours
Glue

1 Using a craft knife, cut a small rectangle at the top of the writing paper, in the centre. Next, choose two pieces of different colour card just large enough to cover the opening, and tear one in half.

2 Glue one of the torn halves onto the other whole rectangle.

3 Glue this onto the back of the letter-head.

4 Instead of using a plain card, a favourite patterned wrapping paper can be put behind the opening. Different shaped openings can be cut for the effect you like. In this step some paper is glued on to card and then slotted in and glued so that it breaks up the top line of the paper.

5 Of course the plain and patterned papers can be mixed.

SPECKLING EFFECTS

Speckling produces a variety of results depending on how the paint is applied, and on how sharply the brush is shaken. Gentle taps produce fine marks, rather like freckles. More boisterous movements can produce a more startling effect.

YOU WILL NEED
A selection of papers
Assorted poster or gouache paints
Length of wood or other object to tap
*   brush against*
Nail brush
Stiff cardboard

1 Lay the sheet of paper to be speckled on a flat surface. Mix the paint to a fairly thin consistency and load a paint brush with it. Hold the length of wood over the paper and bring the brush down on the wood, tapping along its length over the paper to produce a speckled effect.

2 More than one colour of speckling can be applied; colours that tone in with the first layer of paint or even those which contrast sharply with it can look very effective. To obtain a fine spray of speckles dip a nail brush in thin paint and position it over the paper, holding it with the bristles uppermost. Pull a strip of cardboard over the bristles (taking care to pull it *towards* your body so that you do not splash yourself with paint), moving the brush around the paper to create an even coating of paint.

CURVY-EDGED BOX

This unusual box is almost as pretty in two halves as it is when assembled. To get the maximum effect choose two contrasting or complementary colours for the two halves so that the pattern of the curves stands out.

YOU WILL NEED
Thin card in two different colours
Craft knife
Glue

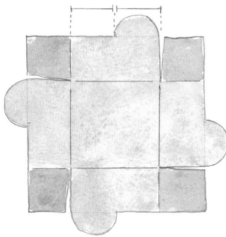

1 Scale up the template to the size required and transfer the pattern twice to a piece of card, once for each half of the box. Cut out the patterns using a craft knife, taking extra care around the curves. Both halves are made in the same way: fold and glue each tab beneath the semi-circles to form the sides.

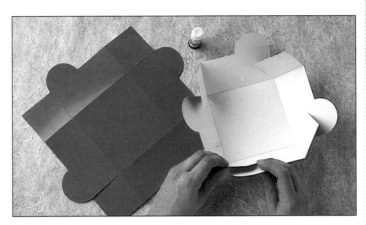

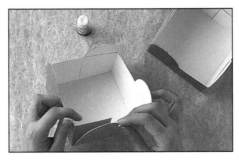

2 Repeat the process with the other half, gluing each side firmly.

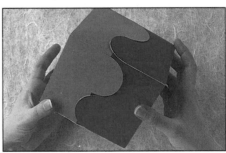

3 To assemble the box, interlock the two halves, making sure each semi-circle overlaps on the outside of the box.

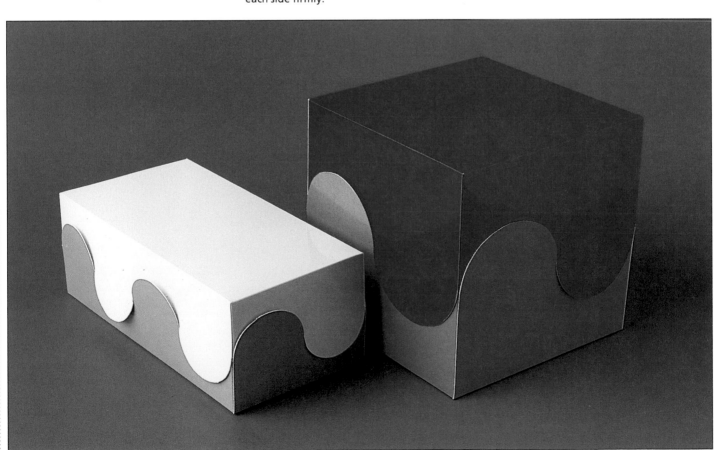

QUILLS
AND COILS

Quilling is a traditional way of rolling strips of coloured paper and then squeezing them into different shapes; they are used here to decorate cards.

YOU WILL NEED
Coloured paper
Glue
Contrasting coloured card
Hole punch
Ribbon

1 To make up the individual quills, cut strips of coloured paper 7 × 25 cm (2¾ × 10 in). Starting with one end, roll the paper up.

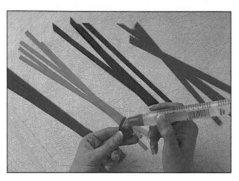

2 When you have rolled it completely, let it uncoil slightly and glue the end to hold it.

3 Once the strip has been coiled and glued it can be shaped into one of the many traditional quill styles, such as the triangle, or the pear, or the scroll or the eye.

4 Take a piece of folded card in a good background colour and arrange the quills into a pattern. Punch a hole with a hole punch and thread a ribbon through to make an original and delightful miniature card or gift tag.

BOOKLET CARD

Just a small piece of wrapping paper from your gift is enough to make this booklet card or gift tag. Secure with embroidery thread to match.

YOU WILL NEED
White card
Wrapping paper
Glue
Ruler
Craft knife
Writing paper
Needle
Embroidery thread

1 Take a piece of white card 28 × 7 cm (11 × 2¾ in) and cut out a piece of wrapping paper the same size. Glue this paper onto the card.

2 On the reverse, lightly score a line at the centre using a ruler and craft knife, and fold in two to make the outer card.

3 Then cut a piece of white writing paper so that it is just smaller than the card and fold this in two.

4 With a needle and some embroidery thread to match the wrapping paper, sew the two layers together with one stitch, and tie the threads into a knot to secure the booklet.

DECORATIVE PAPERCRAFTS

361

THIS LITTLE PIGGY

Great for children's parties or for a more adult gathering, this piggy place setting will bring oinks of delight! Choose bright pink, or a pale pink for a Miss Piggy.

YOU WILL NEED
Circular plate
Pink, green and blue card
Glue
Craft knife
Felt-tip pen

1 Place mat
▬ Using a plate as a template, mark and cut out a circle about 24 cm (10 in) in diameter in pink card, remembering to include two ear shapes.

2 Using green and blue card, cut out and glue all the features of the face into position.

3 Then attach the curly tail to the right-hand side in order to give the finishing touch to your pig place mat.

4 Name place card
▬ To make up the name card, take a piece of green card measuring 9 cm (3½ in) square. Draw a line down the centre and around the top half of the pig's head and ears. Score along the head and ears only and then gently fold, and the pig's head will stand up.

5 Glue the piggy's features as before onto a piece of pink card and then attach the finished face on to the folded card. Add the curly tail.

6 Napkin holder
▬ Take a strip of pink card measuring 22 × 5 cm (8½ × 2 in) and glue the ends together.

Before the glue has dried, slip a green curly tail card under the join and hold firmly until it is dry.

TIGER STRIPES AND
HOPPING FROGS

Here are some ideas for making writing paper with an animal theme. You can use these ideas to design original writing paper, based on your favourite animal.

YOU WILL NEED
Orange, black, blue and green paper
Glue
Writing paper

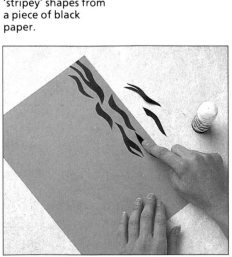

1 To make a jungle theme take a piece of orange paper and cut out 'stripey' shapes from a piece of black paper.

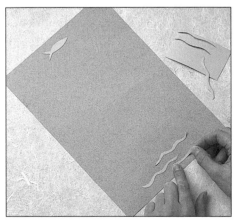

2 Arrange the tiger stripes down one side of the paper and glue them into position.
To add colour to a sheet of white writing paper you can also cut out an abstract squiggle and glue it onto the right hand side.

3 For a fishy theme cut out shapes of watery ripples and a swimming fish from blue paper and then stick them at the top and bottom of the page.

4 This hopping frog theme is made by cutting out a frog shape in green paper and fixing it to the top of the page. You will then need to cut out and glue small squares of green paper to represent its hop!

PAPER-MAKING

Paper-making is an ancient art form, practised for many centuries since the process was first discovered by the Chinese. It can be very satisfying to make your own paper. If you want to make paper of writing quality, dissolve two teaspoons of size powder in a pint of warm water and add it to your pulp. It is possible to produce many interesting effects in your paper. Small pieces of coloured paper can be added to the pulp to give a speckled effect; this can also be achieved by adding organic material such as tea leaves, seeds, hair, leaves and flower petals. It is also possible to colour and perfume your paper by adding waterproof ink or a few drops of scent to the pulp.

YOU WILL NEED
Waste paper
Blender or liquidizer
Fine sieve
Rectangular bowl
Kitchen cloths (one for each piece of paper to be made) or towelling
Newspaper
Paper-making frame (deckle and mould)
Two wooden boards

MAKING PULP

To make paper pulp, tear up waste paper into small pieces. The lighter the colour of waste paper used, the paler the result; newspaper will produce a greyish paper. Old computer printout paper is good. Place the torn paper in a bucket of warm water and let it soak overnight. To reduce the paper to a pulp, squeeze out as much water as possible, and place a small handful of the mushy paper into a blender or liquidizer, covering it with two parts of water. Blend the paper and water together for a few seconds at a time. Add more water if the pulp is too thick for the blender to rotate freely.

---

1 When you have pulped all the soaked paper, drain it through a fine sieve, and place three or four handfuls in the rectangular bowl. Cover the pulp with warm water. You will need roughly three parts of water to one part pulp.

Before you start to make your paper, prepare a 'couching mound'. This is a small pile of wet material such as kitchen cloths or towelling, cut or folded to the same size as the frame and placed on top of a thick wedge of newspaper. The pulp is transferred from the mould onto this mound to dry.

2 Take your paper-making frame. The mesh-covered frame is called the mould, and the open frame is the deckle. Position the mould mesh-side up, and place the deckle on top of it.

3 Put the frame into the far end of the bowl, with the deckle facing you.

4 Next, submerge the frame in the pulp.

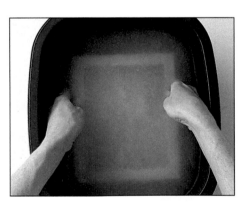

5 Pull the frame gently towards you, while holding on to keep it tightly closed and completely submerged. Lift the frame from the bowl, keeping it horizontal. Let the frame rest on the side of the bowl for a minute to drain, and then remove the deckle.

6 Stand the mould on its short side and lower it onto the couching mound, pressing it down firmly. Then lift the bottom edge off the couching cloth, and remove the frame. The pulp will stick to the cloth. Cover the pulp with an opened-out kitchen cloth, and continue couching sheets of paper, covering each new piece with another kitchen cloth.

7 When you have used all the pulp, or feel that you have made enough paper, cover the last piece with a kitchen cloth, and transfer the pile of cloths containing your paper on its couching mound and pile of newspaper onto one of the wooden boards. The board should be placed on a surface that is easy to mop dry as a great deal of water will come out of the paper.

Place the second board on top of the pile, and then stand or lean heavily on it to press the paper flat. Press on the paper for a couple of minutes.

Remove the pile of cloths from the newspaper, then gently lift the top cloth, uncovering the last piece of paper that you made, and lay it out, still on its cloth, on a flat surface to dry. Do the same with every piece of paper. The sheets may take two days to dry properly. To remove the paper from its drying cloth, slip a blunt knife under its edge and gently separate the two.

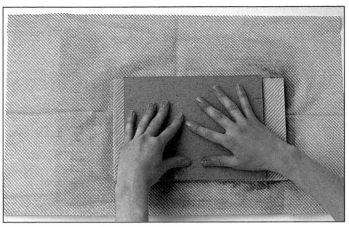

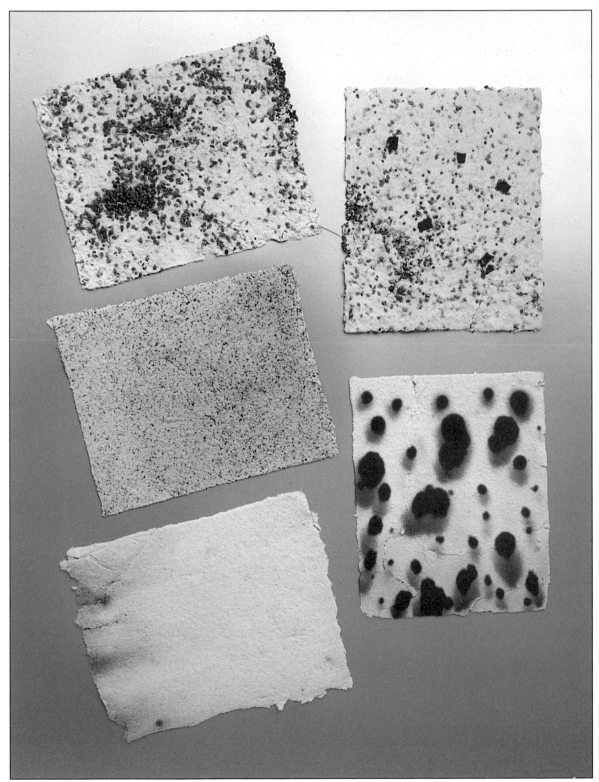

DECORATIVE SPONGING

Sponging has been used as a form of decoration for many years, especially on pottery. The process gives a pleasing mottled effect to plain surfaces, and can be very bold and dramatic; or, if you prefer, a more subtle background pattern can also be obtained.

YOU WILL NEED
Selection of poster or gouache paints
Piece of natural sponge
Paper
Newspaper

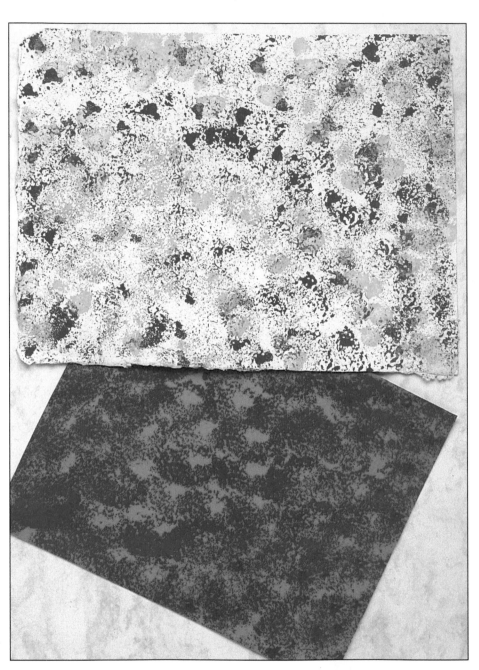

1 Mix a little paint in a saucer or on a small palette. The paint should be fairly sticky. Dip the sponge into the paint and dab it lightly over the surface of the paper, making a random pattern. If you want to be certain of the thickness of the pattern, test the density of the paint first by dabbing the sponge on newspaper.

2 To create patterns with two or more colours, wash the sponge thoroughly and squeeze it almost dry. When the first layer of sponging has dried, add more colours one by one, making sure each has time to dry before the next coat.

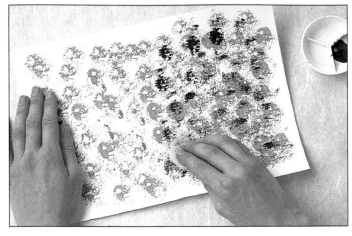

RIBBON
ROSETTES

Make gifts look extra special with ribbon rosettes that match your wrapping paper. There are many ways of making ribbons into rosettes, pom-poms or just simple bows. Choose from all the types of plain and fancy ribbons available, or make your own by cutting strips from the wrapping paper.

YOU WILL NEED
Ribbon
Double-sided tape

1 Cut eight lengths of ribbon, four 30 cm (12 in) long and the other four measuring 24 cm (9 in). Make each one into a loop by using double-sided tape.

2 Assemble the rosette by crossing two of the longer loops and taping them in the middle. Then make another cross and join to the first cross, making the bottom layer.

3 Repeat with the shorter loops and join these to the base.

4 Finish off by putting a small loop into the centre and fixing it onto your wrapped gift.

5 To make a different ribbon trim, grade the loops to start with a 30 cm (12 in) loop and make each layer smaller by 5 cm (2 in). Holding the loops in the middle, glue them one on top of the other, starting with the largest at the bottom and getting smaller to form a fan shape.

TO MY VALENTINE

This centre opening style of card can be used for any type of message. It could be to wish a Happy Christmas or just an abstract design to say Hello! Some variations are shown below.

YOU WILL NEED
Thin card in two colours
Tissue paper
Glue

1 Take a piece of card 34 × 14 cm (13½ × 5½ in). Instead of folding the card in the usual way, mark the centre of the card and fold each side to the centre point so that they meet. In another colour of card draw and cut out a heart shape. Cut the heart in half.

2 Cut out long strips of tissue paper and fold in half lengthways. Spread glue around the outer edge on the back of the heart shape and then make a frill with the tissue by gathering it up and sticking down. Finally glue both halves of the heart onto the two opening flaps of the card.

CUT-AND-THREAD PAPER

Make plain writing paper extra special with simple strips of crêpe paper threaded through in unusual patterns. Practise first on spare paper to get the right effect.

YOU WILL NEED
Sheet of writing paper
Craft knife
Crêpe paper

1 Take a sheet of writing paper and mark two sets of two vertical lines at the top, in the centre. The lines should be approximately 2 cm (¾ in) long and 2½ cm (1 in) apart. Cut through the lines using a craft knife.

2 Cut a piece of crêpe paper in a toning colour to your writing paper. Thread it under the 'bridges' taking care not to break them.

3 Once the crêpe paper is centred arrange the bow by fanning out the sides.

4 Repeat the bow design on the extended back flap of an envelope to complete the writing set.

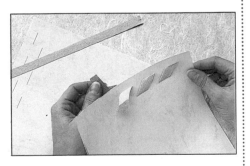

5 Another effect can be achieved by marking and cutting out a series of vertical lines across the top of the page. Cut a piece of crêpe paper the same width as the slots, and a thinner strip in a stronger colour.

6 Fold the paper in half to thread the strips through easily, and then open up.

7 Instead of using vertical lines this version uses two staggered lines of horizontal slits. Once again thread the strip of crêpe paper through and see the diagonal pattern it makes.

BLOCK PRINTING

Quite sophisticated printing blocks can be cut from potatoes, and some lovely effects are possible. To make a more permanent block, use pieces of eraser. These can be used with paint or an ink pad.

YOU WILL NEED
Potatoes
Craft knife
Erasers
Poster or gouache paints
Ink pad
Paper
Nail brush
Stiff cardboard

1 To make a potato block, first cut the potato in half, making sure that the cut surface is straight and flat so that the design will print evenly onto the paper. The design can be cut directly into the potato, or else it can be drawn first with a pencil and then carefully pared away using a craft knife. Use the same process to make blocks from erasers.

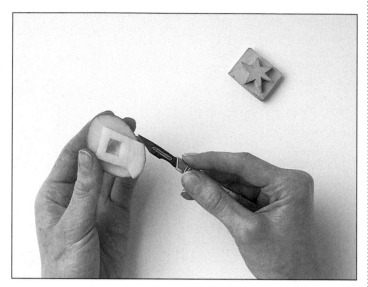

2 Mix the paint with a little water and dab it onto the surface of the block with a paint brush.

Firmly press the block onto a piece of paper and lift it up again, taking care to use a direct upwards movement to avoid smudging the printed image.

3 Rubber blocks can be used with ink pads as well as with paint.

4 Block printing can be combined with speckling in contrasting colours to create a very lively effect. Here, purple paper with a black block design is speckled using a nail brush dipped in yellow paint. Hold the brush over the paper and draw a piece of stiff cardboard over the bristles, making sure the cardboard is pulled towards the body (to avoid splashing yourself with paint!).

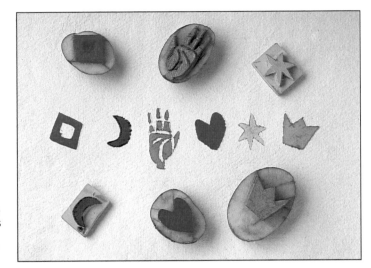

5 Cut a set of symbols into some erasers and use them on letter-heads and envelopes for a personalized look to your stationery.

DECORATIVE WALLET

Make this tidy wallet out of a favourite colour paper or piece of wrapping paper. You could even design the pattern yourself. Use the wallet to store banknotes, photographs or special letters.

YOU WILL NEED
Stiff paper or wrapping paper
Craft knife
Glue

1 Scale up the template to the size required and transfer the pattern onto the paper. Cut around the edges using a craft knife. Fold the sides inwards and glue one long edge to the other.

2 Glue the bottom flap to seal the end of the wallet, and it is ready for use.

21ST BIRTHDAY POP-UP

This unusual card is perfect for celebrating a special birthday. Once you have mastered the simple pop-up technique you could use different numbers for a variety of birthday years.

YOU WILL NEED
Craft knife
Stiff white and coloured paper
Paints
Glue

2 Next, fold a piece of stiff paper into two to form a card shape. Glue one tab to one half of the backing card, so that the bottom of the crease down the middle of '21' exactly touches the crease on the card.

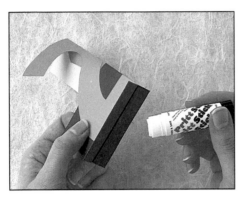

1 Scale up the '21' shape to the size required and transfer to a piece of white paper. Cut it out using a craft knife and paint the numbers. When the paint is dry, fold the '21' in half and glue the underside of each tab.

3 To finish off, apply glue to the second tab and fold the empty half of the backing card over the top of the second tab. When unfolded, the card will stick to this second tab, pulling up the '21'.

COLLAGE TAGS

When you want to keep things simple and have perhaps used a plain paper to wrap your present, a collaged gift tag can be the perfect finishing touch. They can be as easy or as complicated as you want to make them.

YOU WILL NEED
Orange card
Green paper
Glue
Coloured thread

1 For the Grecian-style tag cut out a Grecian urn and decorative dots in green paper.

2 Glue them onto a folded piece of orange card.

3 Punch a hole and thread through a length of coloured thread.

■ WRAPPING A SPHERE

A sphere-shaped present is always a difficult shape to wrap up and it can be approached in two ways. The gift can either be placed in the centre of a piece of paper which can then be gathered up into a bunch above the present and tied with ribbon, or the paper can be pleated. Alternatively, pleat the paper as here.

YOU WILL NEED
Wrapping paper
Sticky tape
Double-sided tape

1 Place the present in the centre of a square piece of paper. Make the square into a circle by rounding off the corners.

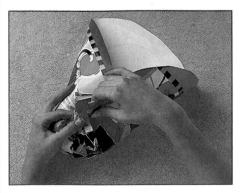

2 Start by bringing one section of the paper up to the top. Now work around the circle by pleating the paper so that it hugs the shape of the sphere. Use tape to secure the pleats as you go round.

3 Continue to pleat neatly until you have gone all the way around. To finish off the top, make a pleated fan. Take a long strip of paper and fold in half with the right side outside. Pleat the paper along its length.

4 Then, pinch the pleats together at the bottom and fan out the sides. Attach it to the present by fixing with double-sided tape.

■ PLACES ON A THEME

Simple ideas are often the most striking, and so here are some suggestions for place cards made using a collage technique, creating a theme for your table setting.

YOU WILL NEED
Two pieces of contrasting coloured
card or paper
Glue
Gold metallic pen
Metallic crêpe paper

1 Draw and cut out a snail shape from coloured paper. Glue it onto the front of a contrasting place card. Use any animal image: you could even give each person an individual animal!

2 For a Mexican theme for your table setting, cut out a cactus shape in green paper or card and stick it onto a yellow place card. Draw on small dots with a gold pen to indicate the prickles.

3 To introduce a touch of frivolity to your table, make up this jolly bow-tie card. Take a rectangle of metallic crêpe paper and fold the ends to the middle. Glue ends in place. Take a smaller strip of crêpe paper and wrap around the centre of the bow to pull into shape. Glue ends in place.

4 Finally glue the bow-tie to the top of the place card.

DECORATIVE DOILY

A circle of lightweight coloured card in a contrasting colour forms a base for this tissue paper doily and sets it off to best effect.

YOU WILL NEED
Lightweight card
Tissue paper
Glue

1 To get a good-sized doily, draw around a dinner plate and cut out two circles, one in card and the other in tissue paper.

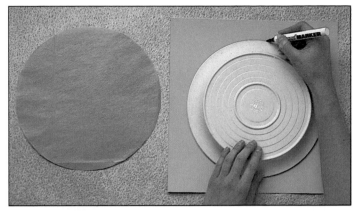

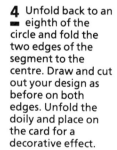

2 Fold the tissue paper in half three times to form an eighth and cut a scalloped pattern around the curved edge.

3 Fold it in half again and lightly draw a small geometric design along the edge and then cut these shapes out.

4 Unfold back to an eighth of the circle and fold the two edges of the segment to the centre. Draw and cut out your design as before on both edges. Unfold the doily and place on the card for a decorative effect.

CONE HATS

With a simple change of decoration this basic cone hat can make a clown's hat or an elegant medieval headdress fit for a lady.

YOU WILL NEED
Card
Crêpe paper
Glue
Sticky tape

1 For the basic cone you will need to cut out a 60 cm (23 in) diameter semi-circle in card. You can make this measurement larger or smaller depending on the finished size you require. Roll the semi-circle into a cone and fasten with tape or glue.

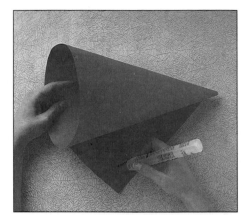

2 To make the medieval cone cut streamers of crêpe paper in three different colours and push them through the end of the hat. Secure with sticky tape on the inside.

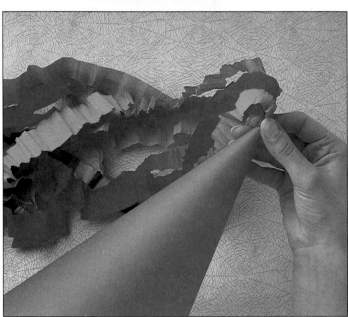

3 Now plait wider strips of the three colours of crêpe paper. Stick the plait onto the base of the cone.

4 To make the clown's hat make up pom-poms by cutting out three 20 cm (8 in) diameter circles of crêpe paper. Pinch each circle in the centre and twist. Now scrunch up the excess paper and mould it into a ball shape.

5 Push the first pom-pom through the top of the cone, then carefully make two slots one above the other down the front of the cone. Push the centre of the pom-poms through the slots and tape them on the inside to secure.

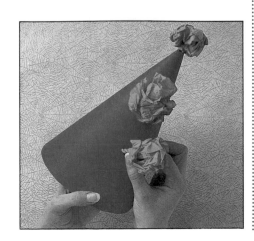

CHRISTMAS GIFT TAGS

If you want to get away from the traditionally shaped gift tag, here is an idea for making them with a stand-out effect.

YOU WILL NEED
Red and green card
Glue
Red paper

1 Take a long strip of red card and fold it so that one end is slightly longer. Draw and cut out a Christmas tree shape on a separate piece of green card.

2 Stick the tree onto the front flap and now cut away the part above the top branches so that it has a shaped top.

3 Then, glue on circles of red paper to decorate the tree.

4 Experiment by making up abstract designs in card, sticking these onto the front and then cutting around the shapes you have created.

SECRET MESSAGES

Give a sense of mystery to your gifts by adding a tag tied with a ribbon bow to conceal your message. A perfect idea for sending notes to loved ones.

YOU WILL NEED
Coloured card
Contrasting coloured paper
Gold metallic pen
Glue
Ribbon

1 Take a rectangle of card and fold in half. Open out the card and make a small narrow slit for the ribbon on the centre of both leading edges, back and front.

2 On a separate piece of black paper draw a design with a gold pen and stick this onto the card.

3 Write your message inside and then thread a length of gold ribbon through the slits and tie a bow to keep the wording a secret.

COMBING AND FEATHERING

Paint can be mixed with cellulose wallpaper paste to make a coloured 'gel' which can be used to create a variety of effects.

YOU WILL NEED
Poster or gouache paints
Large bowl
Cellulose wallpaper paste mixed according to manufacturer's instructions
Paper
Small piece of cardboard
Craft knife
Serrated pottery tools or forks

1 Feathering
■ Add a quantity of paint to the bowl of paste and mix it thoroughly until the desired colour is obtained. Test the depth of colour on a scrap of paper before you use it. Next, take two pieces of paper of the same size (trim if necessary) and, with a paint brush, coat them with a layer of coloured paste.

2 Put one piece of
■ paper on top of the other so that the pasted sides touch. Then gently pull the sheets apart, starting at one corner. This process results in a delicate feathered pattern.

3 Combing
■ To make your own combing implement take a scrap of cardboard and cut 'teeth' into one end using a craft knife. Alternatively, ready-made implements such as pottery tools and forks can be used to achieve the combing effects. First, coat a piece of coloured paper with a layer of the paste. Then draw the combing tool through the paste, leaving behind a trail. This method produces many intricate effects when a variety of tools with different size 'teeth' are used on the same sheet of paper.

LIDDED BOX

This box can be used to keep things safe – or to conceal a surprise. Make several in a variety of colours to form a set or give one to each of your friends.

YOU WILL NEED
Thin coloured card
Craft knife
Glue

1 The box and its lid are made in the same way. Scale up the template to the size required and transfer the pattern to thin coloured card. Carefully cut out the pieces using a craft knife. Fold in the side tabs to form the upright sides.

2 Next, assemble the box by applying glue to the central tabs and folding them over the sides, fixing down firmly. Repeat this process to make the lid, and slide it over the base to complete the box.

CANDY CONES

Pretty and simple ideas for arranging sweets at a wedding or party. For another alternative wrap a red ribbon upwards around a cone made from elegant wrapping paper and use matching red tissue paper inside.

YOU WILL NEED
Square of wrapping paper
Glue
Rosette
Tissue paper
Sugared almonds

1 All you need is a 20 cm (8 in) square of coloured paper in patterned or plain design. Roll the paper into a cone, starting with a corner and shaping it into a rounded form.

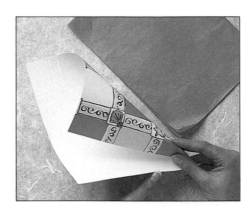

2 Glue the cone together along the edge and stick a rosette on the overlapping point. Flatten the cone at the closed end.

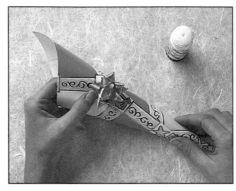

3 Scrunch up some matching tissue paper and push this into the open end. Fill with sugared almonds or candies.

DECORATIVE PAPERCRAFTS

You can vary the design of the cones, depending on the occasion, using different paper and ribbons.

YOU WILL NEED
Black and gold paper
Glue
Ribbon or bow
Tissue paper
Chocolate coins

1 For a variation, cut one square in black paper and another in gold paper. Zigzag the edges along two adjacent sides of the black square, first drawing a line about 1½ cm (¾ in) from the edge as a guideline.

2 Then glue the black paper onto the gold and roll up into a cone form, gluing along the overlapping edges.

3 Slightly flatten the end of the cone and stick on a bow or pieces of ribbon.

4 Take some tissue paper and scrunch it up and insert it into the cone. Fill with chocolate coins.

ACROSS THE BORDER

By making the back half of this card slightly wider than the front it enables you to decorate the created border in many ways.

YOU WILL NEED
Assorted coloured paper or card
Silver metallic pen
Glue
Felt-tip pens
Tissue paper

1 To make the basic card fold a rectangle in two so that the top side is slightly shorter than the back.

2 Now shape the front fold by cutting a zigzag border.

3 Stick a contrasting coloured card behind to make the serrated edge stand out.

4 Alternatively, cut out a wavy edge on the front side and then decorate it with a silver line following the curved line. To finish the decoration draw a row of whirls.

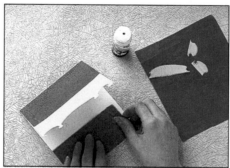

5 This version is slightly more complicated. Take a piece of bright card and fold into the basic shape, then glue a panel of contrasting wrapping paper onto the front. When it is fixed, trim at the sides and then draw an arch and bauble design onto the leading edge. Cut out the arch and bauble shape.

6 On the inside of the card glue down a panel of contrasting tissue paper.

7 Cut further small circles in the tissue paper and glue them along the border.

SPOT-ON NAPKINS

This is a quick and bright way to decorate your paper napkins for children's parties or a special theme dinner. The basic idea is to split the layers of two different coloured napkins, then join them together and cut out shapes in one colour in order to reveal the other.

YOU WILL NEED
Two packets of contrasting coloured paper napkins
Glue

1 Take two paper napkins of different colours. Here a light and a dark colour are used. They should be the same size and preferably the same make so that they fit together exactly. Most napkins are three-ply (three layers). Start by splitting them so that you are working with two layers of each colour. The reason for this is so that the finished napkin is not too thick.

2 Fold the lighter coloured napkin diagonally and cut into two.

3 Carefully glue one half onto the darker napkin. Cut out light-coloured spots from the other half and glue them onto the dark triangle.

4 Now cut out spots from another dark napkin and glue these to the lighter triangle.

GIFT BAG

This gift bag is simple to make and adds a touch of elegance to any present. It can be used instead of separate wrapping paper and is sturdy enough to hold a variety of gifts.

YOU WILL NEED
Decorated paper
Craft knife
Glue
Hole punch
Ribbon

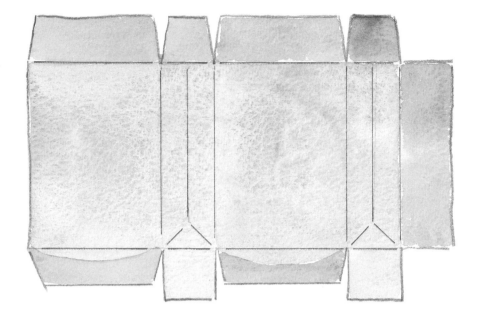

1 Scale up the template to the size required and transfer the pattern onto the decorated paper. Cut out carefully using a craft knife. Score lightly along the back of the creases so that they will fold more easily. Fold down and glue the flaps along the *top* edge of the bag.

2 Next, glue the long, side tab to form the bag shape.

3 Then glue the base of the bag, folding in the short end tabs first.

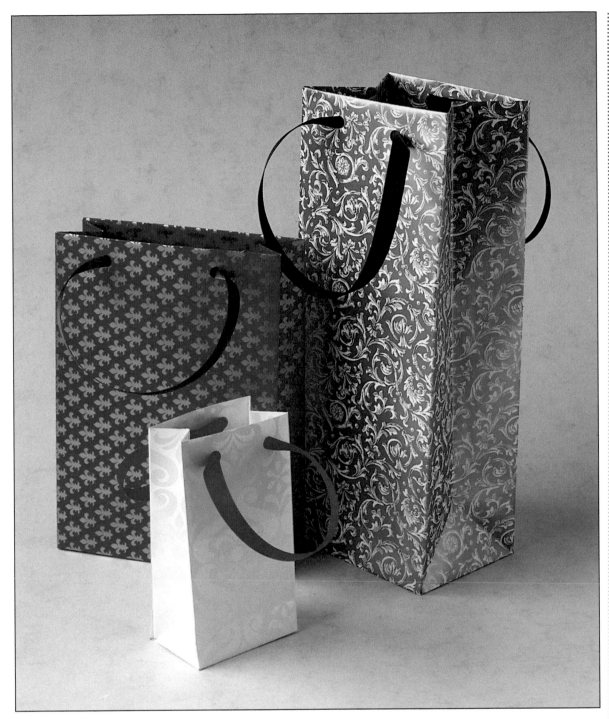

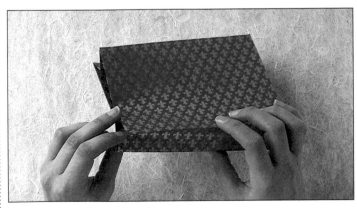

4 Form the pleats down the sides of the bag by pressing the long edges together gently so that the paper is pushed inwards.

5 Using the hole punch, make two holes on each of the top sides near the upper edge. Cut two short lengths of ribbon and thread each end through the holes to make two looped handles. Knot the ends at the back of the holes to secure.

STENCIL STYLE

Use ready-made or cut your own stencils to make this stylish writing paper. Dab on stencil paints or colour with soft crayons for speedy results.

YOU WILL NEED
Stencilling card
Craft knife
Paint
Stencil brush
Writing paper
Crayon

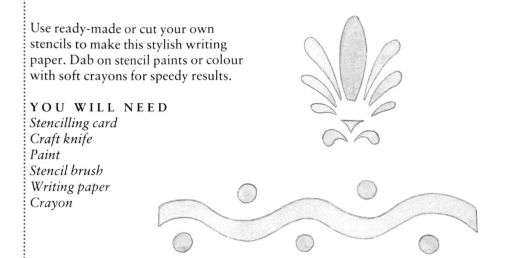

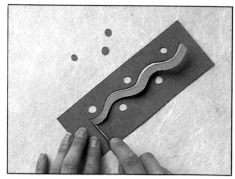

1 Using the template transfer the motif onto stencilling card in the size you require and cut out using a craft knife.

2 Prepare the paint on a saucer and collect the colour onto a stencil brush. Then, holding the stencilling card firmly with one hand, use the other to dab the brush onto the writing paper using a circular movement.

3 Instead of using paint, a coloured crayon could be used. Once again hold the stencilling card firmly in one hand and lightly fill in the pattern, remembering to work the crayon strokes in the same direction each time.

PLACES PLEASE!

Here is a selection of attractive name cards for the table, using a technique of slotting decorative paper shapes through the card to create an interesting three-dimensional effect. Experiment with your own ideas!

YOU WILL NEED
Black, orange and white card
Craft knife
Red, orange and green paper
Sticky tape
Wrapping paper
Glue
Crêpe paper
Gold metallic pen

1 First, fold a piece of black card, 13 × 10 cm (5 × 4 in) in half lengthways. Open out again and place flat. On the bottom half of the card, cut two short lines just above each other in the top left hand corner area, using a craft knife. Then, cut out flame shapes in red and orange paper.

2 Push the flame shapes through the slots, from the back to the front of the card, and arrange so that they extend at varying angles and lengths.

3 Turn the card over, and secure the ends on the back with sticky tape.

4 For this fishy collage card, make an orange card and glue on a green fish. Cut a slot at the bottom of the card. Cut wavy strips of green paper for weeds, and push them up through the slot and arrange. Secure on the back as before.

5 As a decorative alternative, you could cover the card with patterned wrapping paper. Fold the card in half, then cut a long slot in the top edge of the front side. Cut two lengths of crêpe paper twice as long as the slot and fold up to make a frill, a little longer than the slot. Push the frills through the slot. Secure at the back with tape as before. To complete, stick a small piece of white card in the centre, and decorate with a gold pen.

NOTELET HOLDER

Take an ordinary writing pad and envelopes and dress them up in a special notelet holder. All kinds of versions are possible, made from decorative papers and cards.

YOU WILL NEED
Writing paper and envelopes
Card
Glue
Brown paper or wrapping paper
Gold metallic pen
String
2 paper fasteners

1 To make the notelet holder use one of the envelopes to determine the size, and cut a piece of card, measuring the length of the envelope and adding 8 cm (3 in), by three times the height of the envelope plus 8 cm (3 in).

2 Cut out the card with or without the pointed flap according to the finished style that you require.

3 Apply glue to the unmarked side of the cut out card, and then cover in brown paper, trimming the edges where necessary. In this example the paper covering is decorated by hand, but you could use a favourite wrapping paper or a piece of wallpaper.

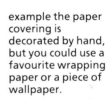

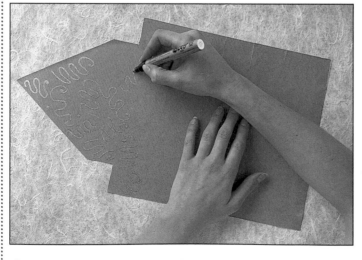

4 Taking a gold pen draw a design onto the brown paper.

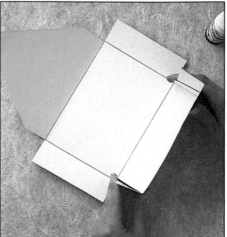
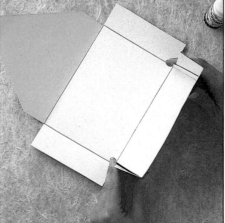

5 On the inside, score along the marked lines and cut the tab lines.

7 Decorate the brown paper with the gold pen as before. Fold the paper in half and pop the six notelets and envelopes into the notelet holder.

6 To make the notelets take six sheets of paper from the writing pad and glue a piece of brown paper or wrapping paper onto each sheet of writing paper. Trim to size.

8 Now fold and glue the notelet holder together. To make the closure push the fasteners through the paper at the point of envelope flap and in the front of the box to one side of the flap. Secure the case with a loop of string round the fasteners.

CONCENTRIC TWIST

Hang this impressive paper sculpture in a window; if it is made from metallic-coated card it will catch the light as it moves gently in the air currents.

YOU WILL NEED
Thin coloured card
Craft knife

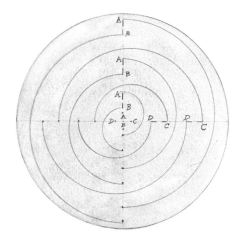

1 Scale up the template to the required size and transfer to coloured card. Cut the slits using a craft knife. Gently twist the central circle away from its frame.

2 Starting at the rim, form the first twist again by gently turning the central section at an angle of 90 degrees to the outer ring.

3 Continue to form the twists by turning each ring at the same angle, moving progressively towards the centre, until the twist-out is complete.

3-D CHRISTMAS TREE

Make a paper Christmas tree stand out by adding extra layers. Smother it with self-adhesive stars for a quick and easy decorative touch.

YOU WILL NEED
Coloured card in three colours
Glue
Self-adhesive stars
Ribbon

1 Cut out three Christmas tree shapes, in three different colours, so that they are gradually smaller in size.

2 Now cut twelve small squares of card and glue six of them together one on top of the other to make a block. Glue the other six in the same way. Glue one card block onto the top of the largest tree and the second one onto the middle-sized tree.

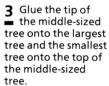

3 Glue the tip of the middle-sized tree onto the largest tree and the smallest tree onto the top of the middle-sized tree.

4 Now decorate all three trees with sticky stars. Attach a ribbon at the back so that it can be hung up to be displayed.

ABSTRACT POP-UP

This stunning pop-up sculpture is always impressive. Once you have mastered the basic technique you can start to experiment with your own designs.

YOU WILL NEED
Sheet of stiff paper
Metal rule
Craft knife
Sharp blade

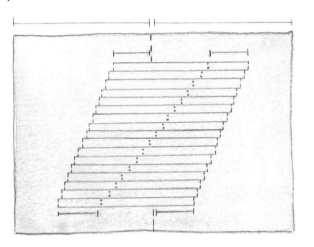

1 Scale up the template to the size required and transfer onto the paper. Place a metal rule or other strong, straight edge along each strip and cut through each line with a craft knife.

2 Next, score along all the short creases with a scissor blade or similar implement, taking care not to cut right through the paper.

3 Take the piece of paper in both hands and very carefully begin to bend the pop-up in half. The strips of paper should begin to bend outwards but remain parallel to each other.

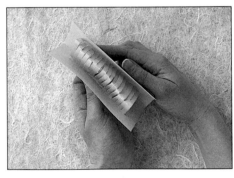

4 Close the two sides of the sheet of paper, ensuring that all the strands are lying side by side, folded evenly.

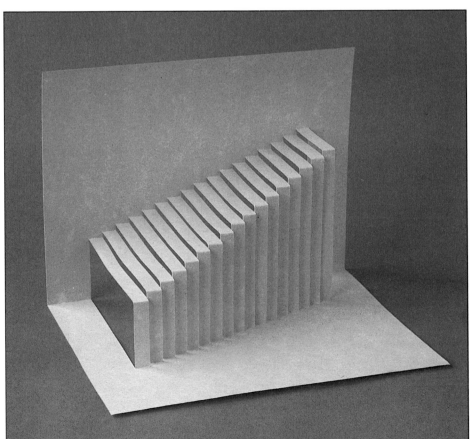

5 Lay the paper flat and, using gentle pressure, push down on all the creases to strengthen them. Open out the card and watch the design appear.

PRACTICAL ENVELOPE

Home-made envelopes can be cheaper and a lot more fun than shop-bought ones. Make a set from a variety of different papers, both plain and patterned. In order to write the address on a patterned paper simply add a little white label.

YOU WILL NEED
Stiff paper
Glue

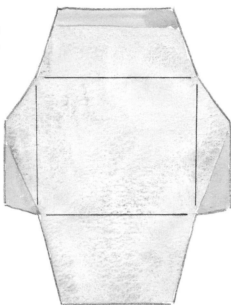

1 Scale up the template to the size required and transfer to the stiff paper. Using a scissor blade, gently score along the back of the creases that are to be folded. Next, fold in the side flaps.

2 Glue the bottom flap to the side flaps to form the envelope. Pop in your letter or card, seal with a dab of glue and send it off!

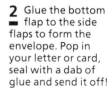

RING THE CHANGES

Using small pieces of coloured card you can create several different eyecatching napkin rings. Add contrasting coloured motifs, or simply cut and slot them into interesting shapes.

YOU WILL NEED
Coloured card
Contrasting coloured paper
Glue

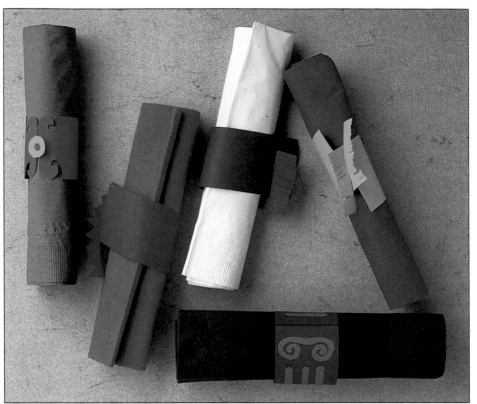

1 Take a plain band of card measuring 15 × 5 cm (6 × 2 in). For the classical column design cut out the 'capital' and 'flutes' from contrasting colour paper and stick them onto the plain strip.

2 When the strip has been decorated, dab some glue onto one end and bring the other end around to join. Hold the ends in place until the glue has dried.

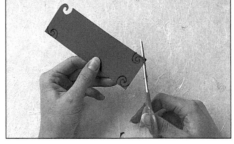

3 For the blue napkin ring, shape the ends by drawing and cutting out a design, so that when the ends are brought together the band looks more interesting.

5 For the asymmetrical rings, take a strip the same size as before and cut a 4 cm (1¼ in) slot, 1 cm (⅜ in) in from the end and parallel to it. Repeat the same on the other end but making sure that the slot is cut from the opposite edge.

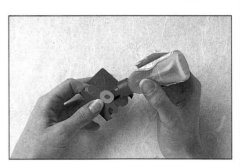

4 To finish off add a contrasting colour circle with a blue dot in the centre.

6 Now cut the ends and interlink the slots so that they hold together. Decorate the ends by fringing or cutting triangles in them. By varying the size of the darts you can experiment with different effects.

BOW-TIE
GIFTWRAP

Here is an interesting way to present
your gifts by making your own three-
dimensional bow-tie wrapping paper.

YOU WILL NEED
*Crêpe paper in two or three contrasting
colours*
Double-sided tape or glue

1 First wrap your
gift in a plain
crêpe paper. To
make the bows, cut
out 5 cm (2 in) wide
strips of contrasting
crêpe paper and
then cut them into 6
cm (2½ in) lengths.

2 Gather each piece
in the middle and
then twist to make
the bow shape.

3 Now attach the
bows to the
wrapped gift either
with double-sided
tape or some glue.

4 To make your
present really
stand out, make up
the bows in two
different colours
twisted together.

CUT-OUT STATIONERY

A fleur-de-lys motif is used for this writing paper cut-out, but you could choose a simple heart shape or your initial as decoration.

YOU WILL NEED
Plain writing paper
Craft knife
Contrasting coloured paper
Glue

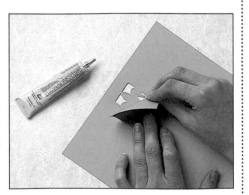

1 Scale the motif from the template up or down to the required size or design your own and transfer it onto the centre of the top of the writing paper.

2 Carefully cut out the background area with a craft knife. Using a pair of scissors cut out a small rectangle of a different coloured card just larger than the motif.

3 Turn the writing paper over, glue around the opening and then stick down the contrasting coloured card. Turn the paper back again and see how the motif stands out.

TEARING HURRY

Using pieces of torn paper to create an abstract design, these cards are unusual and unique! Experiment with colours and cards for the best effect.

YOU WILL NEED
Envelope
Card
Ruler
Craft knife
Paper scraps
Glue

1 Using the size of an envelope as a guide, cut out a piece of complementary card three times as wide. Divide and mark the card into three equal parts. In the central panel cut out an opening with a ruler and a craft knife to create the frame.

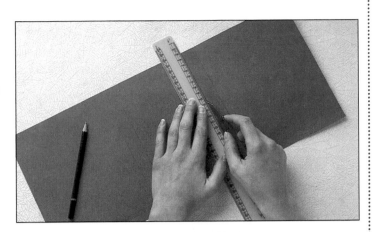

2 Tear up pieces of paper into similarly-sized, irregular shapes and start to arrange them on the left hand panel.

3 Once you are happy with the arrangement of the collage pieces they can be glued into position. Complete the card by gluing around the frame in the centre panel and sticking it down over the artwork. Fold the blank sheet round to form the card shape and add your message.

DESK TIDY

Simple boxes can be used for many purposes; this one is ideal for keeping all those essential bits and pieces in one place on a desk.

YOU WILL NEED
Thin card
Craft knife
Glue

1 Scale up the pattern to the size required. Transfer onto a piece of thin card and cut it out using a craft knife. First of all fold in the side tabs.

2 Next, 'lock' the box by applying glue to the central tab and folding it over the side tabs, sticking it down firmly. Fill the box with pencils, pens and ink or other useful items.

ANTIQUE MARBLING

There are several methods of marbling paper to achieve the beautiful effects seen on old bookbinding and traditional Italian stationery. The process involves suspending pigment on top of water, arranging the colour into patterns, and transferring these to paper.

YOU WILL NEED
Metal roasting pan or deep tray
Paper
Oil paints in various colours
White spirit
Paint brush or metal skewer

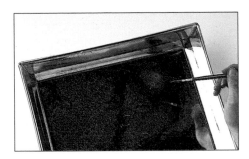

1 Half fill a clean metal roasting pan or a deep tray with cold water. Cut a piece of paper to fit the size of the tray. Thin a little oil paint with white spirit, and dot the diluted paint onto the surface of the water with a brush.

2 The paint will disperse, creating patterns on the surface of the water. Hold the paper by the top right- and bottom left-hand corners and lower it across the surface of the water in a rolling movement.

3 Carefully lift the paper from the tray. The paint will adhere to the paper, giving a marbled effect. Lay the sheets out to dry at room temperature.

4 To create multi-coloured patterns add two or more colours of oil paint to the surface of the water. Use the end of a paint brush or a metal skewer to move the colours around before laying the paper down on the water. Before marbling subsequent pieces of paper, skim the surface of the water with scrap paper to pick up excess paint and keep the water clean.

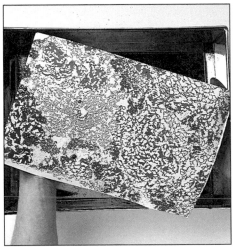

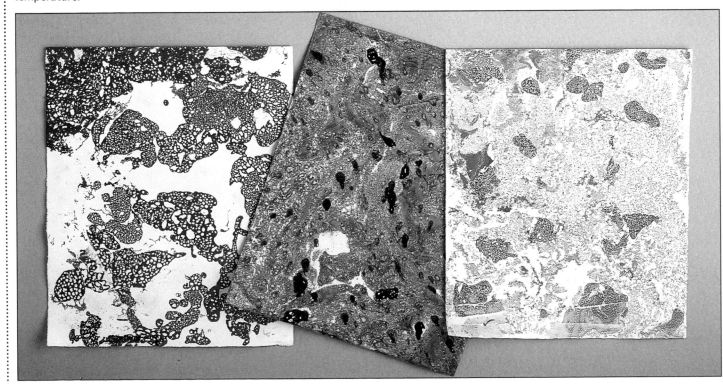

ONE-PIECE GIFT BOXES

This box is constructed from a single piece of card and can be closed tightly, making it an ideal container, either vertical or horizontal, for sweets or small biscuits.

YOU WILL NEED
Thin card
Craft knife
Glue

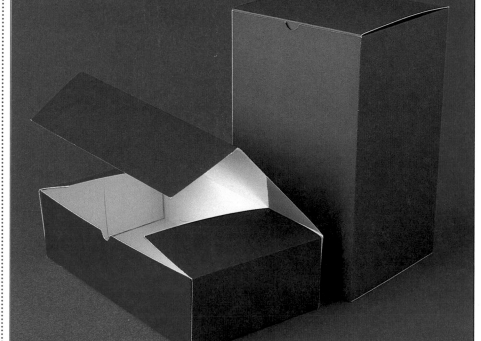

Vertical version

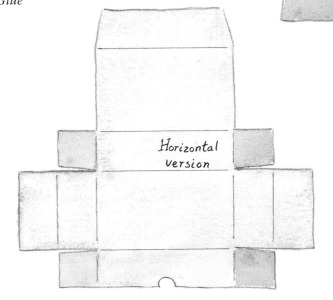

Horizontal version

1 Scale up the template to the size required, and transfer it to the card. Cut it out using a craft knife. Score along the back folds of the tabs. Fold up the sides of the box and glue the end tab to make a tube shape.

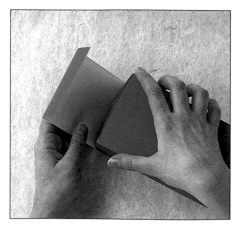

2 Interlock the tabs at the base of the box and the base should lock securely without glue.

VALENTINE'S HEART

This pop-up surprise will add a touch of fun to Valentine's Day. The same technique can be used to make cards for other occasions, such as a tree for Christmas time, or a house for a friend's moving day.

YOU WILL NEED
Stiff paper in two different colours
Glue

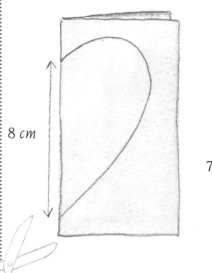
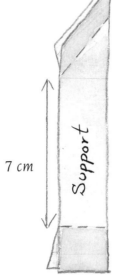

8 cm

7 cm

Support

1 Scale up the support from the template to the required size and cut out of a piece of stiff paper. Then fold a matching piece of paper into two halves to form a card. Fold the support to the correct shape, creasing the tabs upwards.

2 Next, glue the support to the backing card near the top, ensuring that the crease on the support exactly touches the crease on the card. Note that the support is symmetrically placed over the crease.

3 Cut out a heart shape in red paper and glue it to the tabs at the top of the support. Decorate the inside border of the card to match. When the card is opened the heart will spring out and surprise the recipient!

EGYPTIAN EVENING

Ancient Egypt is the inspiration for this exotic place setting of place mat, napkin holder and name card embellished in bronze and gold.

YOU WILL NEED
Thin card
Bronze, black and blue paper
Glue
Gold metallic pen
Black felt-tip pen (optional)
Sticky tape

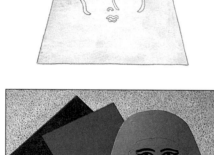

1 Place mat
■ In order to make up this place mat, cut out a piece of card in the shape of a Pharoah's head which should measure 30 cm (12 in) across the bottom and have a height of 27 cm (11 in). Cover the card in bronze coloured paper and, in the centre area, very lightly mark out the shape of the face in pencil. Cut the beard out of black paper, glue in place, and then make a criss-cross design on it with a gold pen. Scale up to the size required the features of the face from the template and cut out of black paper and glue into position or use a black felt-tip pen to draw them in.

2 Cut strips of blue paper 2 cm (¾ in) wide for the headdress decoration and start to glue them in parallel lines onto the bronze card. The strips at the top of the head are slightly curved. Add blue dots for the earrings.

3 Napkin holder
■ To make the Egyptian napkin holder, first cut out an 18 cm (7 in) square of card. Cover one side in bronze paper and the other side in black paper. Fold up one side not quite half-way, with the bronze side inside, and add blue strips, fanning them out as shown. Trim the strips level with the edge of card. Cut out an Egyptian eye motif in bronze paper and fix it onto the front.

4 Name place card
■ Cut out two triangles in card. Cover one side in black paper. Join them at the top by cutting off the top corner and taping them together at the back. Cut out a bronze motif, glue on the front then use a gold pen to write on the names required.

BROWN PAPER STATIONERY

Sometimes you need very little to make a good impression. For this project recycled brown paper is used to decorate the sheets of writing paper.

YOU WILL NEED
Brown paper
Plain writing paper
Glue
Gold metallic pen
Black felt-tip pen

1 For the first idea, tear a thin strip of the brown paper and glue it down, either on the right-hand side of the page or across the top as illustrated.

2 Then take a gold pen and draw a design along the strip. Remember that you can invent your own designs.

3 As an alternative suggestion, stick down pieces of brown paper to make two corner strips. Take the gold pen, draw in a design and then give it a three-dimensional effect by outlining it in a black felt-tip pen.

4 Another variation on the same theme is to tear a wider strip of brown paper and then tear it into four squares. Glue these down at the top of the paper and then decorate with black spots using a felt-tip pen.

FLOWER POWER

A simple idea for a get well or Mother's Day card. As an alternative, choose yellow backing paper for a birthday design.

YOU WILL NEED
Thin card in three colours
Craft knife
Glue

1 Take a rectangle of card and fold it in half. Draw the 'daisy' pattern onto one half of the card and with the card opened out flat cut out the shapes using a craft knife.

2 Cut a piece of pink card to the same size as the folded card. On the inside of the main card spread glue around the cut-out areas and place over the pink card.

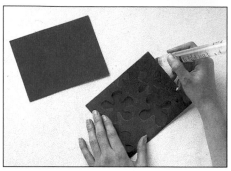

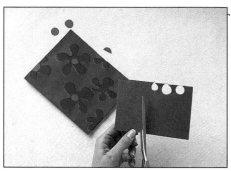

3 Cut out orange circles from the remaining card and glue in place to make the centres of the daisies.

DECORATIVE PAPERCRAFTS

FRUIT 'N' VEG

Here is a fruity number that makes a collection of fun gift tags. These are just a few ideas from the wide variety of interesting shapes that can be found in fruit and vegetables, such as peas and bananas.

YOU WILL NEED
Orange, green and yellow card
Sticky tape
Coloured felt-tip pens

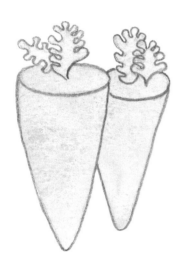

1 For a carrot gift tag scale up the template and transfer to the orange card. Cut out the pair of carrots, making sure that the top is not cut in order to leave the fold intact. Now cut out some greenery.

2 Open out the card and cut two slots with a craft knife at the top of the carrots.

3 Next, push the greenery through the slots and secure on the back with some tape.

4 The last stage is to draw the shading marks onto the carrot with a brown felt-tip pen.

BEAUTIFUL BINDING

If you have an old book or album and want to brighten them up you can learn how to cover your own pages. For this project you will need to determine the size of your book. If you are making a photograph album, for instance, the size will be determined by the album pages.

YOU WILL NEED
Book or photograph album
Thick card
Adhesive cloth tape
Patterned and plain wrapping paper
Glue
Hole punch
Ribbon

1 First cut two pieces of thick card that are about 1 cm (½ in) wider and longer than the pages to be covered. If you are covering a loose-leaf album, measure the side strip of the album sheet which has the holes punched in it, and mark the same amount onto the top of one of the cards, which will eventually be the top cover. Cut a small strip off one side of this.

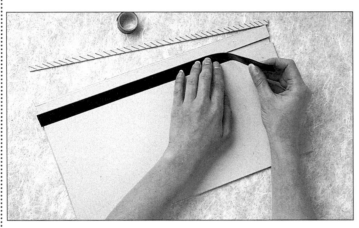

2 Using the other back card as a measure, place the trimmed top card onto it and put the narrow strip above so that there is a gap between them where the strip has been removed. Tape the pieces together using adhesive cloth tape. Turn the block over and put another piece of the cloth tape onto the other side. This will make the hinge for the top cover.

3 Now glue on a decorative paper to cover the outsides. A toning or contrasting plain colour is used to cover the inside.

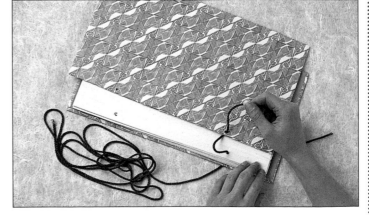

4 Next lay an album or page sheet on to the bottom cover and draw where the holes are onto it. Punch them through using a hole punch. Repeat the process with the front cover.

5 Now place the pages onto the back cover so that the holes are aligned and put the front cover on top. To finish off, thread a good quality ribbon through the holes.

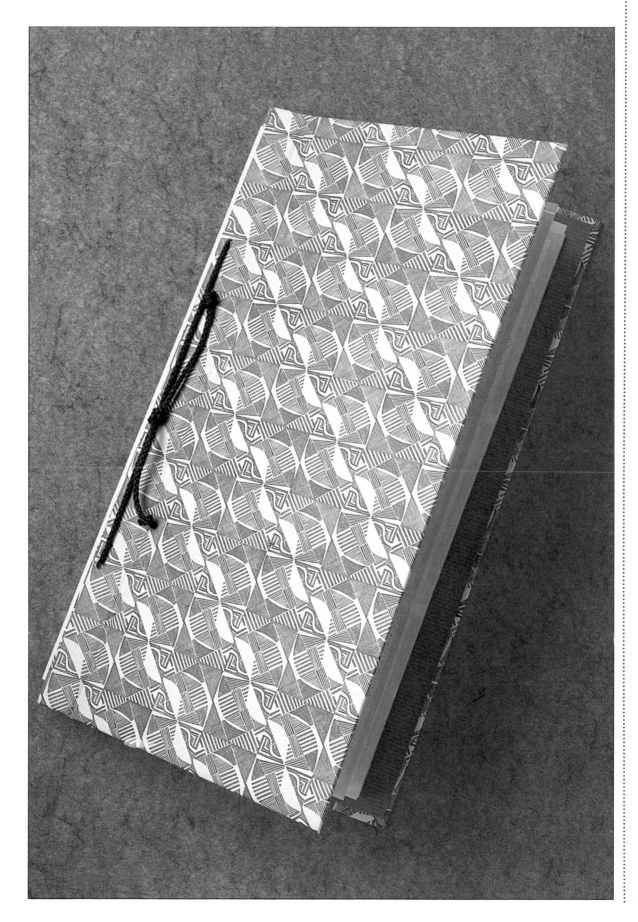

MARBLED TAGS

Inevitably, after wrapping presents with marbled or decorated paper, there are small scraps left over that are too large to justify throwing away. Matching gift tags will make good use of these scraps as well as brightening up your present even further. You could even make them into a collection of ten gift tags and present them as a gift for a friend.

YOU WILL NEED
Marbled wrapping paper
Contrasting coloured card
Glue
Ribbon

 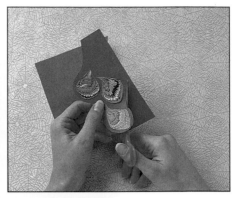

1 First of all cut out some interesting shapes from the left-over marbled paper.

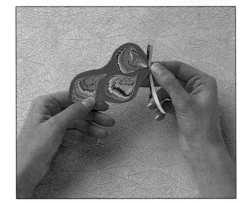

2 Then choose some contrasting coloured card which will bring out the beautiful colours in the marbelling. Glue the marbled motif onto the card and trim the card to suit the shape of the motif.

3 Make a hole in the tag to thread some ribbon through.

■ STAND-UP PLACE NAMES

Make your place cards really stand out with these novelty motifs that project above the cards. Choose simple, recognizable shapes cut out from contrasting coloured card.

YOU WILL NEED
Green, orange, red and white card
Glue
Gold metallic pen
Craft knife

1 Take a square of green card and fold in half. Cut out an octopus shape from orange card but instead of gluing it directly onto the green card, position it so that the top half is above the fold line. Cut out the facial features from the green card and glue in place.

2 For a festive name place, cut out two holly leaves in green. Fix them onto the top of a red place card so that the holly is sticking upwards. Cut out and glue on red dots to make the berries.

3 To make this rocket name card, fold then unfold the name card and lay flat. Draw on the spaceship shape onto the lower half with gold pen so that the top of the rocket extends over the halfway line. With a craft knife, cut around the top part of the rocket only. Then fold the card in half again and the rocket will stand up.

LOCKING BAG

This bag has a flap which 'locks', keeping the contents safe inside. Choose a favourite paper or decorate plain paper with your own design.

YOU WILL NEED
Decorated paper
Craft knife
Glue

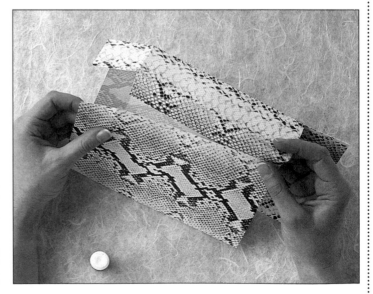

1 Scale up the template to the size required and transfer it to the decorated paper.

Cut out the shape using a craft knife. Score along the back edges of the creases to allow them to

fold more easily. Fold down and glue all flaps along the *top* edge except for the lid flap.

2 Next, glue the end tab to form the bag shape.

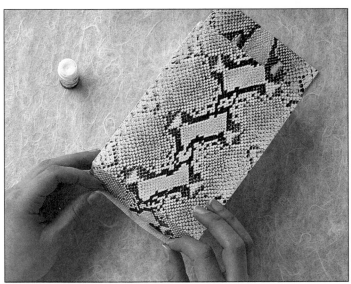

3 Glue the base of the bag, folding in the short end tabs first.

4 Form the pleats down the short sides of the bag by gently pressing the long edges together so that the paper inbetween is pushed inwards. Close the top by folding the excess tab down into the *front* half of each pleat.

SCULPTURED TOPS

For this style of card it is best to have a tall image so that the majority of the folded card remains intact and is able to stand up. A palm tree card is described here, but you could use similar techniques to create the architectural variations shown.

YOU WILL NEED
Assorted coloured card
Orange and brown
*   paper*
Glue

1 Take a square of coloured card and fold in half. Draw out the shape of the palm tree leaves on the front and cut out the uppermost ones through both layers.

2 Then cut out coconuts from orange and brown paper and stick them onto the card at the base of the leaves.

3 Draw a tree trunk shape on light green card and cut out. Cut a zigzag edge along one side and glue this onto the card.

ENVELOPE LETTERS

There is no need for an envelope if you make this clever stationery that folds up like a notelet. Seal it with a sequin and pop it in the post.

YOU WILL NEED
Sheet of writing paper
Glue
Sequin
Double-sided tape

1 Fold a sheet of writing paper into three parts so that the top third is slightly smaller than the others.

2 On the top fold draw a line from the centre to each corner to make an envelope flap and then cut off the corner triangles.

3 To decorate the top, glue a sequin at the point. A piece of gold, metallic or shiny card would work as well.

4 Just under the flap attach a small piece of double-sided sticky tape and then draw in address lines on the reverse.

5 There are lots of different ways to decorate the envelope letter. You can glue on strips of contrasting coloured paper so that when the paper is folded up it looks like a present.

BEETLE STATIONERY

Hunt through nineteenth-century
natural history books for engravings
of weird and wonderful beetles,
which you can use to decorate a
matching set of greetings cards,
envelopes, gift tags and postcards.

YOU WILL NEED
Thin card and writing paper in
  various colours and white
Craft knife
Ruler
Cutting mat
Ready-made envelopes
Scissors
Hole punch
Photocopies of beetles
Matt gold paper
Glue
Gold cord

1 For postcards, use
a craft knife and
ruler to cut the
coloured card to a
suitable size.
Measure your
envelopes and cut
the greetings cards
to fit neatly inside
when folded. Score
down the centre
with the blunt edge
of the scissors. You
can use the offcuts
for gift tags,
punching a single
hole in the top.

2 Cut round the
beetle motifs
with the craft knife
and ruler, making
neat rectangles.

Tear squares and
rectangles of various
sizes from the
coloured card and
gold paper.

3 Arrange the
beetle shapes in a
pleasing design on
the paper or card.
Stick each piece
down with glue.
Make sure the glue
reaches right to the
edges so that they
don't curl up. Stick

single motifs on the
flaps of the
envelopes and at
the top of the
writing paper. To
complete the tags,
thread a length of
gold cord through
each hole.

DECORATIVE PAPERCRAFTS

RECYCLED LOOK

There is a huge variety of rough-textured, hand-made papers and cards around, many imported from the East and made from unusual exotic plants. Some have visible fibres, flowers or leaves and others are finer, with embossed textures applied to them.

YOU WILL NEED
Selection of tissue paper scraps
Scissors
3 contrasting sheets of hand-made textured paper
PVA (white) glue
Hole punch
Coarse string
Corrugated black card
Eyelets
Raffia

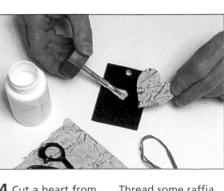

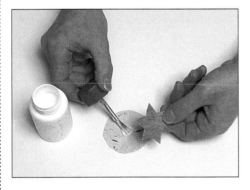

1 For a star tag, draw a star and cut the shape from tissue paper. Cut a hand-made paper disc, spread it lightly with PVA glue and press the star on to it.

2 Cut a square to give a 1cm (½in) border to the disc, from contrasting hand-made paper. Punch a hole in one corner and thread it with coarse string. Tie a knot and untwist the end to make a tassle.

3 To make a heart and bow, cut a rectangle from the black corrugated card and fix an eyelet in the centre at one end.

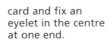

4 Cut a heart from textured paper, glue it, point down, at the other end of the rectangle. Thread some raffia through the eyelet and tie a neat bow that rests just above the heart.

Paper projects

The projects shown in this chapter share a degree of levity and are all extremely easy and cheap to make. Many of the projects are ideally suited for once-only use by children and could be suitable for parties. Some of the extremely simple cut-out items, such as the various flat masks, the crown and the wonderful stand up cut-out dolls and finger puppets are great fun. Slightly more intricate projects, requiring a little more skill and effort to construct, include card boxes and containers, colourful crackers, paper flowers, Christmas tree decorations, a smart letter rack, a handsome pencil holder, picture frames, various mobiles and even a kite that can be flown. There are also more ambitious projects showing how to make simple decorative plaques for walls and unusual window hangings that resemble stained glass designs when they are placed in front of a window pane.

Among the several papier-mâché projects are ideas for making beads, rings and bangles, puppets, animals and decorative bowls. Any of these can be altered to make different designs using the same techniques. The idea for the papier-mâché pear, for instance, could be extended to fill an entire bowl with luscious looking fruit. This section is packed with ideas you will find hard to resist.

TIGER, TIGER

Dress up as a big cat with this colourful tiger mask that will set the scene for a jungle theme party.

YOU WILL NEED

Orange card
Black felt-tip pen
Black ribbon
Craft knife
Sticky tape
Sewing needle
Elastic

3 For the whiskers cut thin strips of black ribbon about 12 × ½ cm (5 × ¼ in). Using a craft knife make four small slots on either side of the nose.

4 Push the whisker strips through the slots and use tape on the back to secure them.

1 Use the template, scaled up to size required, and cut out the tiger mask in some bright orange card.

2 Now draw on the tiger stripes with a black felt-tip pen.

5 Now sew on some elastic to either side of the mask and adjust to fit.

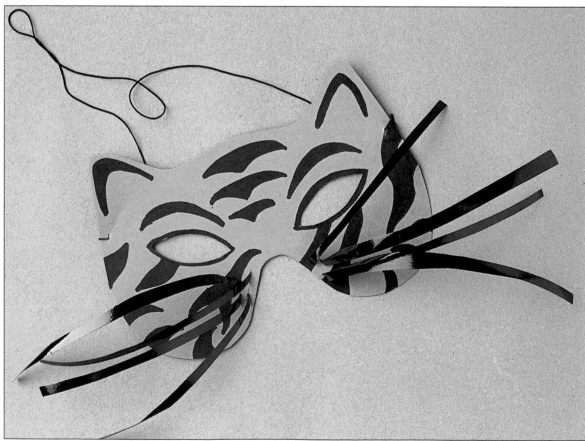

■ EASTER EGG BASKET

Make Easter egg-stra special by giving this pretty gift-wrapped basket of eggs. Choose daffodil yellow card and tissue, or bright pink as here.

YOU WILL NEED
Old bowl-shaped container
Coloured card
Glue
Metallic tissue paper
Pink tissue paper
Pink ribbon
Chocolate eggs

1 Cut a strip of card large enough to go around the bowl and just a bit deeper. Then cut a wavy line along the top edge.

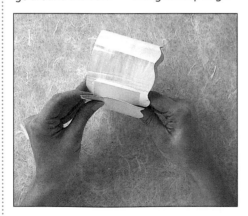

2 Glue the strip onto the bowl.

3 Now take a square of metallic tissue paper and place it in the bottom of the bowl.

4 Scrunch up a large sheet of bright pink tissue paper and arrange it in the bottom of the bowl. Place the chocolate eggs inside on the pink tissue paper. Bring the metallic tissue paper around and tie together with some pink ribbon.

CHOCOLATE BOX

This box is quick and easy to assemble. It needs only a spot of glue and a few tucks. Fill it with chocolates or homemade truffles for the perfect gift.

YOU WILL NEED
Thin coloured card
Craft knife
Glue

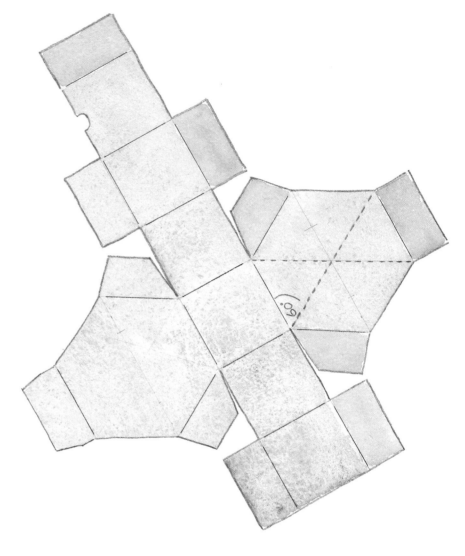

1 First, scale up the pattern from the template to the size required and transfer to the piece of card. Cut out using a craft knife, scoring along the back of the creases. Glue the end tab to form the basic box shape.

2 Next, interlock the tabs at the base of the box. If the pattern has been carefully cut out, the base will lock strongly without glue. Fill the box with sweets and fold down the lid.

RING AND BANGLE

A very simple way to make attractive jewellery is by twisting paper. Sheets of newspaper are twisted into a tight 'rope' and fitted around the wrist or throat to form bangles and rings, which can be covered with papier-mâché and decorated.

YOU WILL NEED
Newspaper
Masking tape
Diluted PVA glue
Fine sandpaper
White paint
Selection of poster paints
Glass 'gems', sequins, shells etc.
Non-toxic clear gloss varnish

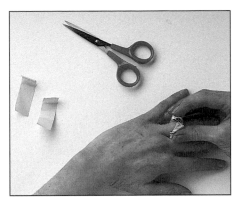

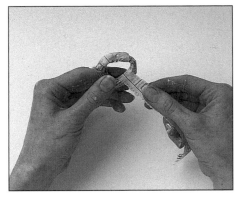

1 Ring
Take quarter of a sheet of newspaper and roll and twist it into a thin rope. Secure the rope along its length with strips of masking tape. Hold the rope around your finger, cut it to size, and tape the ends firmly together.

2 Tear small thin strips of newspaper, about 1 × 5 cm (½ × 2 in), coat them with diluted PVA glue, and stick them around the ring. Three layers of papier-mâché strips will be sufficient.

3 To add decorative knobbles to the ring, perhaps to imitate jewels, squash short pieces of newspaper between your fingers to form pellets, and stick in place.

4 Allow the ring to dry for 24 hours in a warm place. Lightly sand down the ring, and prime it with two coats of white paint.

5 Bangle
To make the bangle, simply roll up a double sheet of newspaper to make a thicker rope, cut it to fit your wrist and then follow the same process you used to make the ring. Decorate the ring and bangle with poster paints. You may like to paint them in one colour, and then augment them with sequins, 'gems' or shells. Leave them to dry overnight, and then seal with two coats of non-toxic clear gloss varnish.

■ P L A Q U E

Your family may have a coat of arms or a heraldic device that could be displayed on a wall plaque – if it hasn't, why not invent one? Add a Latin motto or phrase for authenticity – the wittier the better!

YOU WILL NEED
Thick cardboard
Strong clear glue
Masking tape
Diluted PVA glue
2 picture hangers
Newspaper
Fine sandpaper
White paint
Selection of poster paints
Non-toxic clear gloss varnish
Chain or cord to hang plaque

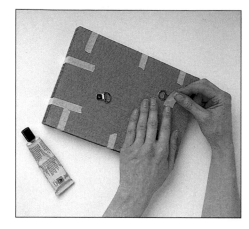

1 Cut three identical pieces of cardboard to the required dimensions, and stick them together with strong clear glue, securing the edges with masking tape. Paint the plaque with a coat of diluted PVA glue and allow it to dry. Stick two picture hangers to the reverse of the plaque with strong clear glue, and secure the stem of each hanger with a piece of masking tape.

2 Next, let the glue behind the hangers dry for at least an hour, and then cover the plaque with five layers of papier-mâché, using strips of newspaper approximately 2½ cm (1 in) wide, soaked in PVA glue.

3 Lightly sand down the surface of the plaque, and then apply two layers of white paint. Leave time for the paint to dry thoroughly.

4 Finally, draw in your design with pencil, and decorate the plaque with poster paints. Seal the finished plaque with two coats of non-toxic clear gloss varnish. Attach a chain or cord to the hangers on the reverse side to suspend it from the wall.

FRAMED
PIECE

If you have a spare frame or a gap on a wall that you have been wondering how to fill, here is a way to make a charming abstract seashore scene. You can vary the images to make a series of pieces for different sized frames.

YOU WILL NEED
Stencilling card
Craft knife
Assortment of coloured papers
Glue

1 Scale up the design on the template to the size that you require for your frame. Draw it out onto a piece of stencilling card and carefully cut out the lines using a craft knife so that the shapes show through. Take care not to cut through any 'bridges' in the card.

2 Next, place the cut-out stencil onto the piece of coloured paper which will form the main background. Then cut out squares or rectangles of different coloured papers until you have enough to fill the spaces in the stencil design.

3 Arrange the coloured papers by placing them between the stencilling card and the background paper, and see how they give form to the shapes.

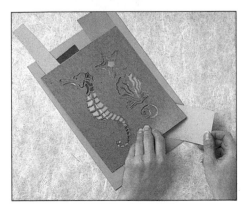

4 When you have decided on the colours for the final picture, glue all the pieces into position. Finally, trim the pieces of coloured paper that extend beyond the stencil and secure the picture into a frame.

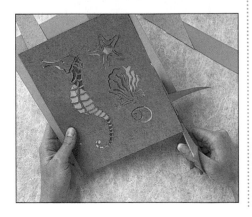

PIRATES AHOY!

This hat is simple to make, but looks good and would make a very realistic pirate outfit. For added authenticity cut out an eye patch and tie with elastic.

YOU WILL NEED
Gold card
Stiff black paper
White paint
Double-sided tape
Black elastic

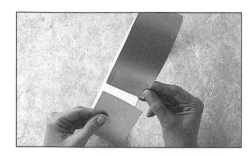

1 Cut out a strip of gold card measuring 6 × 60 cm (2¼ × 23½ in) and join the ends together to make the basic headband.

2 Next cut out two pirate hat shapes in stiff black paper. On the front piece mark out a skull and cross bones (the pirate's hallmark) and paint it in white.

3 Apply two pieces of double-sided tape to the back and front of the headband and stick on the black paper hat shapes.

4 Now stick a small square of double-sided tape at either end of the hat so that the back and front sides join together.

5 For the eye patch, cut out a small triangle in the same black paper just large enough to fit over your eye. Attach elastic to either side so that it can be worn around your head to make the eye patch.

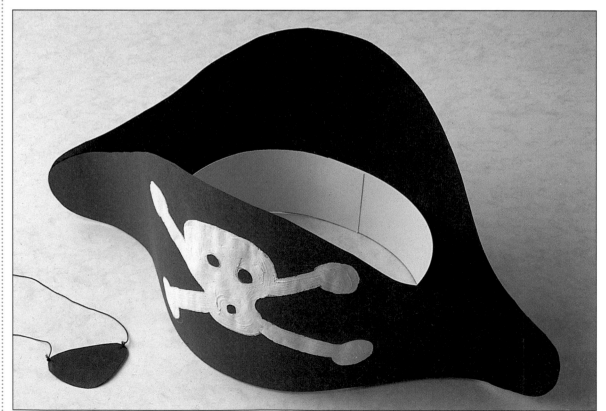

■ S A N T A ' S   S T O C K I N G

Children will love these Santa tree decorations to hang on the tree. Make a larger one to hang up by the fireplace on Christmas Eve.

YOU WILL NEED
Red card
Pale pink and dark pink paper
Glue
Black felt-tip pen
Cotton wool
  (surgical cotton)
Ribbon

1 Scale up the Santa from the template to the size required and transfer to the red card. Cut out carefully.

2 Next cut out the face shape in a pink paper and cut out two rosy cheeks in a darker coloured pink paper. Stick these onto the face area on the red card. Alternatively, colour in cheeks with felt-tip pen.

3 Draw in the smiling eyes and mouth with a black felt-tip pen.

4 Now glue the cotton wool (surgical cotton) onto the hat, the cuffs, the top of the Christmas stocking, and finally Santa's beard. Make a loop with some coloured ribbon and attach it to the back of the stocking so that it can hang on the Christmas tree.

PAPIER-MÂCHÉ PUPPET

Papier-mâché has long been associated with puppet-making, being a cheap, lightweight alternative to wood or clay. The simple construction of this puppet makes it easy to handle, and sumptuous costumes can be made out of exotic fabric scraps.

YOU WILL NEED
Newspaper
Masking tape
Diluted PVA glue
Fine sandpaper
White paint
Selection of poster paints
Black ink (optional)
Non-toxic clear gloss varnish
Piece of doweling rod about 40 cm
*   (16 in) long*
Thin string
Strong clear glue
Scraps of fabric, torn or cut into strips

1 Beginning with the puppet's head, crumple a double newspaper page into a ball, then sculpt it with masking tape into the desired shape. Do not forget to give your puppet a neck, as the top of the doweling crossbar will be glued inside.

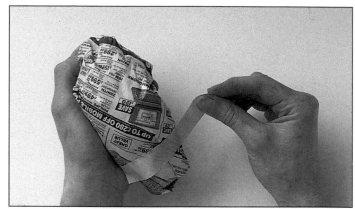

2 Tear newspaper into strips and soak in diluted PVA glue. Cover the puppet's head with four layers of papier-mâché.

3 Form the puppet's features by squashing glue-soaked strips of newspaper into small pellets of pulp and sticking them in place. Cover over the pulp with two layers of short thin news-paper strips.

4 Allow the head to dry overnight in a warm place. Lightly smooth it with fine sandpaper and then prime it with two coats of white paint. When it is quite dry, draw in the puppet's features, and decorate the head with poster paints, adding detail with black ink if desired. Let the head dry overnight and seal it with two coats of clear gloss varnish.

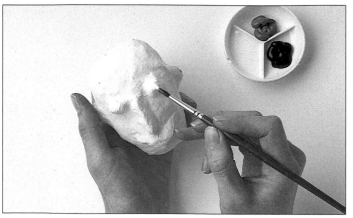

5 Cut the doweling rod into two pieces 10 cm (4 in) and 30 cm (12 in) long. Place the shorter piece of rod across the longer piece, and tie them together in a cross. Make a hole in the puppet's neck and glue in the rod. Leave in a warm place to dry overnight.

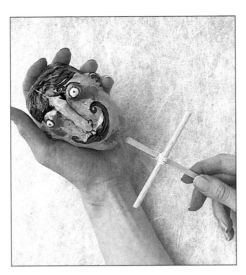

6 Finally, tear or cut strips of fabric about 2½ cm (1 in) wide and long enough to cover the doweling rod. Tie the strips along the length of crossbar that forms the puppet's arms. You might like to tie some fabric around the puppet's neck as well, to disguise the point where it joins the rod.

MASK

This handsome king mask could be used for plays or pantomimes, or for fancy-dress parties. It is made from heavy-weight paper and is strong but still flexible. By using the same basic face shape, and changing the crown to hair or a hat, you could make all sorts of masks, both male and female. Remember to cut the chin round rather than pointed if you do not want the mask to have a beard!

YOU WILL NEED
Thick paper in various colours
Gold paper
Glue
Thin elastic
Darning needle

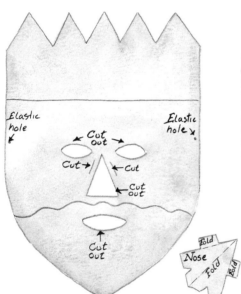

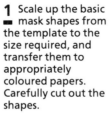

1 Scale up the basic mask shapes from the template to the size required, and transfer them to appropriately coloured papers. Carefully cut out the shapes.

2 Next, take the face shape and stick the nose, beard and gold crown onto it using a thin coating of glue.

3 Decorate using smaller pieces of coloured paper. Embellish the crown with jewels, and define the beard with strips of lighter coloured paper. Before wearing, carefully push a length of thin elastic through the mask using a darning needle. Knot the ends inside the mask.

SPOTTY DOG

This spotty dog is made from tightly rolled and twisted newspaper. It is a very good method for the construction of other animals, giving a firm armature or support for papier-mâché. It might be fun to make a giraffe or an elephant to go into a papier-mâché ark!

YOU WILL NEED
Newspaper
Masking tape
Diluted PVA glue
Fine sandpaper
White paint
Assortment of poster paints
Non-toxic clear gloss varnish

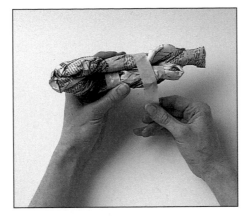

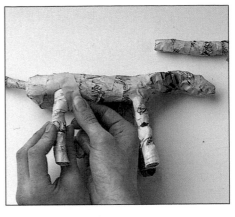

1 Take two double spread sheets of newspaper and twist them tightly to form a 'rope'. Tape the ends of the rope, and then bend it to form a fat rectangle about 15 cm (6 in) long, with one end extending about 5 cm (2 in). This end will form the dog's head. Firmly tape the rectangle to hold it in place.

2 Make the dog's limbs in the same way as the body and head. Using a single sheet of newspaper, form a thinner 'rope', and tape it along its length. Cut it into four pieces about 7–10 cm (3–4 in) long, and fix each one in place on the dog's body using masking tape. Add the dog's ears and tail with small, thin rolls of paper.

3 Soak newspaper strips in diluted PVA glue and cover the dog with three layers of papier-mâché strips. Leave it to dry overnight in a warm place.

4 Sand down the papier-mâché dog shape, and prime it with two coats of white paint. Decorate the dog with poster paints, and then seal with two coats of clear gloss varnish.

STAINED GLASS PENDANT

Hang this 'stained glass' pendant in your window and enjoy the bright colours as the light shines through. You could choose your own design from a plate or a piece of jewellery or you could base it on the Celtic ship used here.

YOU WILL NEED
Black cartridge paper
Craft knife
Coloured tissue paper
Glue
Ribbon

1 Trace and draw out your designs twice in black cartridge paper and then cut out the shapes with a sharp craft knife. Be careful to cut inside the lines so that the shape remains intact.

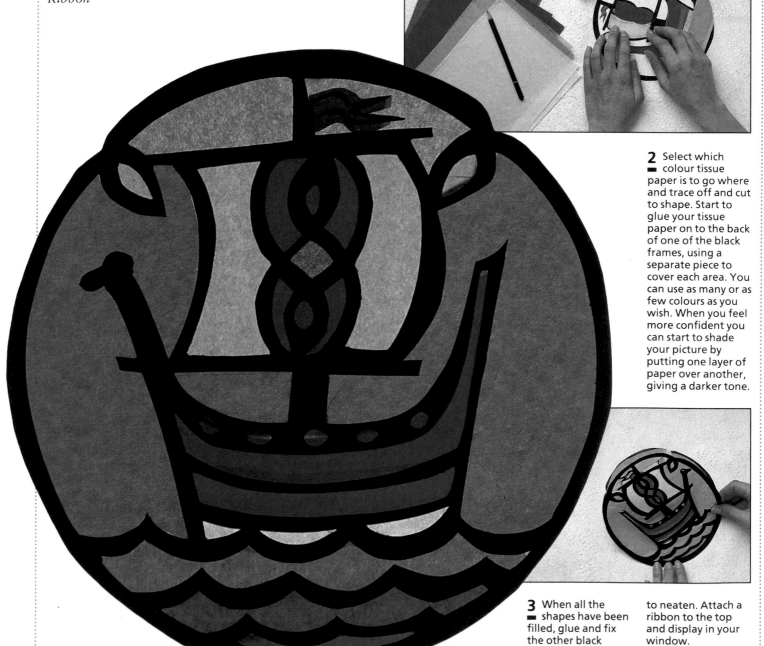

2 Select which colour tissue paper is to go where and trace off and cut to shape. Start to glue your tissue paper on to the back of one of the black frames, using a separate piece to cover each area. You can use as many or as few colours as you wish. When you feel more confident you can start to shade your picture by putting one layer of paper over another, giving a darker tone.

3 When all the shapes have been filled, glue and fix the other black frame on to the back to neaten. Attach a ribbon to the top and display in your window.

ABSTRACT STAINED GLASS

This is a very effective but easy way to make an abstract piece of 'stained glass' work, which is great fun to do and because the pieces are torn it is always slightly unpredictable.

YOU WILL NEED
Two sheets of black paper
Coloured tissue paper
Glue

1 Cut out two identical frames from the sheets of black paper. Take the coloured tissue papers and tear them into strips.

2 Cut out two pieces of tissue paper just larger than the frame opening, one in a light colour and one in a darker colour. Glue the lighter one onto the back of one of the frames. Arrange the torn strips so that they overlap the edges of the lighter tissue paper, and glue them into place.

3 Finally, stick down the darker piece of tissue paper, sandwiching the strips in place. Glue down the other black frame on top.

▪ V A S E

This vase is not waterproof, but it can be used to hold artificial or dried flowers, and is a very decorative 'objet d'art' in its own right. It is made using a simple basic method that can be easily adapted to make other shapes or sizes of vase.

YOU WILL NEED
Heavy corrugated cardboard
Strong clear glue
Masking tape
Newspaper
Diluted PVA glue
Fine sandpaper
White paint
Assorted poster paints
Non-toxic clear gloss varnish

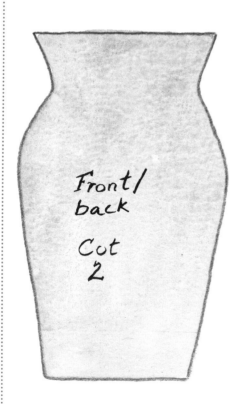

Front/back

Cut 2

Wall of vase

1 Scale up the shapes from the template to the size required and transfer onto heavy corrugated cardboard and cut out. The vase wall should be placed on the cardboard so that the corrugations run vertically down the wall's width. This will make it easier to bend the wall into

shape. Glue and tape the wall into place right around the inside edge of one of the vase pieces. Cover the pieces with a coat of diluted PVA glue to help prevent warping, and let them dry for three to four hours in a warm place.

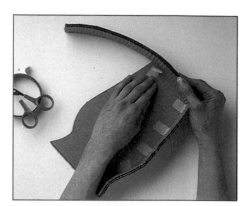

2 Next, tear narrow strips of newspaper and soak in diluted PVA glue. Cover the pieces of vase with four layers of papier-mâché strips. Leave to dry flat in a warm place overnight, and then smooth them lightly with fine sandpaper. Cover the inside of the vase and wall, and the remaining vase piece with two coats of white paint.

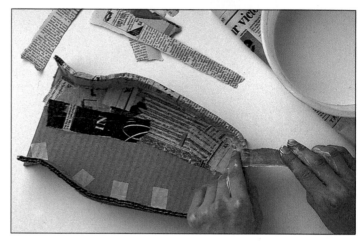

3 Join the vase together, with the painted surfaces to the inside. Glue the pieces together with strong clear glue and tape over the join with masking tape.

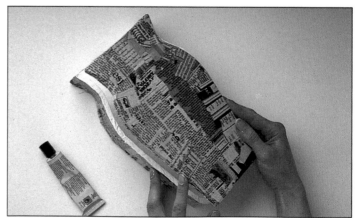

4 Leave the vase to dry for at least an hour. When dry seal its joined edge with three layers of papier-mâché strips, taking care to ensure a smooth surface by pushing out any small air bubbles or excess glue.

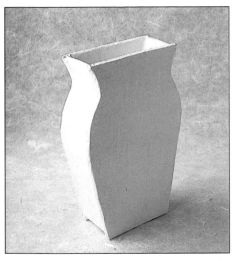

6 To decorate, lightly draw on the design with a pencil and then fill in using poster paints. When the paint is completely dry, apply a coat of clear gloss varnish.

5 Let the vase dry overnight, sand it lightly, and prime with two coats of white paint.

PERFORMING PIERROT

Children will love to watch the clever movements of this traditional Pierrot puppet. Why not make a couple and put on a show?

YOU WILL NEED
Blue, white and red paper
Black felt-tip pen
Glue
4 paper fasteners
Metal skewer or scissor blade
Curtain ring
Thin string

1 Scale up the pieces from the template to the size required and transfer to the coloured paper. Cut out the shapes for the clown: one body, two legs, two arms and a hat in blue, collar, cuffs and pom-poms in white. Mark on reference dots with a black pen. First make up the face by gluing on his hat and rosy cheeks. Draw the face details in with a black felt-tip pen.

2 Glue the pom-poms onto the hat, front and Pierrot's boots, and stick on the collar and cuffs.

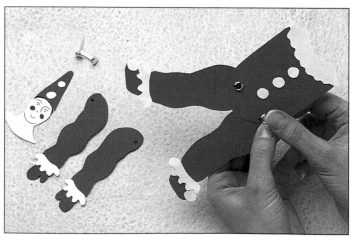

3 Match up the dots on the body and limbs and join them all together by pushing the paper fasteners through both layers. Open out the fasteners on the back.

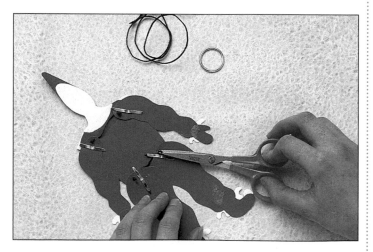

4 On the reverse side, pull the limbs downwards and pierce a hole at the top of each arm using a skewer or scissor blade. Thread a length of thin string through each hole and knot at both ends, on the reverse side. Repeat this with the legs to form two 'cross bars'.

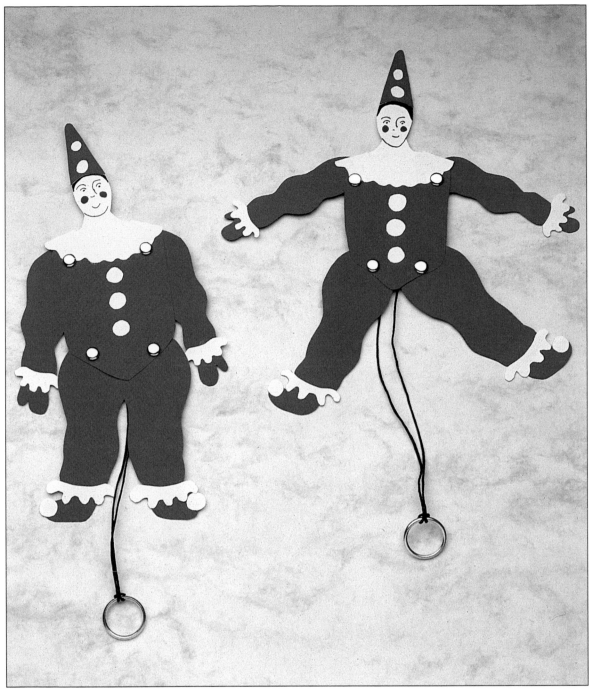

5 Thread a long piece of string through a curtain ring. Attach one end to the centre of the arm string and the other end to the centre of the leg string. Trim where necessary. The strings should not be slack when the limbs are 'at rest'. When the strings are firmly fixed, pull the ring and watch Pierrot perform.

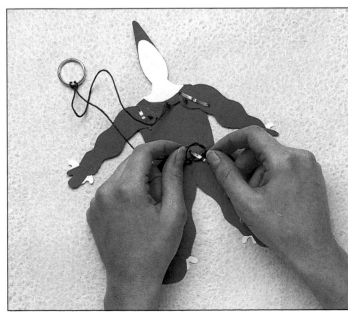

PICTURE CALENDAR

A simple idea that even children can make to give as presents. Calendar booklets are available from stationery shops.

YOU WILL NEED
Chosen picture
Card
Coloured paper
Glue
Calendar booklet
Matching ribbon
Sticky tape

1 Cut out a favourite picture from an old greetings card or a magazine.

2 Now cut out a larger piece of card and then choose a coloured paper which will match the colours in your picture. Glue the paper onto the card to cover.

3 Position and glue the picture onto the card, making sure that it is centred, but leaving more space at the bottom in order to accommodate the calendar booklet. Glue the calendar in place. Make a loop at the top with some matching coloured ribbon, and fix it at the back with sticky tape. For an added detail, make a little bow from the same ribbon and glue it just above the booklet.

A GREAT CATCH

This handsome fish is displayed proudly on a papier-mâché stand, rather like a trophy. It would be fun to make a papier-mâché case displaying a similar 'catch' to hang on the wall!

YOU WILL NEED
Heavy corrugated card
Strong clear glue
Masking tape
Diluted PVA glue
Newspaper
Fine sandpaper
White paint
Assortment of poster paints
Black ink (optional)
Non-toxic clear gloss varnish

1 Scale up the fish shape and stand from the template to the required size, and transfer onto the corrugated card. Remember to cut out two pieces for the stand. Stick the two halves of the stand together with strong clear glue, hold the joins with masking tape and leave to dry.

2 Soak newspaper strips in diluted PVA glue and apply three layers of papier-mâché to the fish and stand. Leave them to dry overnight in a warm place.

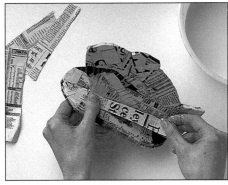

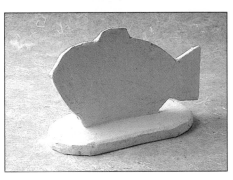

3 Lightly sand down the fish and stand. Prime with white paint.

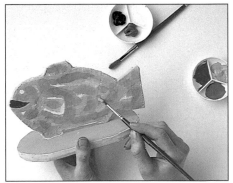

4 Draw in the fish's face, fins and other features, and then decorate it with poster paints. Use black ink to draw in the detail, if required. Let the fish dry overnight and then seal it with two coats of clear gloss varnish.

SOPHISTICATED CRACKER

1 Cut a piece of crêpe paper 30 × 20 cm (12 × 8 in). Wrap the crêpe paper around the cardboard tube and glue in place.

This cracker is easy to make and will add a designer look to your dinner table. Choose sophisticated black and white or match colours to your table setting.

YOU WILL NEED
Crêpe paper
Cardboard tube, 10 cm (4 in) long
Glue
Acetate paper
Silver metallic pen
Ribbon

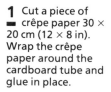

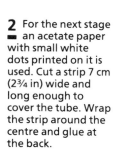

2 For the next stage an acetate paper with small white dots printed on it is used. Cut a strip 7 cm (2¾ in) wide and long enough to cover the tube. Wrap the strip around the centre and glue at the back.

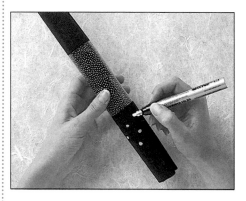

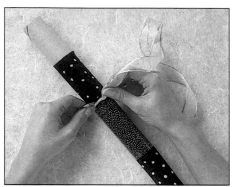

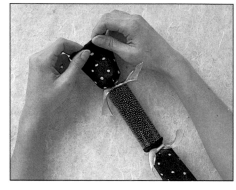

3 On either end of the cracker paint silver dots with a metallic pen.

4 Now ease an extra piece of tube into one end, and tie a piece of silver ribbon between the rolls to make the cracker shape. The tube will give form to the end. Remove the extra tube and repeat with the other end of the cracker.

5 Frill the ends of the cracker by stretching the paper between the finger tips.

WHIRLING CIRCLES

Festoon your room with garlands of whirling circles. Double-sided crêpe paper is used here so that one side is a slightly darker colour.

YOU WILL NEED
Drinking glass
Double-sided crêpe paper
Wide ribbon
Craft knife

1 First of all draw round a drinking glass and cut out circles of crêpe paper in all different colours. Now cut a spiral towards the centre leaving a small 'bobble' in the middle.

2 When you have cut out enough circles in all the different colours, take some wide ribbon and, using a craft knife, make small cuts parallel to the sides, at intervals along the tape.

3 Now push the 'bobble' centre of the whirls through the cut in the ribbon so that they are held in position. Make sure that you alternate the colours along the ribbon.

CHINESE HAT

Celebrate Chinese New Year with a stylish Oriental hat. There is no fixed design to follow, so you can have fun adding your own characters.

YOU WILL NEED
Beige and white card
Black ink or paint
Double-sided tape

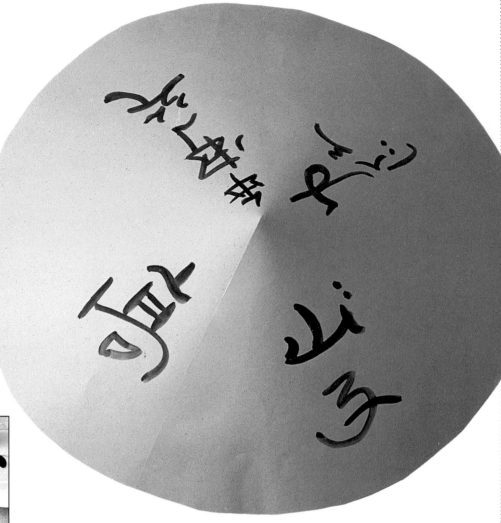

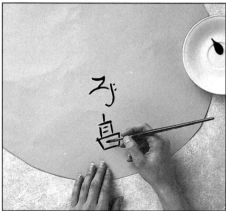

1 Cut a 48 cm (19 in) diameter circle out of beige card. Using black ink or paint, make up Chinese characters and decorate the beige card with them.

2 Now cut a line from the edge of the circle to the centre and overlap one edge over the other to give form to the hat. Stick in position with double-sided tape.

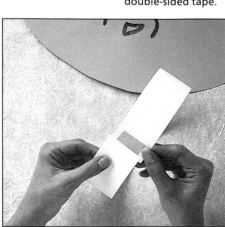

3 Take a strip of narrow card, long enough to go around your head, and tape the ends together to make a headband.

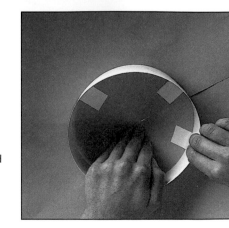

4 Fix the headband to the underneath of the Chinese hat with pieces of tape as illustrated.

POT-POURRI PUNNET

Bring the sweet smell of your favourite flowers into the room all year round with a basket of pot-pourri. Stir it occasionally to bring out the scent.

YOU WILL NEED
Small basket
Tissue paper
Needle
Silver thread
Pot-pourri

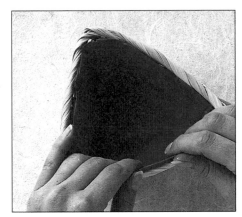

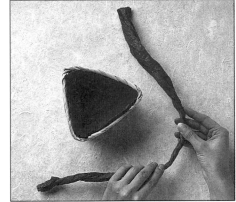

1 Take a small gift basket and line it with coloured tissue paper. A bright pink has been chosen here to bring out the colours of the pot-pourri.

2 Now take another piece of the same tissue paper and roll it up into a sausage shape and twist.

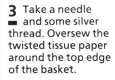

3 Take a needle and some silver thread. Oversew the twisted tissue paper around the top edge of the basket.

4 Fix the two ends of the sausage so that they overlap and secure them with a couple of stitches or a dab of glue. Now place the pot-pourri into the basket to give your room a lovely aroma as well as look attractive.

POPULAR POPPIES

The stark simplicity of bright red poppies with their black centres makes them an ideal flower to craft in paper.

YOU WILL NEED
Garden wire
Cotton wool (surgical cotton)
Green, black and red crêpe paper
Glue
Sticky tape

1 To make the stem cut a length of garden wire. Bend the top to make a loop and trap a small amount of cotton wool in the loop. Cover this in a cut-out circle of green crêpe paper. Secure by wrapping tape around.

2 Next cut three small circles of black crêpe paper. Fringe the outer edges and then poke the other end of the wire through the centre and slide up to the green bud.

3 Cut out five petal shapes in red crêpe paper and stretch the outer edge with your finger tips so that they frill.

4 Glue the petals one by one around the base of the centre.

5 Finally, cover the stem in green crêpe paper by winding a long strip around diagonally and securing it at the base with sticky tape.

▮ LEAFY FOLIAGE

This foliage can be used to add to other flower arrangements you can make out of paper.

YOU WILL NEED
Garden wire
Double-sided tape
Green crêpe paper

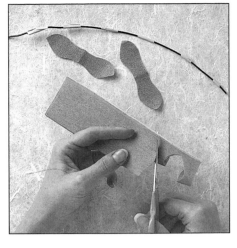

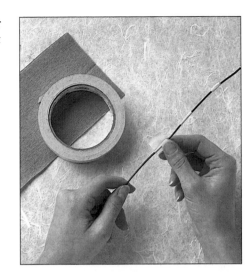

1 Take a length of green garden wire and wrap small pieces of double-sided tape at intervals along the wire.

2 Cut out double leaf shapes in thick green crêpe paper.

3 Twist each leaf shape in the centre and fix them onto the wire by twisting them around the taped parts.

4 Tape a long strip of the same green paper to the bottom of the wire and wind it up the stem, making sure to cover the tape as you go. Bend and mould the finished greenery to suit your flower arrangement.

CHRISTMAS TREE BOWS

Dress up your tree with shimmering bows for a glamorous film-star style Christmas. Match bows to baubles for a co-ordinated look.

YOU WILL NEED
Metallic corrugated paper
Stapler
Metallic tissue paper
Double-sided tape
Ribbon

1 From the metallic corrugated paper cut out an oblong measuring 18 × 12 cm (7 × 4½ in).

Gather in the centre to make the bow shape and staple in position.

2 Now take a length of metallic tissue paper and wrap it around the centre of the bow to cover the staples. However do not

wrap the whole length around but leave some excess to fall at the front. Fix at the back with double-sided tape.

3 Now cut two rectangles for the tails in the metallic paper measuring 20

× 8 cm (8 × 3 in). Cut darts at one end of each tail.

4 Make one pleat at the top of the tails. Staple each

pleat and then staple the tails together.

5 Now attach the tails to the back of the bow with double-sided tape. Make a loop with a

piece of ribbon and stick it to the back of the finished bow for hanging.

SOAP-BOX

Guest soaps come in all shapes and colours. Decorate a box in pretty shades to match your soaps for an attractive present. •

YOU WILL NEED
Empty circular box
Assorted coloured card
Glue
Tissue paper
Soaps

1 Cover the outside of the box by gluing a strip of coloured card around the side.

2 This particular gift uses shell-shaped soaps, so draw shell shapes onto coloured cards that complement the colours of the soaps.

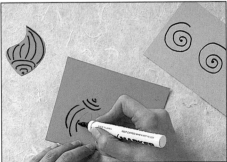

3 Cut out the shell shapes and stick them onto the outside of the box.

4 Scrunch up a large piece of tissue paper and arrange it inside the box. Place the soaps on top of the tissue paper.

BOWLED OVER

This bowl is made by a traditional method where layers of papier-mâché are laid into a greased mould and removed when dry. For this project, an ordinary china bowl has been used, but all sorts of items can make interesting moulds – just remember to grease them first, otherwise they will be permanently lined with paper!

YOU WILL NEED
Bowl suitable for using as a mould
Petroleum jelly
Newspaper
Diluted PVA glue
Heavy corrugated card
Strong clear glue
Masking tape
Fine sandpaper
White paint
Assortment of poster paints
Non-toxic clear gloss varnish

1 Coat the inside of the bowl with five layers of PVA-soaked newspaper strips, allowing for an overlap of 2½ cm (1 in). Leave to dry in a warm place for 48 hours.

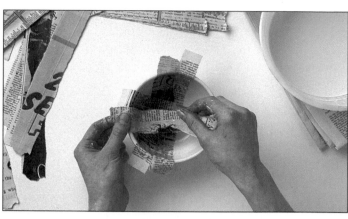

2 Gently prise the paper bowl from its mould with a blunt knife, and leave it upside down to dry for a few hours.

3 Trim the ragged edge to about ½ cm (¼ in).

4 Cut a zigzag bowl rim from the thick cardboard and lay it on the top of the papier-mâché bowl rim. Stick the rim on the bowl with strong clear glue, and hold it in place with masking tape. Allow the glue to dry for an hour or so and then paper over the rim, covering the joins carefully.

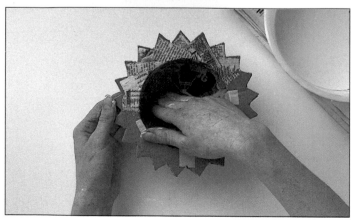

5 Paper the underside of the rim in the same way. Leave the bowl to dry for 24 hours. Lightly sand down the surface of the bowl, and then prime it with two coats of white paint.

6 Draw in any decoration with pencil first, and then decorate the bowl with poster paints. Let the bowl dry thoroughly, and then seal it with two coats of clear gloss varnish.

TAKE A
LETTER

As well as paper and card, this letter rack also requires a block of wood to give it a firm base. Cover it in patterned paper to match your desk accessories.

YOU WILL NEED
Block of wood 19½ × 4½ × 2 cm
(7½ × 1¾ × ¾ in)
Patterned paper
Glue or waterbased wood adhesive
Mounting card

1 Entirely cover the block of wood in the patterned paper and glue in place. Trim it where necessary.

2 Cut three pieces of mounting card, one piece measuring 25 × 13 cm (10 × 5 in) and the other two measuring 20 × 9 cm (8 × 3½ in). With each bit of card, measure and cut out a piece of paper slightly larger than the card itself. Glue the paper onto the card, and mitre the corners carefully by snipping off the corners diagonally and folding the turnings on to the back, making sure that they are well stuck down. Repeat with each piece of card.

3 Now stick a piece of paper slightly smaller than the card onto the back.

4 Using a strong glue or waterbased wood adhesive stick the smaller, front card to the narrow edge of the covered piece of wood, making sure it is centred. Glue the back card in the same way.

5 To complete the letter rack, position and glue it onto the covered base.

ADVENT
CALENDAR

Make the countdown to Christmas even more exciting with this beautiful tree advent calendar. The windows are decorated with pictures cut out from old Christmas cards.

YOU WILL NEED
Red, green and orange card
Thin cardboard
Craft knife
Old greetings cards
Glue
Silver metallic pen

1 Cut out two tree shapes, one in red card and the other in green. Use a 2 cm (¾ in) square template of thin cardboard to mark out 25 windows at random on the green tree. Now cut along three sides of each window with a craft knife.

2 Place the green tree onto the red tree so that it is slightly higher and gives the green tree a red line on the bottom edges.

Carefully open each window and mark their position on the red tree in pencil. Remove the green tree. Cut out 25 small pictures from old Christmas cards and glue them onto the pencilled squares on the red Christmas tree.

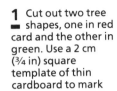

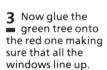

3 Now glue the green tree onto the red one making sure that all the windows line up.

4 Decorate the tree with cut-out circles of red and orange card to suggest the Christmas tree baubles.

5 Using a silver pen draw a bow above each bauble and then number the windows 1 to 25.

WASTE PAPER BOX

Waste paper boxes can make elegant gifts that can be put to use straight away. They can be covered in paper that matches the decor of the room they are intended for, or else in paper of your favourite design.

YOU WILL NEED
Thick card
Dark contrasting or toning paper
Impact adhesive
Decorative paper

1 For this waste paper box, cut out one square in thick card measuring 20 cm (9 in). Now measure and cut out from the same type of card the four sides so that they are 20 cm (9 in) wide, with a height of 25 cm (11 in). Cover one side of all these pieces with a dark toning paper.

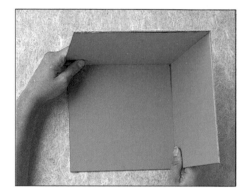

2 Next glue the sides onto the base and to each other using an impact adhesive.

3 Now cut out a square of decorative paper measuring 24 cm (10 in). Firmly glue it onto the base and cut the corners diagonally. Glue the turnings around and up onto the sides of the container to give the box extra strength.

4 To cover, cut a piece of the decorative paper large enough to go around the whole of the box. Stick it on and trim where necessary at the base to create a neat finish.

5 At the top, turn the excess paper over and glue down onto the inside of the box, after mitring the corners. This will produce a very professional look.

ELEGANT LAMPSHADE

Add a designed look to your room by using a left-over piece of wallpaper, or a paper of a complementary colour, to make this lampshade.

YOU WILL NEED
Lampshade frame
Coloured paper or wallpaper
Craft knife
Coin
Glue

1 First of all take a lampshade frame and place it onto your chosen paper. Draw around the shape while slowly moving the frame round to obtain the correct measurement. Now cut out the shape slightly outside the drawn line using scissors or a craft knife to give a piece of paper larger than the frame. Using a coin, draw a scalloped edge along the bottom edge.

2 Then cut along it until the edging is complete.

3 Now apply a layer of glue to the frame and carefully attach the paper to it, smoothing it out to avoid bumps or creases.

4 Finally, cut small darts around the top and glue them down, working around until the frame is completely covered and the shade ready to be fitted to a lamp.

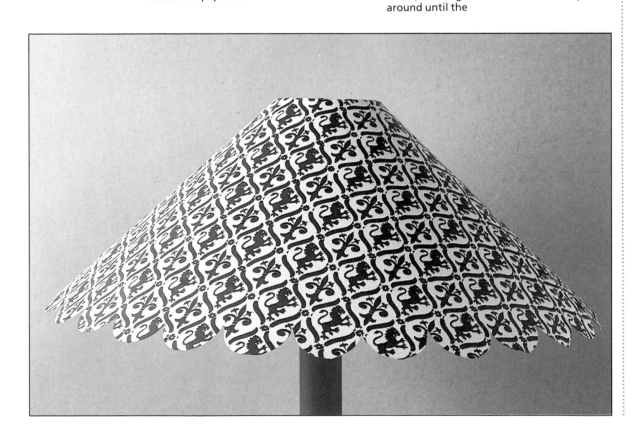

DESIGNER PENCIL POT

This pencil pot is a lovely idea to cheer up your own desk, or it can make a beautiful personalized gift for a friend. The matching pencils add an artistic touch.

YOU WILL NEED
Empty cardboard tube or salt
*   container*
Patterned paper
Glue
Pencils

1 First of all you will need to cover the inside of the container. Measure the height and circumference of the pot and cut out two pieces of paper, slightly larger. You could use wallpaper, wrapping paper or marbled paper.

2 Take one of the pieces, glue it and carefully slot it into the inside of the pot, pressing it around the inside walls.

3 Cut darts on the excess paper at the top and glue them down to the outside one by one.

4 Take the other piece of paper and stick it to the outside so that the edge is flush with the top of the pot.

5 Once again cut darts into the excess length at the bottom and glue them onto the base.

6 Now draw around the base of the pot onto the patterned paper and cut out a circle slightly smaller. Glue this and drop it inside the bottom.

7 Cut out another circle and glue it to the outside base.

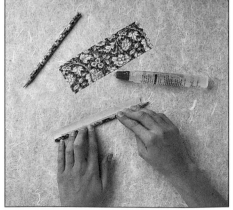

8 To make the matching pencils, cut out a strip of the same patterned paper the length of the pencils and approximately twice the width. Glue it and place the pencil at one edge and roll. Trim the paper where necessary.

DESK BLOTTER

To make the blotter special it is a good idea to select a wrapping paper to suit the type of desk area. You could choose a hand-made marbled paper for a very traditional look, or an abstract paper or two co-ordinating plain papers for a more modern effect.

YOU WILL NEED
Thick card
Patterned paper
Glue
Thin card
Coloured paper
Blotting paper

1 Cut a piece of thick card 46 × 30 cm (18 × 12 in). This will be the finished size of the blotter. Cut your chosen paper 3 cm (1 in) larger all around than the card.

2 Next fold and glue the edges onto the back of the card, mitring the corners by trimming them diagonally.

3 For the corner pieces cut four triangles in thin card measuring 10 × 10 × 14 cm (4 × 4 × 5½ in) and cover them in coloured paper cut to the same size first. Glue and turn down the bottom edge and the top point. Repeat this for all four corner pieces.

4 Position the corner pieces onto the corners of the blotter. Turn the board over and fold the edges around, gluing them securely.

5 Cut another piece of coloured paper the same size as the blotter and glue it on to the back. Trim where necessary.

6 Insert a piece of blotting paper under the corners.

■ SWEET THOUGHT

Chocolates are always a treat, especially when they are gift-wrapped. Simply cover an empty container with vibrant tissue paper and fill with sweets.

YOU WILL NEED
Empty bowl-shaped food container
Tissue paper
Glue or tape
Metallic card
Pencil or paint brush

1 Cover the bowl with tissue paper by placing the centre of the paper inside, pushing it down and then moulding it out and around the sides.

2 Glue or tape the tissue paper to the underside, trimming where necessary.

3 Now cut two strips measuring 3 × 50 cm (1¼ × 20 in) of coloured metallic card. Tightly roll each end of the card strips around a pencil or paint brush so that it curls.

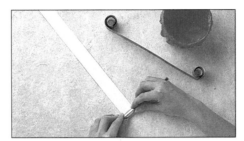

4 Now glue the centre of the cards and place them into the bowl at right angles. Place another piece of tissue paper that has been scrunched up into the bottom of the container, and arrange the chocolates on the top.

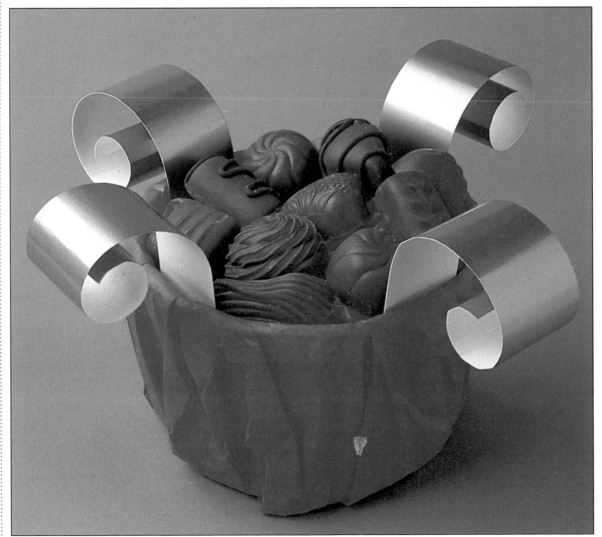

NECKLACE AND EARRINGS

This beautiful necklace with matching earrings is created from only a small piece of decorative paper. A printed feather marbled pattern is used here.

YOU WILL NEED
Patterned paper
Pair of earring fittings
Leather cord
Glue

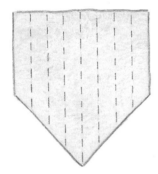

1 For the earrings, cut out two tab shapes from the decorative paper, using the template as a guide to the shape. Now fold the tab in half to the point and continue to pleat out from the centre.

2 Pierce the top and push an earring fitting through to create a fan shape. Make a second earring in the same way.

3 For the necklace you will need to make five 'fans' in the same way and then pierce them at the top.

4 To make the beads which sit inbetween the fans, cut 30 cm (12 in) strips of paper into elongated triangles measuring 4 cm (1½ in) at the base and tapering to 1 cm (½ in) at the tip. Starting at the wide end, roll up the strips around a pencil and glue the end. Now thread a piece of leather cord through the tops of the fans, alternating them with the beads.

FESTIVE CRACKERS

Here is an economical way to make your own festive crackers as well as to give your guests a personal surprise present by adding a small gift.

YOU WILL NEED
Crêpe paper in two colours
Thin writing paper
Cracker snaps
Thin card
Two cardboard tubes
Glue
Strong thread
Double-sided tape

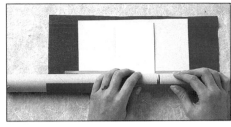

1 First of all cut a length of crêpe paper measuring 35 × 20 cm (14 × 8 in). Lay it flat and place a piece of thin writing paper centrally on top. Place a cracker snap on top and then place a piece of card measuring 15 × 8 cm (6 × 3 in), across the centre.

2 Place two cardboard tubes onto the papers so that their ends meet in line with the right hand side of the piece of card. Roll the crêpe paper around and glue at the edges.

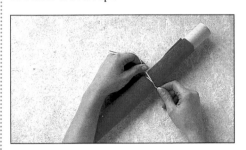

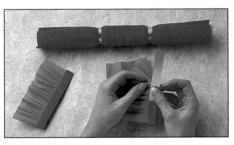

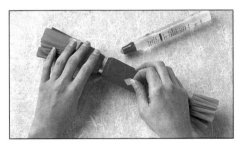

3 Pull the right hand tube out slightly and use some strong thread to tie inbetween the tubes and gather the paper as illustrated. Now pop your gift in at the other end. Pull the other cardboard tube so that you can feel a gap between the tube and the inner card, and tie the end as before with some strong thread.

4 Remove the cardboard tubes and, using a strip of contrasting coloured card, stick over the threads to neaten. Now cut another strip of the same card and a strip of contrasting coloured crêpe paper twice this length. Put double-sided tape on the back of the card and gather up the crêpe paper onto it.

5 To finish off decorate the cracker with a diamond of card.

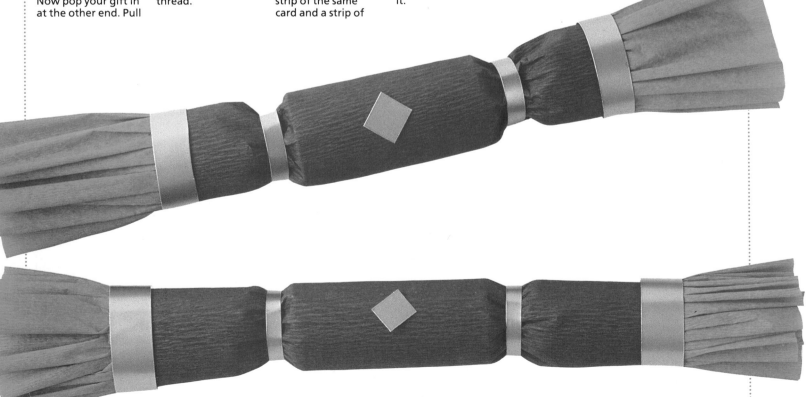

SUNNY MOBILE

Mobiles come in many forms, from very simple brightly coloured abstract shapes, to highly sophisticated motor-driven extravaganzas. This one is made in a traditional way and features a soothing arrangement of the sun with clouds, which will move gently if hung in a breeze.

YOU WILL NEED
Thin card
Thin wire jewellery hangers, one for each piece of mobile
Strong clear glue
Masking tape
Newspaper
Diluted PVA glue
Fine sandpaper
White paint
Assortment of poster paints
Black ink (optional)
Non-toxic clear gloss varnish
Fishing line or similar nylon cord
Thin florists' or model-makers' wire

1 Scale up the mobile shapes from the template to the size required and transfer them to the thin card. Make a total of four cloud shapes. Cut out each shape. Stick a wire hanger to the back of each mobile piece with strong clear glue, and secure the hangers with a piece of masking tape.

2 Let the glue dry for an hour, and then cover each card shape with three layers of papier-mâché, using short, narrow strips of newspaper soaked in diluted PVA glue. Allow the shapes to dry overnight in a warm place.

3 Lightly sand down each piece of mobile, and then prime them with two even coats of white paint.

4 Draw in any
design with
pencil first, and then
decorate the mobile
shapes with poster
paint. Accentuate
details with black ink
if desired. When the
decoration has
thoroughly dried,
seal all the pieces
with two coats of
clear gloss varnish.
   To assemble the
mobile, cut two
pieces of thin
florists' or model-
makers' wire to a
length of about 15
cm (6 in). Suspend
one piece of wire
from the centre of
the other. Attach the
shapes to the wires
using short lengths
of nylon cord tied
through the
fasteners. Attach a
length of cord to the
middle of the top
wire and hang the
mobile in place.

This traditional toy is easy to make as well as being fun to watch turn in the wind. For a children's party you could make one for each guest in a variety of colours.

YOU WILL NEED
Square of stiff paper
Map pin
Empty ballpoint pen casing
Piece of cork
Plastic drinking straw or short bamboo cane

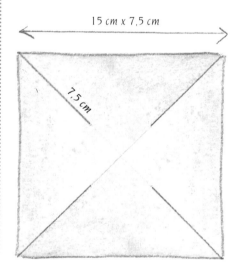

15 cm x 7,5 cm

7,5 cm

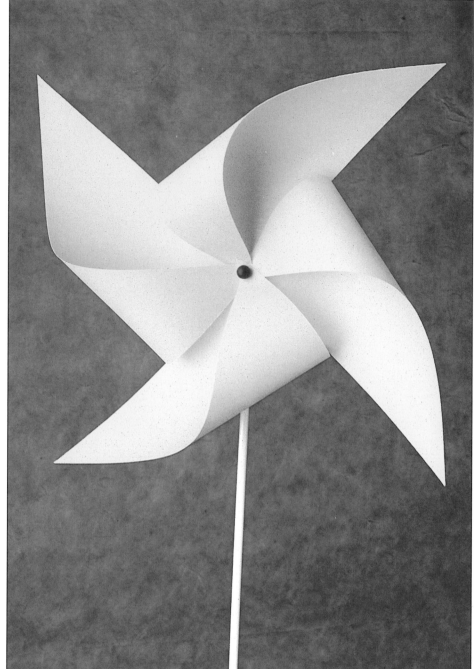

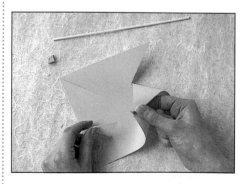

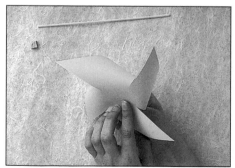

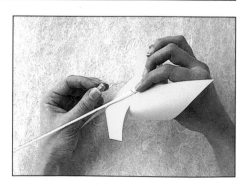

1 First, scale up the pattern from the template to the size required and transfer it to the square of paper. Cut along the lines from each corner nearly to the centre. Bend each alternate corner to the centre, securing each one with a map pin. It is easier to create the pin hole when the sheet is flat.

2 Next, push the pin through the centre of the windmill to the back.

3 Cut a small piece off the end of a ballpoint pen ink casing to act as a bearing, and put it onto the point of the pin behind the paper. Push the pin through a drinking straw, and then into a small piece of cork for safety.

Alternatively, push the pin into a garden cane, making sure the point is well inside the wood so that no sharp end is protruding.

DANCING FINGER PUPPETS

Finger puppets are traditional toys that have been made to amuse children (and adults!) for many years. Here are a flying Scotsman and a member of the corps de ballet for you to make.

YOU WILL NEED
Thick white paper
Felt-tip pens or coloured pencils
Glue
Thin card
Craft knife

1 Scale up the puppet designs from the template to the size required and transfer them to the paper.

2 Colour in the Scotsman and the ballerina with felt-tip pens or coloured pencils.

3 Then stick the puppets onto the thin card, and cut carefully around each one with a craft knife. Cut out the finger holes with a craft knife, and your puppets are ready to dance the night away!

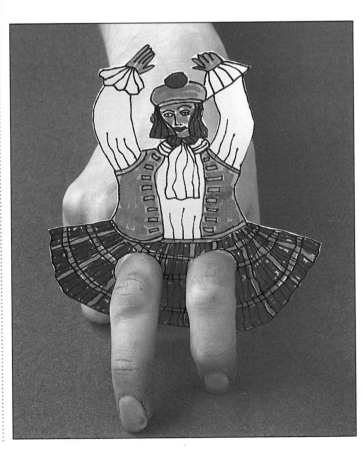

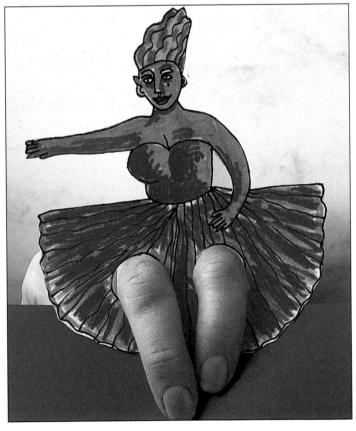

NECK TIES AND BOW-TIES

A tie always creates a good impression, and these paper ties add a touch of fun without the formality. All you need is a sheet of wrapping paper or crêpe paper.

YOU WILL NEED
Neck tie
Wrapping paper
Glue
String or elastic
Crêpe paper
Double-sided tape

1 To make this party tie cut out a piece of suitable wrapping paper using the front part of a real neck tie as a guide. Make sure that the paper is slightly larger all round to allow for turnings.

2 Glue and fold back the turnings to get a good finish.

3 To make the 'knot', cut out a fairly large rectangle of paper. Cut a piece of string or elastic long enough to go around your neck, and place it across the rectangle. Glue and fold the rectangle in half. Now glue the 'knot' to the top of the tie and knot the elastic at the ends.

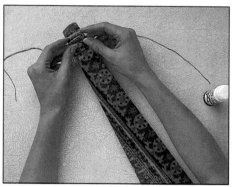

4 To make a bow-tie, use some crêpe paper, measuring 25 × 10 cm (10 × 4 in). Join the ends together to form a ring with double-sided tape.

5 Gather in the centre and cut a thin strip of crêpe paper and wind it around the middle.

Apply glue to the end, but before sticking it down, insert a neck-length of elastic.

6 Glue on coloured spots to make an impression at the party!

PAPER PEAR

You could make any sort of fruit or vegetable from papier-mâché using this method. It is possible to make quite convincing shapes by 'sculpting' the crumpled newspaper with masking tape. You might even be inspired to attempt something really exotic, like a star fruit!

YOU WILL NEED
Newspaper
Masking tape
Diluted PVA glue
Fine sandpaper
White paint
Assortment of poster paints
Non-toxic clear gloss varnish

1 Loosely crumple a sheet of newspaper into a large egg shape. Twist and tape the paper. You may have to add smaller wedges of crumpled paper to achieve the shape you want.

2 To make the stalk, roll a small piece of newspaper into a thin tube, bend the top over, and tape it firmly. Make a hole in the top of your pear, and push the stalk in, fixing it with masking tape.

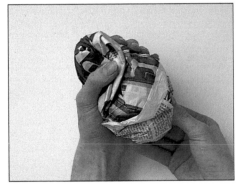

3 Soak strips of newspaper in diluted PVA glue. Cover the pear with three layers of paper strips. Smooth its surface with your hands.

4 Let the pear dry overnight in a warm place, such as an airing cupboard. Lightly sand the surface of the fruit, and prime it with two coats of white paint.

5 Colour your pear with poster paints. When it has dried, seal the surface with two coats of clear varnish. You might like to use satin finish rather than gloss varnish to give a more naturalistic look.

■ DECORATIVE CUP

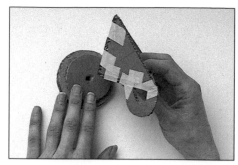

This papier-mâché cup is formed in an exotic style from heavy cardboard. This method of making a frame which can be built up with layers of papier-mâché allows great versatility of style: almost any design on paper can be reproduced in card with a little planning.

YOU WILL NEED
Heavy cardboard
Diluted PVA glue
Masking tape
Newspaper
Fine sandpaper
White paint
Selection of poster paints
Non-toxic clear gloss varnish

1 Scale up the cup pieces from the template to the size required and transfer them onto heavy cardboard. Assemble the cup by first sticking the three triangles of card together using PVA glue. Strengthen with strips of masking tape, and then assemble the base.

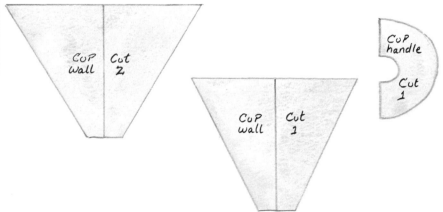

2 Stick the handle to one side of the cup and secure with masking tape. To stick the bowl and base together, make a hole in the centre of the base using a sharp pencil. Apply glue to the 'point' of the bowl and rest this on the base. Finally, fix in place with masking tape for extra strength.

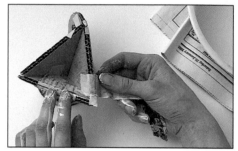

3 Next, paint the cup with one coat of diluted PVA glue to prevent it from warping, and then cover it with four layers of papier-mâché. Use short thin pieces of newspaper soaked in diluted PVA glue. Make sure the pieces of newspaper are thin enough to go around the handle.

4 Leave the cup to dry overnight in a warm place. Then lightly sand down the dried cup, and prime it with two coats of white paint.

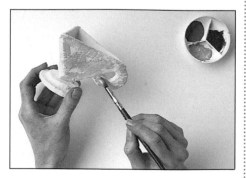

5 Decorate the cup with poster paint. When the paint has dried thoroughly, apply a coat of clear gloss varnish.

MASKED BALL

Keep the guests at the party guessing with this stylish evening mask. Choose crêpe paper to match your ballgown and trim with matching ribbon.

YOU WILL NEED
Gold foil card
Gold doily
Glue
Foil crêpe paper
Sticky tape
Doweling rod
Ribbon

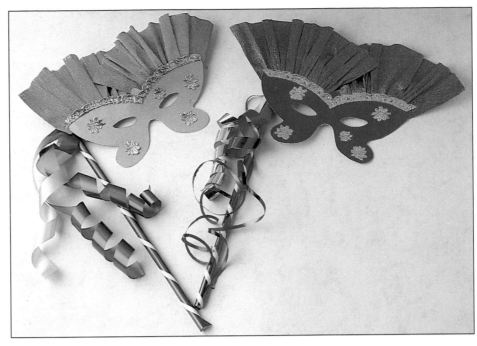

1 Scale up the template to the size required and cut out a mask shape in gold foil card.

2 Now cut the scalloped edge from a gold doily and glue it to the top of the mask.

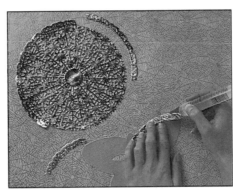

3 Gather a strip of foil crêpe paper and stick it to the back of the mask along the top edge. You might need to secure this further with some tape.

4 Now cut out some other motifs from the doily and stick them onto the mask front to decorate.

5 Take a piece of doweling rod, wrap a length of ribbon around it and glue the ends. Curl further pieces of ribbon and stick them to the top of the doweling. Tape the doweling rod onto one side of the mask and set off for the ball.

INDIAN CHIEF

Transform a strip of card into an exciting headband fit for an Indian chief. Why not make one each for the whole tribe?

YOU WILL NEED
Coloured card
Assorted coloured card
Glue
Sticky tape

1 First of all cut out a length of stiff coloured card measuring 60 × 6 cm (24 × 2½ in). Now decorate it by cutting out zigzag lines from brightly-coloured card and sticking them onto the band.

2 Draw and cut out feather shapes from the brightly coloured card and make lots of small scissor cuts along the sides of the feathers to make them more realistic.

3 Apply glue to the inside of the band and stick the feathers in place. To secure them really well use a strip of tape on top.

4 Fold the two ends together, adjust the size and tape to fit.

SUNFLOWER

Brighten up a room with some crêpe paper sunflowers that will bring a ray of sunshine all year round.

YOU WILL NEED
Brown card
Brown and green crêpe paper
Glue
Bright yellow paper
Doweling rod
Green paper
Sticky tape

1 Cut out two 10 cm (4 in) diameter circles from brown card. Next cut 4 cm (1½ in) squares of brown crêpe paper and attach them to one side of one of the brown circles by screwing up each one and gluing it on.

2 Using the petal template, scaled up to the size required, cut out petals in bright yellow paper.

5 Attach the leaf stems to the doweling rod at intervals, securing with tape.

3 Pleat and glue them into position onto the back of the covered brown circle so that they follow the edge.

6 Cover the stick completely by winding a long strip of green crêpe paper around it.

4 To make the stem take a piece of doweling rod approximately 50 cm (20 in) long. Cut leaf shapes in green paper and twist the ends to make a small stem.

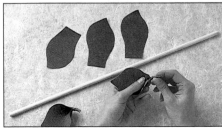

7 Tape the flower head to the front of the stick, then turn over and glue the remaining brown circle to the back to neaten.

FLYING IN THE WIND

This regal kite will look very grand flying in a blue sky with its gold bows trailing behind. If it is made with fairly stiff paper, it should withstand quite strong gusts of wind. It is possible to make the kite in a variety of sizes: just follow the basic rule that the cross bar is two-thirds the length of the long doweling rod.

YOU WILL NEED

Two lengths of wooden doweling rod, one measuring 40 cm (16 in) and one 60 cm (24 in)
Lengths of strong thin string
Craft knife
Large sheet of stiff coloured paper
Strong glue
Curtain ring
Ball of kite string
Contrasting scraps of coloured paper for decoration and tail ribbons
Length of coloured ribbon for kite tail

1 First, take the two pieces of doweling rod. Using a pen, mark the shorter piece halfway along its length. Mark the longer piece a third of the way down its length. Join the pieces of doweling rod together so that the marks touch; the shorter piece should lie horizontally across the longer, forming a cross. Tie the sticks tightly together with thin string.

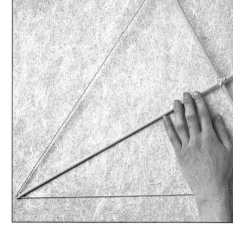

2 Using a craft knife, make a notch at the end of each piece of doweling rod. Then tie the end of a length of string around the notch in the top of the kite frame, and wind the string around the outside, securing it around each notch in turn. Tie the ends of the string together when you reach the top of the frame again.

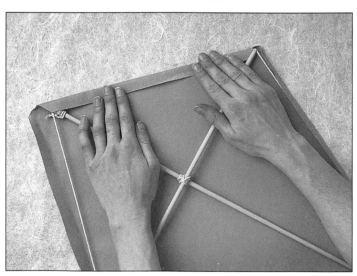

3 Next, place the kite frame on the large piece of coloured paper and cut around it, leaving 1 cm (½ in) of paper spare outside the edges of the string. Cut the corners of the paper back to the ends of each piece of doweling rod, and then smear glue along the edges of the paper, folding them over to enclose the string.
    Tie a length of string to each end of the short rod, and a piece to either end of the long one. Pull the strings together so that they overlap, and secure them where they touch with a curtain ring. Tie the ball of kite string to the curtain ring.

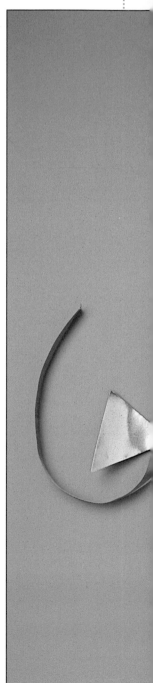

4 Decide on the colour of the tail decoration and stick it to the front of the kite with strong glue. Secure the tail ribbon at the bottom of the kite frame, and stick paper bows in place along its length with a dab of glue or small pieces of tape. Alternatively, tie the kite tail around each bow to keep them firmly in place.

CANDLE DECORATIONS

This is a very quick and decorative way to display candles, but remember that lit candles should never be left unattended under any circumstances.

YOU WILL NEED
Oasis or florist's sponge
Tissue paper
Candle
Thin paint brush

1 To make the candle holder, first cut a block of oasis or florist's sponge to the size that you require.

2 Now cut out small squares of tissue paper. This tissue paper is black on one side and gold on the other so that it has a two-tone effect, intended to match the elegant black candles used.

3 Push the base of the candle into the oasis so that it can stand by itself.

4 Taking a square of tissue paper, place the end of a paint brush in the centre of the paper and poke it into the oasis so that it is held in place. Continue to do this until the block is covered.

STAR GARLAND

For this star garland you will need lots of different colours of tissue paper. Four colours have been used here, but it is up to you how many you choose.

YOU WILL NEED
Coloured tissue paper
Double-sided tape

1 First of all fold up the sheets of tissue paper in individual colours and draw a star shape on top. Now cut out the stars and repeat in all the colours.

2 Stick double-sided tape onto four points of one star and place another star of a different colour on top.

3 Put a further piece of double-sided tape into the centre of the second star and place the next coloured star on top of this. Continue to build up the garland, sticking the stars alternately at sides and centre, until you have a chain long enough for the length that you require.

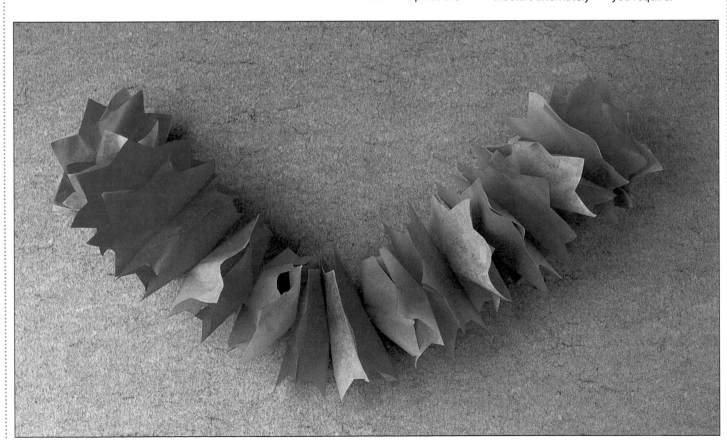

SPACE ALIEN

A hair band simply covered in shiny paper makes an effective alien headdress. Team with T-shirt or leotard and tights for a double-quick space outfit.

YOU WILL NEED
Rigid hair band
Blue metallic crêpe paper
Glue
Sticky tape

1 Use an old hair band and wind a strip of blue metallic crêpe paper around it, taking care not to tear the paper. Secure the end with glue or sticky tape.

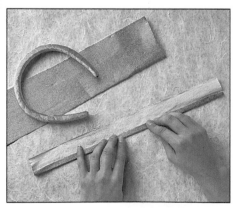

2 Next cut two lengths of the crêpe paper and roll them up lengthways, gluing them to make a tube.

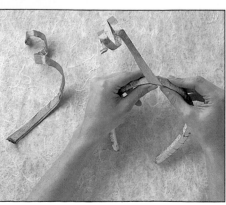

3 Now tightly wind the top part of the tube around a pencil or paint brush to make it curl. Repeat with the other length. Fix the Space Alien 'antennae' onto the hair band with clear tape and mould into a suitable shape.

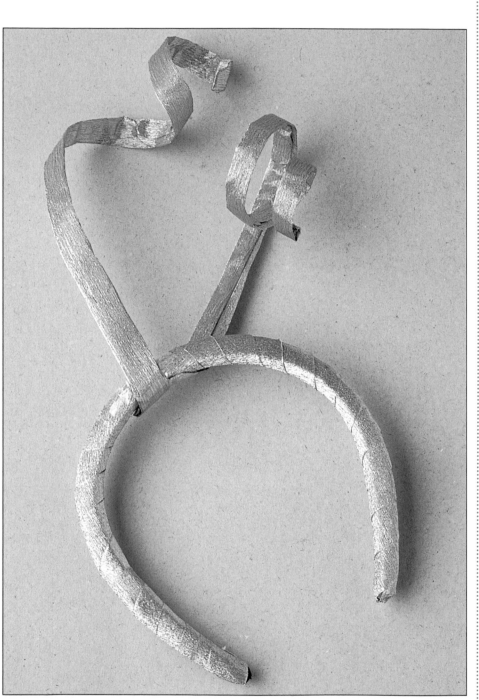

CHRISTMAS TREE GIFT BOX

Here is a way to make a very attractive Christmas decoration to hang on the tree. Pop a sweet or small gift inside or leave it empty simply for decoration.

YOU WILL NEED
White card
Craft knife
Ruler
Glue
Wrapping paper
Ribbon

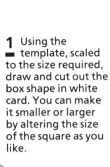

1 Using the template, scaled to the size required, draw and cut out the box shape in white card. You can make it smaller or larger by altering the size of the square as you like.

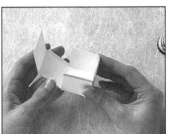

2 Score along all the lines using a craft knife and ruler, taking care not to cut through the card completely.

3 Shape the box by folding the sides up along the scored lines. Apply glue to the tabs and hold the box in position until it is fixed.

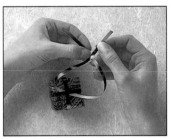

4 Now cover the box in an appropriate wrapping paper.

5 Finish off by tying a ribbon decoratively, and making a loop to hang the box on the tree.

SPARKLING FRAME

This frame is decorated with two different coloured foils, and will take standard-sized photographs. It opens at the side and could easily be made larger to accommodate bigger pictures.

YOU WILL NEED
Heavy corrugated cardboard
Thin corrugated cardboard
Strong clear glue
Diluted PVA glue
2 picture hangers
Masking tape
Newspaper
Fine sandpaper
White paint
Silver foil
Gold foil
Cord for hanging

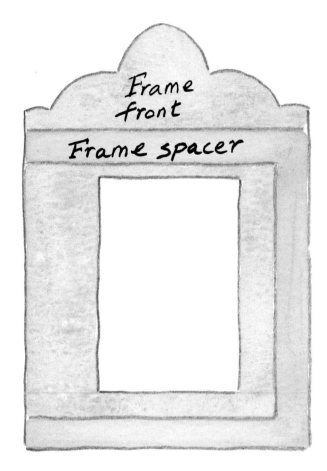

Frame front

Frame spacer

1 Scale up the frame pieces from the template to the size required. Transfer the front to heavy cardboard and the spacer to thin cardboard. Cut a rectangle in thick cardboard to form the back of the frame. Stick the spacer to three sides of the reverse of this rectangle and secure with tape. One side is left open for inserting the picture. When the glue is dry, prime the pieces with diluted PVA glue to help prevent warping. Allow to dry for three or four hours. Glue and tape the hangers to the back.

2 Now cover both pieces of frame with three layers of papier-mâché, using strips of newspaper about 2½ cm (1 in) wide. Let the papier-mâché dry overnight, and then sand the layers lightly with fine sandpaper.

3 When they are dry, prime the frame pieces with two coats of white paint *before* they are joined. Although the paint will eventually be covered, you will be able to see much more easily where to stick the foil if the surface of the frame is white. Stick the back to the front of the frame with strong, clear glue, and hold the joins together with tape. Cover the joins with two layers of papier-mâché strips, and apply another coat of white paint.

4 When everything
is dry, decorate
the frame. Cut strips
of silver foil to fit on
the frame and glue
them in place. Make
sure that you cover
the inside edges of
the frame. Next, cut
shapes from gold foil
and stick them
around the frame.
Finally, attach some
cord to the back of
the frame, around
the hangers.

MOSAIC STYLE

Mosaic tiling is a very ancient form of art and was used as a practical way to decorate floors. It is also an attractive way to make a picture using paper. It does need patience and the finished result makes a beautiful piece to frame and display.

YOU WILL NEED
White and brown card
Coloured papers
Glue
Craft knife

1 Scale up the design from the template to the size required and transfer it onto a piece of white card 30 × 20 cm (12 × 8 in).

3 Organize the various squares of colours into separate piles and start to glue them onto the picture.

4 Continue to build up the squares in colour sections. In order to achieve a smooth line, it may be necessary to use a craft knife to trim the edges of the squares once they have been glued.

2 Select the coloured papers you would like to use and cut them into strips first of all and then into squares. They do not have to be perfect as the variety of shapes and edges will add to the mosaic effect.

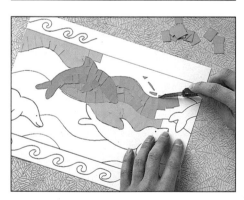

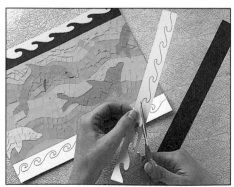

5 To make the border, cut two strips of the brown card 3 cm (1¼ in) wide and the length of the white board. Cut two yellow strips of paper in the same size and draw and cut the wave design onto them. Fix the yellow strips onto the brown and glue them onto the card. When all the areas have been covered, cut pieces to make the eyes and the mouths and glue them into place.

PAPER PROJECTS

CIRCLE GARLAND

Festoon your room with these simple circular garlands made from vivid tissue paper. Alternate the colours individually or place together in blocks of colour.

YOU WILL NEED
Card
Coloured tissue paper
Glue

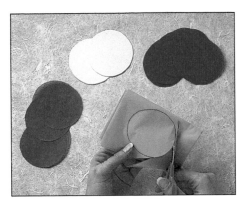

1 Cut two circles of card and lots of circles in different colours of tissue paper.

2 Take ten of the tissue paper circles and fold them in half, then half again into a quarter. Do not use any more than ten pieces as they will not fold properly. Now make a cut from the double-folded edge, following the line of the outside of the circle, two thirds down the wedge.

3 Undo the circle and fold again in half the other way. Fold again into a quarter so that you have a new fold line. Make a cut nearer the centre, following the outside line as illustrated. Undo the circle and lay it flat.

4 Glue the first circle onto one of the circular cards and then attach another tissue circle onto it by gluing it at the centre.

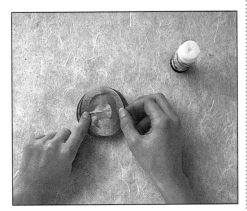

5 Glue the next circle to the top and bottom of the first. Continue to glue together alternately gluing them at the centre, and the top and bottom. Finally, glue the other circular card to the last tissue circle. Pull the cards away from each other to reveal the garland.

PARTY BOATER

Perfect for a fancy dress party, a theatrical production or a summer picnic, this boater is both elegant and easy to make.

YOU WILL NEED
Coloured card
Glue

1 Measure and draw a 24 cm (10 in) diameter circle on to a piece of coloured card and then draw a second circle with a 19 cm (7 in) diameter inside the first one. Cut out the larger circle.

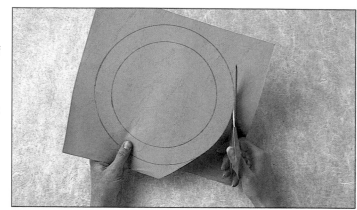

2 Cut darts around the larger circle so that they end at the inner circle. Fold the darts down once they have all been cut. This allows the hat to fit perfectly.

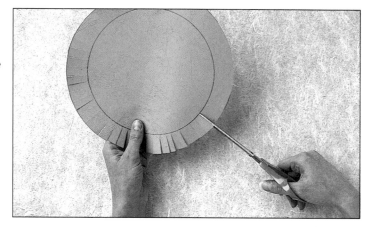

3 Next measure and cut out a strip of card in the same colour measuring 8 × 60 cm (3 × 23½ in). Draw a straight line down the centre of the strip and carefully cut darts down one half. Glue the strip and then fix it to the circle by attaching the darts onto it in order to form the top of the boater.

4 Now push the side darts outwards; cut out a ring of coloured card that has an outside diameter of 30 cm (13 in) and an inside diameter of 19 cm (8 in).

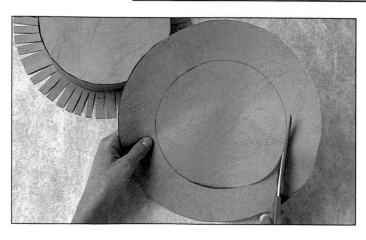

5 Place the card ring over the top and onto the out-turned darts and glue into position.

6 Decorate by putting a band of suitable wrapping paper around it, to create a colourful band. You could make several hats and give each one a different band.

BRIGHT BEADS

Papier-mâché can be used to make beads in a huge variety of sizes, shapes and colours, and because of its lightweight nature you can make the most enormous necklaces, bracelets and earrings without being weighed down!

YOU WILL NEED
Newspaper
Diluted PVA glue
Darning needle
White paint
Assortment of poster paints
Non-toxic clear gloss varnish
Thin nylon cord or elastic to string beads

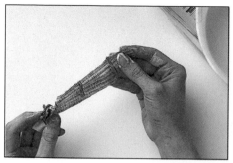

1 Tear the newspaper into long strips about 2½ cm (1 in) wide, and soak them in the diluted PVA glue for a few seconds. Shake off the excess glue, and roll up the paper between your fingers so that it forms round pellets of pulp.

2 Squash each ball of pulp so that it is tightly compacted, and most of the glue is squeezed out. Lay the beads in a warm place to dry for a couple of hours.

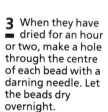

3 When they have dried for an hour or two, make a hole through the centre of each bead with a darning needle. Let the beads dry overnight.

4 When the beads are completely dry, prime each one with two coats of white paint. Let the paint dry, and then decorate the beads with poster paints.

5 Varnish each bead with two coats of clear gloss varnish, and when dry, string them onto thin nylon cord or elastic using a darning needle.

CUT-OUT
ANIMALS

The chicken, frog, and elephant are held together with paper fasteners and have moveable limbs. They are very simple in construction, and many other animals could be attempted using the same process.

YOU WILL NEED
Heavy paper or thin card
Felt-tip pens or coloured pencils
Craft knife
Paper fasteners
Glue

1 Scale up your chosen animal from the template to the required size, and transfer the pieces to paper or card. Cut two bodies for each animal. Remember that one will have to be cut *in reverse* so that the bodies can be stuck together. Next, cut two of each leg, wing, ear and so on. To transfer the pattern in reverse, simply turn it over.

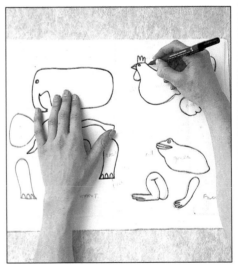

2 Next, colour each piece of animal with felt-tip pen or coloured pencils, and cut them all out, keeping the parts separate.

3 To fix the animal together, make a small incision with a craft knife at the limb positions in each body, and at the top of each body part. Push a paper fastener through the front of each body part, through the body, and open it out on the other side to secure the animal.

4 To join the two halves together, spread a little glue along the top edge of one half of the animal's body, and stick it to the other.

MONOCHROME
DECOUPAGE

Decoupage is the traditional art of decorating surfaces with paper cut-outs of Victorian-style images. This project has a contemporary feel, however, by using monochrome cut-outs and a modern box covered in brown paper.

YOU WILL NEED
Black and white pictures
Card or wooden box
Glue
Varnish (if needed)

1 Start by choosing your images. The ones used here are from a wrapping paper. Cut them out carefully following their outlines.

2 Arrange the images on a box and then glue them into position. A card gift box is used here but you could apply the paper cut-outs to a wooden box such as an old cigar box. However, you would need to coat the decorated box with a layer of varnish.

BANGLES AND BEADS

If you want some new accessories and to wear something that nobody else will have, this jewellery that is made from paper could be just what you are looking for.

YOU WILL NEED
Patterned paper
Contrasting coloured card
Pencil or paint brush
Glue
Bead thread
Sticky tape

1 To start, cut 30 cm (12 in) strips of marbled or decorated paper and taper them so that they measure 4 cm (1½ in) at the base and 1 cm (½ in) at the tip. Then cut a small length of contrasting coloured card, wrap it around a pencil or paint brush and fix it with glue.

2 Now apply some more glue to the length of the triangular strip and, beginning with the wider end, start to wrap around the card, so that the strip is kept central. Make several more of these beads, and thread them onto a length of bead thread to form a necklace.

3 To make a matching bangle, cut a long strip of white card and curl it round into a ring, large enough to slip over your hand. Fix by taping it.

4 Now cut long strips of your chosen decorated paper and after gluing them at one end, start to wind them one by one around the bangle shape.

CUT-OUT DOLLS

This charming couple are modern versions of the cut-out dolls that have been popular for several centuries. They have 'casual' and 'smart' outfits, so are ready for any occasion!

YOU WILL NEED
Thick white paper
Felt-tip pens or coloured pencils
Glue
Thin card
Craft knife

1 Start by scaling up the designs from the template to the size required. Next transfer them to white paper.

2 Colour in the dolls and their clothes with felt-tip pens or coloured pencils according to your own fashion scheme.

3 Stick the dolls onto the thin card. Cut carefully around the dolls and their clothes with scissors. Using a craft knife, lightly score the fold line of the stand at the bottom of each doll, making sure you do not cut right through. Fold along the scored line to make a prop to help the dolls stand upright. To dress the dolls, simply fold each white tab over to the back of the body.

'BAROQUE' CHRISTMAS WREATH

The base for this beautiful wreath is an embroidery hoop. An oval one is used here but a round one would work just as well.

YOU WILL NEED
Gold crêpe paper
Glue
Oval embroidery hoop
Gold card
Paint brush or pencil
Black felt-tip pen

2 Now cut a strip of gold card approximately 1 × 30 cm (½ × 12 in) and wrap it tightly around a paint brush or pencil.

3 Attach one end of the curled gold strip half-way up the right-hand side of the hoop, wind round the hoop and fix the other end just beyond the bottom point.

1 First cut a long strip of gold crêpe paper, glue it at one end of the hoop and start to wind it around the hoop until it is completely covered.

4 Using the template, scaled to the size required, draw the angel playing the trumpet onto the back of some gold card and cut out. Draw on the features in a black felt-tip pen. Make a bow out of gold crêpe paper and stick it on to the top of the wreath.

5 Now fix the angel to the left hand side of the wreath.

■ FRAME UP

Make your own designer-look photograph frames from thick card and wrapping paper. Choose paper to pick out colours in the photographs or to co-ordinate with furnishings.

YOU WILL NEED
Thick card
Ruler
Craft knife
Wrapping or marbled paper
Glue

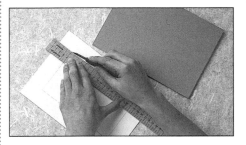

1 Cut two pieces of thick card to the required size and cut a window in one of them using a ruler and craft knife. As a guide allow 3 cm (1 in) for the frame but this can be varied depending on the photograph.

2 For the backing card, cut a piece of marbled paper to the same width but slightly longer, then glue and turn the excess length around the top edge.

3 Take the frame front, place it onto another piece of marbled paper and lightly mark and cut out a smaller window so that you have turnings of about 1½ cm (½ in). Glue the turnings on the window to the inside of the frame. Cut across the external corners of the paper and glue the top edge down.

4 Cut spacing strips out of thick card and stick them along the three sides of the back panel.

5 Apply glue to the strips and carefully fix the front frame on top. Glue and turn the edges at the side and base front so that they wrap around the three remaining sides of the back panel.

6 Now cut a piece of marbled paper exactly the same size as the frame and stick it onto the back to neaten.

7 To make the support strut cut out a piece of card approximately half the length of frame and cut a pointed end. Cover in paper leaving a long overlap of excess paper at the blunt end.

8 Use the excess paper to glue and attach the strut to the back of the frame.

9 Make a support strap from the same paper, and glue it to the back of the frame and the support.

TREE DECORATIONS

Good, unusual Christmas decorations are often hard to find. If you want an alternative to glittery baubles then you may like to design and make your own decorations in papier-mâché. These are very simple in design and structure, but you could easily make quite ornate, even three-dimensional, decorations to dress your tree.

YOU WILL NEED

Thin card
Craft knife
*Small metal jewellery hangers, one for
    each decoration*
Strong clear glue
Masking tape
Newspaper
Diluted PVA glue
Fine sandpaper
White paint
Assortment of poster paints
Black ink (optional)
Non-toxic clear gloss varnish
Cord to hang decorations

1 Trace the decoration shapes from the template, scaling up to the size required, and transfer them to the thin card. Cut out each shape.

Stick a hanger onto the back of each decoration with strong clear glue, and hold it in place with masking tape.

2 Allow the glue to dry for an hour, and then cover each decoration with three layers of small, thin newspaper strips soaked in diluted PVA glue. Let the decorations dry in a warm place overnight.

3 Then, sand the dry decorations lightly with fine sandpaper, and prime each one with two coats of white paint.

4 Draw in any design first with pencil, and then colour your decorations with poster paints. Define details with black ink if required.
    Allow the decorations to dry thoroughly, and then seal them with two coats of clear gloss varnish. When they are dry, tie a loop of cord to the top of each decoration.

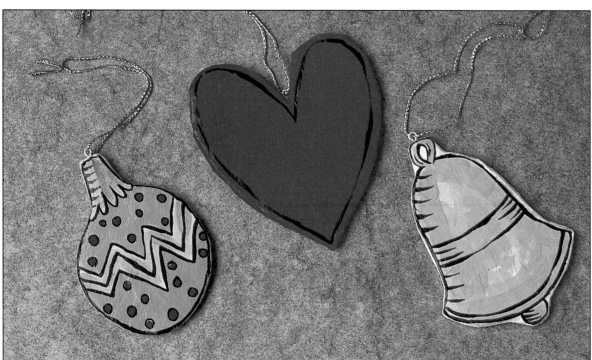

VICTORIAN BOOKLET

What could be more evocative of the Victorian age than a notebook that has been decorated by decoupage. This little book could be used as a diary, a notebook or a sketch pad.

YOU WILL NEED
Writing paper
Needle and embroidery thread
Victorian-style scraps or magazine pictures
Glue

1 First fold some sheets of writing paper in half to make the booklet, and press down in the centre to create the crease.

2 Now open out the book and, taking a needle and embroidery thread, make three large stitches to bind the booklet.

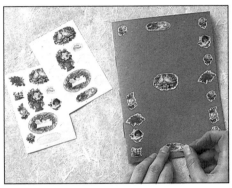

3 To give the booklet a nostalgic feel use Victorian-style scraps which can be cut out from magazines, or purchased. Arrange and stick them onto the cover of the notebook.

ROYAL CROWN

A regal crown fit for a king, queen, prince or princess! Make your decorations as simple or elaborate as you like, for a right royal celebration.

YOU WILL NEED
Foil card
Silver paper
Glue
Coloured foil paper
Double-sided tape
Foil crêpe paper

1 To make the crown, cut out a length of foil card about 55 cm (22 in) long and 15 cm (6 in) wide. On the back of the card draw out a shaped crown design and cut it out.

2 Now cut out small circles of silver paper and glue them onto the finials. Cut out diamond shapes in different coloured foil paper to make up the 'jewels' and glue them onto the crown.

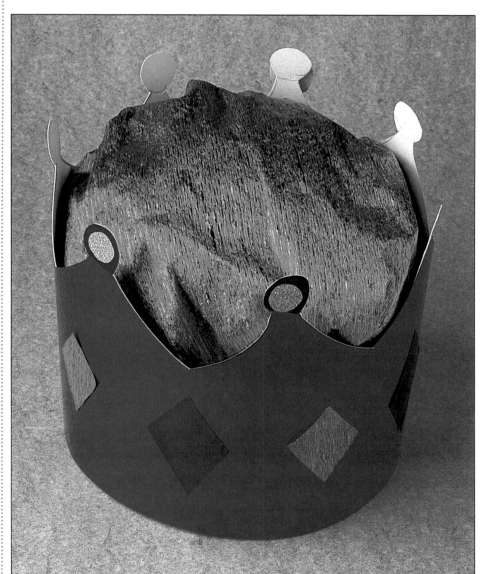

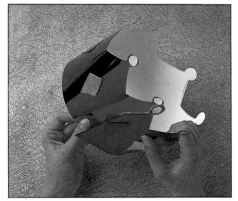

3 Join the ends of the crown together with glue and stick a long piece of double- sided tape all the way around on the inside about half- way down.

4 Take a circle of matching foil crêpe paper, which is just larger than the crown, and carefully place it inside the top so that it is fixed to the tape. Make it billow out by pushing it up from underneath, to represent the velvet in a crown.

CHRISTMAS RING

This is a quick and easy way to make a new collection of Christmas decorations to hang on your tree without spending a fortune. They are made from wooden curtain rings, covered in vivid crêpe paper.

YOU WILL NEED
Crêpe paper
Wooden curtain rings
Glue
Thin ribbon

1 Cut 2 cm (¾ in) wide strips of coloured crêpe paper. Take a wooden curtain ring and wind the strips of crêpe paper around the ring to cover. Glue ends in place.

2 Now take a thin ribbon and secure it at the top of the ring. As before, wind it around the ring leaving gaps to reveal the paper. When you have worked the ribbon back to the top, secure it and then make a loop for hanging.

3 To finish off, make a bow out of the crêpe paper and stick it on at the top of the ring.

BUTTERFLY MOBILE

Mobiles can drift gently in the slightest breeze or draught, entertaining young and old alike. Here the pretty butterfly wings are particularly eye-catching as they sparkle in the light.

YOU WILL NEED
Brightly coloured card in different shades
Sequins or glitter (optional)
Glue
Cotton thread
Sewing needle
Sticky tape
Three mobile wires, or three thin lengths of thin wooden rod

1 Scale up the template to the required size and trace four butterflies onto different coloured cards and then cut them out. Then cut out a fifth butterfly, using a smaller scale so that it is approximately half the size of the other four.

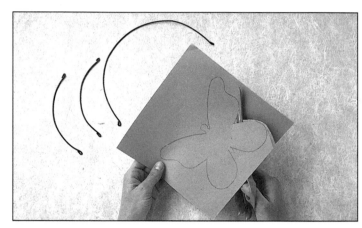

2 Next start to decorate the butterflies by sticking on small pieces of card, making sure that the colours are strong and bright. You could use other materials such as sequins or glitter to add extra sparkle.

3 Thread a long length of cotton through the top of each of the large butterflies, knotting the end securely and fixing it with sticky tape. Attach the other end of each piece of thread to the mobile wires. Each piece of thread should be a different length to add variety to the positions of the butterflies.

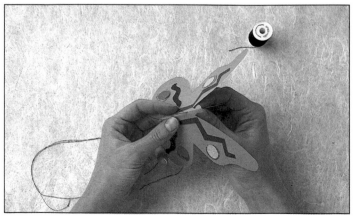

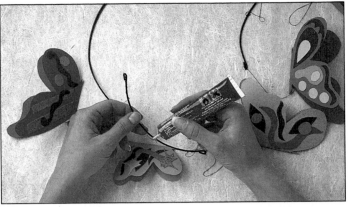

4 Last, but not
■ least, decorate
the smallest
butterfly and stick it
onto the top wire of
the mobile, to make
it look as if it is
having a rest from
flying around!

BAUBLE
BOX

This box can be made in a variety of sizes, and could be filled with handmade sweets as a gift on a special occasion. It may be decorated in a variety of ways, perhaps with small pieces of brightly coloured pottery to emulate mosaic, or glass 'gems' from a theatrical costumiers.

YOU WILL NEED
Heavy and thin corrugated cardboard
Craft knife
Strong clear glue
Masking tape
Newspaper
Diluted PVA glue
Fine sandpaper
White paint
Assorted poster paints
Non-toxic clear gloss varnish

Base and lid Cut 2

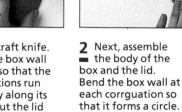

Box wall

Handle Cut 1

1 Scale up the box pieces from the template to the size required and, apart from the lid handle, transfer to heavy corrugated cardboard. Cut out using a craft knife. Place the box wall pattern so that the corrugations run vertically along its width. Cut the lid handle from thin corrugated card.

2 Next, assemble the body of the box and the lid. Bend the box wall at each corrugation so that it forms a circle. Glue and tape it in position on the box base. Then glue and tape the lip to the underside of the lid, and fix the handle in position.

3 Tear newspaper into thin strips and soak in diluted PVA glue. Cover the body of the box and the lid with four layers of papier-mâché. Make sure the strips of paper are thin enough to ensure a smooth surface, especially around the curved edges.

4 Leave the box to dry overnight in a warm place. When quite dry, lightly smooth the surface of the box with fine sandpaper, and prime it with two coats of white paint. Leave to dry thoroughly in a warm place.

5 Decorate the box and its lid, both inside and out, using poster paints. When the paint is completely dry, apply a coat of clear gloss varnish.

DOLL

This doll is formed from tightly taped and compacted newspaper twists. The resulting structure is very sturdy and quite large dolls or other toys could be constructed using this method.

YOU WILL NEED
Newspaper
Masking tape
Diluted PVA glue
Fine sandpaper
White paint
Selection of poster paints
Black ink (optional)
Non-toxic clear gloss varnish

1 First, twist a double sheet of newspaper together to form a 'rope' and tape the top, about 5 cm (2 in) down, to form the doll's head. Cut the remaining paper 'rope' to the desired length to form the body, and secure it with masking tape.

2 Cover the body and head with strips of masking tape to add extra strength. Next, make the arms and legs by the same process, twisting smaller pieces of paper and taping them along their length. Cut the resulting 'ropes' to the right length, and tape them firmly in place on the doll's body.

3 Tear some newspaper into thin strips and soak in diluted PVA glue. Then cover the doll with four layers of papier-mâché. To make the doll's hair, hands and feet, roll up small strips of glue-soaked paper between finger and thumb to form pellets of pulp and stick them in place on the head. Paper over the pulp hair with short, thin strips of paper.

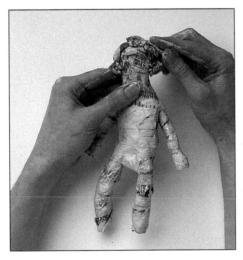

4 Let the doll dry overnight in a warm place. When completely dry, lightly smooth the surface with fine sandpaper and prime it with two coats of white paint.

5 When the paint has dried thoroughly, draw in the features of the doll with pencil and fill in the design with poster paints. Define the decoration with black ink if more detail is needed. Seal the doll with two coats of non-toxic clear gloss varnish and allow to dry.

CHRISTMAS CRACKERS

Making your own Christmas crackers is really rewarding and it's great fun watching friends and family pull them open to discover the treats inside. Make exactly the number you need for your party and collect small gifts to put in them.

YOU WILL NEED

Double-sided crêpe paper in
 bright colours
Craft knife
Metal ruler
Cutting mat
Thin card in black and white
Double-sided adhesive tape
Gold crêpe paper
Gold paper-backed foil
Corrugated cardboard
Fine gold cord
Cracker snaps
Paper hats, jokes and gifts to go in
 the crackers
Narrow black ribbon

1 For each cracker, cut two rectangles of crêpe paper measuring 25 x 20 cm (10 x 8 in). Join, overlapping the ends, to make a rectangle 45 x 20 cm (18 x 8 in). Cut three pieces of thin white card 22 x 10 cm (9 x 4 in). Roll each into a cylinder, overlapping the short ends by 3.5 cm (1¼ in).

2 Lay strips of double-sided adhesive tape across the crêpe paper rectangles with which to attach the card cylinders: one in the centre and the other two about 4 cm (1½ in) in from each end of the rectangle. Roll up and secure the edge with double-sided tape.

3 Decorate the cracker with strips of the gold papers. Lay a strip of paper-backed foil over a piece of corrugated cardboard and ease the foil into the ridges with your thumb. Cut a simple star shape out of thin black card, wrap some fine gold cord around it and stick it on top of the gold decorations.

4 Insert the snap and place the novelties and a paper hat in the central section of the cracker.

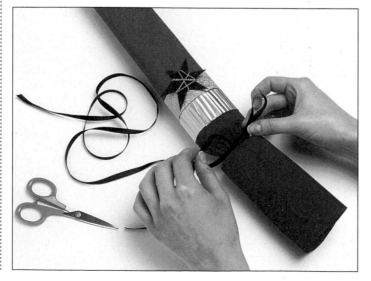

5 Tie up the ends with narrow black ribbon, easing the crêpe paper gently so that you can tie the knot very tightly.

6 Complete the cracker by folding the edges of the crêpe paper over the ends of the cardboard cylinders.

PAPER FLOWERS

These everlasting blooms are made by folding and cutting squares of coloured paper into a variety of shapes. Experiment with the technique to make some really fabulous flowers.

YOU WILL NEED
Scissors
Thin paper: variety of colours
  including green
Ruler
Pencil
Paper glue
Strong glue
Pipe cleaners

1 Cut out squares of coloured paper measuring 10 x 10 cm (4 x 4 in) and then fold each one into quarters.

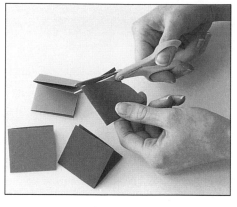

2 Cut a curve into each folded square so that it will form a circle when opened.

3 Cut a variety of petal shapes into the curved shape. Open out each paper flower.

4 Cut circles and other details from contrasting paper and stick them with paper glue to the middle of each flower.

5 Using strong glue, stick a pipe cleaner to the back of each flower to make a stem. Cut the pipe cleaners first if you want to make stems of different lengths.

6 Cut leaf shapes from the thin green paper. Stick these to short lengths of pipe cleaner with strong glue leaving a 3 cm (1¼ in) stem below each leaf. Wrap this short stem around the main stem of the flower to attach the leaves.

■ I N D E X

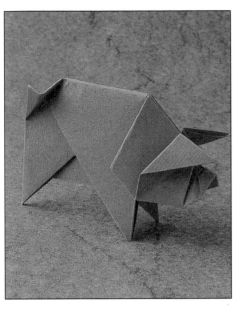

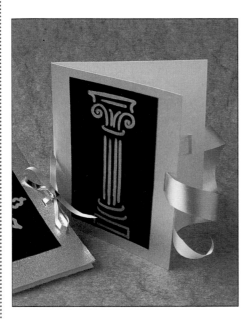

ACKNOWLEDGEMENTS

The publishers would like to thank the following contributors:
Ofer Acoo (page 80), Madeleine Adams (pages 36, 58), Juliet Bawden (pages 38, 106, 141, 210), Deena Beverley (page 228), Petra Boase (pages 111, 200, 212), Penny Boylan (pages 146, 190, 219), Victoria Brown (pages 46, 64, 76, 228), Louise Brownlow (pages 135, 196), Diana Civil (pages 126, 214), Marion Elliot (pages 28, 30, 32, 40, 42, 48, 50, 52, 54, 60, 63, 100, 104, 130, 140, 147, 148, 184, 198, 201, 232, 234, 242), Tessa Evelegh (pages 35, 82, 88, 134), Lucinda Ganderton (pages 37, 75, 144, 145), Emma Hardy (pages 142, 206, 224, 234, 244), Mary Maguire (page 152), Deborah Schneebeli-Morrell (page 118), Kim Rowley (page 56), Judy Smith (page 156), Andrea Spencer (pages 72, 86, 216), Isabel Stanley (page 194), Liz Trigg (pages 82, 88, 191), Liz Wagstaff (page 188) Stewart and Sally Walton (pages 34, 82, 88, 96, 112, 116, 119, 120, 122, 124, 128, 132, 136, 138, 150, 162, 166, 167, 168, 173, 174, 176, 178, 180, 186, 199, 208, 213, 218, 220, 222, 226, 240, 246), Emma Whitfield (page 154), Josephine Whitfield (pages 78, 84, 90, 94, 102, 108, 110, 170, 171, 172, 238) and Dorothy Wood (page 92) plus Paul Jackson for the chapter on Origami (pages 252–337) and Angela A'Court and Marion Elliot for the chapters on Decorative papercrafts (pages 338–419) and Paper projects (pages 420–499).

SUPPLIERS

For many of the projects in this book you can use paper that you have on hand. If you want to buy paper, the range available today is enormous. There are speciality stores, and most craft and hobby stores stock a good collection.

Cardboard can be bought from many different shops and packaging suppliers. Craft and art shops and stationery stores sell a wide range of decorative card and cardboard in quite small quantities. For large amounts of heavy-duty cardboard, contact packaging companies.

Listed here are a few addresses of craft and paper specialists:

UK

Falkiner Fine Papers Ltd.
76 Southhampton Row
London WC1B 4AR

Mara Amats
ADAE Associates
c/o 8 Wendover Court
Chiltern Street
London W1M 1PB

Neal Street East
5 Neal Street
London WC2H 9PU

One Four Nine Paper Supplies
PO Box A13
Huddersfield
West Yorkshire HD3 4LW

Paperchase
213 Tottenham Court Road
London W1A 4US

Paperpoint
130 Long Acre
London WC2E 9AL

Paperpoint
26 Calthorpe Road
Edgbaston
Birmingham, B15 1RP

Robert Horne Paper Company
Huntsman House
Mansion Close
Moulton Park
Northampton NN3 1LA

USA

The Art Store
935 Erie Blvd. E.
Syracuse, NY 13210

Kate's Paperie
8 West 13th Street
New York, NY 10011

Papersource Inc.
730 N Franklin Suite 111
Chicago, Il 60610

Australia

ACT Papers Pty Ltd.
10 McGlone Street
Micham
Victoria 3132